Systematic Classroom Observation

Social Research and Educational Studies Series

Series Editor
Robert G. Burgess
Senior Lecturer in Sociology
University of Warwick

Social Research and Educational Studies Series: 3

Systematic Classroom Observation

Paul Croll

 The Falmer Press

(A member of the Taylor & Francis Group)
London and Philadelphia

UK	The Falmer Press, Falmer House, Barcombe, Lewes, East Sussex, BN8 5DL
USA	The Falmer Press, Taylor & Francis Inc., 242 Cherry Street, Philadelphia, PA 19106-1906

First published 1986

Library of Congress Cataloging in Publication Data

Croll, Paul.
  Systematic classroom observation.

  (Social research and educational studies series; 3)
  1. Education—Research. 2. Observation (Educational method). I. Title. II. Series.
LB1028.C745 1986 370'.7'8 86-11675
ISBN 1-85000-106-5
ISBN 1-85000-107-3 (pbk.)

Typeset in 11/13 Garamond by
Imago Publishing Ltd, Thame, Oxon

Printed in Great Britain by Taylor & Francis (Printers) Ltd, Basingstoke

Contents

Series Editor's Preface

The purpose of the *Social Research and Educational Studies* series is to provide authoritative guides to key issues in educational research. The series includes overviews of fields, guidance on good practice and discussions of the practical implications of social and educational research. In particular, the series deals with a variety of approaches to conducting social and educational research. Contributors to this series review recent work, raise critical concerns that are particular to the field of education, and reflect on the implications of research for educational policy and practice.

Each volume in the series draws on material that will be relevant for an international audience. The contributors to this series all have wide experience of teaching, conducting and using educational research. The volumes are written so that they will appeal to a wide audience of students, teachers and researchers. Altogether, the volumes in the *Social Research and Educational Studies* series provide a comprehensive guide for anyone concerned with contemporary educational research.

The series will include individually authored books and edited volumes on a range of themes in education including: qualitative research, survey research, the interpretation of data, self-evaluation, research and social policy, analyzing data, action research, the politics and ethics of research.

Paul Croll examines a style of investigation that has been widely used in the USA and more recently in British educational studies. He discusses the use of systematic observation in studies of classrooms making reference to the schedules and recording sheets. He outlines strategies for the collection and analysis of data and examines the use of this approach by teachers working together as well as researchers. Finally, he reflects on critiques of systematic observation and points to ways in which this approach can be used to develop educational research. Paul Croll discusses research processes and research techniques as well as data collection and data analysis. This book brings together a range of material which will help students and teachers consider how systematic classroom observation can be conducted.

Robert Burgess
University of Warwick

Preface

One of the major developments in educational research in Britain over the past ten years has been a growing interest in classroom processes and a movement towards locating research in classrooms. This has sometimes been characterized as a movement away from a 'black box' model of classrooms where research was concerned with inputs and outputs to a 'glass box' model where the teaching process itself is the focus of study. This new focus for research activity has been accompanied by new developments in research methodology including the development of ethnographic approaches to studying school and classroom life and an involvement of teachers in research on their own educational settings. Another major development has been the introduction of systematic observation techniques for studying classrooms which is the subject of this book.

Systematic observation in classrooms is a research method which uses a system of highly structured observation procedures applied by trained observers in order to gather data on patterns of behaviour and interaction in classrooms. Its key elements are, first, that the observation procedures are carefully defined and highly explicit so that it is absolutely clear how descriptions have been arrived at and the idiosyncracies in an individual's selection and perception of events are eliminated. Second, the results are expressed in quantitative terms. The careful definition of variables and categories in systematic observation make it suitable for large-scale, comparative studies, in a way that is not generally true of other approaches to the study of classrooms. However, the methodology is also suitable for small-scale research and case studies. Consequently this book is intended not only for researchers planning or conducting large-scale surveys of classroom practice but also for researchers who may want to consider the value of incorporating systematic observation methods into studies of individual schools and classrooms and also for teachers conducting research in their own educational settings.

Although systematic classroom observation has a long history in the United States it has only relatively recently been used by British researchers and does not appear in standard textbooks of educational research methods. This book is intended to fill that gap and to provide an introduction to the methodology of systematic classroom observation. The approach used is to engage with the issues involved in studying classrooms rather than to present a set of procedures in 'cookbook' fashion. Most of the issues and principles to be considered in working with systematic observation are extensions of more general issues in educational research and considering them here provides the opportunity for a discussion of the nature and role of empirical enquiry in education and to outline criteria relevant to good research practice. Systematic observation has been the subject of a variety of criticisms and the discussion of these necessarily involves wider issues in educational research. It is therefore intended then that this book should contribute generally to a discussion of the role of empirical research in education and, in particular, to the place of quantitative methods within it.

Chapter 1 consists of an overview of systematic observation explaining the principles involved and some of the uses to which it is put. In chapter 2 a number of studies using systematic observation are described. It is hoped that these will clarify the general issues as well as giving the reader a feel for systematic observation in action. In chapter 3 the issues involved in designing a systematic observation system are presented and in chapter 4 the difficulties that may arise in conducting research in classrooms are discussed. The processing and analysis of observational data are dealt with in chapter 5 and this is developed in chapter 6 with a discussion of multivariate data analysis techniques. The suggestions in this chapter could equally well apply to the analysis of other educational and social research data. Finally, in chapter 7 some of the criticisms which have been made of systematic classroom observation are addressed and the relevance of research using these methods for teachers and others concerned with education are discussed.

I have been fortunate in that my own involvement in research using systematic classroom observation came about as a result of work pioneered by Professor Brian Simon who was one of the first people to develop this approach to educational research in Britain and who, together with Deanne Boydell, devized observation systems for studying British classrooms. It was this work which led to the

SSRC-funded ORACLE (Observational Research and Classroom Learning Evaluation) project in which I took part. I later acted as Co-director of a DES-funded study, The Assessment and Incidence of Special Educational Needs, which also used observational methods.

I should like to thank my colleagues on both of these projects, Brian Simon, Maurice Galton, John Willcocks and Anne Jasman, and Gerald Bernbaum, Diana Moses and Jane Wright, with all of whom I have discussed the problems involved in doing observational research. As with all such research these studies have depended heavily on the goodwill and forbearance of teachers and children in the classrooms where observation was conducted.

I must thank Bob Burgess, the editor of this series, and Diana Moses, who first suggested that I should write this book, for their careful reading of a draft of the text. Both suggested improvements to phrasing and argument which were of great help in producing the final version.

1 Introduction

Approaches to Classroom Research

It is probably fair to say that there is general agreement about the
value of direct observation of classrooms in educational research but
there is very much less agreement about the appropriate methodology
for such observation. Broadly speaking observational research can be
divided into two approaches. The approach being outlined here is
that of systematic observation. This is the process whereby an
observer or a group of observers devize a systematic set of rules for
recording and classifying classroom events. Such a process is sometimes said to be an objective approach to observation although the
meaning of this claim and the extent to which it can be substantiated
will be the focus of later discussion. The results of such observations
are normally reported in numerical or quantitative terms as percentages or averages and may then form the basis for a variety of
statistical analyses. The second approach is that associated with
ethnographic or qualitative observational techniques in which the
observer (often called a participant-observer, although this term is
sometimes used rather imprecisely) attempts to arrive at an understanding of the meaning of social relations and social processes in the
classrooms for the subjects being observed and conveys this, typically, by means of field-notes and verbatim accounts of selected episodes
rather than by quantitative analysis. There has been considerable
controversy over the appropriateness and methodological adequacy
of these two approaches. Proponents of systematic techniques have
suggested that qualitative approaches can be subjective and unreliable
(Croll, 1981; McIntyre and MacLeod, 1978), while ethnographic
observers have argued that the claim to objectivity of the results of
systematic observations are largely spurious and that by concentrat-

ing on that which can be classified and measured such techniques miss out that which is most important in classrooms (Hamilton and Delamont, 1974; Delamont and Hamilton, 1984).

It is not intended in this volume to engage in a controversy over research methods although aspects of this controversy will inevitably be discussed in what follows. Clearly, presenting a guide to systematic observation implies that such an approach is thought to be valid and important and this is indeed the case. However, the claim for its value does not depend on minimizing the value of other research approaches and at certain points in the text it will be indicated that some research problems may be better tackled by ethnographic than by systematic methods.[1] It will be necessary to discuss criticisms which are sometimes made of systematic approaches. It will also be suggested that the claim, sometimes heard, that 'the appropriate research technique should be determined by the particular problem being studied' should be treated carefully and that the relationship between a research problem and a methodology is more complex than this suggests.

Teachers and Researchers

This book is explicitly addressed to both teachers and researchers interested in using systematic observation techniques in classrooms and it is useful to consider whether there are differences in the way these different groups might use the techniques presented here. Teachers may wish to monitor some aspect of their own or their pupils' classroom activities for very particular and specific purposes concerned with a particular problem or concern while a researcher may be observing a classroom in order to compile a description of activities across a large number of teaching settings or to test a psychological or sociological theory. Nevertheless, a simple distinction between teacher and researcher cannot be sustained. Teachers may carry out observations in other classrooms than their own or may invite a colleague to observe some aspect of their classroom. Groups of teachers may carry out a collaborative programme of observations in respect of teaching concerns which they have in common or which have arisen as a shared problem. In these cases teachers conducting observations are moving to some extent towards a researcher as well as a practitioner model of classroom observation. The idea of 'the teacher-as-researcher' has received a lot of attention recently as an aspect of the professional development of teachers and also as a model for how educational research should be conducted.[2]

As will be shown in subsequent chapters one of the distinctive features of systematic classroom observation is that the observer is outside the situation which is observed. The role problems of the observer are similar for a teacher and an outsider coming into the classroom. The purposes for which teachers and professional researchers conduct observations may often, but by no means always, be different but the problems they confront in designing and carrying out programmes of observation contain many of the same elements.

Systematic Observation: An Overview

If any of us was asked to spend a period of time observing a classroom and was then asked to describe what we had seen we would inevitably find that the content of our descriptions was heavily influenced by the purpose for which we had been asked (or thought we had been asked) to carry out the observation. An external examiner asked to observe a student on teaching practice would probably describe what he or she had seen in terms of lesson organization, the presentation of material and the relationships the student had established with pupils. A fellow student, writing a dissertation on classroom interaction, might describe the period of observation entirely in terms of the ratio of pupil to teacher talk or the number of questions the teacher had asked of the class. An educational psychologist visiting the classroom because of a concern with a particular child would concentrate the description on that child and on the way the teacher's activities affected him or her. The head of the maths department visiting the classroom might give a description of what had been seen in terms of the levels of a maths work programme that various children had reached.

All of these descriptions may be perfectly accurate in their own terms but they will almost certainly differ from one another to the point where they may not even be recognizable as referring to the same classroom. There is no such thing as *the* description of a classroom (or other social setting). There are an infinite variety of descriptions which are more or less adequate for particular purposes, and in order to judge the adequacy of descriptions it is absolutely necessary (although not, usually, sufficient) to know the purpose for which it has been arrived at. This point should always be kept in mind when devizing or discussing systematic (and other) observations. Like all reports in social science, descriptions of classrooms involve abstracting from the totality of the social world certain aspects thought to be relevant for particular investigatory purposes.

Even where two or more observers agree about the purpose of their observation and description, their reports on identical settings and events are still likely to differ to some extent. If a group of people (for example, a group of teachers on an in-service course) decide to observe a variety of classrooms for a particular purpose (for example, to describe the extent of cooperation between pupils in their work), when they come to compare their descriptions they will certainly find that there are differences between the accounts of cooperation in different classrooms not only because the classrooms differ but also because their definitions of cooperation and the procedures they have used to observe it will also differ. The set of descriptions may be very rich in detail and in the 'feel' it gives for the various classrooms but it will have limitations as a basis for an analysis of classroom cooperation. It is not just (or principally) that it will be impossible to compare classrooms with regard to the degree of cooperation or to give an overall 'cooperation score' but that it will be impossible to tell if something which emerges as an important feature of one classroom but does not appear in the account of another was really absent in the second or was not thought relevant or important by the observer. Similarly, it is easy to imagine that in discussion of the various results it emerges that the group do not agree about what they include as cooperation and that this has also influenced their accounts. It is also easy to imagine that the discussion reveals that some members of the group have concentrated their description on a group of pupils who had engaged in cooperation while another had thought it more interesting to describe instances where opportunities for cooperation were not taken up, while a third group were mainly concerned with the extent to which the teachers set up cooperative activities.

This problem of comparing the accounts of different individuals occurs both because of different purposes underlying the observations and also because of differences in the way different people respond to the same events. Systematic classroom observation attempts to arrive at descriptions of classrooms which are absolutely explicit in their purposes and which remove part of the subjectivity which occurs when individuals describe events. To follow through the example above, the group of in-service teachers might decide not only that they had a common purpose in observing classrooms (that of describing pupil-pupil cooperation) but that they were also going to arrive at a common definition of what constitutes cooperative activity between pupils and a common procedure for describing it.

They might decide that whenever they saw an instance of cooperative activity or whenever an instance occurred during a particular interval or at a particular point in time, depending on the procedures used for sampling events and locating them in time, they would record the number and sex of children involved, the area of the curriculum on which they were cooperating (this would involve an agreement between them on how to define curriculum content as well as on how to define cooperation) and whether or not the cooperating group were working directly with the teacher.

This procedure would result in very exact information on those aspects of cooperation included in their definition and recording procedure. They would describe the overall level of cooperation and the extent to which it varied from school to school and classroom to classroom and could relate this variation to the type of school or to characteristics of the teacher. They could also describe the sorts of groups in which cooperation occurred in terms of the size of the group and whether they were single sex or mixed groups. They could describe the curriculum content of the activities on which coopera- tion occurred. If they had also observed children when they were not cooperating they could say which kinds of group setting and curriculum areas were most likely to be associated with cooperative activity and the extent to which this varied across classrooms and schools. If they wished to extend the research they might gather further, non-observational, data and relate the extent of pupil-pupil cooperation to the value their class teachers said in interviews that they placed on such activities or to the level of pupil achievement in different areas of the curriculum measured by exam results or by specially administered assessment exercises.

This example illustrates some fundamental aspects of systematic observation as a research procedure:

(i)   It is explicit in its purpose or purposes and the purposes have to be worked out before data collection is conducted.

(ii)   It is explicit and rigorous in its definition of categories and in its criteria for classifying phenomena into these categor- ies.

(iii)   It produces data which can be presented in quantitative form and which can be summarized and related to other data using statistical techniques.

(iv)   Once the procedures for recording and criteria for using categories have been arrived at the role of the observer is essentially one of following instructions to the letter and any observer should record a particular event in an identical fashion to any other.

It is this uniformity between observers which underlies the claim of systematic observation systems to provide an objective account of the situation they describe. By setting out a predetermined set of categories and an absolutely explicit set of criteria for assigning occurrences to them, the researcher or research group using a system of systematic observation has eliminated one aspect of the subjectivity which normally occurs in an individual's description of events. The account of cooperation in classrooms offered by the hypothetical in-service group reflects the judgment of the group that cooperation in classrooms is worth studying in the first place which probably depends on subjective views of what is important in classrooms or what is likely to be related to other educational outcomes. Their definition of what constitutes cooperation will also reflect personal and subjective criteria. But, if they have successfully constructed an observation system which different observers can use in an identical fashion, then they have made this personal view of cooperation absolutely clear and explicit. Someone reading their description knows exactly by what principles it was arrived at. The reader may not agree that this is what constitutes cooperation (or a teacher question or a maths task) but he or she knows exactly what the researcher means by it.

This limited objectivity, an objectivity given the focus of the enquiry and the criteria employed, has the epistemological advantage that the reader knows exactly where he or she stands. It has practical advantages in that it allows data to be collected on a substantial scale — across a large number of classrooms and a long period of time using large numbers of observers all engaged on a common purpose. It also has the practical advantage that it allows results to be expressed in exact quantitative terms. If a researcher wants to describe patterns of similarity and variation across a large number of classrooms or to correlate some aspect of the observations with some other measure such as test results then such numerical exactness is essential. Similarily if a teacher wants to compare children's engagement on task (or level of pupil-pupil cooperation) during different types of work organization or group composition then, unless differences are very dramatic, it is likely that the results will be needed in numerical form. It has further advantages in that it makes research results cumulative and replicable. A teacher or researcher working alone can use previously tested observation systems and may have large amounts of previous data with which to compare their own results. A researcher who feels that certain aspects of someone else's research procedures give misleading results in certain settings or that a minor change in a definition will lead to major differences in findings can test these concerns as can a teacher who feels that certain conclusions are specific to the classrooms originally studied and will not apply in the teacher's own classroom.

All these arguments suggests that there are many areas of educational enquiry which would profit from the use of systematic observation and that the in-service group will have learned a great deal from using identical definitions and procedures in a variety of classrooms. However, it should be said that some of the group may be unhappy about the majority decision to study classroom cooperation in this way. Some of them may feel that the definition of cooperation that the group has decided to work with leaves out something that they consider important or includes activities which they do not regard as true cooperation. They may also feel that the additional information being collected on group size and curriculum content is not the most relevant and that they would rather focus their observations on something like the process of cooperation — the way that a group comes together to engage on a cooperative task. These group members may decided to devize their own systematic obervation procedure using their preferred definition and collecting the sort of contextual data which they think is most relevant. As was emphasized above there is no single best way to observe a classroom or an aspect of classroom activity. It may be that this sub-group of teachers have exactly the same research questions in mind as the main group but differ about the correct way of operationalizing them. It is more likely they will turn out to have somewhat different research questions in mind although these still fall under the general heading of classroom cooperation. The process of deciding on exact systematic procedures forces the researcher or research group to confront their research purposes in a very direct fashion as decisions about procedures can only be made by reference to these purposes.

Such differences about procedures or definitions within a programme of systematic observation may lead to the development of an alternative systematic observation system providing information on other aspects of pupil-pupil cooperation. Alternatively it may be possible for a single observational research project to incorporate more than one definition of aspects of classroom activity being observed and it should certainly be possible for a single observational system to collect information relevant to more than one research question and even to competing perspectives on some aspect of classroom activities.

What is likely to create greater difficulties is if some of the original group of teacher-researchers are unhappy about the idea of using a systematic, quantitative approach to studying the phenomena of interest to them. Perhaps this group feels that classroom cooperation is simply not amenable to observation along pre-determined lines either because its complexity is such that they do not believe that an appropriate systematic observation schedule can adequately reflect it or because they are mainly interested in how the participants understand the process of classroom cooperation and the meanings which it has for them. This group may decide that their research interests are better met by a qualitative, ethnographic approach to classroom observation. Before they abandon systematic observation, however, there are three points which they should consider. First, the complexity of the phenomena being studied is not in itself a reason for abandoning exact operational definitions and predetermined observational procedures. If it is not possible to arrive at such procedures this may be because the research problem has not been conceptualized sufficiently clearly to be the subject of empirical investigation. Second, qualitative and quantitative techniques should not be regarded as mutually exclusive approaches but may be complementary. A period of qualitative observation can provide researchers with procedures, definitions and hypotheses for an investigation using systematic techniques. Alternatively (or additionally) the results from systematic observational research may provide a starting point for an ethnographic investigation by showing statistical regularities in patterns of behaviour and interaction which need to be further investigated in terms of the understandings the participants have of them (for example, Delamont, 1976). This leads into the third point which is concerned with the relationship between reporting social events and coming to an understanding of the meaning of the events for participants.

At the most basic level, all reports of social phenomena require a degree of intersubjectivity between the researcher, the subject and the audience for the research and this is implied in any systematic observation system. Also, however, accounts which attempt to come to an understanding of the meanings participants give to events depend initially on accurate reports of these events. These three issues will be taken up again in the final chapter. The present argument is merely concerned to establish that the techniques of systematic observation are likely to prove of value in most studies concerned to describe classroom processes and that a familiarity with such techniques is valuable both for practising researchers and for teachers wishing to develop a research orientation to their professional activities.

The Purposes of Systematic Classroom Observation

In the most general sense the purpose of systematic classroom observation is to provide an accurate description of selected features of activities and interactions in classrooms. The principles involved in designing and conducting such research will apply to a wide variety of specific projects. As has been emphasized above, however, the specific purpose for which an observation is being conducted is crucially important in deciding on appropriate procedures and definitions. The purposes listed below are not intended to be exhaustive of possible uses but rather to give an indication of some of the major purposes for which systematic observation techniques have been employed.

Providing a Representative Description of Classrooms

The purpose of many systematic observation studies is to give a descriptive overview of certain features of the educational system. For example, the research reported as *The Teacher's Day* (Hilsum and Cane, 1971) sets out to use observational techniques to provide a descriptive account of teachers' work in terms of a careful breakdown of activities which make up a teacher's day both at school and when engaged on professional activities out of school. The first stage of the ORACLE research project reported as *Inside the Primary Classroom* (Galton, Simon and Croll, 1980) describes teacher and pupil behaviour and interactions in a large number of junior school classes. These two studies will be discussed in more detail in chapter 2. The American project 'A Study of Schooling' also provides an extremely detailed account of a variety of aspects of classrooms — physical layout, curriculum materials, teaching methods, pupil-teacher interactions — in schools throughout the United States (Sirotnik, 1983).

Descriptive accounts of this sort are typically conducted on a large scale across a representative sample of classrooms as the purpose is to make generalizations about what teachers or classrooms are typically like. (Or about how they vary. Such research is not just concerned with describing averages but is also concerned with the extent of variation among those studied and may be used to describe sub-groups within a sample.)

The main purpose of such research is to provide reports on aspects of the educational system; how teachers and pupils spend their time, what teaching methods are used, what life is like inside classrooms. The educational system is a major social institution absorbing vast resources as well as much of the time of all children and many adults and is a focus for both individual and collective hopes for the future. Large-scale representative data of the type to emerge from the projects mentioned above provide a valuable source of information by which educators, policy makers, parents and others can come to learn more about a major social institution.

Sometimes such information is set against other accounts of classroom activities, either assertions about what is actually happening or claims about what should or could be made to happen. For example, the authors of *Inside the Primary Classroom* point out that the picture which emerges from their study of orderly industrious classrooms contrasts with the claims made by a variety of politicians, journalists and educationalists in the middle 1970s that primary schools had abandoned a concern with basic skills and were frequently unruly and undisciplined (Galton, Simon and Croll, 1980, pp. 155–6. In the same volume it is also suggested that the low frequency of what the authors call 'higher cognitive level' questions and statements by teachers is a disappointing feature of junior classrooms. Similarly, the title of an article reporting the results of the American project mentioned above, 'What You See Is What You Get' (Sirotnik, 1983) implies a critical view of the results reported and the author claims that they show a limited and unimaginative approach to teaching in most classrooms.

Such evaluative responses to the results of observations cannot be justified by reference to the observation alone but must reflect the values or experience or other sources of information of those making them. It is open to any readers of such reports to make evaluations of this kind or to use the results for specific purposes. (As, for example, teacher unions might have used the data from *The Teacher's Day* in salary negotiations.)

Such studies provide a valuable source of information both for those within and outside the educational system but when reading and judging such results it is important to keep in mind what has been said earlier in this chapter. Such results cannot provide a complete, objective account of what is happening in classrooms or how teachers spend their time. Out of the infinite number of ways of describing what is going on in classrooms or how people live, they have abstracted certain elements and described them according to a particular set of definitions. This is informed by a judgment about what is important and relevant. Such judgments will often be uncontentious and large-scale descriptive studies usually contain a wealth of data relevant to a variety of purposes. But in understanding results from such studies the reader must remember that it is important to be aware of the research procedures and operational definitions employed if the data reported are to be adequately understood.

Measuring Teaching Effectiveness

A second major purpose for which systematic classroom observation has been used is in measuring the effectiveness of different approaches to teaching. Research on teacher and school effects which employs classroom observation is generally described as process-product research. In contrast to earlier studies of the effectiveness of teachers and schools which simply related school outcomes such as test scores and examination results to inputs such as the type of catchment area and previous levels of performance of pupils, process-product studies also relate the outcomes of schooling to observed classroom processes. A simple example of this might involve testing a hypothesis that the amount of praise given by teachers is positively related to the amount of academic progress children make. An observation schedule in which procedures for defining and recording a teacher's use of praise had been operationalized could be used in a large number of classrooms to provide each teacher with an overall 'praise score'. This score could then be correlated with some measure of pupil progress.[3]

A correlational procedure of this kind formed part of the recent research project conducted by Rutter and his colleagues which was reported in *Fifteen Thousand Hours* (Rutter *et al*, 1979). Various features of classrooms and schools including aspects of teacher and pupil activities in and out of the classroom were observed using, in part, systematic observation procedures. Schools were given scores on the basis of this observation which were then correlated with a variety of academic and social outcomes such as exam results, levels of truancy and juvenile court appearances.

A slightly different approach to the use of systematic observation in relating school processes to academic and other outcomes involves using the measures of different aspects of classroom behaviour to construct groups of relatively similar individuals. This procedure, known as cluster analysis, identifies sub-groups within the data and allows the researcher to say that a large sample of classrooms, teachers or pupils is better described as a smaller number of teacher or pupil types. This may be used for purely descriptive purposes but it also allows comparisons to be made between the amount of progress or positive attitudes towards school of children taught by teachers of type A as against those taught by type B or type C. In the ORACLE research project, six teacher types and four pupil types were identified on the basis of observation in junior classrooms. These types were then compared with one another on a variety of measures of outcomes of schooling.

Monitoring Teaching Approaches

Classroom observation may be used to measure the impact of one aspect of classroom process on another as well as to relate classroom processes to other measures such as attitude and test scores. A teacher who is developing a particular curriculum innovation with the intention of increasing the level of children's engagement in their work or increasing cooperative activity or reducing the need for queueing at her desk can use systematic observation (or could ask a colleague or student to use it in her classroom) in order to measure the extent of such behaviour. This may take the form of a comparison of the levels of cooperation or queueing before and after the innovation or might simply be concerned with whether a particular level was obtained regardless of comparisons with other conditions. Teachers may use these procedures to measure various aspects of the relationship between classroom organisation and pupil behaviour. For example, a recent study has compared the level of junior-aged pupil involvement in their work when sitting in rows with that in the more normal condition of groups around tables (Wheldall *et al*, 1981). Studies of this kind cannot tell teachers how they should organize their classrooms but, whether conducted by the teachers themselves or by outside researchers, they can indicate the consequences of and possible difficulties with particular patterns of organization.

Monitoring Individuals

As well as being used to monitor aspects of whole class behaviour systematic observation can also be used to monitor that of particular individuals. This may be done as part of a teacher's recognition of the differing ways that different children react in class. An innovation that increases engagement in work or levels of cooperation overall may have the opposite effect for particular pupils. It may also be used to help to devize, and then to monitor, programmes for children experiencing particular difficulties in the classroom. The techniques of behaviour modification and precision teaching for children with behavioural difficulties or learning problems depend on breaking down behaviours or accomplishments into small measurable components and setting targets for them in quantitative terms (see Presland, 1976; Williams *et al*, 1980). This involves the teacher or other observer in carefully observing and recording aspects of the child's behaviour. Conducting these observations is not likely to involve either the lengthy planning or long periods of an observational research programme but the principles involved in setting up and conducting such observations are the same.

In-Service Teacher Education

Systematic observation is increasingly becoming a part of the in-service education of teachers, partly associated with the increasingly professional basis of in-service work and the idea of the teacher-as-researcher which are coming to influence it. Teachers involved in in-service work may use systematic observation for any of the above purposes but are probably most likely to want to monitor some aspect of their own practice. Some of the issues involved in teachers doing research in their own professional settings will be discussed in the final chapter but it is worth indicating here that one major problem teachers face is the practical one of observing and teaching at once. As will be suggested in chapter 3 the various possible mechanical recording procedures are likely to provide only a partial solution. Many teachers are likely to find that they need to cooperate with a colleague or find some other observer. Current developments in linking in-service work with the initial training of teachers (Ashton, 1983) may provide a useful model for this.

The Initial Training of Teachers

The use of systematic observation in in-service education programmes described above is associated with teachers investigating their
own practice and other issues arising from their professional activities. The same sort of investigation is possible in the case of students
in initial training conducted in collaboration with their tutors and
fellow students. Students engaged in classroom-based investigations
will have little professional experience out of which issues for
investigation and ideas about what to observe can arise. Consequently, in many instances the use of systematic observation in initial
teacher training will be closer to a teaching technique on the part of
tutors than a genuine research process although this does not mean
that students cannot engage in genuine research.

Systematic observation techniques can be used to give students
feedback on their own teaching either in 'real' classes during teaching
practice or in specially devized teaching situations such as those
employed in micro-teaching (see Wragg 1970 and 1984; and Brown,
1975, for examples of these). As well as providing feedback, the
process of acting as an observer can make students more aware of the
dynamics of teaching processes and of classroom interaction. Prior to
acting as either teacher or observer, the process of designing an
observation schedule or of deciding on whether an existing schedule
is appropriate for particular purposes can be valuable in helping to
focus on what it is that the student teachers are actually planning to
do in their lessons and what sort of pupil response they are hoping to
obtain. Used in a way that involves the students in deciding what and
how to observe, the planning of systematic observation can make
students more precise and explicit about what they intend to do in
classrooms and the feedback from observation can give them more
control over and insight into their teaching activities. Incorporating
such an observation exercise into teaching practice supervision can
help to make this a more supportive experience through disscussion
between student and tutor of appropriate categories for observation.
The recently published account of the work of the Teacher Education
Project gives examples of this kind of use of systematic observation
(Wragg, 1984).

The purposes described above are not exhaustive and should not
be seen as necessarily distinct. They are also put in very general terms.
A research project which could be operationalized into an observation system would need to be very much more specific about the
purposes for which observation was being conducted. Some examples

of such specific projects will be discussed in the following chapter. The main intention of this volume is to give a methodological guide to systematic observation but the crucial link between methodology and the substantive aims of research will always be made clear.

A final point which needs to be made concerns the terminology used. Systematic classroom observation, which is the focus of this book is sometimes treated as synonymous with Interaction Analysis or Classroom Interaction Analysis (see, for example, Hamilton and Delamont, 1974; Kerry and Wragg, 1979.) As it will be discussed here systematic classroom observation applies to any procedure for describing events, interactions and material artifacts within classrooms. Many, perhaps most, of such enquiries will be concerned with interactions and many of the examples presented here will be of this sort. But interaction is not the only aspect of classrooms to be of interest to educational researchers and the study of interactions will be subsumed here in a more general consideration of the process of systematic observation.

Notes

1   The term systematic observation is conventionally used for observational research which involves carefully defined rules for recording and observation and which normally reports the results of such observations in quantitative terms. This terminology will be followed here. It is recognized, however, that it carries an unfortunate and unjustified implication when used in the context of a discussion of qualitative research techniques. I am not intending to suggest that such a methodology is unsystematic, at least not in a sense which implies that it is arbitrary or slipshod. (see HAMMERSLEY and ATKINSON, 1983; and BURGESS, 1984a, for a discussion of the methodology of ethnographic research.)

2   The classic statement of 'teacher-as-researcher' is given in STENHOUSE, 1975, chapter 5. This argument is developed in ELLIOTT, 1980. A good recent introduction to the purposes, issues and methods involved is given by HOPKINS, 1985.

3   Measuring pupil progress and relating it to a process measure such as praise involves some complex methodological issues and readers will note that the probable direction of causal effect in this example has been left deliberately ambiguous. (See GALTON and CROLL, 1980; GRAY and SATTERLY, 1976, for a discussion of some of the problems involved in process-product research.) These issues will be taken up in chapter 6.

2 *Systematic Observation in Action: Some Examples*

The purpose of this chapter is to provide illustrations of systematic observation in use by presenting particular pieces of research or particular research approaches that use systematic observational methods. The research presented here has been chosen to illustrate a variety of purposes for systematic observation and a variety of observational techniques. Some results from these research projects will also be briefly discussed to show the kinds of conclusions which can be drawn from the use of systematic observation and also to indicate the interrelationship between research problems, investigatory techniques and the findings of research.

The main purpose is exposition and it is not intended to present a critique of the studies, or to comment upon the criticisms which have been levelled at some of them. These issues will be taken up in the final chapter. Certain technical aspects of the studies such as observer training, methods of data analysis and the reliability of the observation schedules will be dealt with as appropriate in later chapters.

The structure of the chapter is to begin with a detailed presentation of the development and use of a systematic observation system as part of a recent research project for which the author was responsible. This will show the way in which substantive research purposes determine the form of an observation system, and also illustrates some of the technical issues involved in devizing such a system. The listing of categories of the variables and procedures for making observations may be helpful for other researchers engaged in devizing observational procedures.

The remainder of the chapter is taken up with shorter presentations of other observational studies. These are included to show the variety of forms of systematic observation and as a focus for discussion of methodological issues arising from them. These studies are, for the most part, well known and further details of them are readily available in published sources.

One in Five

The first observational research study, which will be presented in some detail here, is the research carried out as part of the Department of Education and Science funded project, the Assessment and Incidence of Special Educational Needs and reported in *One in Five* (Croll and Moses, 1985). Many of the procedures were based on those of Moses (1982).

The *One in Five* research was concerned with children with special educational needs in mainstream primary schools and the observational part of the study was designed to investigate differences between the classroom activities and interactions of these children and those of other pupils in primary classrooms. Areas to be investigated were: (a) whether the classroom experiences of children with special needs in terms of areas of the curriculum and types of teaching situations differed between children with special needs and other children; (b) whether children with special needs differed from other pupils in terms of their involvement in their work, the extent and type of their interactions with the teacher and the extent and type of their interactions with fellow pupils; (c) whether the classroom behaviour of children influenced whether or not the teacher regarded them as having special educational needs.

These areas of interest determined the form that the observational system had to take. It was clearly necessary that observations would need to focus mainly on pupils and that observations would have to be made of both pupils who had been identified as having special educational needs and, for comparative purposes, of a control sample of other pupils. This meant that the observation system had to be suitable for use with specific, identified pupils and had to be applicable to them across a representative sample of their classroom activities.

The procedure adopted was that in each of the thirty-four classrooms where the observation was taking place, the teacher was interviewed and asked about children with special educational needs in the class. This provided the basis for the identification of children with special needs but, in addition, tests of reading and of non-verbal reasoning were administered in each classroom and children with unusual patterns of scores (for example, high non-verbal reasoning scores and low reading ages) and children with low scores who had not been identified by their teacher were also identified for possible observation. From this list of children, up to six were selected at random for observation. From the remainder of the class four children, two boys and two girls, were also selected for observation as a control sample. This meant that between four and ten children might be observed in each class depending on the number of pupils identified by the teacher or as a result of the tests. The teachers did not know which children were to be observed although they did know that some of the children they discussed with the researchers were likely to be included.

All the time that the children spent in the classroom (or specialist teaching areas such as the hall or a craftroom) with the teacher was to be observed with the purpose of obtaining a substantial and representative sample of the behaviour of the various children. The observational procedure was to observe each child for a few minutes at a time, moving from child to child in pre-determined random order. An observer spent about twenty hours in the classroom and each child was observed for a total of two hours made up of a large number of short periods of observation.

After deciding on the pupils to be observed and the procedure for organizing the observation it is necessary to decide on the variables and categories to be used in classifying children's activities in the classroom. These are determined by the research questions which the observation is designed to answer. The first major research question was whether children with special educational needs had the same classroom experience as other children with regard to their contact with different areas of the curriculum and patterns of teaching organization. Two basic variables were, therefore, the area of the curriculum on which pupils were engaged and the sort of organization of learning (a class lesson, group work, individual work, etc.) in which they were involved. Secondly, the observation was intended to show if children with special educational needs had different levels of engagement in work and different levels and types of interaction with the teacher than other pupils. This meant that variables had to describe pupils' work activities and types of pupil-teacher interaction. Other areas of interest included aspects of children's behaviour which might cause problems in the classroom or which might affect the teacher's assessment of a child. These included aggressive behaviour, fidgeting and moving around the classroom and were included either as new variables or as categories of another variable. Finally, there was a concern about the response of children who had reading problems to curriculum tasks which involved reading and so a measure of whether a piece of work involved reading was incorporated as an extra variable.

The variables used to observe and describe pupil activities in class are described below. As with the other pieces of research presented here they must be considered in terms of the questions being asked in a particular research project and not in terms of a single 'best' approach to classroom observation.

The first three variables to be coded were intended to establish the context of a child's activity and related to the child's situation in class with regard to teaching organization and curriculum content.

Variable 1 — Teaching Organisation

Categories:

Class contact	— the child is part of a class lesson or similar whole class activity.
Group contact	— the child is part of a group working with the teacher.
Cooperative activity	— the child is in a group who have a cooperative task.
Individual activity	— the child's activity does not involve class or group work.
No directed activity	— there is no pattern of organized activity (for example, beginning and end of lessons).

The categories of this variable refer to the context in which a child is placed rather than to the child's actual activity. During a class lesson a child who is part of the class is coded 'class contact' whether or not that particular child is paying attention to the lesson. Similarly a child who is part of a group or pair which has been set a cooperative task is coded 'cooperative activity' whether or not any cooperation is going on.

Variable 2 — Reading/Non Reading

Categories:

Reading	— the content of the child's activity requires the reading of text.
Non-reading	— the reading of text is not required.

This variable established whether or not the task on which the child is engaged requires the reading of text. Like Variable 1, it is not necessary for the observer to say whether or not the child is actually reading but only whether or not the activity requires reading. The 'reading' code does not mean that reading is the main content of the child's curriculum activity, or even that the child is engaged in a curriculum activity at all. A mathematics task may require that a problem or instruction has to be read as may a task concerned with classroom organization.

Variable 3 — Curriculum Content

Categories:

Reading	— reading is the main focus of the child's curriculum activity (for example, silent reading of a library book, reading to the teacher).
Writing	— writing text is the main focus of the child's curriculum activity (for example, creative writing, grammar exercises).
Maths	— number work is the main curriculum activity.
Other 'literacy'	— the curriculum activity is related to literacy but does not involve writing and is not primarily a reading activity (for example, oral vocabulary or spelling work, drama, listening to a story).
Other non-literacy	— curriculum activities not falling into the above categories (for example, craft, P.E.).
Non-curriculum	— activities which are not directly part of the curriculum such as registration and classroom organization.

These categories provide an overall classification of the pattern of curriculum content which children experience. As with variables 1 and 2, the categories relate to the content of the child's curriculum task rather than what he or she is actually doing at any particular moment.

Variables, 1, 2 and 3 establish the immediate classroom and

curriculum setting of the child being observed, for example, that the child is part of a class lesson on mathematics which does not involve reading text, or that the child is alone with a reading book or similar material. Variables 4, 5 and 6 refer to aspects of the child's activities and interactions within this context and are coded on the basis of what the child is actually doing at each moment when the child is observed.

Variable 4 — Child Activity

Categories:

Work	— the child is working directly on a curriculum task.
Work related	— the child is engaged on an activity associated with a curriculum task (for example, fetching materials, waiting to see the teacher).
Distracted	— the child is not engaged on the task or other activity which is his or her curriculum context and is not involved in other activity categories.
Aggression to person	— physical or verbal aggression.
Aggression to property	— the child is damaging the school's or an individual's property.
Discipline	— the child is the subject of a disciplinary interaction by the teacher individually or together with others.
Class business	— the child is involved in activities associated with classroom organization and management (for example, registration, queueing to leave the classroom, listening to instructions which do not have a curriculum focus).
Other (neutral)	— this is not a conventional 'other' category to be used when nothing else applies. It is coded when the teaching organization

> code is 'no directed activity' so
> that a child who is not working
> cannot be described as 'dis-
> tracted'.

This variable describes the actual activities of the children being observed at each of the large number of occasions when observations are made. The categories reflect the main interests of the research project.

Variable 5 — Pupil Interaction

Categories:

Alone	— child is not interacting.
One other child	— interaction with one other.
Group of children	— child is interacting simultaneously with two or more other children
Teacher alone	— child is interacting with the teacher on a one-to-one basis.
Teacher group	— child is part of a group of children with whom the teacher is interacting.
Teacher group star	— child is part of a group with whom the teacher is interacting and is the main focus of the teacher's inter-action.
Class	— the child is part of a whole class with whom the teacher is interacting.
Class star	— the child is part of a whole class with whom the teacher is interacting and is the main focus of the teacher's interaction.
Another adult	— the child is interacting with an adult other than the teacher.

This set of categories provides a simple description of the classroom interactions which may be involved in interacting with another child, more than one other child and the teacher. Types of teacher interaction are classified in some detail; not only are individual, group and class interactions distinguished, but, in addition, situations when a child is the main focus of the teacher's attention but the teacher is also interacting with a group or class (for example, when a child answers a question asked of the whole class or group or is singled out by the teacher during a class lesson) are distinguished from simple one-to-one teacher-pupil interactions and from other class and group interactions. This makes it possible to use the categories in a variety of ways in data analysis. A measure of simple one-to-one pupil-teacher interaction is given by the 'teacher alone' category. A measure of the total amount of time when a child is the main focus of the teacher's attention is given by adding 'teacher alone' to 'teacher group star' and 'class star'. An overall measure of teacher interaction with the class can be obtained by adding 'class' and 'class star', and, similarily, the amount of group interaction a child is involved in can be obtained by adding 'teacher group' and 'teacher group star'.

Variable 6 — Mobility/Fidgeting.

Categories:

Mobile	— the child is moving around (not just out of place).
Fidgeting	— the child is fidgeting (swinging on the back legs of a chair, playing with a pencil or ruler, etc.) but not moving around.
Neither	

This variable was included because in discussions with teachers as part of the pilot study for the research, moving around and fidgeting were descriptions often applied to children said by their teachers to have special educational needs. It should be noted that there is a hierarchy of categories for this variable. A child who is moving around is coded as 'mobile' whether or not he or she is also fidgeting but a child who is fidgeting is only coded as such if he or she is not also moving around.

The six variables described above provide a way of describing the organizational and curriculum context in which children are observed in the classroom and some features of their behaviour and interactions. For each of them there was also a 'not coded/other' category. The fact that this was used extremely infrequently provides a check on the adequacy of the coding system.

The procedure for making the observations was a time-sampling system. Observations were made at ten-second intervals and the variables are coded according to what the child is doing at that instant. The observers wore a small tape-recorder feeding a pre-recorded 'bleep' into an earpiece every ten seconds and recorded the appropriate categories at that instant.

In principle, the six variables could each be coded at every observation point, that is, at ten second intervals. However, this would be difficult for the observers to cope with and proved unnecessary in practice. The first three variables, because they refer to the context in which the child is located rather than to the child's immediate activities are likely to remain constant through several minutes, or longer, of observation time. Variables 4 to 6, on the other hand, may well change between the ten-second intervals. Therefore, the procedure used is to code variables 1, 2 and 3 at the beginning of a period of observation of a particular child and only to code them again if they change during the time that the child is being observed. Variables 4, 5 and 6 are coded at each ten-second interval.

The coding form used in this observation system is presented in figure 1 and the coding procedure is best explained with reference to it.

Figure 1 is based on the form which the observer actually uses in the classroom. On the extreme right are listed the categories of the six variables for quick reference if necessary. On the immediate left of the list of categories is a block of empty boxes into which numbers are written. Each coding sheet contains eighty boxes which are to have numbers entered into them and which are regarded as a group of observations.[1] One coding sheet will be filled in in four minutes of observation if codes are made at ten-second intervals and a one-hour teaching session will use up about sixteen forms.[2]

The first thing the observer has to do is to identify the child, the classroom and the lesson being observed. This is done in the first group of five boxes marked A in figure 1. The first two boxes provide a two digit identification number for the teacher which, of course, also acts as a classroom identification number. The third box is used for the child identification number. (In the *One in Five* research there were never more than ten children observed in each classroom and so a single digit identification, 0–9, was sufficient. If more than ten children are being observed then a two digit child identification number is required and two boxes would have to be used.) The two digit teacher and the one digit child identification number, read together, provide a three digit number which uniquely identifies any child observed in the study and also indicates which class he or she is in. The fourth and fifth boxes of row A are used for a two digit number which identifies the particular lesson or teaching session being observed. A separate list is kept of the lessons observed so that the lesson identification number can be used to identify the date and time of day and other features of the lesson when the observa-

Systematic Classroom Observation

Figure 1: One in Five: Coding Form for Classroom Observation.

ROW A ⬚⬚⬚⬚⬚	1 TEACHING ORGANISATION
ROW B ⬚⬚⬚⬚⬚⬚	1 Class contact 2 Group contact 3 Cooperative activity
ROW C ⬚⬚⬚	4 Individual activity 5 No directed activity
ROW D ⬚⬚⬚	
ROW E ⬚⬚⬚	2 READING/ NON-READING
ROW F ⬚⬚⬚	1 Reading 2 Non-reading
ROW G ⬚⬚⬚	3 CURRICULUM CONTENT 1 Reading
ROW H ⬚⬚⬚	2 Writing 3 Maths 4 Other literacy
ROW I ⬚⬚⬚	5 Other non-literacy (details) 6 Non curriculum
ROW J ⬚⬚⬚	
ROW K ⬚⬚⬚	
ROW L ⬚⬚⬚	4 CHILD ACTIVITY
ROW M ⬚⬚⬚	1 Work 2 Work related
ROW N ⬚⬚⬚	3 Distracted 4 Aggression to person 5 Aggression to property
ROW O ⬚⬚⬚	6 Discipline 7 Class business 8 Other (neutral)
ROW P ⬚⬚⬚	5 PUPIL INTERACTION
ROW Q ⬚⬚⬚	1 Alone 2 One other child
ROW R ⬚⬚⬚	3 Group of children 4 Teacher alone 5 Teacher group
ROW S ⬚⬚⬚	6 Teacher group star 7 Class 8 Class star
ROW T ⬚⬚⬚	9 Another adult
ROW U ⬚⬚⬚	6 MOBILITY/FIDGETING
ROW V ⬚⬚⬚	1 Mobile 2 Fidgeting 3 Neither
ROW W ⬚⬚⬚	
ROW X ⬚⬚⬚	
ROW Y ⬚⬚⬚	

tions were made. The teacher, pupil and lesson identification codes in row A can be filled in before the lesson begins. The observer simply needs to know which number corresponds to each of the children to be observed.

The remainder of the boxes are used for the 'live' observations. When the observer starts to observe a child, the first three variables are coded in the first three boxes of the second row, marked B in figure 1. In the first box of row B a number is written corresponding to the appropriate category of variable 1, *Teaching Organization*. Then variables 2 and 3, *Reading — Non-reading* and *Curriculum Content*, are coded in the second and third boxes. This establishes a context for the subsequent observations recorded in this particular block of boxes and will not normally be coded again during the four minutes for which that particular child is observed.

Variables 4, 5 and 6 *Child Activity*, *Pupil Interaction* and *Mobility/Fidgeting* are coded at each ten second interval. When the first observation of the sequence is made of a child and variables 1, 2 and 3 are coded in the first three boxes of row B, variables 4, 5 and 6 are also coded in the fourth to sixth boxes of row B. Variable 4 is coded in the fourth box, variable 5 in the fifth box and variable 6 in the sixth box. To give a concrete example, if a child is working on his or her own with a reading book sitting still at a desk, row B will read: 4, 1, 1, 1, 1, 3. If a child is in a class lesson in which the teacher is reading a story, but the child is whispering to another child, row B will read: 1, 2, 4, 3, 2, 3.

Row B is the first row to be coded when the observer initially focusses on a child. At the next ten-second interval row C is coded. This does not involve coding variables 1, 2 and 3. Only variables 4, 5 and 6 are coded. Variable 4, *Child Activity*, is coded in the first box of row C, variable 5, *Interaction* is coded in the second box and variable 6, *Mobility/Fidgeting* is coded in the third box. At the next ten-second interval, variables 4, 5 and 6 are coded in row D, then row E and so on until row Y has been coded and twenty-four separate observations have been made of the particular child. At this point the observer moves on to the next child to be observed and starts at the top of another block of boxes.

The above procedure is followed for the great majority of cases when the teaching and curriculum contexts described in variables 1, 2 and 3 do not change during the four minutes when the twenty-four observations are made. If the teaching organization or curriculum content does change, the observer breaks off coding the block of boxes, moves to a new block, codes row B as appropriate for the new teaching or curriculum context and completes however many codes are remaining in the new block of boxes. For example, if an observer is about to code row N when the teacher moves from individual work to a class lesson, the first three boxes of row B are coded in a new block of boxes and row N onwards of the new block are coded. This is the equivalent of coding the teaching and curriculum context at each ten-second interval, but is a more economical way of obtaining the information. It should be noted that this procedure only works if the teaching context and curriculum content are relatively stable. The system would not work in classrooms where there were frequent changes.

The observation procedure gathers information about a child at twenty-four separate instants spread over four minutes. The observer then moves on to another child. If ten children are being observed in a classroom each child's turn will come round every forty minutes. In the *One in Five* research the observer spent about twenty hours in each classroom, observing each child for a total of two hours or on 720 separate occasions.

The large amount of data generated by this procedure can then be used in a variety of analyses. The main analysis involved a comparison of the children with special education needs and the control children and this is the way in which the data are presented in the main report on the project (Croll and Moses, 1985). It is also possible, however, to make other comparisons such as between male and female pupils (Croll, 1985). As well as these comparisons of pupils the data can be used to compare the levels of different kinds of activity in different classrooms or levels of various sorts of pupil behaviour at different times of the day.

The simplest form of such comparisons is to consider the variables one at a time to see what proportion of the observations made of various groups of children fall into each category of the variable under consideration. For example, in *One in Five* the comparison of children with special educational needs and control children on variables 1 to 3 showed that the classroom and curriculum contexts within which the children spent their time at school was very similar for the two groups. The children with special needs were just as likely as other children to be part of a class lesson or to have individual tasks and also experienced the same broad categories of curriculum content.

In contrast, the actual classroom behaviour and interactions of the children with special needs, described in variables 4 to 6, differed from those of the other children. The children identified as having special needs spent less time on their work than other pupils, spent more time engaged in aggressive behaviour (although the overall level of aggressive behaviour was still very low), spent more time fidgeting (but not moving around the classroom) and received about double the level of individual teacher attention as that received by the other children in the class.

It is also possible to go beyond this analysis of the variables one at a time and to consider the interrelationships between variables. For example, by looking at the co-occurrence of categories of variable 1 and categories of variable 4, it is possible to see if different sorts of pupil behaviour such as working on a curriculum task is more likely to occur in the the context of one pattern of organization than during another. This can be established generally and also for particular groups of children. In *One in Five* it is shown that while for the control pupils different patterns of classroom organization are characterized by generally similar levels of work engagement, for the children with special needs levels of involvement in work differ considerably across different patterns of organization. These children's involvement in their work can be shown to be more influenced than that of other children by the teaching approaches used. As the relatively low levels of work involvement of these children is one of the main problems that teachers have with such children these results are clearly of relevance to classroom practice.

It is also possible to look at interrelationships between categories of the immediate behavioural variables. A cross-tabulation of variable 4 and variable 5 makes it possible to look at the co-occurrence of the various categories of activity and interaction. An example of such an analysis is a description of how much of the time pupils spend interacting with other pupils is work-orientated or, put the other way around, how much of the work pupils do is done in cooperation with others. In *One in Five* it is shown that pupils with special needs spend an unusually high proportion of the time they are distracted from work, distracted on their own rather than in interaction with other pupils.

One way of thinking of these cross-tabulations is as the creation of a large number of additional variables. Two variables such as the categories of pupil activity and the categories of pupil interactions can be used to create a variety of other measures such as 'Working with another pupil', 'Distracted from work with a group of others' or 'Working on a one-to-one basis with the teacher'. Introducing another variable such as curriculum content or type of work organization extends the possible number of new variables.

The ORACLE Project

The second project to be described here is the first large-scale study of classroom interaction to be undertaken in Britain and involves an observational methodology very similar to that just described. This was a five-year research project funded by the Social Science Research Council (now the Economic and Social Research Council) at the University of Leicester between 1975 and 1980. Although the original title of the research programme was 'The Nature of Classroom Learning in Primary Schools, and Related Studies', it became generally known as ORACLE, an acronym for Observational Research and Classroom Learning Evaluation. The basic programme of observation and the results obtained are described in *Inside the Primary Classroom* (Galton, Simon and Croll, 1980). Other research work based on this project is contained in Galton and Simon (1980) Simon and Willcocks (1981) and Galton and Willcocks (1982).

The main aim of the study was to describe and analyze pupil and teacher activities and interactions in the primary school classroom and to relate these to the progress children were making in their school achievements. The research involved two separate observation systems: a *Pupil Record* and a *Teacher Record*. Both of these had been developed prior to the ORACLE programme by Deanne Boydell (Boydell, 1974 and 1975). The *Pupil Record* is based on the American PROSE system (Personal Record of School Experience, Medley *et al*, 1973) while the *Teacher Record* was specially designed to record teacher activities and interactions in English classrooms.

Both observation schedules involve selecting moments of time when a record is made by means of *time-sampling*. The observer uses a mechanical timing procedure (a small tape recorder with an earpiece sounding a 'bleep' to the observer at specified intervals, in this case twenty-five seconds) and codes the observation schedule in terms of the activities and interactions of the child or teacher being observed at the moment. This can be likened to a snap-shot of this individual at that moment in time. The coding process continues so that a series of such snap-shots are taken, building up a large sample of aspects of the behaviour of a particular individual or of people in a particular class or lesson.

Each of the observation systems consists of a series of variables relating to an aspect of behaviour or interaction. In the case of the *Pupil Record* a pupil's basic activity is coded according to one of a set of fourteen mutually exclusive categories . These include: directly engaged on a curriculum task, engaged on routine activities supporting a curriculum task such as giving out text-books or sharpening a pencil, waiting for the teacher (including queueing at the teacher's desk or waiting in place with hand up) and disrupting another child's work. As well as the basic fourteen categories, a code is made according to whether a child is moving around the room or not and also according to whether a child is in his or her allotted work base or not. These three variables (activity, mobility, in-out of base) are coded each time a child is observed. In addition to these, if the child is interacting with the teacher at the instant sampled, further variables are coded which describe certain aspects of this interaction. One variable describes whether this interaction is on an individual, class or group basis. Another describes whether or not the interaction is concerned with a curriculum task. A further set of variables are coded if the pupil being observed is interacting with another pupil or pupils. If this is the case, then the sex of the other pupil and whether the interaction is with one or more than one other child is recorded, and also whether or not the child being observed began the interaction and whether or not it is with a pupil from the same base area.

The coding schedule is set out in order to allow these aspects of a pupil's behaviour to be recorded rapidly by a set of ticks in the appropriate boxes and one form allows recordings to be made at ten points in time, covering approximately four minutes. Each form is also coded with an identification number for the child being observed and a record is kept of the date and time and the broad category of curriculum content on which the pupil is engaged.

The basic procedure used in the research was to sample four boys and four girls at random from each classroom involved in the study. These eight children were then sorted into random order and observed for ten instances each in sequence. Together with a period of observation focussed on the teacher, this usually occupied a complete lesson. Over a school year, eighteen lessons were observed in each classroom building up a considerable amount of data on the children sampled.

Like the *Pupil Record*, the *Teacher Record* is coded at twenty-five second intervals. The main variable contains twenty-seven mutually exclusive categories into one of which the teacher's activities are coded. These include different kinds of questions and statements, silent marking, reading a story and so on. A second variable records whether the teacher's audience, if interaction is taking place, is the whole class, a smaller group of children or an individual child. This recording procedure makes it possible to measure how much time the teacher spends in interaction with the class, how much of this is with group, individual and the whole class, how much time is spent questioning pupils, how much time is spent making statements (including some details of the types of questions and statements and whether or not they are concerned with curriculum tasks). Cross-tabulating the two variables provides measures of the sorts of interactions most likely to occur with different sorts of audiences.

The purpose of the ORACLE observation system is to provide descriptions of the classroom behaviour and interactions of individual pupils and teachers which can then be combined to provide an overall description of classrooms. Its relevance is in providing a broad overall survey of what is happening in classrooms which is essential in order to inform educational discussion. It also provides descriptions of aspects of classroom life and of some of the consequences of using particular teaching approaches which may not be otherwise apparent to busy teachers. One of the themes of the research is that teaching can often become an isolated activity and that teachers have relatively few opportunities to see classrooms other than their own. Research like the ORACLE programme can provide descriptions of other teachers' experiences.

The results and conclusions from the analysis of the ORACLE data have been published in the four volumes referenced at the beginning of this section. A brief account of some selected results will be given here in order to indicate the sorts of conclusions which can be derived from a study of this kind.

A central conclusion to emerge was the basically orderly and industrious nature of the classrooms observed and the concentration on number and language in the curriculum. This came at a time when it was being suggested, in the notorious Black Papers (Cox and Dyson, 1969a and 1969b) and elsewhere, that English primary schools were becoming anarchic and disorderly and that teachers had abandoned an emphasis on the basic skills. (For a discussion on these claims see Galton, Simon and Croll, 1980.) In contrast, the ORACLE research showed that pupils were spending three quarters of their time in class directly on curriculum or curriculum-related activities, that classrooms were mainly quiet with very low levels of disruptive behaviour and that the curriculum was predominantly concerned with the basic skills of language and number.

Another result of relevance to teachers to emerge was the asymmetry between the teacher's and pupils' view of the classroom. The *Teacher Record* showed the teacher interacting with pupils for four-fifths of lesson time, mainly on an individual, one-to-one basis. The *Pupil Record* shows the pupil typically working alone and only interacting with the teacher for about one-sixth of lesson time. Most of this interaction is as a member of the teacher's class audience and only about 2.5 per cent of lesson time is spent in interaction with the teacher on a one-to-one basis.

These figures show the predominance of an individualized approach to teaching in the primary classroom, but also the difficulties this creates in the context of large classes. For the teacher the primary classroom is characterized by an intensive round of individual interactions. For the pupils it is characterized by solitary work only intermittently broken up by class lessons and characterized by low levels of individual interaction with the teacher.

The results discussed so far have been presented in terms of averages based on all the pupils and teachers who were observed. This provides valuable information but may also hide systematic patterns of variation within the data. The technique of cluster analysis makes if possible to group together sub-sets of teachers or pupils who are similar to one another with regard to the variables being considered and who differ from other sub-sets within the group studied. (Cluster analysis is discussed in chapter 6.) This sort of analysis makes it possible to provide a richer description of the pupils and teachers and enables comparisons to be made between different groups, for example, between the academic progress made by certain types of pupil and between pupils taught by different types of teacher.

The observational procedures of the ORACLE and *One in Five* studies are in most respects very similar. The differences between them illustrate their different research purposes and emphases. In general the ORACLE observation system is more complex than that used in *One in Five* which has fewer variables and, usually, fewer categories. In certain areas, however, the *One in Five* system introduces distinctions and variables not found in ORACLE such as the Mobility/Fidgeting variable and distinctions between types of aggression and types of pupil-teacher interaction.

Because the ORACLE research was concerned with giving a general view of primary classrooms and not with testing specific hypotheses, considerable detail was necessary in the observation system. As *One in Five* was a more specifically focussed study many of the details included in the ORACLE observation system were unnecessary as they did not relate to the concerns of the study. On the other hand, there were times when in order to test the research hypotheses adequately, finer distinctions and additional information were built into the observations.

The Teacher's Day

The next study considered is a project conducted at the National Foundation for Educational Research (NFER) and described in detail in the book *The Teacher's Day* (Hilsum and Cane, 1971). This research is also based on systematic observation but uses an approach very different from that of the two projects described above. It provides a comparison which illustrates the variety of uses to which observational techniques can be put.

As the title suggests, *The Teacher's Day* was intended to provide a representative account of the working day of school teachers, in this case, teachers in junior schools. The researchers decided that the most accurate way of getting such an account was for observers to spend a day or days with each of a sample of teachers and to note the activities of the teacher during the day. In deciding to use an observational methodology the researchers had to make a judgment about the relative advantages and disadvantages of different approaches. To have an observer spend a day or more with each teacher in the sample is time consuming and involves potential difficulties in securing the agreement of teachers and making arrangements for observation and may also involve a danger that the observer will influence what is being observed. Set against such considerations is the enormous gain in accuracy and detail which becomes possible by using an observer to note the teachers' activities as they occur. It was felt that other methods such as interviewing or asking the teachers to complete a diary would suffer from incompleteness and other inaccuracy. Teachers are too busy during most of their working day to keep a record of what they are doing and later recall is likely to be partial and inaccurate, possibly with the unusual or memorable getting more emphasis than the ordinary and routine. Using an observer also makes it possible to ensure that activities are recorded by all observers in an identical fashion in a way that would be almost impossible if teachers were making an unsystematic record of their own activities.

The basic procedure therefore was for teachers and schools to be asked to agree to be observed. Following their agreement a familiarization day was arranged when the observer accompanied the teacher throughout the day but did not record activities. The observer would then arrive at the school on a subsequent day without prior notice (the teachers knew that this would happen but did not know when) and spend the day noting the teacher's activities. A total of 129 teachers were observed, some for one day and some for two days, generating a total of 197 days of observation. The teachers were sampled at random within one local education authority and represented over 90 per cent of those in the original sample.

Some general issues emerge from this brief description of procedure. The high response rate shows that teachers will cooperate with observational research if the project is carefully explained and is seen as worthwhile. Such response rates are higher than those typically obtained when people are asked to complete diaries or fill in self-completion questionnaires.[3] The familiarization day when the observer goes through the research procedures but does not collect or does not utilize the data is also important. This reassures the teacher that observation will not interfere with the work of the school and also allows teachers and their pupils to get used to the presence of an observer, so reducing the likelihood that the observer will influence the situation. The fact that the observer arrived unannounced to carry out observation also makes it less likely that anything special will happen because the research is being conducted.

In addition, this procedure generates a random sample of days in order to give an accurate overall picture of teachers' work. Observing on a day when school sports are taking place provides an unrepresentative account of that particular teacher's work, but to exclude such days would misrepresent the totality of teaching activities. The researchers in *The Teacher's Day* project were concerned with aggregate features of the junior school teachers' work rather than with giving an accurate picture of the work of particular individuals. Consequently, they sampled a small part of the activities of a large number of people. A research project which wanted data that gave an accurate view of particular individuals would spend much longer with each of the teachers and would probably only have the time and resources to look at a smaller number of them.

The procedure described so far was for a trained observer to spend complete school days with teachers recording their activities. (In addition teachers were asked to keep a record of their work activities in the evenings and at weekends but this was not part of the observational study which is the focus of this description.) Fundamental to the research was the system by which observations were made and noted. The research was planned as a systematic observational study which means that the observers were to record according to a pre-determined set of categories and an agreed procedure for using them.

As with any observational research the categories used were determined by the purpose for which the research was being conducted and the questions which the investigators wanted to answer.

The research was concerned to describe teachers' work commitments and therefore needed categories which would reflect the range of work-related activities in which teachers are engaged. It was not concerned with teaching methods or curriculum content or teacher-pupil relationships but rather with the amount of time spent on instruction, organization, marking, consultation, pastoral work and so on and the categories used reflected these interests. Consequently the categories are usually very broad such as 'teaching' (including direct instruction, demonstrating on a lesson topic, marking work in interaction with a pupil), 'organization' (including organizing assignments, seating and equipment), 'marking' (not in interaction with pupils), 'playground duty' and 'professional reading'. The possible range of teacher activities was categorized under fifty-five headings of this type.

These fifty-five categories were generated empirically, that is, they were developed from a consideration of all the sorts of activities which arise during a teacher's day and the best way of categorizing them. This process was based in part on lists of their daily activities drawn up by teachers. An empirical procedure of this sort for devizing categories is not the only approach. Categories could have been generated theoretically in response to the need to test a specific research hypothesis or based on a theoretical model of teaching.

The fifty-five categories and descriptions and definitions of the activities to be placed in them gave the observers a procedure for assigning a single numerical code to any teacher activity during the school day. (It was occasionally necessary to use more than one category to describe any activity but this was unusual and the set of activity categories were intended to provide an exclusive code for any particular activity.) The fact that the categories were exclusive meant that codes could be grouped together in analysis where appropriate. For example, the general category 'organization' includes organizing pupils within the class, consulting with colleagues and planning lessons, but these categories can also be looked at individually and can be put into a variety of groupings. (The coders simply used the individual category codes without regard to possible grouping in analysis.)

Having established a set of categories the researcher had then to decide on the way in which observers would apply these to the on-going activities of teachers. The procedure employed was one of *continuous recording*. This means that a record is kept of the teachers' activity at all times and this record changes at exactly the point when the activity changes rather than noting the teachers' activities at, for example, ten or twenty-second intervals.

Recording sheets were prepared on which each row represented a minute of the day marked off in five second intervals. (An example of such a recording sheet is given in figures 4 and 5 in chapter 3.) The observer writes a number corresponding to the category from the list of fifty-five possible activities which describes what the teacher is doing and then moves the pencil along the row as a minute (indicated by a watch with a sweep second hand attached to the clip board) goes by, returning to the next row at the end of the minute and so on. In this way the observer can mark off the whole of the school day in timed intervals. Whenever the activity of the teacher changes to a new category, the observer marks a downward stroke at the appropriate point on the row and after it writes the number corresponding to the new activity.

The research reported in *The Teacher's Day* is an example of a large-scale survey based on detailed observation using a relatively simple observational system to describe broad features of the teacher's work and can be used to describe all activities throughout a teacher's day. It does not provide any data on what teachers do when they are teaching or engaged in pastoral work but it allows these broad categories to be located in the overall context of the teachers' activities.

Flanders Interaction Analysis Categories (FIAC)

An approach to observational research which provides a contrast to *The Teacher's Day* is the Flanders observational system. This is not a particular research project such as *The Teacher's Day* but is an observation system which has been widely used in a great variety of settings, for a great variety of purposes and sometimes with considerable modifications to the original observation schedule. FIAC is almost certainly the best known of all systematic observation systems and is sometimes, wrongly, regarded as epitomizing systematic observation. It is an American observation system, although it has now been used in many countries, and was originally devized by Ned Flanders. There are many presentations and discussions of the FIAC observation system (Open University, 1976; Delamont, 1983). Flanders' book: *Analyzing Teaching Behaviour* (1970) provides an extensive account of the system and of some of its uses.

FIAC operates by means of classifying teacher-pupil interactions into ten categories. Seven of these categories refer to aspects of teacher talk and two to aspects of pupil talk. The remaining category is 'silence or confusion'. These categories and their definitions are shown in figure 3. The coding procedure is virtually continuous as the observer keeps a constant record by writing down the number corresponding to the content of the interaction which has just occurred. Observers code at a rate of twenty to twenty-five codes per minute or about once every three seconds. A constant tempo of recording is more important than the actual rate.

The recording procedure is very simple. In the sample recording sheet in figure 2 each row represents approximately a minute of time divided into twenty three-second intervals and each box has a number written in it at three-second intervals moving along the row. The example in figure 2 would allow five minutes of classroom interaction to be coded.

Figure 2: Recording Sheet for Flanders Interaction Analysis Categories (FIAC)

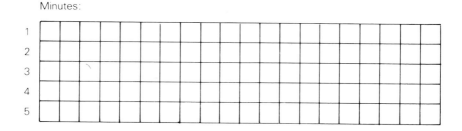

Figure 3:   Flanders' Interaction Analysis Categories (FIAC)

Teacher talk	Response	1	*Accepts feeling* Accepts and clarifies an attitude or the feeling tone of a pupil in a non-threatening manner. Feelings may be positive or negative. Predicting and recalling feelings are included.
		2	*Praises or encourages* Praises or encourages pupil action or behaviour. Jokes that release tension, but not at the expense of another individual; nodding head, or saying 'Um hm?' or 'go on' are included.
		3	*Accepts or uses ideas of pupils* Clarifying, building, or developing ideas suggested by a pupil. Teacher extensions of pupil ideas are included but as the teacher brings more of his own ideas into play, shift to category five.
		4	*Asks questions* Asking a question about content or procedure, based on teacher ideas, with the intent that a pupil will answer.
	Initiation	5	*Lecturing* Giving facts or opinions about content or procedures; expressing *his own* ideas, giving *his own* explanation, or citing an authority other than a pupil.
		6	*Giving directions* Directions, commands, or orders to which a pupil is expected to comply.
		7	*Criticizing or justifying authority* Statements intended to change pupil behaviour from non-acceptable to acceptable pattern; bawling someone out; stating why the teacher is doing what he is doing; extreme self-reference.
Pupil talk	Response	8	*Pupil-talk — response* Talk by pupils in response to teacher. Teacher initiates the contact or solicits pupil statement or structures the

		situation. Freedom to express own ideas is limited.
	Initiation	9 *Pupil-talk — initiation* Talk by pupils which they initiate. Expressing own ideas; initiating a new topic; freedom to develop opinions and a line of thought, like asking thoughtful questions; going beyond the existing structure.
Silence		10 *Silence or confusion* Pauses, short periods of silence and periods of confusion in which communication cannot be understood by the observer.

Source: Flanders (1970) p. 34

This is an extremely simple system, but a combination of the continuing relevance of the distinctions made by the categories with an extremely sophisticated approach to data analysis has meant that the system can provide a wealth of information about teaching processes.

In addition to providing counts of the proportions of utterances in classrooms falling into each of the categories, combinations of the categories and ratios between them provide additional sources of information. Obviously, the ratio of teacher talk to pupil talk or silence/confusion can be calculated. Other ratios can be calculated such as the teacher response ratio, that is, the proportion of categories 1, 2 and 3 to all teacher talk, and the pupil initiation ratio which shows category 9 as a proportion of all pupil talk.

A major feature of analyses of FIAC is the use of the interaction matrix. Because coding is quasi-continuous the record of observations can be treated as a series of pairs of observations, the second member of one pair becoming the first member of the next. These pairs can be entered into a ten-by-ten matrix showing how many times an observation in each category was followed by an observation in each of the others. This makes it possible to identify sequences of interactions and to say how long teachers and pupils spend developing their ideas and how often a particular type of utterance was followed by various other types. A simple version of an interaction matrix is shown in figure 11, chapter 5.

The best known result from the studies using FIAC is the

two-thirds rule. Two-thirds of time pupils and teachers spend in the classroom involves talk and two-thirds of that talking is done by the teacher. This predominance of teacher talk in the classroom has been confirmed by studies using other observational systems (for example, Galton, Simon and Croll, 1980). The system has also been used in a great variety of research studies, some of which are summarized by Flanders (1970) and has also been widely used in providing feed-back to student teachers and in in-service work. Some examples of the uses of FIAC in teacher education are given by Wragg (1970 and 1973).

A Study of Schooling

The final example of research using systematic classroom observation to be discussed here is the American study, *A Study of Schooling* (Gieson and Sirotnik, 1979; Sirotnik, 1983). The particular interest of this research lies in the way that a number of different observation procedures were incorporated within the same study providing a variety of data sources relevant to various aspects of pupils' and teachers' experiences within classrooms. This research was carried out on a large scale and involved observation in over a thousand classrooms in thirty-eight schools in the United States. The research was conducted using four different observation procedures. These were:

(a) *The Physical Environment Inventory* which provides information about the arrangement of seating, the types of furnishings and the materials and equipment in the classroom.

(b) *The Classroom Summary* which provides information about pupil and teacher activities in the classroom particularly with regard to the type and organisation of teaching situations.

(c) *The Five-Minute Interaction Schedule* which describes the detail of pupil-adult interactions.

(d) *The Daily Summary* which provides an overview of space, materials and decision-making in the classroom.

These four observation schedules are all used by each observer in each classroom being observed and illustrate the different types of data which it is necessary to obtain in order to answer different types of research question. The procedure used is that an observer spends a day in a classroom. The day is divided into four approximately one-hour teaching sessions. At the beginning of each session the observer codes the *Physical Environment Inventory* which deals with features of the classroom which are likely to remain constant through the lesson but it can be modified at the end of the lesson if this is not so. The observer uses a checklist to identify whether the desks are in rows or groups or a combination or other arrangement and whether available equipment and materials include: books, magazines, games or puzzles, maps or globes, live animals, plants, various audio-visual equipment and so on. This sort of checklist provides a description of the lesson context as well as enabling a description to be built up of the kind of materials and equipment which are in use in classrooms. The observer then completes a *Classroom Summary* which is completed at the beginning of the lesson and then repeated at fifteen-minute intervals. This results in data being collected four times during a one-hour teaching session. The *Classroom Summary* is essentially a scan of the classroom in which the activities of all the people in it are classified either individually or as groups where they are engaged in identical activities. The observation schedule used for this scan consists of a set of mutually exclusive categories of types of classroom activity. These include: preparation for assignments, explaining/lecturing/reading aloud, discussion, work on written assignments, taking a test, simulation/role-play and adult monitoring/observing pupil activities. For any of these categories which correspond to activities taking place when the scan is made the number of people and the nature of the groups taking part in this activity is noted. Whether or not a teacher or teacher's aide is taking part in the activity, whether it is a cooperative activity and whether it involves students working independently of adults are also noted as is the curriculum content of the activity. *The Classroom Summary* provides a sample of classroom activities which enables a picture to be built up of the nature of teaching and learning activities taking place in the classrooms as well as providing information about, for example, the amount of time the teacher spends with different types of pupil groups and the amount of time that pupils spend working independently of the teacher.

Immediately after each classroom summary is completed the observer begins a *Five Minute Interaction* coding. For five minutes the observer records the details of pupil/teacher interaction using another pre-coded systematic observation system. This is designed to answer the question: 'Who did what to whom and how?' The observer codes each interaction in terms of 'who' — one of nine categories of person or groups of person (for example, teacher, individual student, class as a whole etc.) and 'whom' — the same nine categories. The interaction is then characterised as 'what' — categories include: direct question, response to question, praise etc. The 'context' of the interaction is coded — for example as curriculum instruction, routine or social interaction. Finally there is a multiple-coding of as many categories as appropriate of 'how' — touch, humour, non-verbal etc. This is a procedure similar to the FIAC observation system and provides a detailed account of pupil-teacher interaction in the classroom. On average each five-minute period of coding resulted in just under sixty observations or 'action-frames' (Green and Sirotnik, 1979). The *Five Minute Interaction* is coded after each *Classroom Summary* has been completed giving four such coding periods in each one-hour teaching session.

Finally, at the end of each day's observation in a classroom the observer completes the *Daily Summary*. This relates to three aspects of the lessons which have been observed. The space available for the classes is classified in terms of its adequacy, restrictions on pupil's use of materials are noted and the extent of teacher and student influence on decision-making with regard to seating, grouping, curriculum content, the use of time and certain other features of the work of the class are recorded. The *Daily Summary* provides a rather different approach to data collection to that of the other observation procedures used in *A Study of Schooling*. This final data gathering procedure does not involve classifying specific events into categories or describing concrete states of affairs such as classroom seating arrangements. It depends on the observer making a judgment about the overall content of what has occurred during the day. This judgment is based on observation and involves using a set of pre-determined categories but it is judgmental rather than descriptive in the way that the other observation systems described here are.

What is particularly interesting about *A Study of Schooling* is the ingenious way in which a variety of different approaches to systematic observation are contained within a single research project. These range from moment-by-moment accounts of interaction through descriptions of what is happening in classrooms at fifteen-minute intervals to overall descriptions of physical arrangements and facilities and judgments about the balance of classroom decision-making throughout the day. As well as illustrating a variety of different approaches to classroom observation and the relationship between observational methods and underlying research questions the project also shows how an efficient research design can make the most effective use of time and resources. A single observer spending a day with a class can provide a variety of different sources of information on it.

Some of the results from this study are presented in Sirotnik (1983). As the title of the article 'What You See Is What You Get' implies, these results are interpreted in a fashion very critical of current classroom practice in the United States. The lessons observed are shown to be dominated by pupils either working on written assignments or being lectured to. In contrast, activities such as role-playing, discussion, simulation or demonstrations occupy less than eight per cent of class time. Sirotnik also points out that while 75 per cent of the teachers' time is spent on instruction less than three per cent of time is spent giving corrective feedback. The classrooms are also heavily teacher dominated with decision-making entirely in the hands of the teacher in virtually all elementary schools and between eighty and ninety per cent of secondary schools.

It should be noted that these criticisms cannot be derived from the empirical findings of the observational study but come about as a result of contrasting them with the sorts of classroom practice which Sirotnik would like to see. As he recognizes, the high level of work on curriculum tasks and the teacher concentration on instruction would suggest that a good deal of effective teaching is going on and portrays a practice in line with those recommended by studies of teaching effectiveness. Sirotnik, however, feels that much of value is being lost in what he calls the 'monotonous scenario of teacher talk to total class and student work on written assignments' and that classrooms should exhibit higher levels of discussion, demonstration, praise and student decision-making. This discussion illustrates that we cannot use empirical studies of classroom processes alone to determine how we should teach, but also shows the value of extensive, systematic observational evidence of the kind provided in *A Study of Schooling* which is needed to inform discussion on teaching and which can be approached from a variety of perspectives.

Some Practical Uses of Systematic Observation

Systematic classroom observation is not only a research instrument, it also has practical uses in teaching and teacher education. Two such uses are in behaviour modification and the provision of feedback for student teachers both in micro-teaching and in classroom situations.

Behaviour Modification

The behavioural approach to teaching involves a concentration on the overt behaviours exhibited by children in classrooms, particularly behaviour which gives rise to concern on the part of the teacher. When children exhibit behaviour which concerns the teacher the behavioural approach involves a precise description of the behaviour, its antecedents (the context in which it occurs) and its consequences for the child rather than speculating about assumed mental states or other background factors which may have caused the behaviour. Undesirable behaviour is reduced or eliminated by, wherever possible, removing the antecedent states in which it occurs, removing desirable consequences for the child such as increased attention from teacher and peers, and most importantly by reinforcing desirable behaviour whenever it occurs. For example, teachers may often react strongly when a child is disruptive and be so relieved when he or she is not, that the child is ignored. The behavioural approach ignores disruption if at all possible, or quickly removes the child if the disruption is too severe to ignore, but gives plenty of attention and praise when the child is not disruptive. A good introduction to this approach to classroom management is given by Wheldall and Merrett (1984).

A number of aspects of the behavioural approach make it particularly appropriate to incorporate systematic observation techiques within it. The approach involves a very precise specification of both undesirable behaviour and behaviour to be rewarded in just the same way that activities and characteristics to be observed are specified in an observation schedule. It is not sufficiently precise to say that a child is a 'trouble-maker' or is 'disruptive' or 'lazy'. The behaviour of concern has to be specified such as 'strikes other pupils', 'calls out during lessons', 'only completes two sums during a maths period'. The relevance of systematic observation is not just that behaviour must be exactly defined in observable terms but also that it is valuable to actually produce counts of the behaviour.

A teacher who defines the behaviour of concern can then observe it and produce counts of the occurrence which will serve a number of purposes. The counts will tell the teacher whether the behaviour is actually as frequent as expected. A teacher who has decided that a child who is causing problems in class is doing so by means of certain actions may find that these actions are actually infrequent and must then consider if the child's behaviour is really a problem or if the correct aspects of the behaviour which make the child a problem have been identified. Counting occurrences of problem behaviour (and possibly also of desirable behaviour) also allows the teacher to look at variations in the level of this behaviour, in particular, if it is especially likely to occur in particular teaching settings or social groupings or following other behaviour. This can help the teacher to remove antecedent conditions for the behaviour. Thirdly, counting occurrences of the behaviour provides a base-line measurement with which later situations can be compared. A teacher who is planning an intervention to eliminate or encourage some aspect of behaviour can compare the level of the behaviour before the intervention with that after the behaviour modification programme has been implemented. In this way the success of the intervention can be monitored.

Systematic observation as part of a behavioural approach to teaching usually involves a very simple observation methodology. Often only one aspect of behaviour is coded (calling out, being out of place, physical aggression etc.) and the observation system either counts each occurrence of this behaviour (event recording) or notes at timed intervals whether or not it has taken place (time-sampling). Wheldall and Merrett (1984) provide instances of appropriate recording procedures and give examples of a number of practical applications of the technique by teachers in classrooms.

Systematic Observation as a Feedback System for Student Teachers

A second practical rather than research application for systematic classroom observation is in preparing students training to enter the teaching profession. Systematic observation can be used in microteaching situations where students concentrate on achieving very specific objectives with a small group of pupils over a short period of time, and also in classroom situations either on teaching practice or other school experience.

The purpose of systematic observation in these settings is to help students to better control their own teaching behaviour. Establishing categories, or discussing the categories of a system such as FIAC helps to clarify what teachers are doing by their classroom utterances and other behaviour and by breaking down interactions into small and clearly specified parts helps student teachers to control, direct and change their behaviour. By actually carrying out the observations tutors or fellow students can provide immediate feedback to the student teacher on his or her behaviour and interactions. Examples of this use of systematic observation are given in Wragg (1970) and Brown (1975).

Anthologies of Observation Instruments

Educational observers have developed a large number of systematic observation systems in addition to those discussed above. Looking at other systems will be valuable to researchers beginning to conduct their own classroom observation both to provide ready-made definitions and even whole observation schedules and also to suggest ideas and to give a sense of the variety of aspects of classroom life which have been studied by means of systematic observation.

As will be argued in chapter 3, researchers should not be reluctant to devise their own systems if their research problem demands it. However, it is clearly sensible to consider if there is already an appropriate observation schedule before developing a new one and, if possible, researchers should attempt to incorporate 'benchmark' measures in their own research by including variables or categories from large-scale studies which can be used to make comparisons between their own results and the results of other studies. This helps to make classroom enquiry a genuinely cumulative exercise and incorporates an element of replication into studies.

Major anthologies of observation systems have been produced by the American corporation, Research for Better Schools Inc. Summaries are given in the two-volume *Mirrors for Behaviour* (Simon and Boyer, 1970) and in the most recent version, *Mirrors for Behaviour III* (Simon and Boyer, 1974). A more recent British anthology is *British Mirrors* (Galton, 1978) which provides information on British observation systems. Examples of observation systems are also included in the collection of educational research instruments, *Educational Research in Classrooms and Schools* (Cohen, 1976). A review of some recent British research is given by Galton (1979) and McIntyre (1980).

Researchers who find useful observation procedures in these or other sources should be sure to check on the original source of the system. These anthologies usually present the categories and procedures without making clear the rationale for these procedures or the purpose for which the systems were designed. As has been emphasized throughout, research procedures can only be understood with reference to these purposes.

Notes

1   Eighty is the number of columns on a standard punched card which was, until recently, the basis for input for computer processing. The terminals for computer input which have now replaced punched cards in many installations usually have an eighty column wide display.

2   In practise, it is possible to economise on coding forms and reduce the number of pieces of paper which the coder has to handle by having more than one eighty column block of boxes on each form.

3   Among surveys of the general population a response rate of 70 per cent for a self-completion postal questionnaire is regarded as very high and much lower rates are common. In the Schools Council research project reported in *The Aims of Primary Education* (ASHTON *et al*, 1975,) 64.5 per cent of heads originally approached agreed to distribute questionnaires to their staff and 75.5 per cent of the teachers filled in the questionnaires. In the survey of primary school teaching methods on which the book *Teaching Styles and Pupil Progress* (BENNETT, 1976) is based, a response rate of 88 per cent from headteachers is described as 'extremely high' (BENNETT and JORDAN, 1975) and just over 80 per cent of teachers completed questionnaires. Even these very high figures involve a substantial possible bias from non-response and much lower response rates are more common; 65 per cent (BENNETT, O'HARE and LEE, 1983), 53 per cent (BEATTY and WOOLNOUGH, 1982), 43 per cent (KELLY *et al*, 1985).

3 Designing an Observational Research Programme

Operationalizing Research Ideas

A crucial step in any programme of research is the process of turning research ideas into a set of procedures for generating empirical data. This is the process of operationalization, of turning a set of theoretical concerns into concrete research operations. It is not just a question of designing an observational system (or a questionnaire or assessment procedure) but of arriving at a complete research design involving decisions about the subjects of the research and any sampling to be conducted from them as well as deciding on the aspects of these subjects to be studied and defining these aspects into variables. Decisions about research design sampling and data analysis are interdependent and it is important that the researcher should have a clear idea about the form and purpose of his analysis, the questions the research is designed to answer and what will count as answers before making decisions about who and what to observe by what procedures and in what circumstances.

Like all research designs the adequacy of an observational system can only be judged with reference to its purposes. It is impossible to evaluate an observational system in isolation without reference to the purpose it is intended to achieve. Experienced researchers will often believe that they can see obvious flaws in an observation system or other research instrument but this is only possible because they can, in a general way, infer its purposes. Such judgments are always vulnerable to being overturned if the purposes are other than those assumed.

It is because empirical data gathering procedures have their validity only with reference to a specific investigatory purpose that researchers should not be afraid to devize new observational systems when this is appropriate to the aims of their research. It is sometimes suggested that a proliferation of classroom observation systems is undesirable in educational research (for example, Rosenshine, 1970; or Atkinson and Delamont, 1980, who write that 'we need new (classroom observation) systems like a hole in the head'). There is no doubt that there is much scope for further investigations using existing observational systems and for replication of previous research in classrooms but it is a mistake to make any judgment about observational systems without reference to what their authors are trying to achieve. This sort of argument also has echoes of the view that there may be a single *true* description of what is happening in classrooms rather than recognizing that all procedures involve abstracting from the infinity of things which could be said about any social setting those which are relevant for a particular investigatory purpose.

Having said this, it is nevertheless true that a researcher confronted with a research question requiring classroom observation would be wise to consider whether an existing system would meet his purposes before designing a new one of his own. Anthologies of observational instruments such as the American *Mirrors for Behaviour* (Simon and Boyer, 1970 and 1974) and *British Mirrors* (Galton, 1978) are likely to be useful in identifying possible systems and some existing observational research in classrooms has already been discussed.

It is also the case that a researcher embarking on classroom research for the first time will find it valuable to spend some time in classrooms using one or more established systems and looking at the data these provide in order to obtain a feel for conducting observation and to gain experience of the kind of issues which will arise in turning his or her own research questions into a set of criteria and definitions for use in classrooms.

A final point to be made about designing new observational systems is that when a researcher decides that the research questions being addressed require a new system rather than using an existing one it will almost certainly be of value to incorporate some aspects of a well established schedule. By this means it will be possible to provide 'bench-mark' measures of some aspects of the classrooms being researched which can be compared with data from other samples of classrooms. Such a procedure, if generally adopted, would do much towards making classroom observation more of a cumulative research activity than has previously been the case and would allow comparisons to be made across a whole variety of different studies. This would normally be of value to the individual researcher as well as providing information which others can draw upon. Some of the ways in which more than one definition of what is basically the same feature of a behaviour or interaction can be incorporated in an observation schedule and procedures for observing a number of variables simultaneously which may be useful in incorporating aspects of other schedules will be discussed later in this chapter. Using aspects of other schedules also has the advantage of forcing individual researchers to be absolutely explicit about their own procedures and to keep carefully to these procedures in practice. Otherwise, the comparisons facilitated by this incorporation are impossible and apparent differences between the results from different studies become uninterpretable.

Recording Events in Classrooms

The most commonly used procedure for conducting systematic observation in classrooms is that of *Live Observation* by a researcher using some kind of paper and pencil recording procedure, often together with a simple time-keeping device. In this approach the observation is truly 'live'. The process of observing and making a record of the observation is virtually simultaneous. The researcher does not have mechanical aids to help reconstruct what happened and does not rely on memory to write a description following the period of observation.

The advantage of this procedure is that it is relatively unobtrusive in the classroom and that it takes advantage of the flexibility of a human observer. A single observer (or sometimes, perhaps, a pair of observers) can avoid becoming intrusive in most classroom situations and can easily switch their attention between different individuals or different aspect of events and can adapt themselves rapidly to respond to what is going on.

The problems with the use of a live observation system are that the events being observed can only be recreated in terms of the observation system used and that the nature of the systematic observation system is limited by the requirement that it must be possible for an observer to observe and record virtually simultaneously. Anything that is not part of the systematic observation system cannot be subsequently recovered after a period of live observation and only a limited number of observers (perhaps one or two) can conduct a particular period of live observation. There is a considerable limit on the complexity of the observation system that can be used when observing and recording are done at the same time. It must be possible to make the appropriate record or records very quickly, a tick or number or similar mark, rather than making notes is necessary if the recording procedure is to be continuous. The system of categories and the rules for assigning events to them must also be simple enough for a trained observer to remember them; the live observer cannot look up coding decisions in the manual while observation is proceeding.

This problem of the complexity with which observers can cope is the major limitation on live observation as a research technique. However, the examples of successful observation systems already discussed show that trained observers using a carefully organized observation system can reliably code events into more complex categories than might at first be supposed possible, and relatively simple systems can be applied and analyzed in ways which can generate detailed and rich descriptions of classroom events.

An alternative approach to live observation in classrooms is that of *video recording*. A videotape of a lesson or section of a lesson can be subjected to a more complex and more flexible analysis than is possible in any live observation. The researcher can play and replay the tape, can stop while making notes or considering coding decisions and can replay particular events if the appropriate coding is in doubt. The researcher can also change and develop the observation system during the period of analysis and does not even have to decide on details of the system until after viewing the data. In contrast, a live observer who finds that a schedule is not working or omits something of interest may find that observations made before this decision are wasted. A further advantage of video recording is that a large number of observers can view the same material. This may facilitate a multi-faceted approach to the same research problem or may involve using the same videotaped material for quite different purposes. In this latter instance a set of videotapes of classrooms can become a data resource of use to many different researchers. Despite these advantages there are a number of problems with using video-recording which account for the relative scarcity of research studies using such techniques. These involve both practical difficulties and difficulties associated with the adequacy of the view of classrooms which emerges from such recordings.

The most obvious practical difficulties are the question of resources and the physical difficulties of actually making video-recordings. Video-recording is a relatively expensive activity involving expensive equipment and video tape and skilled technical assistance. For a large-scale research project requiring large, representative samples of classroom activities (750 hours and 2500 hours respectively in the *One in Five* and ORACLE studies discussed in chapter 2) the level of resources required are prohibitive, while for an individual researcher engaged on a small-scale study even the more limited resources required may not be available. It is not just a question of resources however. Recording in classrooms requires considerably more organization and creates considerably more disruption than a single researcher carrying out observations. Space must be found for the recording equipment, lighting levels have to be suitable, it will probably be necessary for the teacher or pupils being observed to wear radio microphones or some other sound recording device. All this makes the practical problems of setting up the research and gaining cooperation from schools and teachers very much greater than with most forms of research.

A further difficulty relates to the adequacy of the view of classroom activities which emerges from video-tapes made in classrooms. There is a problem in all observational studies of the possible effect of the process of observation on the situation being observed. This is obviously much more acute in the case of video-recording. The intrusivenesss of the equipment and the auxillary devices involved (radio microphones, etc.) as well as the associations of 'being on television' make it more difficult for the researcher using video-recording than for the live observer to overcome the danger of influencing the situation being observed. This does not mean that valid classroom data cannot be obtained by such procedures and ways of minimizing and checking this effect in various kinds of observation procedures will be discussed later. But it does mean that there is yet another, possibly serious, problem for the researcher using these procedures to contend with.

Another aspect of the adequacy of the view of the classroom presented by video recordings comes not from problems of bias but from problems of completeness. The video camera lacks the flexibility of the human observer both in terms of moving rapidly between different points of focus and also being able to rapidly scan a whole classroom. If the situation being observed is not static or involves observations of a scattered group of people then the camera is unlikely to be able to adjust quickly enough to the demands of observation. Video-recording can give a satisfactory record of a particular activity, especially when it is appropriate to 'set-up' the situation to be observed. A teacher giving a lecture from the front of a class or a small group of children organised to work together around a desk are possible examples. But it is less likely to be able to reflect a variety of naturally occurring classroom activities.

The researcher deciding between live and video observation will have to judge between the advantages of economy, relative simplicity of organization and the flexibility of what can be observed of live observation compared with the possibility of a very much more complex analysis offered by video-recording. It will usually be a mistake for researchers to decide on video-recording simply because it allows them to postpone decisions about detailed coding procedures. If systematic observation procedures are to be used then decision about categories and definitions have to be made at some point. The work involved in conducting live pilot studies and experimenting with procedures is almost certainly less demanding of resources than video-recording for an observation system which could have been used 'live'.

Video-recording has mainly been used by researchers with very specific research interests or in the context of providing feedback in teacher education, often in micro-teaching situations (Wragg, 1974). For most researchers video-recordings have been used to help develop observation systems and to train observers rather than as sources of data.

Other kinds of recording procedures, in particular *audio recording*, have usually been used alongside rather than replacing live observation. Tape recorders are both cheaper and less intrusive than video equipment but for most research purposes they do not by themselves allow the situations being observed to be reconstructed in a useful fashion. As would be expected, audio recording techniques have generally been used in studies concerned with linguistic analysis, most notably the extensive recordings of children, parents and teachers made as part of the Bristol Language Project (Wells, 1981). This research is outside the scope of the techniques being presented here and audio recordings will only be considered as part of the video-recording process or as an occasional supplement to live observation techniques.

Most of what follows will assume that the researcher is basically using live observation and the examples discussed earlier are of this kind. Much of the discussion will also be relevant to the analysis of video or audio tapes although many of the constraints on the complexity and detail of the analysis which are assumed here will not apply. Some of the research strategies presented, particularly those concerned with locating the behaviour of individuals within a classroom context and moving between different levels of aggregation when conducting observation will be impossible to apply in any but a live observational setting.

Defining Variables for Observation

The process of designing a programme of systematic observation and analyzing its results will be presented here in terms of the definition and analysis of variables. The idea of a *variable* is a fundamental one in quantitative social research. A variable represents the process by which a concept which is of interest to the researcher but which exists at a theoretical level is turned into a set of working definitions whereby the results of observation or some other data collecting process can be categorized and measured. Sometimes, this movement between the theoretical and the operational is very straightforward. 'Age' or 'sex' present relatively few difficulties in moving from our theoretical interest to a procedure for classification at least in classroom observation[1]. Other concepts are more difficult such as 'attainment in mathematics' or 'attitude towards mathematics'. Here the operational procedures, tests, attitude scales etc. have a more problematic relationship to our theoretical understanding of the concepts being studied. In systematic classroom observation variables typically take the form of categories of behaviour or interaction together with a set of rules for assigning behaviour or interaction to these categories. The reason for using particular sets of categories will reflect the purposes of the research as has been discussed earlier but the results will reflect the particular working definitions and procedures for assigning events to categories which define the variables.

A particular category of behaviour or interaction — a teacher's question, a pupil reading — forms the most basic unit of an observational system. (The units may, of course, be smaller than this — a teacher asking a specific type of question, a pupil reading a particular type of material). Where these units or categories are organized into a classification they will be referred to as a variable (Galtung, 1970). This classification may be very simple, for example, a dichotomous system of categories such as 'the child is writing/the child is not writing' or it may involve a large number of categories or a system of scores such as an IQ test. What is important is that any observation which is to be made as part of the observational system should be capable of being classified according to the categories of the variable or variables in accordance with a pre-determined set of rules.

The use of variables in a systematic observation system is best described by some simple examples. For the moment, these will be presented without considering the question of locating the variables at points in time. This is a crucial part of the definition of the variable but will be dealt with in the next section. The examples will also be presented as single, isolated aspects of a classroom, the idea of a system of variables will also be presented later.

A researcher starting with a theoretical interest in the incidence of individual instruction, whole class teaching and the teacher working with groups will want to operationalize this in a way that makes it possible to describe classrooms in terms of the incidence of such activities. The researcher can define a variable; *teaching focus* by which a teacher's focus of attention can be described as falling into one of these types of interaction. This variable might initially have three *categories* or *values*; individual, group and class. The researcher will then have to formulate a set of definitions whereby any instance to be coded can be placed uniquely into one of these categories. This example has been deliberately chosen to be very simple but even so, some problems of definition will occur. Unless the procedures for locating instances in time are such that codes are only made when the teacher is working with children it will be necessary to provide a category to be used when the teacher is not interacting. Consequently, an extra category of 'not interacting' might be used. More generally, the completeness of a system of categories can always be guaranteed by the inclusion of an 'other' category. However, if many occurrences fall into this category some other procedure should be employed.

Even including the 'no interaction' category does not solve the problems of definition. If the teacher is walking silently around the class, is this an interaction? Similarly, if the teacher is silently waiting for an answer? When interaction is undoubtedly taking place there may still be problems of definition. Is a class from which a few pupils have been withdrawn a class or a group within a class? When a particular pupil is singled out to answer a question during a class lesson is this an individual interaction or a whole class interaction? Such problems may be solved by a coding definition. In terms of the researcher's theoretical interest, it may be that silent monitoring is not to count as interaction but silent waiting for an answer is or that interaction with an individual in front of the class counts as class teaching. They may also be solved by incorporating new categories into the variable; 'monitoring' may become an extra category as may 'individual + class'. Using new categories to resolve coding problems has the advantage of greater flexibility, the new category of 'individual + class' not only presents a new piece of information but it also allows the 'class' and the 'individual' categories to be counted either on their own or together with 'individual + class', whichever is more appropriate in particular analyses. However, categories cannot be allowed to continually multiply. There is no point in incorporating distinctions which are not of relevance for the purposes of the research. Decisions about coding definitions and new categories must be made in terms of the theoretical purposes of the study. They should also be made in advance of data gathering and not made on an *ad hoc* basis as the work proceeds.

In the above example, the original set of categories, class/group/individual might be operationalized into a variable with a set of categories as follows:

INDIVIDUAL INTERACTION
INDIVIDUAL WITH CLASS LISTENING
INDIVIDUAL WITH GROUP LISTENING
GROUP INTERACTION
CLASS INTERACTION
NO INTERACTION

This would have to be accompanied by a set of definitions and coding rules specifying, for example, the conditions or number of children present which would count as a 'class' interaction and whether a teacher silently watching children work should be counted as interacting or not.

The second example arises from a research interest in the use of questioning by teachers. Initially, this interest could be operationalized into a dichotomous variable of the simple form;

TEACHER IS ASKING A QUESTION
TEACHER IS NOT ASKING A QUESTION

(as before, the problem of locating this in time will be left until later).

In principle, all classroom occurrences can be accurately categorized in this fashion although certain problems of definition will still occur. Rules will have to be constructed to decide, for example, how rhetorical questions ('Why can't I get any peace and quiet?') are to be coded. This might involve a coding rule (for example, all utterances with the formal structure of questions are to be coded as such) or a new category (for example, 'quasi-questions' or 'rhetorical questions').

However, the researcher will almost certainly want to make

more sensitive distinctions than that between 'question' and 'not-question'. He or she may want to distinguish between questions such as 'Who succeeded Queen Victoria?' and 'Who has got the glue?' and may want to further distinguish questions such as 'Who succeeded Queen Victoria?' and 'How different do you think it would have been to be at school in Victorian times?'.

A concern to make such distinctions might lead to a more complex series of categories making up the variable. For instance;

QUESTIONS — CLASSROOM MANAGEMENT
QUESTIONS — FACTUAL RECALL
QUESTIONS — OPEN ENDED IDEAS
OTHER QUESTIONS
NOT QUESTION

This might serve the purposes of a particular piece of research but it is more likely that the researcher will want to further breakdown the category of 'other questions' and may also want to incorporate other aspects of the teacher's use of questions. To go back to the first example, there may be an interest in whether questions are asked of the whole class or of groups or of individuals (or of individuals in the context of a class lesson). This can be accomplished by devising a longer set of categories to take all these possibilities into account;

QUESTION-CLASSROOM MANAGEMENT	WHOLE CLASS
QUESTION-CLASSROOM MANAGEMENT	GROUP
QUESTION-CLASSROOM MANAGEMENT	INDIVIDUAL
QUESTION-FACTUAL RECALL	WHOLE CLASS
QUESTION-FACTUAL RECALL	GROUP
QUESTION-FACTUAL RECALL	INDIVIDUAL
QUESTION-OPEN ENDED IDEAS	WHOLE CLASS
QUESTION-OPEN ENDED IDEAS	GROUP
QUESTION-OPEN ENDED IDEAS	INDIVIDUAL
OTHER QUESTION	WHOLE CLASS
OTHER QUESTION	GROUP
OTHER QUESTION	INDIVIDUAL
NOT QUESTION	

This, as it stands, is fairly manageable; a variable with thirteen categories into which any instant of classroom life can be coded (most instants presumably falling into 'not question'). However, if it is decided to make the category 'other question' more meaningful by turning it into a number of separate categories then the list of categories may begin to get long enough to present a problem for the observer trying to use it. If additional aspects of the questions asked are also to be included (such as the area of the curriculum the question refers to) the list of categories will almost certainly become unmanageable.

In this sort of instance, where a long list of categories of a variable result from an interest in different aspects of questioning, then the information required is best organised into a number of separate variables. Rather than use a single category to indicate that a question was concerned with classroom management and was asked of an individual, three separate variables can be coded to indicate whether a question is being asked, whether it is managerial or concerned with curriculum content and whether it is asked of the class, group or individual. The single variable above would be replaced by:

QUESTION-FACTUAL	MANAGERIAL	INDIVIDUAL
QUESTION-OPEN ENDED	CURRICULUM CONTENT	INDIVIDUAL/CLASS
OTHER QUESTION	OTHER	INDIVIDUAL/GROUP
NOT QUESTION		GROUP
		CLASS

All instances to be coded will be assigned to a category of each of the three variables and in the analysis it will be straightforward to reconstruct any of the detailed categories of the original single variable. Categories of any of the three new variables can be further divided or new categories added without complicating the other variables and if an additional aspect of questioning is to be investigated a fourth variable can be included. The only constraint on the number of variables is that of the number which can be accurately coded by an observer within the observation procedure being used.

As well as being easier to use, this arrangement of breaking up a complex variable into several simpler ones has the potential for gathering additional information. If the category 'not a question' is divided into 'other interactions' and 'no interaction' then all interactions can be characterized as being 'managerial' or 'curriculum content' and as being addressed to the 'class' 'group' or 'individual' and the proportion of class interactions which are managerial and so on can also be calculated. This not only gives a great deal of information about what is going on when questions are not being asked but also allows information gathered about questions to be put into context. It is possible, for example, to say not just how many questions are asked and how many of them are asked of individuals but also what proportion questions are of all interactions and whether questions are more or less likely than other interactions to be directed to individuals.

This process of reducing complex variables to simpler ones is only possible in certain cases. In the example given, the different aspects of questions can be separated into distinct sets of categories which can be coded independently in a system of variables. In other instances the observer wishing to make detailed distinctions may find that this only is possible by increasing the categories of a single variable. Decisions about the number of variables and about the number of categories within them will also be influenced by the procedures for locating observations in time to be discussed below.

The presentation of variables so far has involved constructing sets of categories into which occurrences can be coded unambiguously according to the rules and criteria which define the variables and categories. These are called *low-inference* measures because they reduce the role of observer judgment to a minimum. Other types of variables, however, involve the observer in judgments which cannot easily be made in terms of pre-determined criteria. These are *high-inference* variables which involve the observer in making a personal response to what is seen.

Typically, high-inference measures are presented in the form of *rating scales*. Such variables consists of bi-polar constructs such as 'dull — stimulating' or 'harsh — kind' on which people or events are rated. The scales may involve explicitly described categories matched to each point on the scale (for example, Powell, 1975) or they may simply involve labelling the two ends of the bi-polar constructs and numbering the points in between (for example, Ryans, 1960).

An explicitly labelled rating scale might look as follows;

INFLEXIBLE : keeps to set pattern whatever student response

FAIRLY INFLEXIBLE: only makes minor changes in response to pupils

FAIRLY FLEXIBLE: within overall plan adapts to pupil
response
FLEXIBLE : builds a lesson around pupil response

A numerical rating scale might look as follows;

INFLEXIBLE 1 ---2----3----4---5---6---7 FLEXIBLE

This sort of rating system might be used to give a global rating to a lesson or teaching episode or it might be used to represent a judgment on particular instants in time using one of the procedures for locating observations in time discussed below. The first kind of rating has little in common with the procedures for systematic observation in classrooms. The second type of use, involving local rather than global ratings has more in common with other kinds of systematic classroom observation. However, incorporating subjectivity in a way that may result in difference between observers observing the same events makes it a rather different procedure from the research techniques presented in the previous chapter.

Sometimes, researchers using classroom observation techniques may not be in a position to specify the categories of a variable although they have a fairly specific idea of the kinds of classroom events in which they are interested. This may occur in the early stages of an investigation when the researcher is in the process of moving towards a fully systematic observation procedure. Rather than coding pre-determined categories, researchers at this stage may make a brief note under each of a set of categories to describe aspects of the behaviour or interaction of whoever is being observed. This quasi-systematic procedure may be an early stage in formulating a research design or it may itself generate valuable data, although it will not produce the sort of exact quantitative data, comparable across different settings, of a fully systematic research design.

Another different type of variable occurs where some aspect of the occurrences being described has unique identifiers available to the researcher. For example, children may be identified by name as may particular books or other curriculum materials. In such cases, an exact record can be kept and the variable can then be reclassified for particular purposes in analysis. For example, if teacher interactions with named children have been recorded these might be reclassified into boys and girls or high and low achievers in the analysis. Understanding the process of systematic classroom observation in terms of variables which provide a system for classifying events into a category of one or more of the variables is fundamental to the argument presented here. The variables used reflect the process by which we turn the theoretical concepts which underlie our attempts to describe aspects of classrooms into a set of working definitions which are used to provide actual descriptions. The examples show some of the issues which can arise in the process of providing working definitions of variables and categories within them. They also show how it may be valuable to categorize the same observed event in terms of more than one set of categories. The next section will deal with the complexities which arise and the decisions which have to be made when the idea of placing events into categories of variables is applied in the on-going situation of the classroom.

Locating Observations in Time

Classroom observation is unlike most other data collecting procedures in education and the other social sciences in that it is an attempt to describe and categorize a process which is on-going in time. Observations are located at particular points in time and this may be a crucial factor in understanding them. A number of problems arise due to the fact that observation is concerned with an on-going social process and this affects the ways in which variables are defined and the observational procedures used. It should be emphasized that these difficulties arise because of the time dimension within a particular observational session, for example, a lesson. The problems of analyzing the results of observations conducted over long periods of time are no different from those of analyzing tests or attitude scales or similar data which may have been collected at different points in time.

Some of the difficulties which the time dimension creates can be seen by considering the variables used as examples in the previous section. These examples were presented without reference to the time difficulties but a moment's reflection will show that there is a time-related ambiguity in the idea of teacher questions and the focus of a teacher's interaction. The discussion so far has not considered whether we are concerned with the *frequency* of an activity or interaction or its *duration*. There is a difference between describing how often a teacher asks a question and how much time is spent in questioning. Similarly, if sessions with the class as a whole are longer than those with individuals a teacher may have many more separate individual interactions than class ones but nevertheless spend most of lesson time working with the class. Clearly, this is not just a question of whether we are interested in frequency or duration, but also raises the question of what do we mean by an interaction. Any decisions about procedures for locating observations in time will have to be informed by notions of how we understand the temporal aspects of the activities we are interested in and whether we want to know how much time they occupy or how frequently they occur.

Two further time-related aspects of observations are those of *location* and *sequence*. It may be of interest that particular behaviour or interactions are located at the beginning or end of lessons or in the morning or afternoon. This is an additional complication for the observer but can be dealt with by devizing some procedure for recording the time that a particular observation was made. The problem of sequence is that of locating an observation not just in terms of when it occurred but in terms of when it occurred relative to the occurrence of other observations. If the interest in sequential location is fairly general, for instance, 'lessons which are characterized by type A activities early on usually develop into type B activities' this can be coped with by the same procedures as those for straightforward temporal location although coding and analysis can become very complex. However, an interest in sequences of a specific kind — question type A followed by answer type B and feedback type C — is much more problematic for the researcher.

All of these questions, the relative importance of different aspects of the temporal location of events as well as the structure and complexity of the variables by which events are to be classified, will affect the procedures used for locating observations in time. A number of commonly used procedures will be presented and discussed below. The first type of procedure for locating observations in time to be considered here is that of *continuous recording*. Using this procedure the observer keeps a continuous record of the category into which the behaviour of the subject of the observation is to be categorized on a schedule laid out in such a way as to allow the use of the categories to be precisely timed.

In the example used above of research into the focus of a teacher's interactions the five categories would each be assigned a number or letter as follows:

CLASS	1
GROUP	2
INDIVIDUAL	3
INDIVIDUAL/GLASS	4
INDIVIDUAL/GROUP	5
NON INTERACTION	6

Figure 4:   Section of a continuous observation schedule

| Time | 10 | 20 | 30 | 40 | 50 | 60 |

The schedule would be laid out so that each horizontal line represents for example, one minute, with seconds indicated by sixty dots on the line. The time of day could be indicated in the left hand margin. Figure 4 shows what a small section of such a schedule would look like.

The section of a schedule in figure 4 represents four minutes of time. The actual time can be recorded in the left-hand margin. Each row represents one minute with the seconds indicated by dots and vertical lines indicating ten-second intervals to assist the observer. Using this, together with a large watch with a sweep second hand or a small digital clock showing minutes and seconds, the observer can keep an exact continuous record of the categories into which the behaviour being observed should be classified.

In figure 5, an example of a completed section of such a schedule is given. In this example, the observer has been recording the teacher's interactions for a period of four minutes from 9.00.00 am until 9.03.60 am.

The time is indicated in the left-hand margin. The observer indicates the category of the variable being observed into which the interaction is classified by writing the appropriate number at the point where such an interaction begins. At the point in time when this ceases to be the appropriate category a vertical line is drawn followed by the number of the new category. In figure 5, at the beginning of the observation period the teacher is interacting with an individual pupil. This interaction (coded 3) lasts for seven seconds and is immediately followed by an interaction with the class (coded 1). This class interaction lasts for the rest of the first minute and for six seconds of the second minute. At this point the teacher, still keeping the attention of the class, picks out an individual pupil (code 4). This lasts for five seconds, after which the teacher reverts to an ordinary class interaction. Forty-five seconds of class interaction (code 1) is then followed by seventeen seconds of no interaction (code 6), twenty-one seconds of interaction with an individual or series of individuals (code 3), a two-second period when there is no interaction (code 6), a further one minute and five seconds of individual interaction (code 3), an eight-second interaction with the whole class (code 1), and, completing the four-minute period, twelve seconds with no interaction.

This is the procedure used in the research, reported in *The Teacher's Day* and discussed in the previous chapter.

It is clear that there are many advantages to a continuous recording procedure of this kind. It allows exact measures to be made of both the duration and frequency of the activities in each of the categories. These activities can also be located exactly in time and be placed in sequential relationship to other activities. It is possible to say that a particular activity occurred on a particular number of occasions, took up a certain proportion of time, was more likely to occur at particular times of the day and typically followed or preceded other identified activities. As will be shown in chapter 5, when procedures for analysis of observational data are considered, a continuous observation system is likely to result in a very complex

Figure 5:   Completed section of a continuous observation schedule.

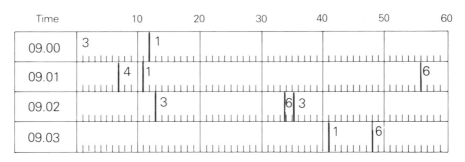

Key   1 : Class interaction   4 : Individual/class interaction
2 : Group interaction   5 : Individual/group interaction
3 : Individual interaction 6 : No interaction

and time-consuming effort of data processing and analysis if all this information is to be retrieved for large numbers of observations, but, in principle, it is all available.

Despite these very considerable advantages it will be clear that there are limitations inherent in this method of observation. The process of keeping a continuous record and changing the code whenever the category of behaviour changes places constraints on what it is possible to observe using this system. In the example given above, and also in the much more complex use of such a system in *The Teacher's Day*, all activities are coded into the categories of a single variable. That is, one and only one category of behaviour can be recorded at any one time. (In *The Teacher's Day* a few examples of multiple coding are given, but this should be thought of as inventing a new category rather than as true multiple coding.)

As has been shown in the earlier discussion it is usually possible to operationalize the research units of interest either into several simple variables or into one complex one. The researchers working on *The Teacher's Day* used a variable 'teacher activity' which had more than fifty categories. However, in this instance, although there were a large number of categories, most of them referred to activities which took place over a relatively extended period of time (play-ground duty, marking, instructing etc.) rather than the rapidly changing activities which are the focus of research such as *One in Five* and ORACLE. In many research projects, it will not be practicable to express the concept of interest as a single variable, only one category of which can be coded at a particular time, and it is likely to prove extremely difficult to keep an accurate continuous record of more than one variable simultaneously. It may be possible for a second observer to code another aspect of classroom activity but there are, of course, limits on how far this process can be extended.

The rapidity of change between the categories to be coded will also influence the practicability of continuous recording and the more complex the system of categories being used, the less rapid the change that can be coped with accurately. Rapid question and answer sessions or similar exchanges are sometimes coded using the quasi-continuous recording system discussed below.

A further difficulty occurs if a coding decision about the appropriate category cannot be made until a sequence of activities has developed. In cases of this sort, it will be virtually impossible to keep a continuous record.

Continuous recording may also prove impracticable, if it is necessary to move at fairly frequent intervals between different observation subjects, for example from the teacher to a pupil or from pupil to pupil.

(It should be noted, for example, that in the instance of continuous recording given above that, although it is possible to describe the amount of time spent interacting with individuals and the frequency of periods of individual interaction, no distinction is made between an interaction with one pupil and a series of consecutive interactions with several pupils occupying the same amount of time. It is therefore not possible to count the number of separate individual interactions. In this particular example, if this extra information was required, it would be relatively simple to incorporate a code for changing individual interactions but many such additions would rapidly become unwieldy.)

A further point which the researcher should keep in mind is that of the implications of the recording technique for the data processing which will be necessary and the kinds of analysis which will be applied. As will be shown in chapter 5, the use of complex analysis on large amounts of continuous record data can be particularly time-consuming.

Despite these reservations about the use of a continuous record, it must be emphasized that, wherever it is practicable, it is likely to be the most satisfactory procedure for locating observations in time. It preserves an exact record of the frequency, duration, exact time and sequence of the categories used. Researchers who decide that the complexity of their variables or of other aspects of their research design, or features of the phenomena being studied preclude the use of this method need to be sure that they are really gaining more than they lose.

A variation of continuous recording is *event recording*. Using this procedure the observer records whenever a particular activity of interest is observed. For example, a researcher interested in teacher questioning techniques could define a series of types of question and mark on a schedule whenever an interaction fell into one of these categories.

An observation schedule for event recording might look very similar to the continuous recording schedule in figures 4 and 5. In this case, the observer would write in a code number or letter for the particular type of question at the appropriate point on the time schedule. A simpler example might involve listing types of question and placing a tick beside each type whenever it occurred.

This procedure provides an accurate count of the frequency of the activity and, depending on the recording procedure used, can provide an exact time location and possibly locate the activity in a sequence. The simple example of ticking a list at appropriate points would only provide a frequency measure but a version of the continuous recording schedule also provides exact time of occurrence and can provide a sequence in terms of other events being coded. (We can say that questions type X always or usually follow answers type Y if 'answer Y' is an event being coded. Where no coded events immediately precede or follow a code, we can only say that it may be part of some other sequence which is not included in the observation system). What this procedure cannot do is to provide a measure of the duration of the activities. Even where the observation system allows for an exact time to be associated with an event, this must be a specific point in time, usually the point where the event commences. If events are timed exactly this logically makes the procedure a straightforward example of continuous recording. Even if coding only begins when specific events occur the rest of the time is implicitly coded as 'other' or 'not applicable'.

Event recording has advantages over continuous recording if it is necessary to code events of too great complexity to allow an exact continuous record to be kept and where the advantages of capturing the complexity outweigh the limitation of losing any measure of duration of an event. A researcher who was interested in certain patterns of question and response may wish to record the type of question asked and which of a variety of responses were elicited in more detail than could be achieved using a strictly continuous record. Alternatively, a researcher may wish to code, or have the possibility of coding, a large number of facets of a particular event. This approach to recording is likely to be most fruitful if the events of interest are not very frequent and are followed by enough time to carry out a fairly complicated coding operation. For events of this kind, the simple version of the recording procedures discussed above rather than something like a continuous recording system is likely to be appropriate. The simpler system loses information about time but is much easier to use if a variety of events as being coded.

In Figure 6, an example of an event recording schedule is given. A number of possible characteristics of events are listed and whenever something which happens in the classroom has one of these characteristics, a tick is made in the appropriate box. In this example, each column represents a moment in time and within each column any number of categories can be ticked. In the first column something with characteristic B has been noted. In the second column an event with characteristic B is again noted, this time also having the characteristic C. In the third column, another instance of C is noted, this time also having the characteristics F and G. This type of recording allows counts to be made of the frequency of occurrence of a fairly large number of possible events. It also allows the researcher to calculate how often these characteristics of events are associated with one another, for example how often B occurs together with C. This is a type of recording which it would be difficult to do accurately with a continuous observation system. However, it is impossible to say how much time these events took up and also impossible to put them in sequence. The apparent sequence of the records is misleading; categories coded in adjacent columns may be separated by varying periods of time. If the location of events during a lesson is of interest, this could be indicated by noting the time that each column was coded or, probably more practically, by having a separate block of columns or a separate coding sheet for different periods within the lesson. Although the columns cannot be used to indicate sequences, specific sequences of interest can be categories of the coding system, for example, category A represents a particular type of answer following one sort of question while category B is the identical answer but given in response to a different sort of question.

It should be noted that the various categories in figure 6 do not form a classification and are not categories of a single variable. They are neither mutually exclusive nor exhaustive as classifications of classroom events. They are seven separate dichotomous variables. Any classroom event is classified independently in terms of each of them as either having that characteristic or not.

Figure 6:   Examples of event recording schedule

(a) Tick whenever an event
      has any of these
      characteristics.

A final point to be made about event recording relates to observational systems in which the observer only begins coding when certain relatively infrequent occurrences take place but then times these occurrences exactly. Such systems may seem like event recording but should logically be regarded as a form of true continuous recording. An implicit negative code is being made throughout most of the observational procedure and ordinary continuous recording procedures are being used at other times.

The recording procedures discussed so far record all occurrences of the categories of the variables of the observation schedule being used. Obviously, this is a desirable feature of an observation system but attempting to achieve this may sometimes defeat the main objective of the observation. Continuous recording places considerable constraints on the kinds of variables which can be used. Event recording sacrifices some of the information obtained from continuous recording in order to allow greater complexity but even here it is clear that it will be very difficult to code relevant events occurring in quick succession unless the coding system is very simple. Consequently, other procedures for locating observations in time have been developed which involve taking a sample of events rather than trying to record continuously. These are called *time sampling* procedures and involve various ways of sampling from the continuous pattern of on-going classroom events.

A time-sampling system which has similarities to event recording is the *one-zero* time sampling technique. In this system, the period of observation is divided into timed intervals, for example, intervals of thirty seconds, or two minutes, or five minutes, and a schedule similar to an event recording schedule is coded in terms of whether any of the categories of behaviour have occurred during the preceding time interval. A simple example of a one-zero recording schedule would look like the example of the event recording schedule in Figure 6. However, in this case, each column would represent not a unique moment in time but an occurrence during the previous timed interval. A ticked category indicates a minimum of one occurrence rather than a single occurrence as in event recording and the fact that two categories in a column are coded only indicates that they occurred within the same period not that a particular event had both characteristics.

An example of the use of a one-zero time sampling system is the Science Teacher Observation Schedule (STOS) used in a study of styles of science teaching (Eggleston, Galton and Jones, 1975b). In STOS, a three-minute time period is used and any of twenty-three categories of behaviour (including types of teacher-pupil interaction and pupil use of resources) are coded if an instance occurs within each three-minute period.

This sort of time sampling has very serious limitations for use in accurately describing aspects of classrooms. It provides a measure of the minimum frequency of events but cannot be used to give any indication of the actual frequency which is not only almost certain to be different but which may also not be associated with the minimum frequency. Events which are clustered at particular times during lessons will be heavily undercounted compared with those that are evenly spread throughout the lesson and relatively brief events will probably be undercounted relative to longer ones. Despite this probable undercounting of brief events, the schedule does not allow anything to be said about the duration of events. The location of events within lessons can be established but not the sequence between events except in so far as sequence is part of the definition of a variable. (See chapter 5 for a discussion of the difference between establishing sequence by locating observations in time and establishing it through the definition of variables.)

The influence of these limitations on the results obtained from one-zero time sampling systems will depend to some extent on the relationship between the time interval and the natural length of the events being sampled. If the events fall fairly neatly into the time intervals, then the system is more likely to be satisfactory. However, the advantage of such systems is that they allow a variety of complex events to be classified (Eggleston and Galton, 1981) and it is very unlikely that all of these events will typically have the same length. A researcher using one-zero systems should be aware of the danger of obtaining highly misleading results (Altman, 1974) and the Science Teacher Observation Schedule referred to above has been subject to criticism on these grounds (Dunkerton and Guy, 1981).

There are two different approaches to one-zero time sampling which have different potential biases. In *Partial Interval* sampling, an occurrence is coded if it has happened at any point in the interval. This potentially overestimates the prevalence of such occurrences. In *Whole Interval* sampling, an occurrence is only coded if it has taken up the full period of the preceding time interval. This procedure underestimates true occurrence as some observed occurrences are uncoded. In an experimental study of time sampling, it was found that the extent of these biases increased with the length of the time interval and errors became large with time intervals of thirty seconds and greater (Powell *et al*, 1977).

Another, generally more satisfactory, approach to time sampling is *instantaneous sampling*. As with one-zero sampling, the observer codes at set intervals, for example every ten seconds or every twenty seconds rather than coding continuously. However, in instantaneous sampling, the codes describe what is happening at that moment in time rather than recording retrospectively whether instances of various kinds of activity have occurred within the last time period. Using a system of this sort, it is possible to categorize fairly complex aspects of occurrences at particular instants. Typically, the observer ticks the appropriate category on each of a set of variables. A simple example of this kind of schedule is given in figure 7. In this example, the observer is coding the behaviour of a particular pupil. Using a timing arrangement such as a digital clock or a pre-recorded 'bleep', the observer places three ticks in each column at every ten-second interval. These ticks represent the activity of the pupil with regard to the three variables at that precise point in time. From this, it is possible to describe the pupil's activities with regard to whether or not he or she was interacting with the teacher and whether this was as a member of the class, a group, or as an individual; whether or not there was interaction with another pupil or more than one other pupil and whether the pupil was concerned with an area of the curriculum, with class organization or with none of these at each of the points in time coded.

In this example, there are three variables with sets of categories but instantaneous time-sampling could also involve a check list of possible characteristics of the interaction, any number or none of which might apply at any particular time interval.

Examples of the use of instantaneous time sampling have already been given in the discussion of the ORACLE and the *One in Five* research projects in chapter 2.

This sort of time-sampling system provides accurate estimate of the duration of different activities over a lesson but cannot usually be used to estimate their frequency. On the basis of calculating the proportion of coded instants when different categories were used the researcher can estimate the proportion of the lesson given over to such categories of activity but not how many separate instances of the activity occurred.

It is easy to use such a system to locate activities at specific times during the lesson but it is not generally possible to establish a sequence of events. An activity can be shown to have occurred ten seconds after another activity but the schedule does not show what happened in between. Instantaneous time-sampling can, of course,

Figure 7:   A simple instantaneous time-sampling schedule

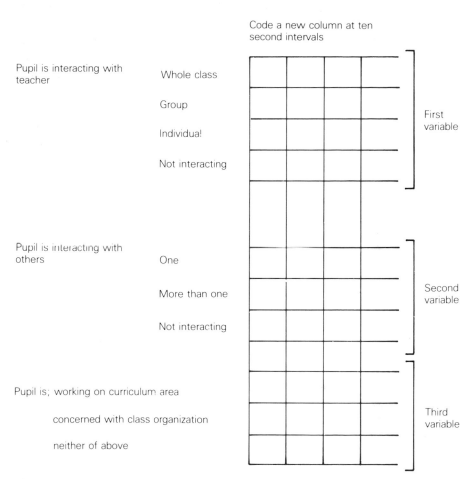

incorporate aspects of sequence into the definition of variables as will be discussed in chapter 5. Occurrences in between the coded instants are not themselves coded but they may still be taken into account. For example, a category of a variable might be the answer to a particular type of question. The category is only coded if the time signal corresponds with the answer but the observer has to take into account what has happened before.

The example in figure 7 shows the complexity of information which can be obtained from even a simple set of variables. Not only can these variables provide estimates of the amount of time the child spent in different sorts of interaction with the teacher, with other pupils and so on, but can also provide data about new categories which can be created from the co-occurrence of the existing categories. For example, the amount of work-oriented interaction with the teacher and with other pupils can be estimated. What the observations cannot describe is how many separate teacher and pupil interactions took place as opposed to how much time they took up.

Instantaneous time-sampling is a good substitute for a continuous record when the complexity of the variables being studied prevents an accurate continuous record being kept. Even the relatively simple example above probably contains more information than could be recorded continuously. However, information about frequency and sequence is lost. It is the loss of this potential for analysis rather than the actual loss of data which is the main drawback of instantaneous sampling. For most research purposes a large number of instants spread over time are likely to be more appropriate than the same amount of data generated continuously over a much shorter period as it will give a more representative selection of classroom events. The choice of sampling interval in the case of instantaneous sampling is far less crucial than in the case of one-zero sampling. The sampling interval does not affect the validity of instantaneous sampling data and the choice should be made in terms of the complexity of the coding procedures and the most efficient use of observation time.

A variation of the technique of instantaneous time sampling is that of *scanning*. In this procedure, categories of activity are coded at timed intervals in the same way as in instantaneous sampling but the timed intervals mark the beginning of a 'scan' of the classroom rather than a code being made of what is happening at that point in time. Such a scan might involve a count of the number of pupils engaged in various activities or of the physical location of everyone in the room. At the time signal the observer looks around the pupils, or looks at various sectors of the room in predetermined order and categorizes each of their activities or marks their position on a plan.

An example of this sort of scanning procedure is a research project which looked at non-work activities in junior classrooms (Lea, 1978). In this study, the observer started a scan at five minutes time intervals and conducted a clockwise sweep of the classroom noting the position and activity of any child not engaged on their work or on another approved activity. A similar example is given in Hopkins (1985).

This procedure is particularly appropriate if information is to be gathered according to relatively simple categories across a wide sample of children in a class. It is a version of instantaneous time sampling and like it can give estimates of the proportion of class time (or of an individual child's time) devoted to various activities but not of the frequency of these activities or the sequence in which they occur.

Unless the categories to be coded are fairly simple the procedure is likely to be unsatisfactory as unlike instantaneous sampling there is no particular instant which identifies the behaviour to be coded. If the categories cannot be coded immediately the scan reaches a child, for example, because the categories imply knowledge of the child's previous behaviour or because they involve coding a number of variables, then the observer will find it impossible to decide on the instant which should be recorded.

It should be noted that in the example given the scan was started every five minutes which gave plenty of time for a full sweep of the classroom to be made. Scanning systems which involve a continuous sweep of the class rather than starting at timed intervals are likely to result in data which is uninterpretable because of the different lengths of time it takes to code different activities.

The advantage of a scanning system is that it can be a more efficient use of observation time when the individual activities of all the children in a class are of interest and the coding system is a simple one. An alternative procedure of scanning the class but coding on the signals of a briefly spaced instantaneous time-sampling arrangement is more cumbersome but avoids the difficulty created by giving observers discretion in deciding the exact moment to be coded.

The procedures for time-sampling of events discussed so far have involved imposing a timing system on the events being studied. Some researchers may feel that it is more satisfactory for their purposes to sample *naturally occurring behavioural units*. A researcher might be interested in such naturally occurring units as 'teacher question — pupil answer — teacher feedback' or 'a pupil starting — working on — completing/failing to complete, a curriculum task'. Such naturally occurring units may be closer to the way that participants experience the activities of the classroom than the ten-second or other intervals imposed by a conventional time-sampling system. In particular research projects it may be possible to work with such units while still maintaining the rigour of systematic observation but in other cases the difficulties of defining appropriate units in advance and having a standard recording procedure which can describe them will mean that some other way of recapturing such 'natural' units must be found. If the researcher is concerned with types of lessons where it is known that the structure of the lesson will allow naturally occurring units to be identified in a predictable fashion then a procedure for sampling from such units can be devised. A question and answer session around the class, pupils bringing up work to be marked one by one or all the pupils taking, completing and returning work cards might be suitable for this sort of sampling. However, in more general classroom situations with less predictable patterns of events it will be impossible to code systematically in this way. This is partly because of the complexity and variety both of type and length of units of behaviour or interaction but also because most of what goes on in classrooms cannot be described in terms of units of behaviour in the same way that the examples given can be. Patterns of behaviour usually have to be discovered at the analysis stage rather than being amenable to straightforward observation.

It should not be thought, as is sometimes suggested, that systematic observation cannot reflect sequences making up exchanges and episodes which naturally structure classroom experience. If the exchanges or episodes of interest can be defined in advance then they can be the categories of an event recording or a one-zero time-sampling system. Even without specifying in advance, a continuous recording system allows sequences consisting of categories of the system to be recreated in analysis and allows the same observation to appear in more than one type of sequence. Instantaneous time sampling is less flexible at recreating sequences, but short sequences can be used as categories of the system while an instantaneous system with short time intervals may also make it possible to recreate episodes in analysis. The developmental structure of a lesson can also be recreated both from continuous recording and from instantaneous time-sampling. Finally, in considering procedures for locating observations in time, the comments made in chapter 2 about the FIAC system should be recalled. This provides a *quasi-continuous* system of recording by using very brief timed intervals. It is effective in certain types of classroom settings, principally those involving a teacher interacting with the class as a whole. As was previously noted, the effectively continuous system of recording is only possible because of the simplicity of the categories and the possibility of bias is built into the flexibility allowed to the observer.

Locating Observations in Context

The presentation so far has mainly concentrated on observation systems which have a single focus; observations of a teacher or of a pupil or the slightly more complicated focus of a teacher-pupil interaction. For some purposes such a simple focus of observation may be all that is required but as a general approach to observation it has obvious limitations. Much of what researchers want to observe about classrooms becomes of interest, or can only be properly understood, within the context in which it takes place. As it stands this is a very general statement and the idea of locating observations within a context must be seen as an issue of research design related to the question of deciding on the variables and categories of an observational system. There are very many aspects of classrooms which could be the focus of observations, and there are also very many contexts in which the observations can be placed. One aspect of the context of observations is the location in time; the place in a sequence or the precise time of occurrence discussed above. The context to be considered now is that provided by observations of different aspects of the classroom.

Most of the examples of observational research mentioned so far have a very simple focus of attention. In *The Teacher's Day* the focus of observation was on individual teachers. The use of the FIAC system and similar systems involves observing the classroom more generally but is only appropriate to teacher-pupil interaction and so, in practice means that the observer focusses on the teacher and whoever is being interacted with. Other research has involved taking a sample of pupils in a class and focussing on each of them individually in a pre-determined order (for example, Bennett 1976).

With any of these simple observation systems it is relatively straightforward to incorporate certain kinds of contextual variables within the observation system. Any features of the situation being observed which can be relied on to be stable throughout an observation session can be incorporated without affecting the basic procedures of the observation system. Aspects of the classroom setting such as the size and other physical features of the classroom are virtually always permanent. Other features such as the number of children present, the seating arrangements, the equipment and materials available and the curriculum content of the lesson may be stable aspects of an observation session in some educational settings but not in others. In some secondary school classrooms these could be coded at the beginning of a lesson to describe the whole of the observation period but in many other settings, especially in primary schools, these could not be relied on to remain unchanged. In addition to relatively permanent features which can be observed in the classroom the researcher should always have recorded such details as an identification of the school and classroom and the date and times of the observation as a basic matter of good research practice.

This information gives a basic context to the detailed observation of individuals. It allows these observations to be described in terms of features of the classroom in which they occur, the time of day when they were noted and perhaps the area of the curriculum and the type of teaching arrangements associated with them. An analysis using this contextual information may be conducted in order to give more of a sense of what the observed occurrences were like or, in some instances, a comparison of contexts may be the major purpose of the research. The researcher may want to compare teaching approaches in different curriculum areas (for example, Willcocks, 1983), or pupil behaviour in different types of seating arrangement (for example, Wheldall *et al*, 1981), or pupil activities in 'formal' and 'informal' primary classrooms (for example, Bennett 1976). In these examples it is the comparison of contexts which gives the observations their point. In other instances, establishing the context of observations may add to the interest of the description.

The contexts described so far have been limited to those features of the classroom which can be described at the beginning or end of a period of observation and which do not have to be incorporated into the observation system itself. A further procedure for establishing context involves using an observation system which has more than one focus within the classroom or separate observation systems, each with a differing focus. Many classroom systems focus on the teacher but there are also procedures for observing pupils and some observational researches have used both at different times in the same classrooms. In the ORACLE project discussed in chapter 2, separate observation systems were used to observe the teacher and to observe selected pupils in the same classrooms and during the same observation sessions (but not at exactly the same times). This makes it possible to describe a classroom in terms of the teacher's activities and interactions and also in terms of the activities and interactions of the pupils. Teacher behaviour and pupil behaviour can therefore be seen in the context of each other and, in some research designs, the influence of each on the other can be isolated.

The use of observations of pupils in a class or of a sample of pupils in a class to establish a class context for behaviour can place an individual child's activities and interactions in context as well as those of the teacher. Particular levels of behaviour and interaction take on more meaning when set against the levels generally prevailing in the class as well as when put in the context of teaching approaches. Some research projects make use of a sample of 'control' children chosen at random from the class in order to provide an overall class context for the behaviour of children identified as being of interest because of the difficulties they are experiencing or other identifying features. An example of this is the *One in Five* research.

In these examples an overall view of a classroom has been obtained by focussing on individual pupils one at a time. Another approach involves some variety of the scanning technique discussed above where an overall view is obtained by counting the numbers of pupils engaged in various activities at particular points in time.

The context established by classroom observation itself provides measures from the analysis of observational data against which particular observations or particular groups of observations can be set. It differs from the context which is established by describing the type of school or physical features of the classroom in that it cannot be specified before the observations are conducted and therefore cannot be fully specified in the research design. (The research design can specify comparisons between different contexts arising from observation but it will not be known in advance exactly what these contexts will be.) Contexts established by observations in the way described above also have the limitation that they cannot be precisely linked to particular observations. We can say that a pupil has a level of engagement in work of half the class average but not what the rest of the class were doing when he was not working. If a more detailed context of this sort is required then it is necessary to incorporate it into the observational system as well as providing contextual information from other observations in the classroom.

In some types of classroom it will be possible to specify considerable contextual detail in terms of curriculum content, classroom organization and styles of work. Often these aspects will change throughout the period of observation or will differ for different children in the same class. In these instances contexts have to emerge from observations rather than being established in advance. One approach to this problem is to treat particular classroom *settings* as the basic units of analysis and to locate specific observations of individuals within these settings (Poppleton, 1975). Settings of this sort might include 'the teacher lecturing to the whole class' or 'the teacher working with a small group'. Greater specificity could be introduced by including a particular curriculum area in the definition of a setting. This procedure provides a context for observations and also introduces the possibility of using slightly different observation systems in different contexts if this is appropriate. It has the limitation that it is necessary to specify the settings which are of interest in advance and also involves difficulties of sampling settings, especially if it is intended to provide a representative picture of classroom activities. A similar sampling problem arises if specific children or a representative sample of children are to be included in the observation.

A slightly different approach to the problem of establishing classroom settings for particular observations was used in the *One in Five* research. Here a record of classroom settings was kept in parallel with the detailed observations of pupil activities and interactions. This meant that any particular observation of a child could be related to the area of the curriculum on which he or she was working and the classroom setting (part of the teacher's class audience, part of a cooperative group, individual work, etc.) in which he or she was located. By coding several variables to describe classroom contexts, a wide variety of organizational and curriculum contexts and combinations of these could be identified. Because these contexts are much more stable than the moment by moment activities and interactions of children it is possible to code them whenever they change and to provide a running record of context but to restrict most observations to immediate behaviour and interaction. In the *One in Five* research this running record was kept of the immediate context of an observed child's activities. If a child's context was that of individual work or a cooperative group the recording procedure did not describe what the rest of the class were doing. In principle it would be possible to incorporate observations of this kind but a single observer will find it difficult to code many details of context while still coding the immediate activities of the subject being observed. In some instances it may be useful to introduce a second observer simultaneously coding contextual data while the first observer concentrates on individuals.

The approaches to locating observations in the context described above have used additional observations either made at the beginning or end of a lesson or part of a lesson or a contextual running record kept simultaneously but changed relatively infrequently. A different approach to recording limited aspects of context is to incorporate contextual information into the variables of the original observation schedule. In this case different categories of the observation system might be used to code the same activities occurring in different contexts. However, coding detailed contextual information in this way rapidly becomes unwieldy.

A final point about context relates back to the question of exact identification of individuals discussed in an earlier part of this chapter. If a procedure can be devised to identify the particular children who are interacting with or are near to a teacher, or the particular children interacting with or in the same group as an identified child being observed, then a detailed picture of the classroom as a social setting, a sort of living sociogram, can be built up which will provide a rich source of contextual data.

Note

1 See BURGESS (1986) for a discussion of some of the issues involved in defining and working with variables. Even apparently simple concepts such as age and sex can involve difficulties in some contexts.

4   Conducting Observational Research in Classrooms

The practical difficulties involved in conducting a systematic observation study in classrooms are influenced by factors such as the complexity of the observation schedule, the focus of the observations and the length of time over which observation is to be conducted. In addition to the difficulties involved in accurately recording classroom events in an appropriate form there are also difficulties concerned with access to the research situation and relationships with the subjects of the research. For many projects there may also be difficulties which arise from using a number of different observers and all researchers must consider the issue of the impact their presence in the classroom may have on the situation being studied.

The extent of these difficulties depends on the relationship of the researcher to the situation being studied and also on the scale of the research. Clearly, a researcher working in his or her own classroom or collaboratively with colleagues will be in a different position to an outside researcher with no other relationship to the school. The situation will also be different for a single researcher compared with that of a group of researchers and, even more so, for researchers conducting their own observation and researchers using a research team whose only or primary role in the research is to conduct classroom observation. The first part of this chapter will deal with practical questions which must be confronted by any observer working in classrooms. The discussion will then move to questions of access and relationships between the researcher and the subjects of research. Finally the issues involved in working with research teams of various kinds will be considered.

Observing in Classrooms

The Observation Schedule

The observation schedule must be one that it is practical to use in classrooms. This means both that the information required to carry out the coding must be accessible to the observer and that the mechanical process of coding should be quick and efficient and not interfere with the observation.

The categories of the schedule must relate to things that the observer can see and hear in the classroom. It will therefore be necessary to establish if coding may involve the observer in moving around the classroom at times to be closer to the individual being observed and, if so, if this will be practical. If not, it may be possible to use one of the aids to observation discussed below. The schedule must also be limited with regard to the number of aspects of the situation to be observed simultaneously. It will normally be possible, for instance, to code both the content of an utterance and the communication context in which it occurs, but it may not be possible to simultaneously code what is going on in another part of the classroom. Issues of this kind will depend to some extent on the type of classroom being studied and on the type of lesson within that classroom. The sorts of observation that can be conducted in an infant classroom may not be practical in a sixth form and *vice versa*, and practical observation problems in a lecture-like lesson situation will differ from those in a situation where all children are working individually.

It is important that these difficulties are confronted before the major phase of data collection starts. The researcher will have to ensure that an observer will have appropriate access to the behaviour being observed in any setting in which the observation takes place. This may involve different coding procedures in different settings or rules about the circumstance in which observation does and does not take place.

The other type of problem the researcher will confront is that of having an observation schedule that is practical to carry, read, write on and move onto subsequent sheets in the classroom situation. These considerations may sometimes conflict with a desire to code the data in a form suitable for immediate computer processing or for convenient analysis by eye but it is obviously important to give priority to the requirements of accurate and efficient coding while the observation is being conducted.

It will usually be found best to have a coding schedule which will fit onto a clipboard. A larger schedule will be unmanageable while a smaller one will mean that fewer codes will be made before the observer must move onto the next sheet. In most observational studies it will be necessary to have a number of coding sheets. As the observer gets to the end of one sheet it will be necessary to have a system of moving it to the bottom of the pile or folding it over and moving on to the sheet underneath.

The complexity of the coding system will determine the form in which the codes are made and the extent to which the actual coding sheets will need to contain information for the observer. In the case of a very simple coding system like FIAC the observer simply writes down a series of single digit numbers (0–9) each corresponding to a moment in time. Almost any layout of the coding sheets will be adequate and the observers are trained to remember the ten categories. In the rather more complex coding schedule shown in figure 1 on page 26, three or more variables are coded and the schedule is laid out in a form to make it simple for the observer to code in sequence at ten-second intervals. At each interval three single digit numbers are written in the three boxes corresponding to the three variables. Observers are trained to remember the appropriate codes but each coding sheet also contains the list of variables and categories and the numbers associated with them for quick reference. The coding sheet on page 26 has sets of boxes corresponding to twenty-four moments in time. These will last for four minutes if coding is at ten-second intervals.

With other coding schedules it may be necessary to set out the variables and categories on the coding sheets and place a tick beside the appropriate category. A simple example of such a system is shown in figure 7 on page 73. This is simpler to use for the observer than a system which involves writing a number. Codes do not have to be memorized and the coding sheet acts as a prompt with regard to the categories. The disadvantage is that more coding sheets will generally be used with the consequence that the observer will have to move on to a new sheet more frequently and that it is more difficult to set up the coding schedule so as to facilitate data processing. Generally speaking, the more complex the coding schedule the more likely it is that it will be necessary to have the variables and categories printed on each coding sheet and to use a system of ticks rather than writing numbers.

Researchers will need to ensure that the process of recording does not interfere with that of observation. Unless the appropriate ticks or numbers can be written very quickly the process of observation will be interrupted. This will be a constraint on the timing of observation intervals as well as on the amount of information to be coded at each coding interval and the form of the coding sheets. The issues involved in designing coding schedules and their relation to data processing will be discussed further in the next chapter.

Timing Observations

The great majority of coding systems require that the observer be aware of the exact time while conducting observation. Time sampling systems involve making a code at precisely regulated times. The observer needs to know that it is ten seconds or thirty seconds or five minutes since the last code. Continuous recording systems are also precisely regulated by time. The observer will probably move onto a new line every minute and each line will be broken up into one-second or five-second intervals. Other systems may not require that the individual observations be precisely timed but will almost certainly require that the time at the beginning and end of the observation period and possibly also of particular events within it be timed. In the case of this last sort of timing it is sufficient that the observer have a reliable wrist watch, but for systems involving the precise timing of observations some other timing device will be necessary. It is both unmanageable and inaccurate for the observer to be constantly looking at a wrist watch.

One arrangement is to have a watch with a sweep second hand attached to the top of the clipboard. A digital display would be even more accurate as long as it is easily readable. For some types of observation it might be sufficient that there is a clock with a second hand easily visible in the classroom. Teachers doing research in their own or colleagues' classrooms may be able to ensure that this or some other timing device is on display. An alternative to a visual time display is an aural timing system. This has the advantage that the observer does not have to look at the time and can watch the situation being observed constantly. It is particularly appropriate for time sampling systems where codes must be very precisely on the time interval and where the observer needs to know how much time has passed rather than the exact time of day. Aural timing devices can be constructed using a small tape recorder and a tape on which a 'bleep' or other time signal has been pre-recorded at the appropriate intervals. If the 'bleep' is recorded on both sides of a tape cassette it can be quickly reversed as one side comes to an end. It will be helpful if some warning that a side is almost at an end is also pre-recorded.

In an observation situation where the observer can conduct the observation without shifting position or getting too close to the people being observed it may be possible to use an ordinary tape recorder and to have a low signal that will not disrupt the classroom. It is more likely, however, that the observer will need to have an earpiece from the tape recorder. If the observer needs to move then a pocket tape recorder or other small portable tape recorder will be required. It has proved practical in a number of studies for observers to move unobtrusively round a classroom with an earpiece leading to a tape recorder in a pocket or handbag or attached to the back of a clipboard.

Selecting Individuals for Observation

In many observation systems individual pupils within the classroom are the focus of the observation. The selection of these pupils may be determined by the definitions embedded in the schedule, for example, the pupil to whom the teacher is talking is observed. In other systems identified pupils may be observed either to provide a representative sample of the pupils in the classroom or for theoretical reasons as part of the observation system.

If pupils are being sampled so as to give a representative sample of pupils in the classroom some element of random sampling should be incorporated in the selection process. Random sampling is the principle of selection so that each individual in the group being represented has an equal chance of being included in the sample. The simplest example is a lottery procedure whereby the names of all the children in a class are written on a set of cards which is then mixed or shuffled and the appropriate numbers of cards drawn. An alternative procedure is to allocate a number to each child and use a table of random numbers in the selection device. It is important to use a formal random selection procedure if a random sample is required. It is not satisfactory to ask the teacher to indicate some 'typical' pupils unless it is teacher perceptions of typicality which are the focus of the research. Researchers should also be careful not to confuse random selection with haphazard selection. To select pupils in an *ad hoc* fashion on no particular basis, either before the observation starts or during the process of observation in the classroom, may feel random to the researcher but risks introducing a variety of biases. For example, the children who are first into the class or whose appearance makes them easily identifiable may not be representative of the rest of the class. Selecting on this basis would therefore be potentially biasing, as would be deliberately not selecting these children. Consequently, if children are selected to be representative then this must be done beforehand using a random procedure.

Random selection can be used alongside other selection processes. For example, if children are to be observed because they are experiencing difficulties then they may be selected by teacher nomination or on the basis of their test scores. It may also be necessary, however, to observe other children for comparative purposes and these could be selected at random from the rest of the class.

Researchers will generally find that when sampling at random from a school class the sampling procedure is more efficient if the sample is stratified. Stratification involves dividing the group to be sampled on the basis of some criteria such as sex or achievement level or both and then sampling at random within these groups. The simplest, and probably most common, example is to sample boys and girls separately. This ensures that boys and girls are represented in the sample in the same proportions as they appear in the class as a whole.

In the ORACLE research (Galton, Simon and Croll, 1980) eight children were sampled from each class by means of dividing the class into boys and girls and then dividing each of these groups into a top quarter, a bottom quarter and a middle group on the basis of test scores. Children were sampled at random within these groups. Each class was therefore represented by a high achieving girl, a high achieving boy, a low achieving girl, a low achieving boy and two girls and two boys from the middle achievers.

A problem which is likely to arise in practice and which is relevant to selection is the procedure to be followed when individuals who have been selected for observation are unavailable through absence from school or because they are out of the room. The researcher must decide whether in such instances individuals should be replaced by another specified child or whether the observer should move on to the next child to be observed or whether, from the perspective of the research, absence is observed behaviour which should be coded. The important considerations are that the solution adopted should be compatible with the research design and that it should be decided on in advance and should not be an *ad hoc* decision by an observer confronted with the situation.

Being in the Classroom

Except in the case of collaborative projects among colleagues the observer is in a social situation which is someone else's workplace. Both from the point of view of the research and a consideration for the teacher and children whose classroom it is the observer will want to be unobtrusive and non-disruptive. The observer will also have to organize his or her presence in the classroom so that accurate observation can take place. Observers should familiarize themselves with the classroom in advance and should work out where they will need to be in order to carry out the observation. It will normally be desirable to arrive early so as to be comfortable in the classroom before observation begins. The observer or some other member of the research group will have discussed the research with the teacher. The pupils may not know that research is taking place and some explanation from the teacher, possibly introducing the observer by name, will usually be appropriate. (The question of who is told what also involves ethical considerations which will be discussed later.)

Observers need to manage their relationships with the children as well as with the teacher. Initial discussion with the teacher should establish that the observer is to be treated as a 'fly on the wall' and will not be taking part in the activities of the class or interacting with teachers or pupils. In the case of older pupils this can also be explained to the class. With younger children, however, it may be difficult to establish initially that the observer is there to watch and not to take part and observers will need to establish strategies for distancing themselves from the class.

King (1984) describes how he used the difference in height between himself and the infant pupils in the classes he was observing to avoid interaction and how he avoided eye contact with pupils 'if you don't look you will not be seen'. (King was not conducting systematic observation but the relationship between himself and his subjects was the same as for the systematic observer.) Observers in the ORACLE and *One in Five* studies were instructed to attempt to avoid interaction with pupils and if directly approached to respond politely but briefly and to refer any questions about work to the teacher.

Observer Influence on the Classroom Setting

The question of the relationship of the observer to pupils and teachers inevitably raises the question of the influence the observer may have on the classroom activities and interactions being observed. Systematic observation is intended to be a non-reactive measure. The researcher wants a description of the on-going activities in the classroom as they would be if the observer was not present but the description necessarily involves the presence of an observer.

Consequently, it is a valuable precaution to include reactions to the observer, either directly or in interactions with others, as a category of the observation system. In the ORACLE research such reactions accounted for less than 1 per cent of observations. Beyond such reactions, pupils get on as normal, quickly forgetting the observer. Discussions with teachers following periods of observation in large-scale observation studies confirm that the teachers are not aware of differences in pupil behaviour when an observer is present. Such 'debriefing' discussions with teachers could be usefully included in all observation studies as a check on the validity of the data.

The question of the extent to which teachers may behave differently when being observed is more difficult. The teacher is likely to be more conscious of the observer's presence than the pupils and may be reluctant to admit afterwards that they have behaved differently. This is partly a question of having good relationships between the researchers and the schools and teachers who are being researched and of the two groups being open with one another. Careful preliminary discussions and explanations, an assurance that the study is not concerned to judge individuals and that the results of observation are confidential should reduce any tensions felt by the teacher. Teachers should be encouraged to be frank with the researchers about their feelings about being observed and should not have undue pressure put on them to take part in the study. It is important that researchers make it clear that they want teachers to carry on as normal and not to set up a teaching situation that they feel the observer would be interested to see.

Inevitably, given the difficulty of collecting data on what happens when observers are not present, there have been few studies which provide evidence of observer effects. Samph (1976), using a covert observation procedure, reports effects from observer presence, but these effects were in levels of 'desirable' teaching behaviour to which teachers had been previously alerted. In an experimental study of behaviour modification, Harrop (1979a) found no effects of observer presence or a biasing effect from observer expectations. Hilsum and Cane, the researchers who conducted the *Teacher's Day* research, interviewed teachers after observation and found very few reports by the teachers of differences in their own or their pupils' behaviour (Hilsum and Cane, 1971, appendix 5).

Procedures for safeguarding studies against such effects include spending long preliminary periods in the classroom before the real observation begins so that pupils and teachers can get used to the presence of an observer and making sure that the observation procedures are non-obtrusive. Establishing good relationships with the teacher being observed is important both so that the teacher is relaxed and does not feel threatened by the observation procedure and also so that it is possible to have a frank discussion with the teacher about possible effects of the observation.

Aids to Observation

In some studies mechanical aids to observation may be appropriate. The use of video recordings and audio recordings where the aim of the recording is to effectively substitute for the observer and preserve a permanent record for later analysis is outside the range of the present discussion. Simpler techniques which are an aid to live observation most commonly involve improving the audibility of interactions. In *The Teacher's Day*, teachers wore small radio microphones and transmitters and the observers wore receivers and earphones so that they could pick up the detail of teachers' interactions. This is most appropriate when a particular individual such as the teacher is the sole focus of observation. Having several microphones on different individuals is very much more difficult to manage. However, if the setting to be observed is fixed for the relevant period it may be possible to use a single microphone, perhaps on a table around which the pupils being observed are working. In general, researchers using systematic observation have preferred not to use these sorts of aids to observation both because of the difficulties of setting up the arrangements and because of the greater risk that the apparatus will disturb the situation being observed. For most purposes an observer who is free to move around the classroom to some extent can code most activities accurately.

Other aids to observation involve simplifying the coding process. A teacher keeping a simple record of a single aspect of a child's behaviour as part of a programme of behaviour modification at the same time as teaching the class may find that a small mechanical counter involving pressing a button is an efficient aid to counting. There are no published studies involving electronic counting procedures for more complex coding systems but it seems likely that such procedures will be developed.

Access to Educational Settings

Like most other forms of educational research, systematic observation requires the cooperation of educational practitioners, especially teachers. Systematic observation, however, requires this to an unusual degree. Teachers in systematic observation studies are not just being asked for their opinions or their pupils' test scores but are being asked to allow an outsider into their classroom, often for considerable periods of time.

Researchers seeking access to classrooms are likely to need to do so at a number of levels. They will certainly need to approach the headteacher and will probably have approached the education authority prior to this. They will then need to seek the cooperation of individual teachers. Researchers should be aware of a number of factors which they should take into account. For some studies, and in particular at the pilot stage of studies, almost any classrooms will be satisfactory for research purposes. A researcher wanting to try out an observation instrument to become sensitized to classroom processes may be happy to use volunteer schools and teachers. For most purposes, however, there will be a purpose behind the selection of schools and classrooms. They will be chosen to be representative (preferably by random sampling) or because other kinds of information are available about them or because children from the school transfer to another school which is also involved in the research. This means that it is extremely important to get a high response rate from the schools and teachers approached. A carefully sampled random selection of classrooms ceases to be representative if only half the teachers agree to take part and a complex research design involving, for example, secondary schools and their feeder primary schools requires that all the schools cooperate. This consideration of the importance of high response rates may conflict with a reluctance on the part of the researcher to put pressure on unwilling teachers to be part of the research project. This unwillingness will arise both from the ethical considerations discussed below and also from an awareness that the quality of the data may suffer in such instances, particularly with regard to the teacher behaving normally during observation.

Fortunately teachers are generally willing to take part in research of this sort. The researchers responsible for *The Teacher's Day* (Hilsum and Cane, 1971) reported a refusal rate of only 6 per cent among the teachers approached; the 58 teachers approached as part of the ORACLE project all agreed to cooperate (Galton, Simon and Croll, 1980); as did the 34 teachers approached in the *One in Five* research (Croll and Moses, 1985). These studies also reported that almost no headteachers declined to allow classes in their schools to be part of the study.

In approaching schools and, even more, when approaching teachers, researchers should be sensitive to the fact that they are moving between levels of a hierarchical system in which they approach the lower levels with the support of higher levels. Researchers often approach headteachers via the chief education officer or other senior officer and will almost always approach teachers via the headteacher. This may put pressure on the teachers to agree to the research, and researchers should always make sure that teachers have had the research properly explained to them and have genuinely consented to take part. To take advantage of this pressure to obtain a sample is dangerous with regard to the validity of the data as well as being ethically dubious.

Observational research involves a number of ethical difficulties although these are probably less of a problem in systematic observations than in other kinds of observational studies. Research ethics require that the researchers inform all research subjects about what is taking place and that all subjects are free not to take part in the study. But achieving this in practice within a hierarchically organized educational system may be a problem. Once the researcher is sponsored by the LEA or headteacher, schools and teachers may feel constrained to take part whatever the researcher says about them having a choice. Not to gain the approval of LEAs and heads is itself ethically dubious and may put teachers who want to cooperate in a difficult position.

There are also problems with regard to the involvement of pupils as research subjects. A researcher who wants to be open with pupils may find that this is in conflict with normal procedures within the school. It is not, in practice, a possibility for a pupil within the school system to object to the presence of an observer in the classroom. In the case of young children it may be difficult even to properly inform them.

Two important considerations for researchers in dealing with these ethical issues are, first, that the research should be conducted in good faith. Subjects should be told the truth and should be asked for consent, and the extent of access offered should be respected. Secondly, the research should be worthwhile and not harmful to the subjects. Any research involves a degree of intrusion into other people's lives and this needs to be justified by the value of the work. Great care should be taken with regard to reporting anything which can damage individuals and researchers should be aware that subjects may not have the appropriate experience to be the best judges of what may be damaging to them. The consent of the subjects does not relieve the researcher of responsibility in this area. Large scale quantitative studies are unlikely to experience the problems of confidentiality and the possibility that research subjects can be identified which are a feature of some research projects. This is particularly so in the case of ethnographic projects where the focus on a small number of settings, and the types of data presented, may make individuals identifiable. However, where systematic research is conducted on a small scale, or as part of a case study of a particular educational setting, issues of confidentiality may arise.

Considerable attention has been given to these problems, mainly in the context of qualitative research (see, for example, Burgess, 1984b, and Delamont, 1984, for examples and discussion of some of the issues). Researchers should remember that even if they successfully keep the identity of the institution and individuals studied publicly hidden they are still identifiable to the research subjects themselves (see Burgess, 1984b; King, 1984).

Researchers will often find that while they want to be open and honest with teachers with regard to the content of the work, they are reluctant to actually show teachers the schedules or discuss details of them because of the possible effect on the situation being studied. It will almost always be acceptable to explain this to the teachers concerned and to offer to explain the procedure fully after observation is complete.

Teachers and heads sometimes complain that having cooperated in a research project and given researchers access to classrooms that this is the last that they hear of the work. It is obviously courteous and helpful to future researchers to give teachers and schools feedback on the work that has been conducted and at the end of the research to send all those who have been involved a short report on the findings of the project.

Teachers conducting research collaboratively have a set of

related problems concerned with who 'owns' the data produced, who controls whether or not it should be published and who has access to it. The appropriate way of treating all these questions will depend on the particular studies and their purposes and the educational settings and individuals involved. The only general point to be made here is that researchers should take note of the methodological principle guiding all systematic observation research which is that procedures for reacting to events should be specified in advance. The researcher should take care not to be ambushed by such problems. Questions of confidentiality, control over the data and the relationship between the researcher and the subjects of the research and between colleagues if appropriate should be negotiated in advance and understood by all concerned. If such arrangements are at all complex or are likely to lead to difficulties they should be written down.

Working with a Research Team

Systematic observation research, more than most educational research, is likely to involve a number of research workers. This may involve a number of researchers working collaboratively but, in the case of large scale surveys, it may also involve the use of paid observers who are not otherwise involved in the research.

The involvement of a number of observers usually arises from the scale of the observational work but the involvement of additional observers at some stage is a necessary feature of all systematic observation. Even where the scale of observation is such that a single researcher can cope with it alone it is still necessary for the researcher to involve other observers to ensure that the categories of the observation system are sufficiently clear and explicit, and to conduct tests for the reliability of the observation system.

Much the same procedure will have to be followed whether researchers are working cooperatively or are employing observers as part of the research. Training procedures must be devized in which the researchers can learn to use the observation system in a uniform fashion. The first, and most important, stage is to produce a manual setting out the observation procedures, the variables and categories and their definitions in an explicit fashion. Ideally, anyone should be able to use the observation system accurately just from reading the manual.

It will probably be useful to try out the system initially with two or more observers viewing and coding a videotape of classroom interaction. At this stage definitions can be clarified if necessary and the observers can obtain practice in using it. The observers will then need to try out the observation system 'live' in classrooms both individually and in pairs. It is almost always easier to use an observation system live than it is to code video-recordings from which only a limited view of the activities to be coded is often available. Paired live observation should be used at the end of the training process to establish reliability figures for the various variables of the observation system. A description of an observer training programme is given by Jasman (1980).

It is important to keep clear the logical distinction between the development of a schedule and the training of observers, even though these are likely to overlap in practice. The process of trying out the schedule, explaining it to others and confronting difficulties and disagreements over interpretation, is part of the process of designing the research. It may lead to redefinition and clarification of categories and possibly some curtailing of the scope of the research. When this has been done it is necessary to see if observers do in fact reach agreement on the use of categories before the system can be implemented.

As was said earlier, ideally it should be possible to learn to use the observation system from a manual. This is because the validity of systematic observation depends on the basis for its data being absolutely explicit so that a reader knows just how descriptions were arrived at. If observers come to agree on the use of categories not because the definitions are explicit but because they have built up together a private understanding of how events are to be coded, then the apparent high reliability obtained will not reflect a genuine clarity in the categories. The development of a private culture of observational definitions among the observers is something the researcher must guard against. This does not mean that the observers should not practise the system, it is possible for an observation system to be perfectly explicit but only usable after the observers have had a lengthy period of practice and training because of the difficulties of learning definitions and applying them at an appropriate speed in the classroom. But it must be possible for the understanding that the observers have of the system to be written down and researchers should publish not only the rules of their observation system but also details of any special training which is necessary in order to be able to use it.

It is worth noting that the extent to which 'tacit' knowledge may underlie research procedures is not unique to systematic observation or to the social sciences. There are examples in the natural sciences where researchers have apparently been unable to use procedures developed by others until they have actually worked closely with them (Collins, 1974). It should also be said, however, that many of the best known observation systems, such as FIAC and the ORACLE observation procedures, have been used successfully, and to obtain comparable results, by a wide variety of researchers.

In addition to training observers and establishing high levels of reliability at the end of the training session it is important that researchers should repeat the reliability checks at intervals through-out the data collection process. This is to make sure that 'observer drift', a movement away from the original definitions, does not occur as the data collection process becomes routinized. The importance of checking on the continued accuracy of data collection is especially important if the people involved in conducting observations are not all full members of the research team but include people employed simply to carry out the observations. The possible dangers of 'hired hand' research are well known (for example, Roth, 1966). Observers who do not feel personally committed to the research may start cutting corners and become careless about the observation. However, researchers should not regard checks on data collection as the principal safeguard against this happening, although they are, of course, important whether or not hired hands are being used as observers. Researchers should bring observers into the research team and develop their commitment to the research. Where the training period overlaps with the development of the observation schedule employed observers can be brought into the development process. Observers should be aware of the purposes of the research and have a commitment to its importance. Regular and extensive debriefing and feedback sessions are particularly important. These will avoid obser-vers becoming isolated and will involve them in the research as well as alerting the researchers to any difficulties which are arising in observation. It is also desirable that those in charge of research projects should themselves be observers on the projects alongside those in more junior roles. This will help in developing the commit-ment of observers to the project and emphasizes the importance of observation as well as alerting researchers to difficulties which the observers may be experiencing.

5 Processing and Analyzing Observational Data

Research Design and Analysis Strategy

One of the most important rules in conducting empirical research is that sampling, data collection procedures and data analysis are all aspects of research design and should be specified in the design. In particular this means that the analysis strategy to be adopted must be decided on before, not after, the process of data gathering. Most statisticians have had the experience of students and others arriving at their office doors carrying armfuls of data and saying 'What do I do now?' or 'Can the computer analyze this?'. All too often the answer is that the way the research was set up or the way the data have been collected and recorded precludes the kind of analysis necessary to investigate the ideas underlying the research.

The textbook advice that, as part of the process of research design, the investigator should set up dummy tables showing how the data are to be analyzed and presented, would, if followed, prevent many of the problems encountered by inexperienced (and sometimes not so inexperienced) researchers. This is partly a question of efficiency, of anticipating problems and setting up data collection and recording so as to facilitate analysis. But also, and more importantly, it implies a recognition that research is directed to specific questions and that the researcher should work out in advance how the research process will address these. The mechanics of data analysis may be a late stage in a research project but planning analysis is an early stage in research design. This argument is true of all social research but it is probably more important in considering observational data than in many other areas because of the complexities of data structure and the possible uncertainties about appropriate units of analysis which will be discussed below.

Variables and Units of Analysis

The process of data collection can be conceptualized as filling in the entries of a data matrix of which the rows represent cases or units of analysis and the columns represent variables (see Galtung, 1970, for an extended presentation of this conceptualization). The variables are derived from the operationalization of the concepts of interest in the research (these may be 'time on task' or 'time spent lecturing to the class' in the case of observational research or 'reading age' or 'father's occupation' in other kinds of research). The units of analysis are the individuals or other units (classes or schools for example) on which information is gathered.

A major decision to be made in observational research is what the units of analysis are to be and this decision is rarely straight-forward. Most classroom observations are of individuals — individual pupils or individual teachers although observations may also be made of groups or of specific interactions. The distinction between an observation of an individual and observation of an interaction may need spelling out. If the observation system focuses on individuals in the way that the ORACLE or *One in Five* research does then an observation of such an individual in a specific interaction should be thought of as an observation of an individual. However, if the observation system calls for a record to be made whenever a particular type of interaction or other activity takes place then the observation should be thought of as being of an interaction or activity even though these were carried out by individuals.

If observations were being made of an individual teacher then it may seem clear that it is the teacher who is the unit of analysis. But the total of observations made of that teacher are made up of a large number of individual observations at various points in time. If a time-sampling procedure is being used then the observations are divided up into a large number of separate observations as determined by the intervals of the time-sampling system. If an event recording system is being used then the observations will be of however many times relevant events occurred during the time the teacher was being observed. Consequently, each individual observation can be regarded as a unit of observation to be used in the analysis. If these individual units are preserved a number of possibilities arise for analysis which would not otherwise be available. For example, it is possible to specify the level of occurrence of particular variables not just as characteristics of this particular teacher but to distinguish between their occurrence during different lessons or at the beginning and end of lessons or as occurring during a particular sequence of behaviour.

It also makes it possible to link the occurrence of particular categories of a variable with categories of other variables being observed simultaneously. For example, if the teacher is regarded as the unit of analysis, an analysis which established a correlation between time spent in asking questions and time spent in groupwork would show that teachers who asked a lot of questions also spent a lot of time working with groups but would not show whether or not group teaching sessions were particularly likely to involve teacher questions. On the other hand, if the individual observations were the unit of analysis, it would be possible to show not only if questioning and group work were likely to be found among the same teachers but also if they tended to occur simultaneously. The same point applies to observation of pupils. An individual pupil can be treated as the unit of analysis with an overall score on each of the variables in the observation system but, in addition, each particular observation can be treated as a unit of analysis which makes possible different descriptions of the pupil during different lessons or at different times of day and also makes it possible to describe the co-occurrence of categories of variables at particular points in time as well as their more general association across individuals.

In some cases when pupils are the focus of observation the individual pupil is not the unit of analysis of interest. It may be that individual observed instances or possible characteristics of the class as a whole are the focus of interest. If an observation system is intended to give data about particular types of occurrence it may not be relevant which pupils engage in behaviours of interest. Event sampling observation procedures are particularly likely to be of this type when an event is recorded as it occurs without it necessarily being identified as associated with a particular individual. Alternatively, pupils may be observed in order to arrive at some overall characterization of a classroom with no interest in particular individuals. Observation systems involving scanning are often of this type. Here the observer looks around a classroom and notes how many pupils are engaged in particular activities but may not identify specific pupils.

Clearly there is a hierarchy among these units of analysis. If individual observations are regarded as the basic units of analysis then the individuals on whom these observations were made can also be treated as units of analysis providing that observations are of identified individuals. Similarly, data on identified individual pupils in a class can be aggregated to provide overall class data so that the class can be treated as a unit of analysis for other purposes. However, if data are collected in such a way as to provide class averages without identifying individuals then it is impossible to move back to individual level data. Similarly, if individual observations are not preserved in the process of data collection and processing it is impossible to recreate them.

Consequently, the individual observation of an identified individual will be treated as the most basic unit of analysis. Such an observation can be combined with others to give overall data on that individual in analyses when the individual is the unit of analysis, and individual observations can be aggregated in order to provide data for analyses in which the class or the school is the unit of analysis. This procedure retains the maximum amount of data and flexibility in analysis. In some studies it may not be necessary to record or process data in a way that preserves individual instances because overall individual or class scores are all that is required. However, an investigation which proceeds in this way is taking an irreversible step while keeping the detail of the observations keeps the researcher's options open. This argument may seem, superficially, in conflict with the earlier statement that the form of the analysis should be specified in the research design but the earlier point does not deny the value of flexibility in analysis. Researchers should specify how their research design and that data they collect can be used to answer their original research question but this should not preclude the possibility of further questions being generated in the process of data collection and analysis.

The existence of different units of analysis in observational research has consequences for the way in which variables are defined in data processing and analysis. As presented in chapter 3 an observation system may consist of one or more variables, each containing a number of mutually exclusive categories. At a particular observed instant one category of each variable will be coded. As long as the individual observations are the units of analysis then it makes sense to treat the data as consisting of a small number of variables, of which one category of each will apply at a particular moment.

However, when data analysis moves beyond individual observations as the units of analysis the nature of the variables also change. If the observation system consists of, for example, three variables, each observation is characterized by a single value of each of the variables. But if these observations are aggregated to give overall scores for an individual or for a class then every category may have a value. This situation is best considered as if each category of each variable is itself a variable. Every individual or classroom treated as a unit of analysis will have a score for each category of each variable in the observation system. Consequently, an observation system which is initially conceptualized as containing three or four variables may have many more times this number for the purposes of data analysis.

These multiple variables will be dichotomous variables at the level of individual observations, that is, any particular category will be true or false for a particular observation. But for individuals or classes they will be interval level variables having a score corresponding to the number of times they were true at the level of individual observations.

While it is convenient to treat categories of variables in this fashion for the purposes of data analysis it is important to remember the procedure by which these variables were derived and the constraints this places on analysis. Categories of a single variable which are then turned into separate variables are not independent of one another and any attempt to consider the interrelationship between them should take their incestuous relationship into account; if one such category was being coded then the others could not be and an individual with a high score for one such category has an inbuilt tendency to a low score on others.

Data Recording and Processing

This discussion of data recording and processing will assume that it is intended to extract the maximum information from the data and therefore that details of individual observations are to be retained, the less information it is intended to preserve then the simpler will be the process of recording and processing.

In setting up a data recording procedure the predominant consideration which will influence the researcher is that observers should be able to use it accurately in the classroom. The convenience of the system for subsequent data processing will necessarily be secondary but, nevertheless, attention to the requirements of data processing may save a great deal of work without adversely affecting the process of classroom observation.

Most research using classroom observation will generate a very considerable amount of data and, unless the analysis to be employed is very simple, will involve computer processing. Consequently most researchers are likely to find that they need to record data in a way that can be easily input into computer files either directly or through some medium such as punched cards. If it is not intended to use a computer then less attention need be given to the exact arrangements for data processing but the general principles discussed here will still apply.

The simplest form of data recording of the observation systems discussed so far is that associated with the Flanders Interaction Analysis Categories (FIAC). FIAC consists of only one variable and the basic unit of analysis is the individual teacher/pupil(s) interaction. Each interaction is described by one single-digit number and the record of an observation session consists of a long series of such numbers. An example of a recording sheet is given in figure 2. For most purposes computer analysis is unnecessary for such data; category counts and the construction of interaction grids (see pp 121–123) can be done by hand. Even if the quantity of data or the complexity of the analysis is such that computer processing is necessary the information can be input as a string of digits and the analysis to be conducted is relatively straightforward.

A more complicated example is the observation system used in *One in Five* and set out in figure 1. For most of the observation period three variables are being coded simultaneously and each group of three digits refers to a particular observation. This observation is the basic unit of analysis but, associated with the three-digit code are also the pupil, teacher and lesson identification codes and the classroom organisation and curriculum content codes which are recorded at the beginning of each four-minute block of observation.

Standard data analysis packages such as the Statistical Package for the Social Sciences (SPSS) or the more recent version, SPSS-X (Nie *et al*, 1975 and 1983) which are the data analysis and statistical packages most commonly used by researchers in higher education, require that data be input case (unit of analysis) by case. The simplest procedure, therefore, would be to treat each three-digit block of data, representing a single observation, as a case. The individual observation would, therefore, form the most basic unit of analysis and cases could be combined to form units at higher levels of analysis. For example, using the AGGREGATE and WRITE CASES procedures within SPSS all the observations on each individual pupil could be combined and a new data file constructed in which the individual pupils were the units of analysis.

To give a concrete example of this, suppose that 100 pupils in ten classrooms had each been observed at 500 separate moments in time using the observation system in figure 1. The initial data file would consist of 50,000 cases (100 pupils × 500 observations). Each case would contain a pupil, teacher and lesson identification number together with values for six variables (teaching organization, reading/ non-reading, curriculum content, activity, interaction and mobile/ fidgeting). This data file could be used to provide information on the overall frequency of each category of each of the six variables and also to compare the frequencies for different pupils and classrooms. If it is known which pupil identification numbers refer to girls and which to boys or which are high and which low achievers then these groups can also be compared. In addition, the pattern of co-occurrence of the categories of the variables can also be studied; whether, for example, a particular category of curriculum content is especially strongly associated with a particular category of pupil activity.

If these data are then aggregated across individuals a new data file can be created in which the individual pupil is the unit of analysis. The new file will consist of 100 cases but will have many more variables than the original file. While the file based on individual observations has six variables, each having the value of one category of the variable, the file based on individuals will have as many variables as there are categories of the original six variables, in this case 33 variables. Each of these will be a score corresponding to the number of occasions an observation was made in the category corresponding to the variable. This file can then be used to compare individuals and groups of individuals or to look for similarities and differences between individuals through cluster analysis (see chapter 6). Although some of the analysis conducted on the individual file will be the same as those conducted on the file of observations, the new file, with only a hundred cases, will be much easier to work with than that containing 50,000 cases, even though the number of variables is much greater.

Although some of the analyses will be identical on the two data files, others, although superficially similar, will actually be different. For example, looking at the association between variables on the file of observations shows if particular categories occur together but correlating variables across individuals shows not whether two things occur at the same time but whether individuals with high values on one also tend to have high (or low in the case of negative correlations) values on another.

As well as creating a file based on overall data about individuals it is also possible to create a file based on data from each individual at particular times of the day or during particular sorts of lessons. Alternatively the file of individuals may contain additional variables giving this information.

Just as the original observations can be aggregated to produce data describing individuals, so they can also be aggregated to provide a file in which a classroom is the unit of analysis. In the example being considered this file would consist of ten cases and would have the same number and type of variables as the individual file.

To try to achieve clarity of presentation the discussion so far has assumed that the cases used as units of analysis are the same as the cases used in computer processing. In practice, however, the construction of a data file in which each observation is a separate case for computing purposes has a number of disadvantages. First, it results in a data file with a very large number of cases which creates problems of storage and processing. Second it involves a great deal of duplication of information as the identical pupil, teacher and lesson identification numbers are repeated many times over and, in the example of the *One in Five* observation system, variables 1 to 3 which virtually always remain constant for a block of 24 observations also have to be repeated for each case.

In the data analysis for the *One in Five* research, although individual observations were regarded as the basic units of analysis they were not treated as separate cases in computer processing. The case, for the purposes of the computer processing, was a set of twenty-four individual observations represented by the complete coding form shown in figure 1. Each case consists of the pupil, teacher and lesson identification number coded once, values for variables 1 to 3, also coded once, and twenty-four observations of the variables 4 to 6. In analysis, the values of the twenty variables which the original variables 4 to 6 have given rise to can be aggregated in order to give overall scores and to output data files based on the individuals as units of analysis. Values of the individual observations on variables 4 to 6 can be linked to the appropriate individuals and to categories of variables 1 to 3 without these having to be repeatedly coded. A complication created by this approach to data processing is that cross tabulations of categories of variables 4 to 6 must be repeated twenty-four times and an overall cross tabulation table constructed by adding the appropriate categories of the twenty-four separate tables. This can either be done by hand or by a simple computer routine by which output tables are stored and their values accumulated.

This discussion of data processing has assumed that observations have been recorded in the classroom in a numerical form. Sometimes, however, observation systems are such that observers tick categories on the form or use some other sort of symbol. Clearly there are great advantages if the recording system is such that the coding forms used in the classroom can be used as the basis for data processing with only a checking/editing procedure in between. This will usually mean indicating the appropriate numbers on the coding form. If a tick system is being used by the observer it may be possible to indicate the appropriate numbers on the form as shown in figure 8. In this example the observer in the classroom only has to make a tick on a form but the computer punch operator sees the ticks as indicating numbers and can therefore work directly from the observer's coding sheets.

Figure 8: Example of a coding sheet

Code a new column at ten-second intervals

Teacher interacts with:	Class	1 1 1 1 1	
	Group	2 2 2 2 2	
	Individual	3 3 3 3 3	
	None	4 4 4 4 4	*Observer rings or ticks the*
Content of interaction:	Work	1 1 1 1 1	*appropriate number*
	Social	2 2 2 2 2	
	Discipline	3 3 3 3 3	
	Other	4 4 4 4 4	
	None	5 5 5 5 5	

A further development of this idea is to use coding sheets suitable for optical mark reading by the computer. This was the procedure used in *A Study of Schooling*. The appropriate codes for each category are marked on the coding sheet in a similar way to figure 8. The observer uses a dark pencil to mark over the appropriate space on the form instead of just ticking it as in figure 8 and the mark is read by an optical scanner and converted into numerical form. This is a much more efficient way of transferring data from the code sheets into computer files but it requires careful organization before-hand and very exact marking by the observer.

The two most important considerations in deciding on procedures for data recording and processing are those of ensuring that the observer can code accurately in the classroom and that the data are recorded in such a way that the appropriate analyses can be conducted.

The first requirement means that the recording procedure should be set up so that it is 'usable' in the classroom even if this creates later problems in processing. This may mean, for example, that ticks are used where it would be better from the point of view of processing to write numbers. Aspects of efficient and accurate recording in the classroom have already been discussed in chapter 4.

The second requirement means that the recording and processing procedures must preserve any information which will be used in the analysis. Consideration must be given to the units of analysis which will be used and what different sorts of information will be linked together in analysis.

The work of linking the live observation and coding in the classrooms with the data files which will be used in analysis will vary according to the complexity of the coding procedure and the form in which the data are required. It may be, as we have already seen, that units of analysis and cases input into the computer are not the same or that distinctions made between separate observed individuals or observed instants do not need to be preserved.

If the research is being conducted on a small scale then computer facilities may not be necessary and processing and analysis will be a relatively simple procedure of manual counting and sorting of the original observations. Conversely, in studies involving very complex observation procedures on a large scale it may be necessary for the researchers to recode all the observations before they are in a form suitable for computer analysis. In most instances, however, it should be possible to set up the study so that the original observation sheets can be used as the basis for computer input, as illustrated in figure 8. If this is possible then care in setting out the observation schedule to facilitate it will save the researchers a great deal of time after the observations have been conducted.

Simple Analysis of Observational Data

In considering how to approach the analysis of observational data it is useful to return to the idea of the *data matrix* discussed earlier. The information obtained from observation can be conceptualized in terms of a matrix, or series of matrices, of which the rows represent the individual units of analysis and the columns represent variables. If the analysis is to take place at more than one level, that is, if some analyses involve moments in time as the basic units while others involve individuals and others class aggregates then there will be as many matrices as there are levels of analysis. In most research projects these matrices are ways of conceptualizing data held on computer files, but in some small-scale studies it may be appropriate to work with the data directly in this form.

Examples of data matrices derived from an observational study are given in figures 9, 10 and 11. These represent a simple observational study in which four children in each of two classrooms have been observed using a schedule which classifies their activity and interaction using an instantaneous time-sampling system. For simplicity of presentation, at each moment when the pupils are observed their activity is coded working (W) or not-working (Nw) and their interactions are coded as not-interacting (Ni), interacting with the teacher (T), interacting with one or more other children (C) or interacting with the teacher and other pupils (TC). In the matrix in figure 9 each row represents an instant when an observation was made and the first two columns represent the two variables just described. In addition, the identification number of the child being observed can be represented as a category of a variable as can the identification number or letter of the classroom in which observation

Figure 9: *Data matrix using individual observation as units of analysis.*

		Activity	Interaction	Variables Pupil ID	Class	Lesson	Times
Observation	1	W	Ni	1	A	10	1
number	2	W	Ni	1	A	10	1
	3	W	T	1	A	10	1
	4	W	Ni	1	A	10	1
	5	NW	C	1	A	10	1
	6	NW	C	1	A	10	1
	7	W	Ni	4	A	10	2
	8	W	Ni	4	A	10	2
		—	—	—	—	—	—
		—	—	—	—	—	—
		—	—	—	—	—	—

Key　W — Working
　　Nw — Not working
　　　Ni — Not interacting
　　　　C — Interacting with other children
　　　　T — Interacting with teacher

Figure 10: Data matrix using individual pupils as units of analysis

Pupil ID	Working (W)	Not working (Nw)	Not interacting (Ni)	Interacting with teacher (T)	Interacting with child (C)	Total observations	Class ID	Working and interacting with child (C/W)	Sex of Pupil
1	320	180	300	90	110	500	A	30	F
2	–	–	–	–	–	–	–	–	–
3	–	–	–	–	–	–	–	–	–
etc	–	–	–	–	–	–	–	–	–

Figure 11: Data matrix using classes as units of analysis

	Working (W)	Not working (Nw)	Not interacting (Ni)	Interacting with teacher (T)	Interacting with child (C)	Total observations	Working and interacting with child (C/W)
Class A	1200	800	1300	300	400	2000	100
B	1400	600	1275	500	225	2000	75

is taking place. The lesson being observed can also be given an identification number. In the example in figure 9 the time during the lesson at which the observation was made has also been recorded as a variable.

The first row of figure 9 represents the first observation made. The child observed was working (W) and was not interacting (Ni). The child being observed was child number 1, the classroom was classroom A and the lesson was lesson number 10. The observation was made during the first minute of the lesson (time = 1). The second observation represented in the matrix is identical to the first and the third is identical except that at the moment of the observation the child was interacting with the teacher (T). After six observations the observer has switched from observing child 1 and has moved onto child 4. These observations take place in the second minute of the lesson as can be seen from the column headed 'time'.

A matrix in this form is the basis for an analysis using individual observations as the units of analysis, although it would not usually be possible to physically represent the data for analysis in this way. Even in the very simple example given here, if each pupil was observed on 500 occasions this would generate a matrix with 4000 rows. If the data were to be input to a standard data analysis package such as SPSS or SPSS-X then each row could be represented as a case, although, as discussed above, it might be more practicable to treat a group of rows as a case.

Figure 9 preserves all the data from the original observations. For many research purposes it is probably preferable to use individual pupils rather than moments in time as the units of analysis and a matrix in this form is presented in figure 10. In figure 10 each row represents a pupil; the first row is child 1, the second row child 2, and so on, in order to combine the observations to give a picture of individual pupils of whom a large number of observations have been made. In the new matrix each category of the observation system becomes a variable with values representing the number of observations of a particular pupil which fell into that category. The two variables 'activity' and 'interaction' of figure 9 become five variables, working (W), not-working (Nw), not-interacting (Ni), interacting with the teacher (T) and interacting with another child (C). Another variable gives the total number of observations made of each child. In the first row of figure 10 it can be seen that of the 500 observations made of pupil 1, 320 were made when she was working and 180 when she was not working. On 300 of the occasions she was not interacting, on ninety she was interacting with the teacher and on 110 she was interacting with another pupil. The matrix also includes a variable C/W representing the number of times an observation of the child involved coding both 'work' and 'child', that is, the occasions when a child was working in interaction with children. In the example given, there were thirty occasions out of 500 observed when pupil 1 was working in interaction with one or more other pupils.

All the these figures can be derived from the complete version of the matrix in figure 9 by counting the number of occurrences of each category for each pupil and by counting the number of joint occurrences of 'C' and 'W' for the 'C/W' variable. (Obviously, other variables involving joint occurrences could also be derived from the matrix.) In addition to these variables which derived from the observations made of pupils, two other variables, the class the pupil is in and the sex of the pupil are also included in the matrix, this allows comparisons between classes and between boys and girls to be made as part of the analysis.

If comparisons of different classes are to be a focus of the analysis it may be appropriate to derive a new data matrix in which classes are the units of analysis. In figure 11 the units are the two classes, A and B. The variables are the same as those for individuals, but the values in the cells are the number of times a child in the class has been observed in the category on which the variable is based.

Describing Individuals and Classes

Using the matrices in figures 10 and 11 as the basis for an analysis of individuals and classes involves the same principles as other data analysis in educational and social reserch. Analysis can be based on the columns of the matrix to provide a *variable-centred* analysis to describe the individual variables by means of, for example, averages, and to look at interrelationships between the variables through correlations or comparisons of means. Analysis can also focus on rows in a *case-centred* analysis to provide profiles of particular individuals or classes or to group together those with similar profiles in a cluster analysis.

Working on the matrices in figures 10 and 11 and taking the columns one at a time it is possible to provide a summary of the data by giving average values of each variable. It should be noted that if the numbers of pupils observed in each class are equal then the averages derived from figure 10 will be identical to those derived from figure 11. If the numbers are not equal then this will not necessarily be the case and the researcher will have to decide which is the most appropriate. In addition to averages it will usually be appropriate to calculate a measure of dispersion for the variable such as the mean deviation or standard deviation. These averages will convey more information if they are presented as percentages or proportions of the total of observations. For example, for class A rather than report that on 400 occasions an observation involved pupil-pupil interaction it conveys more information to report that 20 per cent of observations were of this sort.

In the case of variables made up out of the co-occurrence of other variables such as C/W, some care must be given to calculating appropriate percentages. In figure 11 the two observations of C/W in class A are 5 per cent of all possible observations (100 out of 2000). However, it may also be of interest that 25 per cent of all pupil-pupil interactions were of work-oriented interactions (100 out of 400), and also that 8.3 per cent of all observations of work were of work involving pupil-pupil interaction (100 out of 1200). In contrast, class B has a lower percentage of C/W (3.75 per cent), but a higher percentage of all pupil-pupil interactions are work oriented (33.3 per cent).

These average values of variables can be used as the basis for a more complex analysis in addition to a simple comparison across columns to show the relative prevalence of different activities. They can be used to compare groups of pupils such as boys and girls or high and low achievers, or to compare types of classes such as primary and secondary classrooms or different subject specialist classrooms. It is also possible to conduct correlational analyses by calculating the correlations of variables in the different columns, for example, that the amount of time spent working (values of W) correlates positively (or negatively) with the amount of time spent in interactions with the teacher (T).

This is similar to the sorts of analyses which might be carried out on data from many other sources as well as observations but there are two possible difficulties in carrying out correlational analyses on observation data. The first is the question of the lack of independence between some of the variables. The variables which appear as the columns of the matrices in figures 10 and 11 have been derived from a smaller number of variables making up the columns of figure 9. Variables which have been derived from different columns of the original matrix can be correlated in the ordinary way as the values have been measured independently. Any variable based on activity (that is, W and Nw) can be correlated with any variables based on interaction (that is, Ni, T and C). But a variable based on activity cannot be simply correlated with another activity variable or an interaction variable with another interaction variable as these derive from categories of a single variable in the original observation and there is therefore a built-in negative correlation between them.

This is fairly obvious in the present example. It would not make sense to correlate working and not-working as they are the only two categories of activity and must necessarily have a perfect negative correlation. However, if there are a large number of categories of a variable in the original observation system the researcher must be careful not to correlate variables which are not derived independently. If the association between two such variables is of interest then an allowance must be made in the calculation of the correlation. For example, a variable based on one of a set of mutually exclusive categories could be represented not as a percentage of all observations but as a percentage of all observations excluding observations placed in the other category to be used in the correlation. A similar calculation, excluding the observations falling into the first category, would then be made for the second and the resulting percentages or proportions used as the basis for the calculation. Needless to say that great care could be taken in presenting and interpreting such results.

The second difficulty which can arise in conducting and interpreting correlational analyses on observational data is the different meaning which patterns of association have when different units of analyses are being used.

The simplest case is when the individual observations are the units of analysis as in figure 9. These observations are made in terms of the category of each variable which applies at a particular observation. Consequently, analyzing interrelationships between variables normally involves cross-tabulation rather than calculating correlation co-efficients. Any pattern of association to occur in the joint distribution of observations across categories of the two variables must reflect a co-occurrence of these categories; observations which fall into a particular category of one variable have a tendency to also be in a particular category of the other. For example, it might turn out to be the case that if the variables activity and interaction in figure 9 are cross-tabulated that observations which are coded as teacher interaction (T) for the interaction variable are almost always coded working (W) for the activity variable while a much lower proportion of the observations coded under the other interaction categories are coded 'W'. This would show an association between categories of the variables arising from a straightforward co-occurrence.

Even this simple example of association being demonstrated by co-occurrence may need careful interpretation however. It may be that although almost all the observations coded 'T' are also coded as 'W', only a small proportion of the 'W' codes are also coded 'T'. This would arise if there were many more instances of observations being coded 'W' than of those coded 'T'. Simply to refer to an association between activity and interaction does not adequately describe the form of the relationship. In the example given above it would be necessary to say that when pupils are interacting with a teacher they are nearly always working but when pupils are working they are not usually interacting with a teacher.

Correlational analysis of observational data becomes more complex when individuals, rather than observations, are the units of analysis. Such an analysis will probably involve using the scores for the number of observations (or, more probably, percentage of observations) in a particular category. For example, in figure 10 the set of scores for individuals for 'W' could be correlated with the set of scores for 'T'. A positive correlation indicates that individuals who have high 'W' scores, that is, spend a high proportion of their time working, also have high 'T' scores — that is, have high levels of interaction with the teacher, while individuals with low 'W' scores also tend to have low 'T' scores. Conversely, a negative correlation shows that high 'W' scores are associated with low 'T' scores and *vice-versa*. A zero, or close to zero, correlation shows that there is no pattern of association between the two sets of scores.

In interpreting such results it is important to remember that what has been correlated are characteristics of individuals not of units of behaviour. A positive correlation between 'T' and 'W' shows that the individuals with the highest levels of one variable tend also to be the individuals with the highest levels of the other variable, but this does not mean that the two categories of behaviour necessarily occur together at particular moments in time. This is underlined by the fact that at the level of individuals it is possible to correlate their scores on categories of the same observational variable such as 'T' and 'C', (making allowance for the built-in negative correlation), which by definition could not be occuring at the same moment in time. The researcher must be sure of the questions which correlational and other analysis are designed to answer in choosing the level at which analysis is carried out. Using individuals as the units answers the question of whether people who have one set of behavioural characteristics (such as high levels of time devoted to work) also have another behavioural characteristic (such as high levels of interaction with the teacher) but they do not allow us to say that these two behaviours occur together in time, although they may do so, and, in an example like the one being used here it is very tempting to assume that this must be the case. An analysis based on individual observations is necessary if we want to talk about the co-occurrence in time of particular aspects of behaviour. An observed association between the categories 'W' and 'T' based on cross-tabulation of the 'activity' and 'interaction' variables from figure 9 would demonstrate such a co-occurrence in time. This would be compatible with, but would not itself demonstrate, a correlation at the level of individuals.

Similar distinctions have to be made if classes rather than individuals are to be used as the unit of analysis. If class average scores have been derived from observations of all pupils in them, or a sample of these pupils, then scores can be presented for the different variables as has been done in figure 11 and these variables can be correlated in the same way as for individuals. The results from such an analysis refer to characteristics of the aggregate, the school class, and not to characteristics of individuals. For example, it might be observed at the aggregate level of analysis that classes which had a high level of disciplinary teacher-pupil interactions were also characterized by high levels of work. This would not mean that it was the pupils who received the most disciplinary interactions who worked the most, at an individual level of analysis the opposite might well be the case.

The question of the relationship between correlations at the level of individuals and correlations at the level of class aggregates, as well as requiring care in analysis, also illustrates some of the analytic possibilities which are made available when data are available for a sample of identified pupils within a single class, as is frequently the case with studies using systematic observation. In such cases, a particular characteristic of a pupil can be placed in the context of pupils in general, if data are available from a large number of classes, and also in the context of the particular class in which the pupil is located, if data are available about a large number of children in it. It may be of interest for the purpose of testing particular explanations or hypotheses that a child has a high level of engagement in work or pupil-pupil interaction overall, or, alternatively that the child has a high level of work or interaction in the context of a particular class. For some purposes children may be regarded as similar if they have the highest levels of particular characteristics, while for other purposes they may be considered as similar if they are the highest in their classes with regard to this characteristic. If class average levels of the variable of interest differ then membership of the two groups may not be the same.

Analysis of this kind makes possible investigations of the relative influence of the teacher and the classroom ethos on pupil characteristics compared with the variation which exists between individual pupils.

Observational Descriptions and Observational Variables

In chapter 3 various ways of locating observations in time and in context were discussed. The procedures adopted have implications for the nature of the variables in observational research and the types of descriptions which can be generated from analysis. Procedures for locating observations in time include:

Event sampling — recording whenever a particular event or events occur.

Instantaneous time sampling — recording whatever is happening at particular pre-timed intervals.

One-zero time sampling — recording at pre-timed intervals whether certain events have occurred between that moment and the previous interval.

Scanning — recording, in turn, what all the members of a class are doing or counting how many are engaged in a particular activity, starting at pre-timed intervals.

Continuous recording — keeping an on-going record which changes whenever the activity changes.

Quasi-continuous recording — making discrete observations as in instantaneous time sampling but with such a short time interval that it becomes an effectively continuous record.

These different recording procedures produce variables with differing characteristics and which provide different sorts of information about the relationship between events and time. Aspects of this relationship which a researcher might be concerned with include:

Frequency of occurrence — how often particular sorts of events or types of behaviour occur.

Duration — how much time is taken up by different sorts of events or types of behaviour.

Bout length — how long individual occurrences take.
Location in real time — at what precise time occurrences take place.
Sequence — how are events temporally related to other events.

The different types of observation system being used together with the way that the variables have been defined will provide information on different aspects of the relationship of events to time. (Continuous recording is a special case and will be considered separately.)

Estimates of the frequency of occurrence derive most obviously from event recording systems. The results derived from such observation systems refer directly to frequency and provide a count of all observed instances. It is possible to say that a particular individual engaged in a specified category of interaction or type of activity on an exact number of occasions or, if a whole class is being observed, that such interactions or activities occurred in that class a specified number of times. Other types of time-sampling do not allow this sort of statement about frequency to be made. Instantaneous time-sampling and scanning do not provide information about the frequency of occurrences at moments other than those sampled and one-zero sampling systems provide counts of the minimum level of occurrence but not of the actual level. Quasi-continuous observation systems are sometimes used to provide frequency counts but a degree of caution is necessary in this case. It may be possible for two consecutive observations to refer to different rather than the same occurrence, and also for an event or interaction to take place in between two observations.

Estimates of the proportion of time taken up by different categories of activity or interaction are usually derived from variables which form part of an instantaneous time-sampling system. Although such variables provide data in the form of a count of the number of sampled instances when particular categories were coded these counts should be interpreted as estimates of the proportion of time falling into these categories rather than as counts of instances. This is why the results of instantaneous time-sampling are normally expressed as percentages or proportions of all observations rather than as raw counts. If a pupil has been recorded as interacting with other pupils on one in ten of the observations made this shows that 10 per cent of the pupil's time is spent in this sort of interaction, not that any particular number of interactions took place.

Some elaboration of this procedure is possible however. Analyzing sequences of sampled instants provides some data on the length of individual interactions or other aspects of behaviour which may make possible estimates of the frequency of these. If a particular category rarely occurs again at the subsequent coding instant then the duration of individual occurrences can be seen to be short. Such a category clearly has a higher frequency of occurrence than one with the same overall number of observations which typically occur in a long sequence even though the amount of time taken up by the two categories is the same. Difficulties arise here, however, as it cannot be assumed that two identical observations several seconds apart refer to an unbroken occurrence. Approaches to this problem will be suggested in the discussion of observing sequences below.

Estimates of the amounts of time falling into different categories of observational variables can also be derived from scanning systems which can be seen as a type of instantaneous time-sampling and by quasi-continuous recording which gives a very accurate estimate of the time spent in different activities. Event recording which simply counts the number of occurrences cannot provide time estimates and this is also a limitation of one-zero time sampling systems which record the number of time intervals in which various categories of behaviour occur but not the amount of time they take up.

Descriptions of the exact moments in time when particular observations were made can be incorporated into any observation system. Events can be timed exactly in an event recording system and the coded instants of the various time-sampling systems and quasi-continuous recording systems can have exact times attached to them. This is best conceptualized as introducing time as a variable of the recording system; each observation is coded for time as well as for the various categories of the observational variables and time can then be used as a variable in data analysis. The amount of detail retained in the coding of time will depend on the purpose for which the information is being gathered. It may be sufficient to indicate that observations were made in the first fifteen minutes or second fifteen minutes and so on of a lesson or even simply that an observation was made in the morning or afternoon. This sort of information about time is clearly relevant to analyzing sequences of interactions and other behaviour although having precisely timed observations does not necessarily solve this problem as will be indicated below.

One of the most complex aspects of data analysis concerned with the location of observations in time is that of establishing a sequence of observations. In this discussion a distinction will be made between what will be termed a *weak* analysis of sequence, which is concerned with where events stand in temporal relation to one another in a general sense, usually over relatively extended periods of time such as a lesson or a day, and a *strong* analysis of sequence, which is concerned with an immediate and detailed account of sequences of behaviour or interactions, usually over short periods of time. An example of the first sort of analysis of sequence might be an analysis which establishes that a particular teacher usually begins lessons with a series of questions to the pupils but reduces the level of questioning as the lesson proceeds. An example of the second would be accounts of specific question/answer sequences where specified categories of question could be linked to specified categories of answer.

The weak analysis of sequence can be derived from a system for noting the time at which observations occur as was discussed above. In many cases this sort of analysis may not go beyond the sorts of examples given in the earlier discussion. For example, it may be of interest to establish that certain sorts of observations typically occur in the afternoon and others in the morning or that certain lessons can be divided into beginning, middle and end periods, each characterized by the occurrence of different categories of the observation system. Similarly, the behaviour and interactions of individual pupils can be looked at separately at different times in the day or at different points in the lesson. Classes, pupils or school subjects can be compared with respect to these characteristics.

However, a more elaborate analysis of sequences can also be conducted using timed observations. Profiles of lessons or of individuals over time can be constructed based on one or more variables measured at different points in time. Thus, it is possible to say that a certain lesson began with an exposition from the teacher, moved into individual work by pupils with the teacher silently monitoring and finished with a question and answer session. This could be derived from an observation schedule focussing on the teacher in which these types of activities were categories. A series of observations focussed on a pupil could give, for example, average levels of engagement in work minute by minute throughout the day and present this as a work profile for this pupil.

These sorts of developmental profiles can be used to provide illustrative accounts of particular pupils or lessons but they can also be used to aggregate data across a number of pupils or classrooms. Aggregating similar profiles can provide accounts of ideal types of lesson development or developmental accounts of pupil behaviour with which other lessons or pupils can be compared. This sort of analysis has something in common with cluster analysis which is discussed in chapter 6, but the profiles are made up of the same variable across time rather than different variables as in cluster analysis.

The analysis of the development of a lesson or of a pupil's behaviour over time involves the individual or the class as the unit of analysis and treats sequences as changes in the observed categories over time rather than as specific, explicitly linked observations. The stronger case of analyses of sequences is concerned to make such explicit links and treats the individual observation as the unit of analysis. This is a micro-level analysis of classroom processes rather than a developmental account of individuals or lessons.

The best known way of establishing a sequence for specific observations is with a quasi-continuous observation system such as Flanders Interaction Analysis Categories. A system such as this which categorizes interactions at very brief intervals makes it possible to link together sequences of interactions. The Flanders ten category system can generate results which can be presented in a hundred-cell matrix which was described in chapter 2. However, a simpler example will be given here.

The example presented in figure 12 is a simple interaction analysis system derived from FIAC. All teacher/pupil verbal interactions are coded into one of four categories coding at three-second intervals as in FIAC. The four categories are: teacher asks a question, teacher makes a statement, pupil responds to the teacher, pupil initiates an interaction. An observer can code a period of interaction simply by writing the appropriate number every three seconds. This will generate a sequence of numbers, a possible example of which is given in figure 12. This sequence of numbers can be used as the basis for counts of the various categories in order to say what proportion of instances were of teacher questions, pupil initiation and so on. But they can also be used as the basis for sequences. The series of numbers forms a sequence in a strong sense, not merely that the later numbers represent observations at a later point in time than the earlier ones but that consecutive numbers represent observations made immediately after one another. In consequence, consecutive numbers can be regarded as pairs of observations and these pairs can be represented in a matrix such as that given in figure 12.

The matrix is derived by moving along the series of numbers and identifying all forty-nine paired observations which arise from the fifty individual observations. The first two numbers give rise to the pair 1–3 where 1 is the first and 3 the subsequent observation. The

Figure 12:   *An interaction analysis system to categorize verbal interaction between teacher and pupils.*

Categories: Teacher asks question 1
Teacher makes statement 2
Pupil(s) responds to teacher 3
Pupil(s) initiates interaction 4

Sequence of 50 observations coded at 3-second intervals:
1 3 1 3 1 1 2 2 2 2 2 2 2 1 3 2 2 2 1 3
2 2 2 2 2 2 4 2 2 2 2 1 3 3 3 4 2 2 2
1 1 3 3 1 1 1 3 3 2

Interaction matrix based on observations:

	1	2	3	4	*Total:*
1	4	1	7	0	12
2	4	19	0	1	24
3	3	3	4	1	11
4	0	2	0	0	2

observation 3 then becomes the first observation of the next pair which is 3–1, the 1 from this observation becomes the first observation of the next pair 1–3 and on until the final pair, 3–2. All observations except the first and the last contribute to two cell entries, first as the first observation and then as the second observation of a pair. In the matrix the rows represent the first and the columns the second observation making up the pairs. In the matrix in figure 12 there are four instances of 1–1 pairs, one instance of a 1–2 pair, nineteen instances of a 2–2 pair, three instances of a 3–2 pair and so on.

This form of analysis makes it possible to identify specific, small-scale sequences of interaction. The 1–1 pairs represent occasions when a question occurring in one three-second interval carried over to the next; in contrast the 1–3 code represents question and answer across two intervals. The largest category of all, 2–2, shows how many times a teacher statement carried over into the next coded instant. The row 3 shows what happens after a pupil is observed answering a question; 3–1 shows how often another question follows, 3–2 how often another statement follows, 3–3 how often the answer goes on to the next code and so on. All sorts of complex analyses using different ratios of cell entries and bases for calculating percentages are possible on the basis of even a very simple matrix like this one. Some examples of the information which can be derived from the Flanders matrix were given in chapter 2; further examples are given in Flanders (1970) and Wragg (1973). Analysis does not have to stop at pairs of observations. Sequences of three observations can be represented by four matrices rather than the one in figure 12, although in the case of FIAC such a representation would require ten matrices. Anything beyond this would be impractical to represent visually but it is relatively simple to search the data, either visually or by computer programs, to find specific sequences as long as these can be specified in advance.

It should be noted that although, due to the prominence of the Flanders Interaction Analysis System, such matrices are usually thought of in terms of interactions they are not restricted to interaction analysis and can be used to describe other behavioural sequences.

Establishing strong sequences is only possible when the observation system uses continuous or quasi-continuous recording. It is possible to construct matrices based on pairs of observations from variables of other systems such as instantaneous time sampling systems or event recording systems but they cannot be given the same interpretation. Time sampling systems allow too long between consecutive observations to be able to treat such observations as a true pair occurring immediately after one another. An observation of a teacher asking a question followed by a similar observation may represent an on-going question or two questions split up by a non-observed pupil answer. In the case of event recording the interval is also likely to be too long and is also variable and, possibly, of unknown length.

Any element of sequence which is to be derived from observation systems of this sort must come from the definition of the variables and their categories as they apply to particular observations rather than from the relationship between separate observations. This relates to the discussion in chapter 3 which distinguished between establishing sequence by means of the time location of the observations and establishing sequence by means of the definition of variables.

The categories which make up a variable can refer to sequence as well as to the behaviour or interaction occurring at a particular moment in time. This is probably most easily seen in the case of event recording systems. The recording of an event can refer backwards as when the category into which a particular type of pupil utterance is coded will depend on whether it was in response to a teacher, in response to a pupil, initiates an interaction with teacher or initiates an interaction with a pupil. This provides instances of specific short-term interaction sequences from a single observation similar to those arising from the interaction matrix in figure 12. Similarly, the recording of an event can refer forwards, as when the coding of a teacher's question, which is the event to be recorded, may depend upon who answers it or on what sort of answer is received. Event recording can also treat sequences as events which are recorded continuously over relatively brief periods of time although this depends on the sequences being clearly and unambiguously initiated so that coding can begin.

Time-sampling systems and, in particular, instantaneous time-sampling systems, can also incorporate limited sequences into the definition of their variables. In the ORACLE observation system discussed in chapter 2 the categories used to code pupil-pupil and certain of the teacher-pupil interactions distinguished between interactions which had been on-going since the last code and interactions which had begun since a code was last made. Clearly other aspects of sequence could also be built into this kind of coding system.

These procedures mean that it is possible to take some account of strong as well as weak aspects of sequence in most observational systems (although not in the case of scanning systems) although systems which do not involve continuous or quasi-continuous observation can only do so in a limited way. In these other systems any possible sequences have to be specified in advance in the definition of the variables and only a limited number can be included. In systems like FIAC all sorts of sequences of interest can be explored either simply for pairs of observations through the interaction matrix or, with more difficulty for longer sequences, through searching a series of observations.

Another concern of data analysis in observational research is likely to be that of establishing the context within which observations were made. This also involves a consideration of the nature of observational variables and of the interrelationship of observations at different levels of analysis.

The simplest case of establishing context is where the contextual variables are not themselves derived from the systematic observation procedure. This sort of context may arise in distinguishing observations made of science lessons and English lessons or primary and secondary school classrooms or the lessons of experienced teachers and of student teachers. Making these distinctions creates no special difficulties and is exactly the same as distinguishing observations made at different times of the day or day of the week.

Less straightforward is the attempt to establish context in terms of characteristics of the classroom which themselves require direct observation. A researcher may want to differentiate between observations made during different teaching settings such as a teacher working with the whole class or with small groups or pupils working on individual tasks on their own (Poppleton, 1975). Similarly, a researcher may want to distinguish between interactions in different curriculum areas in a setting such as a primary classroom where the curriculum content of a teaching period differs for different children or cannot be predicted in advance.

In this situation it will be necessary to have additional variables in the observation schedule which establish context simultaneously with the variables which describe behaviour or interaction. It may be possible to simplify this, for example, by shifting to a different coding sheet or even to a different coding schedule. The approach used in the *One in Five* research was to have a system of additional variables establishing context but only to code them on the relatively infrequent occasions when the context changed. This creates an implicit simultaneous coding which avoid the difficulties of attempting the actual simultaneous coding of a large number of variables.

It is also possible to establish context by means of categories of the main variables of interest. For example, categories of teacher-pupil interaction can distinguish interaction in class, group or individual contexts and categories of pupil activity can distinguish between work on an individual task, work on a cooperative task, work within the context of a whole class activity and so on.

These procedures establish the immediate context in which activities or interactions have taken place. By conducting data analysis at different levels of aggregation and interrelating the results it is also possible to establish a more general context for observations. By conducting an analysis at the level of class aggregates it is possible to establish overall levels of various activities for particular classes which can then provide a context for the results of observation of individual children within these classes. This might make it possible to say that a child has a high level of a particular type of activity overall but is average within his or her class. Similarly, characteristics of teachers established by observation can be related to characteristics of pupils and *vice-versa*.

Also related to the problems of establishing context is that of identifying specific individuals and the interactions between them. Most observation systems make it possible to identify the individual who is the focus of observation, although scanning systems cannot normally identify individual pupils, and systems which focus on teacher-pupil interaction like FIAC do not generally identify the individual child. Similarly, when individual pupils are being observed interactions with other specific pupils are not easy to identify. However, a modification of FIAC allows individual pupils engaged in the interaction with the teacher to be identified (Wragg, 1970) and it is possible to give an indentification number to all pupils in a class to use as categories of a variable specifying exactly who teachers or other pupils are interacting with or sitting beside and so on. This can become clumsy and unmanageable if all children in the class are to be identified in this way but simpler versions are also possible. For example, it is simple to specify as a category of an interaction variable whether the interaction is with a male or female pupil and if teacher interactions with a limited number of particular children are of interest then these can be individually identified.

The presentation in this chapter has been concerned with relatively simple aspects of the analysis of observational data involving descriptions of variables one at a time or a consideration of interrelationships between two variables. In many studies such straightforward analyses will be all that is required. In the next chapter, however, some more complex analytic procedures will be presented. These concern multi-variate approaches to data analysis and also the principles involved in relating observed characteristics of pupils and teachers to educational outcomes. Readers who wish to omit the more statistically complex discussion in chapter 6 should nevertheless look at the section of the chapter which deals with calculating the reliability of observational data and is relevant to any systematic observation study.

6   *Further Aspects of Data Analysis*

Multi-variate Analysis of Observational Data

Multi-variate analysis is the process involved in attempting to consider three or more variables simultaneously in data analysis. The simplest form of data analysis is uni-variate analysis where one variable is considered at a time, for example, if levels of time on task, then levels of teacher questioning and so on are the subject of analysis. A more complex analysis involves considering two variables simultaneously. Some of the examples which have already been presented include cross-tabulation (for example, does the category 'working on task' tend to occur together with the category 'interacting with the teacher'?), comparison of means (for example, do high ability children have higher average levels of 'time on task' than low ability children?) and correlation (for example, do children with high levels of interaction with other children also have high (or low) levels of time on task?).

A straightforward extension of these procedures to more than two variables is the simplest form of multi-variate analysis. For example, a cross-tabulation of 'working on task' and 'interacting with the teacher' could be conducted separately for observations made of high achieving and low achieving pupils or for observations made during English lessons and science lessons or for a combination of these (that is, for high achieving pupils in science, for high achieving pupils in English, for low achieving pupils in science, and so on). Similarly, the correlation between pupil-pupil interaction and time on task could be calculated separately for different sorts of teaching settings or for the different subjects.

A slightly more complex case would arise if a researcher wanted to investigate the relationship between pupil achievement and time on task also taking into account pupil-teacher interaction. In this case, a multi-variate analysis might involve comparing the time on task of high achieving pupils with high levels of pupil-teacher interaction with those of low achieving pupils with similarly high levels of pupil-teacher interaction and then repeating the comparison for high and low achieving pupils with low levels of pupil-teacher interaction. Another analysis of the same three variables might involve comparing the level of time on task of high and low achievers, only counting those observations which did not involve pupil-teacher interaction. It should be noted that these two analyses are not simple alternatives but imply different sorts of interrelationship between the variables. The first analysis is investigating the extent to which different levels of time on task for high and low achievers (or the absence of such differences) is associated with the possibility that the two groups receive different levels of teacher attention. The second is concerned with the possibility that differences might arise because individual observations of time on tasks are associated with individual observations of pupil-teacher interaction.

The examples given so far have involved considering the relationships between two variables separately for different categories of a third variable either with the purpose of controlling for the influence of the third variable or in order to investigate interrelationships between the first two variables in different contexts. This approach to elaborating analysis through introducing a third variable is statistically simple and can, in principle, be extended to fourth, fifth and sixth variables and so on. The two practical limitations are, first, that extended analysis of this kind involves lengthy presentation and description and, second, that even with large samples of individuals or observations, considering relationships separately for categories of several controlling or contextual variables can result in analyses being based on unacceptably small numbers of cases.

Other approaches to multi-variate analysis involve rather more complex statistical procedures. These will only be described briefly here but researchers using such techniques should ensure that they have a thorough grasp of them. Two techniques concerned with data reduction which can be used to describe patterns among a large number of observations are *factor analysis* and *cluster analysis*. Other commonly used multi-variate techniques such as *multiple regression* and *analysis of co-variance* are normally used when it is intended to relate observed processes (or other variables) to outcomes such as pupil achievement. This sort of analysis will be considered in a later section.

Factor analysis and cluster analysis have in common that they take a data matrix consisting of a large number of variables and units of analysis (pupils, teachers, classes etc.) and simplify these data by looking for systematic patterns which underlie the large number of individual observations. Two warnings should be given before these techniques are considered further. It is very important that researchers should understand the nature of the statistical procedures being applied to the data and the assumptions about the characteristics of the variables and the structure of the data which are built into the various versions of these techniques. It is easy to fall into the trap of thinking that these very powerful computer-based techniques can be applied to data to 'make sense' of them in an 'untouched by human hand' kind of way. This is not the case and researchers should be clear about the purpose of the analysis and the assumptions about data structures which are built into it before conducting factor and cluster analyses. Secondly, the presentation which follows assumes that the variables have been measured independently and that the kind of incestuous in-built negative correlation referred to earlier is not present or has been corrected.

Factor Analysis

Factor analysis is a technique for the analysis of variables. That is, the analysis is based on the columns of the data matrix. If a number of variables are interrelated, factor anlaysis can be seen as an attempt to establish if a smaller number of underlying dimensions can account for the observed interrelationship. This has been described as a process of 'orderly simplification' (Child, 1970), or reducing the complexity of the data by providing an economical description of its structure.

The simplest example of factor analysis is where all the variables being considered are strongly related to one another in a way that can be accounted for by the presence of a single, uni-dimensional underlying variable. This is unlikely to occur in observational research but might well happen in the case of attitudinal or attainment variables. Thus, it might well be the case that the interrelationship among a series of attitudinal variables can be accounted for by a common underlying variable such as 'conservatism' or the interrelationship between a set of measures of achievement by an underlying dimension such as 'mathematical ability'.

Much more likely, however, in most cases of data analysis is that more than one underlying dimension (or factor) will be required to account for the observed interrelationships. In the case of attainment test data this might mean that a series of test scores could be described by a few underlying dimensions such as 'mathematical ability', 'linguistic ability', 'general knowledge', etc. In the case of observational data a large number of variables might interrelate in a way that can be described by underlying dimensions such as 'sociability', 'aggressiveness' and 'work orientation'.

Factor analysis starts from the matrix of correlations between the original variables. The first outcome of the analysis of this matrix is a factor which gives the single best linear summary of the observed correlations. In the case of a basically uni-dimensional matrix such as that likely to be produced by variables making up an attitude scale, this single best summary will be a good description of the matrix as a whole (that is, will account for a high proportion of the variance) and will be the main outcome of interest. More usually, however, the single best linear summary will account for only a modest proportion of the overall variance and subsequent factors will also be of interest. It is possible to continue to extract factors until all the variance is accounted for which, unless two or more variables are perfectly correlated, will result in as many factors as variables but only the first few are likely to be of interest. Consequently, the researcher needs to set some criterion for how many factors are of interest (most computer programs for conducting factor analysis use the default criterion of only considering factors with eigen values greater than unity). The factors selected are then subjected to a rotation procedure to see which variables they are most strongly related to. This results in a matrix of factor loadings which is the main outcome of interest in most factor analyses. This matrix has rows made up of the variables and columns made up of the factors. The values of the loadings range from unity (+1 or −1) to zero. The higher the loading the more strongly related to that factor is the variable. A factor is normally defined by those variables which have the highest loadings on it. If these variables can be interpreted as having something in common then this is the meaning attributed to the factor. In this way it may be possible to represent a large number of variables to a smaller number of underlying factors which account for the observed interrelationships between them.

Factor analysis is not a purely inductive procedure for making sense of data. The researcher has to make decisions such as what variables should be entered into the analysis, how many factors should be extracted and whether the factors should be independent of one another (orthogonal) or may be themselves interrelated (oblique). The researcher should also have some understanding of what is happening when a set of factor loadings is produced. A relatively accessible account of factor analysis is given in Child (1970).

Cluster Analysis

Cluster analysis is similar to factor analysis in that it is an attempt to simplify a large amount of data into a more economical description by looking for structures and patterns within the data. But while factor analysis bases the process of data reduction on patterns of interrelationships between variables, cluster analysis is based on patterns of interrelationship or similarity between individuals or other units of analysis. Cluster analysis is, therefore, a *case-centred* analysis, operating on the rows of the data matrix, rather than a *variable-centred* analysis operating on the columns of the matrix.

Cluster analysis starts by considering the similarity between individuals such as individual teachers or pupils. (It can also be used for other units of analysis such as classes but the discussion here will refer to individuals. The principles and statistical procedures are the same in either case). If groups of individuals can be identified on the basis of the relative similarity of group members to one another in terms of the variables used in the analysis and their relative distinctness from other groups then the data can be economically described in terms of a small number of groups rather than a large number of separate individuals. The general aim of cluster analysis is to identify groups (clusters) which are relatively homogeneous internally with respect to the variables being considered while differing from other groups.

Such an analysis can have a number of purposes. The most basic of these is data reduction. Cluster analysis, like factor analysis, provides a way of reducing a large amount of data to a more manageable form. If a researcher presents results as individual descriptions of 200 individuals characterized by measures on a dozen variables this large amount of information, paradoxically, conveys no information; there is too much data for the reader (and probably also for the researcher) to make sense of. If, however, the researcher is able to say that there are basically three (or four or five etc.) types of individual with regard to the variables of interest, and that the three groups have certain characteristics, very much more information will have been conveyed.

Within the overall context of data reduction, clustering can also serve the purpose of providing the basis for a more meaningful presentation of the analysis of particular variables and of the inter-relationship between them. A simple example is that of a variable which has high values for some individuals and low ones for other individuals with very few people falling in the middle. In this case the average value of the variable is not a very meaningful description, but if those with high values are in one cluster and those with low values in another the presentation of within-cluster means and standard deviations provides a much more accurate description. Similarly, patterns of correlation or association between variables may differ for different clusters. An apparently weak correlation between two variables when all individuals in the sample are considered may actually consist of a strong correlation within some clusters and no correlation within others.

A further purpose for which cluster analysis is sometimes used is to identify groups which can then be used as the basis for a comparison of the effectiveness of different teaching methods or for comparison with regard to some other outcome or product measure. This use will be considered in more detail in the following section.

As with factor analysis the actual process of clustering is usually accomplished by computer. A number of clustering programs are available, many based on *Clustan* (Wishart, 1969). Although these programs are very easy to use it is important that researchers understand the principles involved in the analyses.

The first point that should be made clear is that cluster analysis is a general term for a family of techniques each using different procedures. The aim of all these procedures is to establish clusters of similar individuals but the assumption about the structure of the data, the meaning of similarity and the sorts of groups likely to be produced, differ for different types of cluster analysis.

A basic stage in most approaches to cluster analysis is that of establishing measures of similarity, or, alternatively of distance, between individuals. If all possible pairs of individuals who have been observed can be given a score for similarity or distance then the similarity matrix or distance matrix can be used as the basis for sorting the individuals into groups. One measure of the similarity between individuals is the correlation coefficient. This is calculated in the same way as the correlation between two variables except that in the case of correlations between variables there are two variables and many cases and the pairs of values all come from the same two variables but for different cases, while the correlation between individuals involves two cases and many variables and the pairs of values are all from the same cases but for different variables. This procedure results in a correlation coefficient for each pair of individuals which, as with the more conventional correlation between variables, can take values between 1 (or −1) indicating perfect correlation (i.e. the two individuals have identical profiles of values for the variables) to 0 indicating no association between the two sets of values for the variables.

The use of correlation as a measure of similarity requires that the individuals have scores on the variables to be used in the analysis. If the variables consist of categories or dichotomous attributes a matching coefficient can be calculated. This is a very simple measure which defines similarity in terms of the proportion of all the variables of interest on which the value for one individual is the same as that for the other. If there are fifteen binary variables on which two people fall into identical categories to one another on ten, then the matching coefficient will be 0.67. (Observational variables for individuals or classes will not usually consist of dichotomous data or discrete categories as these variables will be based on a large number of observations and will generally be analyzed as scores. But if the individual observations themselves were to be grouped in a cluster analysis then the variables would almost certainly be sets of categories or dichotomies.)

An alternative procedure to calculating the similarity between individuals is to calculate the difference or distance between them. This can then be used as the basis for a distance matrix which has a parallel interpretation to a similarity matrix with the exception that high values indicate that individuals are unlike one another.

One of the best known distance measures is that of squared Euclidean distance. This is based on the square of the absolute difference between the value of a variable for the pair of individuals summed across all variables in the analysis. Individuals who have similar values on all or most of the variables will have low scores on this measure while individuals who have very different values for all or most of the variables will have high scores.

It may not be immediately apparent that these, and other, approaches to calculating difference and similarity are not simply different computational procedures but, in some cases, involve different definitions of what is to count as difference and similarity. To illustrate this, consider the following set of figures:

| | Classroom | | |
	A	*B*	*C*
Percentage of time spent on:			
Spelling exercises	10	20	25
Creative writing	15	30	25
Grammar exercises	10	20	25

A decision as to which two classrooms are more similar and should be placed in the same cluster depends on what criterion of similarity/distance is being used. Classrooms A and B have similar profiles in that in both cases the levels of time devoted to spelling and grammar are equal while the time devoted to creative writing is higher. But A and B differ with regard to the absolute level of these variables while classrooms B and C are similar. A measure using the correlation coefficient would classify A and B together (they are, in fact, perfectly correlated) but a measure based on Euclidean distance will classify B and C together. There are no statistical criteria for deciding which is the most appropriate level of similarity and the researcher must decide on the basis of the substantive purposes of the classification which is the most appropriate. In the example above if it is the relative amount of time devoted to the three activities which is important, A and B are identical, but if the absolute amount of time is important B and C are similar. These are substantive questions but it is clearly important that the researcher should understand the methodological principles involved.

Having established measures of similarity between individuals the second major issue in conducting a cluster analysis is deciding on a grouping technique. Two differing approaches to this are hierarchical and optimizing techniques. In hierarchical methods the two most similar (or least distant) individuals are placed together in a cluster as the first step of the analysis. The next step is to join the next two most similar individuals to make a second cluster or to bring a third individual into the first cluster if the similarity is greatest here. In this way individuals and clusters are progressively merged until the original number of individuals has been reduced to a single cluster. This can be represented by a tree diagram (known as a dendogram) which is a map of the structure of the data showing the similarity groupings at each stage of the analysis. Similarities are calculated for clusters either on the basis of the cluster average or by using a variety of other methods including the most similar and the least dissimilar member. It is also possible to conduct a hierarchical cluster analysis by progressively dividing the group studied rather than by progressively merging individuals and groups, but even with using modern computers this involves an impracticabal amount of computing time unless the number of individuals involved in the analysis is very small.

Hierarchical techniques have a number of advantages for the researcher. The first of these is that it is easy to see intuitively what is happening in the analysis and the procedure is in accord with a common sense understanding of similarity and of grouping. All pairs of individuals are described in terms of their similarity and difference. The two most similar are grouped together, then the next two most similar and so on. As well as the simplicity of these procedures, its hierarchical nature means that it results in a kind of map of the data in which the structure of similarity between individuals and groups can be seen and where particular individuals can be followed through the analysis. This means that the researcher can inspect the analysis to see at what stage of the clustering process the groups produced should be used as the basis for further analysis and also allows more than one level of clustering to be employed. There are two main disadvantages with this grouping procedure. The first is the imposition of a hierarchical structure which may not accurately represent the structure of the data. (Hierarchical methods are used in biological classification where the structure of species, subspecies etc. is more obviously appropriate for this approach than is classroom observation data.) The second disadvantage is the fact that an individual's membership of a cluster is determined at the point of merger and cannot change at later stages of the analysis. It is possible that the nature of particular clusters changes as the process of merger is carried on, and that an individual initially allocated to one group has more in common with another group at a later stage in the analysis. Hierarchical methods cannot correct this misallocation.

Optimizing procedures create groupings which will optimize a particular clustering criterion. The criterion most commonly used is that of minimizing the within cluster sum of squares for the variables in the analysis. It is necessary to specify the number of clusters for which the criterion is to be optimized. The optimizing procedure then works by initially placing the individuals at random into however many groups the solution is being sought for and then relocating the individuals between groups in order to see if this reduces or increases the value of the criterion. Clearly, this is an extremely time consuming procedure and is only feasible through the use of computers.

The technique involves specifying in advance the number of

clusters into which individuals are to be placed but the researcher is often not in a position to do this. Consequently, most cluster analyses which use optimization are actually a series of separate analyses each using a different number of clusters. The usual procedure is to find a solution for a fairly large (perhaps twelve-fifteen) number of clusters, then for one fewer and so on until a two-cluster solution is reached. Using a large number of clusters will optimize the criterion more successfully than a small number of clusters because as the number of clusters gets smaller individuals who are more unlike one another are forced into the same cluster while a large number of clusters means that individuals will only be in the same cluster if they are very similar. This means that the value of the criterion (for example the within group sum of squares) can be plotted against the number of clusters for which solutions have been obtained. This plot will result in a series of points which can be connected by a curved line showing how the amount of error (that is, non-optimal values of the criterion) increases as the number of clusters decrease. The usual procedure in analysis is to examine this curve looking for discontinuities — a sudden increase in the amount of error associated with a particular decrease in the number of clusters. If, for example, a smooth curve showing a steady increase in error as the number of clusters goes down is interrupted by a bigger than normal increase in error between the five and four cluster solutions, this suggests that forcing the data into four clusters involves putting some fairly dissimilar individuals into the same cluster and that a five cluster solution is therefore to be preferred.

Clustering techniques using optimization avoid imposing a hierarchical structure on the data and allow individuals to be placed in the most appropriate cluster at each stage of the analysis. They also have the advantage of allowing the researcher to plot the criterion against the number of clusters which shows the extent to which placing individuals into fewer and fewer clusters involves moving away from homogeneous clusters of relatively similar individuals. Disadvantages with the technique include the fact that assumptions about the shape of clusters are built into the choice of criterion but the researcher will often not have any real basis for making that choice. A further difficulty is that, except with very small data sets, it is impossible to consider all possible patterns of allocation to clusters and, therefore, the solution may be influenced by the initial, usually random, allocation of individuals to clusters before the relocation process begins. (In technical terms, what is arrived at is a local rather than a global solution). Researchers can protect themselves against this to some extent by repeating the analysis with a different initial allocation. If the same cluster pattern emerges this gives greater confidence that it reflects a true structure in the data.

Difficulties which apply to all the clustering procedures discussed above are the lack of any clear definition of what counts as a cluster and the fact that cluster analysis is not a true statistical technique in the sense that sampling distributions can be derived and statistical hypotheses tested. Some progress has been made in these areas (see, for example, Aitken, Bennett and Hesketh, 1981) but it is not possible to describe this work here. A good overview of cluster analysis is given by Everitt (1974).

A simple alternative to both cluster analysis and factor analysis is provided by the technique of *Elementary Linkage Analysis* (sometimes called McQuitty's Elementary Linkage Analysis after its originator (McQuitty, 1957)). This technique was developed when the availability of both computer power and appropriate programs necessary for clustering and factoring was much more limited than it is today, but it still provides a useful tool both for researchers who do not have easy access to these facilities, and also for conducting rapid investigations into the structure of data 'by hand' in a way that can be directly controlled by the researcher.

Elementary Linkage Analysis can be used to group variables in a similar fashion to factor analysis or to group individuals (or other units of analysis) as in cluster analysis. The analysis begins with a matrix indicating the association between each of the variables, or individuals, to be grouped. If variables are to be grouped this matrix will be an ordinary correlation matrix showing the correlation between each pair of variables. If individuals are to be grouped the matrix will be a matrix of distance or similarity coefficients and will have as many rows and columns as there are individuals in the analysis. In the case of individuals the similarity measure may also be a correlation coefficient. The process of analysis will be made simpler if a full square matrix is constructed even though for most purposes half of this is redundant as the entries below the diagonal are a mirror image of those above.

The first step is to underline the highest entry in every column of the matrix. (If a distance measure is used read lowest for highest throughout.) The highest entry of all is then identified as the starting point. The two individuals or variables linked by this entry become the core of the first group. The analysis then identifies others who are most like one or other of these entries by reading along the two rows in which the entries occur looking for other underlined coefficients.

For any which occur the other half of the pair joins the group. All entries identified in this way then become the focus of an identical procedure in which other entries (individuals or variables) most like them are linked to the group. When no further links can be found all the variables or individuals who have been identified as members of the first group are removed from the matrix and the process begins again to identify a second group. This continues until the whole matrix has been classified.

This process results in a set of groupings where all the members of a group are more similar to another member of the group than they are to any other individual or variable. An extended discussion is given in McQuitty, (1957) and brief details in Cohen (1976).

Process-Product Analysis

Systematic classroom observation is concerned with describing aspects of the process of education as it occurs in the classroom. An interest of many researchers is to relate these classroom processes to educational outcomes or products, in particular, to patterns of pupil achievement. A recent example of this kind of process-product analysis is the ORACLE project discussed in chapter 2 where cluster analyses of pupils and of teachers based on classroom observation data produced groupings who were then compared in order to see which groups had made most progress on standardized tests of achievement (Galton and Croll, 1980; Croll, 1983). Process-product analyses do not necessarily involve observational data. *Teaching Styles and Pupil Progress* (Bennett, 1976) is an example of a study where teachers were grouped on the basis of their questionnaire responses and these groups then compared in terms of test outcomes. However, observational research is particularly appropriate for establishing educationally relevant descriptions of the teaching and learning activities of teachers and pupils and a concern with educational processes seems to lead naturally to descriptions based on direct observation of these processes in action.

One of the main concerns of process-product research has been to consider the relative effectiveness of different approaches to teaching in influencing student achievement. One approach to this problem is a classical experimental research design.[1] Students (and possibly also teachers) could be assigned at random into groups to be taught by different methods and the outcomes, in terms of achievement, of the various groups compared. There are, however, both practical and ethical problems in conducting such an experiment in educational settings, especially when the processes of interest are likely to be long-term. Consequently, most researchers who are interested in comparing the different outcomes of different approaches to teaching look for naturally occurring examples of such differences and make comparisons between them. While the experimental approach sets up teaching methods and compares them, the process-product approach samples a large number of classrooms and looks for naturally occurring patterns of difference between them which can be the basis for a comparison of outcomes. Some of the methodological issues which arise in such research are briefly set out below.

The first issue to be considered relates to the way in which processes should be analyzed in order to relate them to products. One approach to this is to group similar individuals (or classrooms) using cluster analysis as described above. If groups of teachers who have similar patterns of behaviour on the variables observed can be identified then these groups can be used as a basis for a comparison of outcomes (for example, test scores) for pupils in their classes. This provides an approximation to an experimental procedure, a natural experiment in which naturally occurring different methods rather than artificially contrived ones are compared, although the lack of experimental control through random assignment of subjects to treatments means that the kinds of causal inferences which can be made from true experiments cannot be made here. Examples of this kind of approach are the ORACLE research (Galton and Croll, 1980; Croll, 1983) and the Lancaster research (Bennett, 1976), although the latter did not base its clusters on observational data.

A weakness of this approach is that because the groupings being compared are constructed from an analysis of the joint occurrence of a large number of variables it is not possible to establish the relative importance of the different variables in producing any effect found. It is possible to say that teachers of type A produce greater gains than teachers of type B but not what it is about these teachers that produces the effect. If the various characteristics of teachers within a group are logically connected in a way that makes them a 'package' this may not matter, but if teachers can change one aspect of their behaviour without necessarily changing another it is a limitation of the analysis.

An alternative to the cluster analysis approach to the process side of process-product studies is to focus on the variables rather than on groups of people and to conduct a correlational analysis of some kind. At its simplest this might involve taking the observational variables one at a time and correlating them with some measure of outcome. For example, if teacher questions are a variable on the observation schedule it would be possible to calculate a correlation coefficient to show if teachers with high levels of questioning also had classes with high levels of achievement. A similar analysis could be conducted for pupil time-on-task and individual pupil achievement. Analyses of this kind have the advantage of specifying exactly what is associated with what. As long as a researcher is in a position to specify a hypothesis about which variable or variables are expected to correlate with specified products then this sort of simple analysis is appropriate. However, if there is no theoretical reason to expect some variables rather than others to be associated with particular outcomes and the exercise is essentially exploratory it is probably best to investigate the structure of the process data before looking for correlations between individual process variables and outcomes.

Even where the correlation between an individual observational variable and an outcome measure has been calculated in order to test a previous hypothesis the researcher will still probably want to investigate it in the context of its association with other variables. This is because observed correlations in non-experimental data may arise from a variety of causes including spurious correlations. In the example given above a possible explanation of a correlation between levels of teacher questions and levels of pupil achievement would be that high levels of teacher talk are associated with increased pupil achievement and that teachers who talk a lot usually also ask a lot of questions. This would be a spurious correlation between questioning and achievement coming about because high levels of teacher talk are associated with both.

Introducing extra variables into correlational analysis may be done through partial correlation or multiple regression. In partial correlation the correlation between two variables is calculated after the effect of a third variable has been controlled for. In the example above, if the apparent relationship between questioning and achievement is spurious then the partial correlation between the two variables controlling for teacher talk will be close to zero.

(In technical terms the partial correlation between two variables is the correlation between their residuals when the regression of each on the third variable has been calculated. This is the same as saying that it is the extent of correlation after the effect of the third variable has been allowed for.)

Multiple regression involves constructing an equation which will predict a dependent variable (the outcome or product variable) from a linear combination of a set of independent variables (the process variables). This takes the form of a prediction equation showing how values of the dependent variable can be predicted from those of the independent variables. The coefficients for each of the independent variables indicates their influence on the dependent variables, taking the other variables into account. Multiple regression can therefore be used as a way of simultaneously considering the association between a number of observational (or other) variables on a particular educational outcome. A particular problem with this technique is that if two or more of the independent variables are themselves strongly correlated measurement unrcliability will make it impossible to distinguish their relative influence in the equation.

Another approach to considering the association between a number of process variables and a product variable is to use the process variables to create one or more indices which can be correlated with the product. Factor analysis provides a way of reducing a large number of variables to a smaller number of under-lying dimensions. If this fits the structure of an observational data set then it is probably more appropriate to identify the underlying dimensions, combine the variables which make it up to provide a single score for each individual on each dimension and to correlate these with the outcome.

In certain instances the researcher may have to decide whether the structure of the data best suits the kind of factorial analysis just described or best suits a cluster-type analysis in which distinct groups of teachers are compared. For example, if a number of observational variables are relevant to the question of the extent of structure the teacher imposes on the learning situation this could result in two forms of analysis. A cluster analysis could divide the teachers into three groups: 'high structure', 'low structure' and 'intermediate'. Alternatively, a composite variable 'degree of structure' could be derived from the original variables and each teacher located along this dimension. This point will arise again in the discussion of teaching styles at the end of the chapter.

Having decided upon ways of organizing the process variables the researcher must decide on ways of treating products and, in particular, ways of establishing a connection between the products and the process. Products are usually measures of children's achieve-ment such as test scores of various kinds, although attitudinal or other measures may also be treated as products. Products may be one-off measures such as a test taken at a particular point in time but to relate a single measure to an on-going process such as that studied in classroom observation is a very limited procedure. It is usually of far greater interest to relate the on-going process within the classroom to developments in product measures, in particular to changes in achievement over time.

Consequently, a common model for process-product analysis is a pre-test post-test design where measurements are taken at the beginning and end of some educationally relevant time span (a school year, the duration of a course, etc.) and the relationship between pre-test and post-test is related to the educational process observed during that period of time.

The pre-test and post-test may be tests of the same aspect of achievement or even identical tests but this kind of analysis can also be conducted with a post-text measuring achievement and a pre-text measuring ability or aptitude. What is important is that the pre-test score for an individual should be expected to relate to the post-text score either because they are tests of the same area of skill or knowledge or because there is reason to believe that whatever is measured in the pre-test will predict to some extent the performance in what the post-text measures.

An obvious analysis would be to measure simple gain over the period of the study, that is, to use post-test minus pre-test as the product of interest. However, this would not be appropriate if the pre-test is not a direct measure of the achievement measured by the post-test and there are technical statistical reasons why simple gain is not a good product measure. (Measurement unreliability results in some pre-test scores being lower than the true score and others being higher. Similar effects in the post-test will be independent of pre-test unreliability with the result that some people with low pre-tests will have higher post-tests, not because of true gains but because of earlier measurement error and *vice-versa* for some people with high pre-tests. This results in an in-built negative correlation between simple gain scores and pre-test scores.)

Because of this effect the measure of gain used is derived from the residual scores of the post-test on the pre-test. A regression equation is set up in which post-test scores are predicted from the pre-test. The pre-test score is very likely to be a good predictor of post-test score (that is, to correlate with it reasonably strongly) either because they are measures of the same aspects of achievement or because the pre-test is a measure of an ability or aptitude associated with the post-test. However, it is very unlikely to be a perfect predictor and most individuals will have post-test scores different from those predicted. An individual's gain can therefore be regarded as the extent to which the actual score is higher or lower than that predicted; an individual who has a higher score than predicted has made positive gains while an individual who has a lower score than predicted has negative gains. (This is a comparative analysis. Even if everyone has made progress, those who have made less progress than would be expected from their pre-test scores are described as making negative gains. If everyone had lost ground on the assessments those losing less ground than expected would be described as making positive gains. The purpose of this analysis is to compare the effects of different treatments or to assess the effects relative to one another, not in absolute terms.)

This approach to measuring gains is the basis of both the cluster analysis based procedure of comparing groups and of analyses which concentrate on the effects of variables. Where groups have been identified for comparison using cluster analysis, the statistical procedure for analyzing gains is known as analysis of co-variance. Essentially, this involves predicting post-test from pre-test scores and then considering whether the classes or individuals with higher than expected scores tend to fall in particular groups while those with lower than expected scores tend to fall into others. If this is in fact the case the hypothesis that the different groups produce different gains is supported. (The above account is a slight simplification of the actual statistical procedures involved which also allow for group membership in calculating predicted scores. A full account of analysis of co-variance is given in Winer (1971) and more accessible accounts of some of the issues involved in these procedures are given in some of the publications discussed briefly in the bibliography.)

Analysis concerned with the effects of a number of variables also utilizes the notion of post-test scores being higher or lower than expected from pre-test scores. In the multiple regression analysis the post-test score is the dependent variable and the pre-test is entered as the first stage of the regression. Variation in the post-test scores which cannot be accounted for by the pre-test can be associated with the other independent variables which are entered at the next stage. The most easily available system of computer programs for performing analysis of co-variance and multiple regression analysis as well as all the other statistical procedures discussed here (with the exception of cluster analysis) is the Statistical Package for the Social Sciences (SPSS). The manual for this system of programmes provides a good account of the statistical basis of the procedures as well as being an easy to use guide to the SPSS package (Nie *et al*, 1975 and 1983).

It is important to note that the statistical procedures described here are based on the notion of variation in the scores of individuals (or other units of analysis). Where test scores or the difference between a predicted and actual score differ between units of analysis, then these differences can be related to other differences such as differences in process variables or differences in membership of the groups which emerge from cluster analysis of process variables. This means that conclusions about the success or failure of different approaches are being made not against some absolute criteria but are relative judgments about the effectiveness of the different approaches studied. If there was no variation in the product scores between individuals, or between the average of different groups or between people with high and low scores on one of the process variables then no effects would emerge from the analysis. This would not mean that there were no effects of the different approaches but that there were no differences in effects between them.

An issue which has caused a great deal of controversy in process-product studies is the appropriate unit of analysis for calculating gains and, in particular, for testing the statistical significance of the results. The products (test results etc.) are characteristics of individuals and the processes (for example, teaching methods) are experienced by individuals and so it might seem natural to regard individuals as the units of analysis. However, in process-product research individuals are virtually never sampled independently of one another and therefore do not experience the process independently. Usually, whole classes or a sample of pupils within a class are sampled. This is administratively convenient, a relatively small number of classes generates a large sample of pupils, but also has advantages for our understanding of educational processes by establishing class contexts within which individual characteristics can be located. However, this creates problems for statistical analysis due to the lack of independence between subjects.

Tests of statistical significance such as those used in analysis of co-variance and multiple regression assume that the units of analysis have been sampled independently so that there is no systematic relationship between chance sampling variations and the variables being studied. Where school classes have been sampled it is clear that the individuals within them have not been sampled independently of one another and also that they are exposed to the same teaching method and also to some of the same chance factors such as an unusually gifted teacher or an especially poor working environment.

Process-product studies which have used individuals as units of analysis such as the Lancaster Research (Bennett, 1976) have been criticized for these reasons (see, for example, Gray and Satterley, 1976). Statistical rigour imposes the use of class average scores as the appropriate unit of analysis (Aitken *et al*, 1981; Gray and Satterley, 1981). This has the effect of dramatically reducing the sample size in most studies but this reduction should be seen as a recognition of the statistical restraints imposed on studies which aim both to be representative and also to study specific educational contexts. A more serious objection to the use of class means is the amount of potential information and possibilities for analysis which are lost. Taking the class average as a measure means that any differential impact of a teaching method on particular individuals or types of individuals cannot be studied and that the interrelationship of variables can only be analyzed at an aggregate level. For example, there may be a different form of relationship between class averages for achievement and time-on-task and individual achievement and individual time-on-task within particular classes. In the ORACLE project, the conflict between statistical rigour and analytic richness was dealt with by producing two sets of analyses. Analyses were conducted using class averages to establish the statistical significance of the results but analyses were also conducted using individuals as the units of analysis which allowed an exploration of some of the relationships between individual characteristics, teaching methods and achievement (Galton and Croll, 1980). Further checks on the validity of the results were made in later replication (Croll, 1983). Another approach to reconciling an interest in individual characteristics with the use of classes as the sampling unit is to treat sub-groups of interest within a class as if they provided separate measures from the same randomly sampled units of analysis. This employs a repeated measures design within analysis of co-variance (Page, 1975; Solomon and Kendall, 1979).

Finally, a problem that any researcher conducting process-product studies must confront is the possible confounding effects of extraneous variables. If the purpose of the research is to investigate an association between observed classroom processes and particular outcomes such as test scores, in the absence of true experimental controls the researcher must face up to the possibility that an apparent association arises because of other variables influencing both the processes and the outcomes. Researchers can approach this difficulty either by controlling for possible confounding variables in the research design or by taking account of them in analysis. Controlling for outside variables in the research design could mean having the same representation of male and female teachers, experienced and inexperienced teachers, classrooms in schools with different sorts of catchment areas and so on in the groups to be compared. A difficulty which sometimes arises with this is that in many observationally based studies it is not clear what groups are to be compared until observation is complete. An alternative approach is to collect measures of these variables, and to introduce them into the analysis, that is, to look at the relationship between process and product controlling for teacher sex and experience and the nature of catchment areas and so on. Different ways of introducing these controls can produce an elaborated analysis that throws new light on the relationships being studied. For example, in one analysis, an association between teacher age and pupil achievement together with the fact that older teachers were over-represented among groups using certain teaching styles could have meant that the apparent relationship between teaching style and achievement was spurious. However, an analysis which correlated teacher age and pupil achievement controlling for teaching style, in addition to one which correlated teaching style and pupil achievement controlling for teacher age, showed that the association between teacher age and pupil achievement disappeared within some teaching styles. Thus, it could be shown that it was aspects of the classroom teaching methods of older teachers which produced higher gains and that these methods were, at least in part, described by the observational methods (Galton and Croll, 1980). A related analysis showed that a relationship between pupil motivation and achievement was much stronger in classrooms using a predominantly individualized approach than in more teacher-directed classrooms (Croll and Willcocks, 1980). These kinds of theoretically coherent elaborations of process-product analysis show that possibly confounding variables should be regarded not as threats to an analysis but as opportunities for gaining further insight into the relationships being studied.

The point about theoretical coherence also applies to the implications of the fact that however many variables are controlled or are introduced into the analysis there is always the logical possibility that other unconsidered variables are really responsible for observed results. This relates to a major theme of this book and applies to all social science research, that the variables selected for study and the procedures for defining them are chosen with regard to specific investigatory purposes and to test theoretical constructions about social reality. They do not represent a purely inductive attempt to 'let facts speak for themselves'. Consequently, researchers will operationalize and control variables which might be expected to confound the relationships being investigated on the basis of theoretical considerations or empirical evidence. Fresh developments in theory or new empirical findings may lead to additional variables being seen as relevant, as in any scientific research programme. Meanwhile, the empirical researcher should not be prevented from investigating interrelationships between aspects of social phenomena by claims that observed results might all be due to something that no one has thought of.

These methodological questions should be placed in the context of an approach to scientific enquiry which emphasizes that the purpose of empirical investigation is not to seek evidence which will confirm the investigators, theories but to attempt to find evidence which will falsify them (Popper, 1963). The conclusions to emerge from these studies are necessarily tentative as are the results of any scientific investigation.

Interrupted Time Series for Behavioural Observations

One of the purposes for systematic classroom observation, particularly when used by teachers in their own classrooms, is to describe behaviour which the teacher is attempting either to eliminate or encourage as part of a programme of behaviour modification in the classroom. Within the context of such a programme observational techniques are used to establish the baseline level for such behaviour and then to monitor the levels of the behaviour as the intervention programme proceeds.

Classroom observation as a basis for behaviour modification is usually very simple. It generally involves counting a single category of behaviour which it is intended either to encourage or to inhibit. This category might be time-on-task or moving around the classroom or calling out. The measure of interest is usually the frequency of such behaviour established either by event recording or instantaneous time sampling. In analyzing the results of such a programme of observation it is particularly important to gather data on its development over time. This is different from the concern with sequence or exact location in time which has been discussed previously. What is of particular interest in monitoring behaviour modification is how the level of a particular behaviour changes over a limited time period — usually on a day-to-day basis.

This sort of analysis is called an interrupted time series. Observations are plotted on a graph such as the ones in figure 13 where the level of the behaviour of interest is shown on successive days. Also shown on the plot is the point at which intervention begins. The first half of the graph is concerned with establishing a baseline level for the behaviour and the second half with plotting what happens when the behaviour modification programme is in operation. In a more extended study the graph might be extended to show what happens when the programme is withdrawn and then reapplied.

Graph (a) in figure 13 is an example of a successful intervention. The observations for days one to five provide a baseline figure for the behaviour and give an indication of day-to-day fluctuation. Days six to ten, after the intervention has begun, show an increased level of the behaviour, also with some day-to-day fluctuation but consistently higher than the baseline figure.

Graph (b) in figure 13 shows the point of providing day-by-day data for frequencies rather than simply relying on average values before and after the intervention. The average values for frequency of the behaviour in the baseline period and the observation period are approximately the same in (a) and (b). However, the values in (a) come about from a distinct shift following the intervention while the different average values in (b) are the result of a long-term trend which does not seem to have been influenced by introducing the behaviour modification programme.

This is a simple example of what can become a much more complex analysis involving several different 'interruptions' to the time series and analyses which allow for the effects of trends and of cyclical processes. The main point is that in analyses designed to investigate the impact of some innovation it is not sufficient to aggregate measurements before and after the innovation. It is also necessary to establish trends and variations in levels of the variable of interest both before and after the implementation of the change to be studied.

Analyzing Data Reliability

The main difficulty in analyzing observational data in order to establish data reliability is the conceptual problem of deciding what is meant by reliability in this context. The idea of data reliability in the statistical sense is strongly associated with establishing the reliability of measurement procedures in attitude scaling and for tests of achievement or ability. Reliability in this sense is concerned with the replicability of the scores established by a test procedure and the

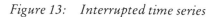

Figure 13:   Interrupted time series

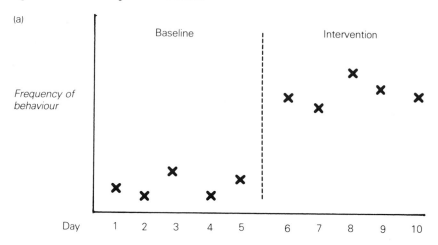

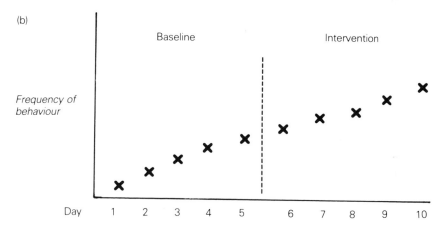

interrelationship of the items in a measuring instrument. Reliability is established by demonstrating that the measurement instrument will establish the same result on a second occasion when that which is being observed is unchanged (test-retest reliability) or else that different combinations of items in the test battery, taken separately, will arrive at the same result (split half reliability or related procedures such as the alpha co-efficient). This concept of reliability is discussed in many standard texts such as Kidder *et al* (1981) and Satterley (1981).

The application of this model causes some confusion in the analysis of observational data where the question of the reliability of the observation instrument as used by different observers is of paramount importance and where there is some dispute over whether the ability to discriminate consistently between different objects of observation should be a criterion for a satisfactory observation instrument. Some researchers use the terminology 'Observer Agreement Coefficient' to refer to the extent to which different observers code the same observed phenomena in an identical fashion and reserve the term 'Reliability Coefficient' to refer to the extent to which individuals are dependably discriminated (for example, Medley and Mitzel, 1963; Frick and Semmel, 1978). The distinction between the two kinds of analysis is a fundamental one which will be followed here. However, the second type of measure will be referred to as stability measures and the two approaches will be treated as different aspects of the problem of reliability.

Observer Agreement

As has been emphasized throughout this book observer agreement is of central importance in the use of systematic observation procedures to describe classroom processes. The distinctive feature of systematic classroom observation is that the observation procedures are such that the basis for the descriptions arrived at are absolutely clear. A good way of establishing this is to show that the procedures can be used by different observers to arrive at identical descriptions of the same events. This is an even more important reason for establishing high inter-observer agreement than the pragmatic one of ensuring that different observers conducting observations in different classrooms or other settings will generate comparable data.

Inter-observer agreement is usually tested by having pairs of observers code the same events in the ways described in chapter 4 and then comparing the two records. An important decision has to be made over whether to test for absolute or for marginal agreement. Absolute agreement means that individual coding decisions are compared in order to see if the categories used by the two observers to code a specified unit of behaviour were the same. Marginal agreement means that the observers are checked to see if their coding has resulted in the same overall description in terms of the totals in each category. Testing for absolute agreement means comparing each individual observation to see if the observers agreed that the individual was on-task or not, interacting with the teacher or not etc.

Clearly absolute agreement is a much stronger test of inter-observer agreement than is marginal agreement as two observers may come to the same overall description while not agreeing about the appropriate coding of particular instances observed. This casts some doubt on the objectivity of the observation schedule. Unfortunately some observation systems such as one-zero time sampling systems (which may also be regarded as unsatisfactory for other reasons as suggested in chapter 3) make it impossible to calculate measures of absolute agreement as the exact instance which is reflected in the coding is not specified. The same is true of event sampling systems unless the event is timed very precisely. For some purposes marginal agreement may be an acceptable measure. Wheldall and Merrett (1984), for example, suggest that in establishing baseline data for a behaviour modification programme it is acceptable to obtain agreement on the overall frequency of the behaviour without having to agree on specific instances. Nevertheless, there is no doubt that in general it is the agreement on particular codings which should be the basis for coefficients of inter-observer agreement.

Calculating inter-observer agreement is relatively straightforward. Separate analyses must be conducted for each variable in the observation system. Clearly it does not make sense to estimate an overall reliability for a system which may have some variables which are very easy to define and get agreement on and others which present difficulties of definition. Each variable therefore has its own reliability coefficient and it may turn out that some parts of an observation system are very much more satisfactory with regard to reliability than others.

It is important to be clear about whether a particular set of categories are all part of one variable or whether they make up separate variables. Only categories which are mutually exclusive can be part of a single variable. If more than one category can be coded simultaneously then they should be treated as separate variables with separate values for inter-observer agreement. Otherwise it is impossible to arrive at a unique value for the coefficient (see Harrop, 1979b, for a discussion of some of the difficulties). A difficulty may also arise if the observation system requires the observer to decide if a particular type of activity is taking place (for example, pupil-teacher interaction) and if it is taking place to code a number of variables describing it. One approach to the analysis is to treat all the occasions when nothing is coded as implicit zero values for the variable. The problem with this is that it may give an inflated picture of the reliability of the variables as most of the agreements will be when there is nothing to code. In this situation it is preferable to calculate observer agreement on whether or not an interaction of this sort is taking place at all and then to calculate agreement on the variables describing it for those occasions when the observers agree that something should be coded. In any case, observer agreement on whether or not this type of interaction or behaviour is happening is a valuable additional piece of information.

The simplest way of expressing observer agreement for an observational variable is as the percentage or proportion of occasions when the two observers agree about the appropriate category to use. This can be expressed as:

$$P = \frac{Na \times 100}{Na + Nd}$$

Where P is the percentage agreement, Na is the number of occasions when the two observers use the same code and Nd is the number of occasions when they use a different code.

A limitation on this procedure is that it does not allow for chance agreement. Depending on the number of categories and the distribution of codes between them, a certain level of agreement will occur due to chance. For example, if two observers are using a two category system at random then they will each put half their codes in each of the two categories and will be in agreement 50 per cent of the time.

This effect can be corrected by means of a coefficient which allows for chance agreement. The Scott coefficient of agreement expresses the agreement between two observers in terms of how much better the observed level of agreement is than the level of agreement that would have been expected if the observed distribution of responses had been generated by random processes (Scott, 1955). This is a more rigorous test of agreement than simple percentage agreement and will always be lower than the percentage agreement unless agreement is perfect. The Scott coefficient is expressed as:

$$\Pi = \frac{Po - Pe}{1 - Pe}$$

where Pe is the proportion of occasions when the observers agree (that is, the percentage agreement divided by 100) and Pe is the proportion of occasions on which they would have agreed by chance. Pe is given by:

$$Pe = \Sigma Pi^2$$

where Pi is the proportion of observations made by all observers falling into the ith category.

In every day terms, we work out what proportion of observations fall into each category, square this value and add up all these squared values for each category of the variable. If there is a variable with two categories each of which is used 50 per cent of the time this results in: $Pe = (0.5 \times 0.5) + (0.5 \times 0.5) = 0.5$; that is, in this situation we could expect 50 per cent agreement by chance. If the categories are used in the ratio 80 per cent to 20 per cent then $Pe = (0.8 \times 0.8) + (0.2 \times 0.2) = 0.68$; that is, agreement by chance will be 68 per cent of observations. Some other agreement coefficients based on the Scott coefficient are given by Frick and Semmel (1978).

There is no absolute way of determining what constitutes a satisfactory level of agreement and the decision will depend to some extent on the purposes for which the observation is being carried out. A number of researchers have suggested that 0.8 or 80 per cent agreement is satisfactory (for example, Galton, Simon and Croll, 1980; Wheldall and Merrett, 1984; Frick and Semmel, 1978).

If a variable does not reach a satisfactory level of agreement then it may need a new or more extensive definition, or the time periods may be too short or the numbers of variables too great for accurate coding. In some cases the solution may be to merge categories. If a distinction between different categories of an activity (for example, different sorts of praise or different types of aggression) cannot be operationalized in a way that observers can agree about, then dropping the distinction will lead to an increase in reliability.

Stability of Observations

The second aspect of reliability refers not to the agreement between observers on the use of categories of a variable but to whether the variables can consistently distinguish between individuals or classrooms which are observed. This is a more problematic application of the concept of reliability to classroom observation data as it is by no means clear that it is necessary for all observational data to be reliable in this sense.

The notion of reliability underlying the calculation of stability coefficients is that if an observation system is to give a reliable description of a teacher or a pupil then it should describe a relatively stable or constant feature of the behaviour of that individual. This means that the variation within the observations made of an individual should be less than the variation between all the individuals studied. This is established by means of an analysis of variance design where the within-group estimates of variance come from observations made of different visits to the same classroom and the between-group estimates of variance come from comparisons of different classrooms. It is then possible to test if differences between individuals or classes can be reliably established given the ratio of within-individual or class variation to between-individual or class variation. (In analysis of variance terms, differences between individuals is explained variation while differences between different observations of the same person is unexplained variation.) The procedures for calculating the stability of observations are fairly complex and are set out in detail in Medley and Mitzel (1963).

The importance of this concept of reliability will depend on the purposes of the particular piece of observational research. In many cases these considerations will not arise at all. Stability of observations depends primarily not on characteristics of the observer or observation system but on the naturally occurring pattern of whatever is being observed. A characteristic on which teachers have over-all very similar levels of occurrence but which varies considerably on different occasions would give rise to unreliable measurements even if individual occurrences are being described accurately. It seems unsatisfactory that an observation procedure that provides a highly accurate description of classroom events should be described as unreliable. In some cases the extent to which a characteristic is a stable feature of individuals and the extent to which it varies for different people may be of interest to the researcher and is itself a focus of analysis rather than a constraint upon whether the data are sufficiently reliable.

However, this concept of reliability does have relevance for certain uses of observational research and researchers should be aware of the extent to which it may constrain their analyses. Where the purpose of observation is to relate the results of the observational variables to other variables in a process-product analysis then the measures on the product variables (for example, test scores) for individual classes or pupils are compared across classes or individuals defined by their process (observational) variables. If the true variation in these process scores is really mainly within individuals rather than across different individuals then the placing of people or classes into groups (for example, by cluster analysis) or on scales (for example, by factor analysis) will be unreliable and will make it impossible to establish differences in outcomes or correlations between process and output variables. Process-product analysis depends on individuals differing from one another with regard to both processes and outcomes or there is no basis for establishing correlations or differences between groups. And to reliably establish individual differences on observational variables requires that different observations of the same individual be relatively stable in proportion to the differences between individuals.

A Note on Teaching Styles

A number of instances of classroom research have been concerned to identify the teaching styles employed by teachers. The research by Bennett (1976), characterized teachers initially into twelve teaching styles and later combined some of these to produce three teaching styles: Formal, Informal and Mixed. The ORACLE research (Galton, Simon and Croll, 1980) identified six teaching styles: classroom enquirers, group instructors, individual monitors, infrequent changers, rotating changers and habitual changers. These were later reduced to five by combining the last two groups. It was suggested in the report of the ORACLE research that systematic observation is particulary appropriate for describing teaching styles as it is based on the direct observation of pupils and teachers in classrooms rather than on people's own accounts of what they do and that observational methods provide a detailed account of the everyday occurrences which are often taken for granted rather than giving general statements or striking instances. They are thus claimed to get closer to classroom reality than other classroom research methods.

The general argument of this book supports the importance of observational studies but also suggests that the notion of teaching style should be used more carefully than has frequently been the case. It has been emphasized throughout this discussion that all social research involves a purposive abstraction from social phenomena and that the validity of descriptions are limited by their purposes. It is not true, as has sometimes been suggested, that observational research can identify some true category of teacher or pupil to which individuals belong. Rather, identifying teaching styles is a process of finding structures in a set of data derived for particular purposes.

This means that it is inappropriate to suggest as is done in the ORACLE research (Galton, Simon and Croll, 1980, pp. 7–10) that systematic observation provides a truer account of teaching styles than teachers' self-reports. All that can be claimed is that a method is better for certain purposes. It also means that cluster analysis methods which are based on a model in which individuals are assigned with specified degrees of probability to an underlying latent class are misconceived (for example, Aitken *et al*, 1981). We have no basis for saying that there is a true class of formal teachers to which individuals' observed characteristics give them different probabilities of belonging (with the necessary implication that there can be a formal teacher who uses the teaching methods characteristic of informal teachers). Nor can we say that certain methods such as observational procedures get closer to the truth about teaching than other methods.

Just as it is mistaken to suggest that teaching styles, whether identified on the basis of observation or other methods, can be a once-and-for-all characterization of teaching, it is worth reconsidering the procedure of assigning individuals to a single teaching style in the way that studies to date have done. It may well be more profitable to think of teaching styles as situationally specific rather than as a more or less fixed characteristic of individuals. It would be valuable to identify teaching approaches on a lesson-by-lesson basis and then to consider individuals in terms of the range of approaches in their repertoire and the extent to which, and circumstances in which, different approaches are employed.

Such an approach to the analysis of teaching styles would also make it possible to consider the nature of the connections between different elements of a teaching style. It would be valuable to identify which elements of a teaching style can be changed without affecting others and which are linked either logically or through the consequences of actually using them in the classroom.

A final point to make about teaching styles arises from the relationship between putting people into groups and placing them on scales as approaches to data analysis. The idea of teaching styles arises from the application of cluster analysis to educational data. Similar individuals are placed in groups which form the basis for comparisons. It is not always clear, however, that this is the most appropriate form of analysis. In the Bennett study teachers are placed into three groups: formal, informal and mixed. An alternative approach is to place the individual teachers on a scale of formality/informality (which is what the variables were originally intended to measure). In this case each individual would have a scale position which could be treated as a score rather than be allocated to a group. This would, in many ways, provide a better test of the hypothesis on the effects of formal and informal teaching. In a similar manner in the ORACLE research, key features of the different clusters involve the amount of class, individual and group teaching and the frequency of organizational change in the classroom. A different approach to analysis would involve treating these as variables which could be correlated with outcome measures.

The general point to be made is that identifying clusters and calling them teaching styles is not the only, or always the best, way of studying teaching. If the variables in the study throw up distinct groups of individuals then using these groups as the basis for the analysis is obviously a sensible strategy. In many cases, however, it may be more profitable to think in terms of dimensions of teaching method based around variables rather than in terms of groups of similar teachers.

Note

1   COHEN and MANNION (1980, chapter 8) give a brief account of the principles of experimental design. COOK and CAMPBELL (1979) provide an extended discussion of the validity of different types of experimental design, in particular, with regard to research in natural settings where full experimental control is impossible.

7   Issues in Systematic Observation

In the previous chapters the characteristics of systematic classroom observation have been discussed, some of the issues and decisions researchers using this approach must confront have been explored and practical procedures have been presented. It is hoped that the reader will have a sense of both the distinctiveness of systematic classroom observation as a research technique and of its essential similarity to other areas of systematic, quantitatively oriented empirical enquiry. The difficulties and issues involved in conducting this sort of empirical research both in classrooms and elsewhere have been presented in a postive fashion and with a conviction as to the value and importance of research of this kind.

Nevertheless, criticisms have been levelled concerning both the validity and value of research using systematic classroom interaction methods. It is necessary therefore in this concluding chapter to consider these criticisms before proceeding to a more general discussion of the place of systematic observation in educational research and the uses which researchers and teachers can make of it. These criticisms will be dealt with under two headings: The Ethnographic Critique and The Critique of Empirical Educational Enquiry.

Many of the criticisms have been made in the context of a contrast between ethnographic research methods and the methodology of systematic observation. It is common for authors of articles presenting the results of ethnographic enquiry to define their own position in contrast to the methods of systematic observation (for example, Atkinson, 1975; Walker and Adelman, 1976; Furlong and Edwards, 1977). It is therefore convenient to deal with these criticisms in the context of a brief consideration of ethnographic approaches to classroom research. Although criticisms will be made of certain studies using these approaches this section should not be read as an attack upon ethnography or on qualitative methods more generally but as a correction of some of the misconceptions which it will be argued are held about systematic observation.

The ethnographic critique, although critical of one particular approach to classroom research, recognizes the value of empirical enquiry within classrooms. The views to be considered under the second heading are a more fundamental critique in that they question the possibility of educationally relevant empirical enquiry as well as the validity of particular studies, although the specific criticisms raised are principally directed at quantitative research. The consideration of these views is therefore relevant to educational research in general as well as to classroom-based studies.

Following these sections will be a discussion of the interrelationship of systematic observation and other research methods including qualitative methods and finally a discussion of the uses that researchers and teachers might make of classroom research and, more generally, of the relevance of research for teachers and teaching. These two concluding sections can be seen as leading on from the earlier discussions. A discussion of the ethnographic critique of systematic observation leads to a consideration of the interrelationship between different research methods, and an argument for the basic validity of empirical educational enquiry leads on to a discussion of the relevance of such enquiry for teaching. In this chapter, however, the four sections are kept separate and the criticisms are presented and considered first before moving to the more positive aspects of the discussion.

The Ethnographic Critique

A well-known example of such a critique is the often-reprinted article by Hamilton and Delamont (1974) (see also Delamont and Hamilton, 1984). This will provide the focus for the discussion here. Similar arguments are presented in substantive articles such as those by Furlong and Edwards (1977) and Walker and Adelman (1976).

In considering these criticisms an important preliminary distinction must be made between criticisms which apply to a particular piece of research, criticisms of general but contingent aspects of a research approach and criticisms of aspects of a research approach which are necessary or logical features of it. These distinctions have not always been made in the critiques referred to and, unfortunately, a consideration of FIAC has tended to dominate them. As was made clear in chapter 2, FIAC is an important contribution to classroom research and undoubtedly the best known example of a systematic observation schedule. But systematic observation is not synonymous with interaction analysis and still less so with FIAC. Even where the criticisms made of FIAC are valid there is no necessary reason why they should apply to other systematic observation systems.

Inevitably, one of the major issues relates to the way that systematic observation utilizes a limited number of pre-defined categories as the basis for describing classroom activities. This gives rise to the related criticisms that observation systems can only give a *partial* view of classrooms (and, it is sometimes suggested, a biased one) and that it is an *inflexible* research instrument because of the way in which the observer is constrained by the categories.

As should be clear from the earlier chapters it is perfectly true that the variables of a systematic observation system only capture a part of what is happening in classrooms. In chapter 1 it was explained that the ways in which observation systems are constructed are determined by the purposes for which the research is being carried out and that they involve a process of abstracting from the totality of the social world those elements thought to be relevant for particular investigatory purposes. It is, therefore, not a criticism of FIAC that it focusses on a few aspects of teacher-pupil interaction when this is what it is intended to do. There is a much more general point, however. This is that the inevitably partial nature of the descriptions offered by systematic observation is not just a limitation of this technique but is inherent in any description of the social world. All descriptions involve selection and in the cases of descriptions of social processes involve the selection of aspects of something which is of its nature evanescent. If we think of being asked to describe a lesson or other teaching episode it is clear that we select from what we see and it is also clear that the selections we make will be influenced by the purposes which the description is to serve.

This has not always been understood by researchers using systematic observation techniques. When researchers claim that it is possible to 'allow no theory to determine the selection of phenomena to be observed' and that it is 'theoretically possible to free the mind of all pre-suppositions about the relationships between events in the classroom and the correlation between these events and possible outcomes' (Eggleston, Galton and Jones, 1975a) they are expressing the reverse side of the error made by those who complain that systematic observation is selective. As has been explained, all observers must make selections and the researcher who thinks that observations are unguided by theory is actually influenced by 'commonsense' everyday assumptions about educational processes which are every bit as theory-laden as the explicitly theoretical formulations of more sophisticated researchers.

Consequently it is misleading to compare the descriptions offered by systematic observation with those offered by qualitative research and to emphasize the 'completeness' or 'fullness' of the latter as though the same process of selection has not occurred. The implication that such descriptions are truer depends on the mistaken view that there is a single best description of what is happening in classrooms and other social settings which can be arrived at independently of the purposes for which it is being sought.

The inflexibility of systematic observation procedures arises from the requirement that observers should strictly follow the coding rules so that the procedures for arriving at the descriptions offered are absolutely explicit. This has the consequence that observers cannot respond imaginatively to classroom events. However, it should be emphasized that it is not research using systematic observation which is inflexible but the actual data-collecting process. Researchers using systematic observation make a clear distinction between the creative, imaginative and flexible stage of research in which ideas are generated and discussed and procedures are suggested, tried and modified and the mechanical stage when these procedures are carried out in a controlled and replicable fashion.

Another pair of related criticisms of systematic observation are that observation systems *de-contextualize* the phenomena being observed and that they result in *atomistic* data, individual isolated bits of behaviour which are in themselves meaningless. These criticisms come about in part from a confusion between characteristics of certain observational systems and necessary features of the method. It is true that FIAC and some other systems are not much concerned with the context of their observations but a concern for context can easily be part of such a system. In chapter 5 a number of ways were discussed of contextualizing observations by means of incorporating a concern with context into individual observations and a more general context can be established by noting the physical arrangements of the classroom and the materials in it at the beginning of a period of observation. The observation systems used in *A Study of Schooling* discussed in chapter 2 of this volume are a good example of this.

It is similarly untrue to say that individual observations are atomized in a way that means that they cannot be related to other observations. In chapter 5 a number of examples were given of ways in which observations could be located in sequence and context and the simultaneous coding of several variables allows detailed analysis of the interrelationship of occurrences. It should also be noted that a particular strength of systematic observation as a technique is that many systems focus observations on one individual at a time but also collect information on many individuals. This makes possible an analysis which can deal with both individual experience and overall classroom processes. For example, in the ORACLE research it was possible to show that even in classrooms characterized by constant interaction and movement the experience of most individual children was predominantly of little interaction or movement. The overview of the observer who is not forced by a systematic observation schedule to focus on individual pupils, whatever they are doing, would not be a true reflection of most pupils' actual classroom experience. This also relates to the unease sometimes generated by reading the very readable and action-packed accounts of classrooms offered by ethnographic researchers that there is a tendency to focus observations 'where the action is' and that these accounts may not accurately reflect the experience of participants. (A similar point is made by Neill, 1985.)

A good deal of criticism which has been directed at systematic observation derives from reservations about quantification and the use of statistical data. Some people have an uneasy feeling that presenting quantitative data about social phenomena is in some way improper and that numbers cannot meaningfully reflect social reality. In considering this argument it is worth considering what it is that happens when a coding decision is made which results in a tick being made in a category or a number written in a box which then goes on to be part of the basis of a quantitative statement. The coder, in placing a behaviour or act in a category, is deciding that it does or does not have certain qualities, that it is a question or an act of aggression or is a one-to-one interaction. This is the kind of decision that is made when we offer any sort of description whether in everyday discussion or in ethnographic research. When we say that something took place or had a particular characteristic we are making a binary coding decision and have implicitly constructed criteria for deciding on its presence or absence. This kind of decision made both on an everyday basis and in qualitative research contains the basis for quantification. If we can say that a particular incident occurred at a certain time and not at another, or in certain lessons and not others, or is a characteristic of one person and not another, then we have an implicit category system for that event or characteristic and can, if we choose, begin to count it. So the coder is only making use of the human capacity for discrimination in making binary judgments that particular characteristics or events are or are not present, although in the case of systematic observation they are being made in a highly organized and self-conscious form.

It may be objected that the coder is forcing the occurrences into one or other categories of the observation system in a way that we do not do in naturalistic observation but in properly conducted systematic observation this is not the case. In some types of coding system there is no compulsion at all to code all events. For example, in event recording systems and one-zero time sampling systems codes are only made when an appropriate event has occurred and the observer is making a perfectly naturalistic judgment about which parts of an on-going process fit the criteria for the presence of certain sorts of behaviour or interactions. With the other systems, especially instantaneous time-sampling systems, the observer does expect that one or other of the categories of each variable in the system should apply but whether or not this will actually turn out to be the case is an empirical question and a test of the adequacy of the observation schedule. Researchers setting up systematic observation systems do not start with the idea that 'everything that occurs will be put into one of these categories come what may' but construct a set of categories based on a theoretical conception of what happens in classrooms and extensive experience and pre-testing such that all or very nearly all occurrences will meet the definition of one of the categories. This is, however, always open to test and observation systems should include the category 'other' or 'not coded'. If such categories are coded more than very infrequently in an instantaneous time-sampling or continuous recording system this may be grounds for questioning its adequacy. If it is accepted that observers can make judgments about the occurrence or non-occurrence of events or the absence or presence of characteristics in social settings such as classrooms, there can be no objection to using these judgments as the basis of counts of such events or characteristics. In fact, descriptions of classrooms and of educational processes virtually always do include quantitative elements even when they come from research in a tradition which ostensibly excludes quantitative statements. Comments such as 'usually', 'typically', 'unusual', 'most of the time' and so on are no different in principal from '10 per cent' or '90 per cent' which are so much objected to by some, they are merely less precise. The extent to which qualitative research is dependent on such terms has been pointed out elsewhere (McIntyre and MacLeod, 1978). It is repeated here not as a criticism of such studies but as an indication of the essential true-to-lifeness of quantitative descriptions.

A further criticism of systematic observation from within the ethnographic perspective and related to the issue of quantification is that a numerical count of incidents may not give a true sense of their relative importance, and that a single event may be more significant than a large number of other occurrences, or, and this may be the more important point, may provide a key insight into the processes being described. There is undoubtedly something in this argument and it requires careful consideration.

In part it is related to the issue of flexibility discussed above. In principle it is possible for a category of events of special significance to be built into an observation schedule and analysis of systematic observation data does not attempt to ascribe importance to events on the basis of frequency (relatively infrequent events like violent acts or open-ended teacher questions have been the focus of some systematic observation studies) but, of course, this can only be done if the characteristics of the events in question have been specified in advance. During actual data collection the systematic observer cannot properly deal with the totally unexpected, but extensive preliminary work in classrooms and pre-testing of schedules should allow the researcher to specify categories for unusual but relevant events.

The term 'relevant' is important here. In everyday terms, an event such as a fire or a fight might be the most significant occurrence of the school day but it may not be relevant to the purposes of the study. A schedule designed to investigate teacher questioning techniques should not be criticized because it does not take account of dramatic but extraneous events such as these.

In considering the place of the unusual in classroom observation it is necessary to be clear whether what is of concern is the frequency or consequence of infrequent events (such as a complete breakdown in classroom discipline) or with establishing that such an event has, on one occasion, occurred. The question of frequency, context, place in a sequence and so on of infrequent events are a problem for systematic observation studies. If such events are significant for research then the study must involve extended pre-testing and lengthy periods of observation. But it is not necessary for an observation system to have a unique recording procedure for any event that takes place. It is not part of the empirical study of education to establish that a particular characteristic or event *can* exist in a classroom. Such an assertion can just as profitably be hypothesized rather than observed and is not available for refutation. In Carnap's terms it is 'almost logically true' (Popper, 1963, pp. 248–50). In fact, observations of key or significant events are usually justified in quantitative terms. For example, Atkinson, after citing such an occurrence in his own field-work conducting research on medical education and using it as the basis for a criticism of systematic observation methods goes on to say that it 'appeared to be a very characteristic facet of this clinician's teaching' (Atkinson, 1975).

Brief mention must also be made of the frequent assertion that systematic observation methods are 'positivist' and 'behaviourist'. These have become all-purpose terms of abuse in some quarters and it must be emphasized that, even where these are accurate descriptions, they do not in themselves constitute a criticism of the research being discussed. It is not true, however, to suggest that there is the kind of simple relationship between theory and epistemology on the one hand and method on the other which the casual use of these terms supposes. Some uses of systematic observation, for example, in behaviour modification programmes, are within an explicitly be-haviourist context but it is the theory of the researcher which is behaviourist not the observation method. It is hard to see the essential epistemological difference between a statement such as 'we often heard X use phrases like . . . .' and '50 per cent of X's utterances were of the type . . . .'. Yet the first is the sort of statement made by qualitative researchers who describe the second as positivist.[1]

In an interesting article Bryman (1984) discusses the relationship between epistemology and research method. He shows that although many discussions of methodology argue for a unique relationship between philosophical views of the nature of knowledge about the social world (such as phenomenology or positivism) and particular research techniques (such as participant observation or social surveys) it is difficult to establish such connections in practice. This raises the question of whether epistemological considerations can determine particular data-gathering procedures. The suggestions presented later in this chapter for the ways in which a research project may draw on different approaches, and similar arguments such as those of Hammersley (1985) and examples such as Delamont (1976) which draws on data based on FIAC and also on qualitative observations, would all suggest that research techniques cannot be judged on philosophical grounds.

Finally, reference should be made to the claim that what makes social behaviour distinctive (in sociological terms what makes behaviour social action) is that it is meaningful both to the actor and to others and that systematic methods cannot provide evidence on these meanings (for example, Jonathon, 1981; Walker and Adelman, 1976). As McIntyre and MacLeod (1978) have pointed out, however, this would only be a limitation on systematic observation if classrooms were private worlds with systems of meaning to which outsiders do not have access. The researcher who describes behaviour in terms of categories such as 'question', 'waiting for the teacher', 'disciplinary interaction' and so on is not making use of a privileged insight into the actors' states of mind but is making use of a system of conventional meanings attached to words and acts which are available to all participants in a culture, and which are the means by which communication and social life are accomplished. If I am talking to a strange class and a student puts up a hand I assume that he or she wants to ask or tell me something. I am very rarely mistaken.

As Runciman (1983) has argued, in considering the difficulties of reporting social events in these terms, a useful way of considering the difficulties involved in arriving at an understanding adequate for the purpose of reporting what occurred is to consider what it would mean to misunderstand. In the context of systematic observation, to misunderstand is to code something in the wrong category. This may occur because the definition used in the observation schedule is unclear or because a particular activity or statement means one thing in one context and something else in another, in a way not allowed for by the observation system. This sort of misunderstanding will show up in reliability tests and observer training as disagreements between observers in the way they code the same event. Any misunderstandings of this sort, which are so unusual that they are not spotted in this way or which crop up on a particular occasion due to the observer mishearing something which is said or missing a cue that changes the appropriate category, will contribute to minor errors in the data which reduce the accuracy of observation but, because they are random, do not bias the observations. Systematic misunderstandings will only occur if the observers agree about the meaning of a particular type of action while the participants in the situation studied attribute a different meaning to it. In terms of the sort of data which is the concern of systematic observation this would mean that conventional definitions of 'question', 'teacher statement to class', 'praise' and so on had become suspended in certain classrooms. As McIntyre and MacLeod (1978) show there is no evidence for this and it seems unlikely that researchers using systematic techniques would remain in ignorance of it.

The Critique of Empirical Educational Enquiry

The previous discussion has been concerned with criticisms of the methodology of systematic classroom observation which arise from different approaches within educational research and social science research more generally. These disagreements come about as a result of differing theoretical and methodological emphases in approaches to studying the social world but researchers taking very different views share a commitment to the central importance of empirical enquiry for education. The sorts of criticisms to be discussed in this section relate to whether the empirical investigation of teaching and learning can have any value for education. Criticis such as Wilson (1972 and 1979) while not totally opposed to the use of empirical evidence to throw light on educational processes, mount a vehement attack on current research practice, while critics such as Barrow (1981 and 1984) and Egan (1983) question the value of all, or very nearly all, empirical investigations both on the grounds that they do not happen to like most contemporary research but also, more importantly, because they claim that most educational questions cannot, logically, be answered by empirical procedures. A particular focus for such criticisms have been quantitative studies of classroom processes and associated process-product analyses.

Although these are extreme and unrepresentative views and are expressed in terms which show major misunderstandings about the nature of the research process they are, nevertheless, worth considering here. This is because they contain, in an extreme form, an instinctive distrust of empirical educational research and its application to educational processes which researchers sometimes encounter, which relates to a residual feeling that researchers cannot really get at what is important about teaching. The latter point will be taken up again in the concluding section of this chapter but it will be useful at this point to clarify what it is that empirical research can achieve in describing educational processes by means of taking up some of the issues raised by the critics.

The first of these issues relates to the claim that because it is not possible to be sure that all relevant variables have been included in a description that this in some way invalidates the description of those aspects which are included. An example of this is the statement: 'It may, for example, be the case that the most important factor in successful teaching is the personality of the teacher and the fact that no adequate research programme has been devised to look into this

... (has) the consequence that all observations of teaching strategies must be imperfect.' (Barrow, 1981, p. 179.)

It should be clear from the earlier discussion that all descriptions of teaching, whether arrived at by observation or other methods, are partial in the sense that they are selective. The use of 'imperfect' rather than selective neatly avoids confronting the real point which is that this selection is a theoretical one. (Consider what would be a 'perfect' description of classrooms.) It is clearly not true to suggest that there cannot be a valid description of a classroom in terms of the balance of teacher and pupil utterances or the ratio of questions to statements or the relative amounts of use made of individual, group and whole class teaching strategies. The relevance of such descriptions is not established by asserting that they are more or less important than teacher personality in absolute terms (a meaningless concept) but that they relate to the purposes of the research.

It should also be noted how obsessed these critics are with inner and unmeasurable characteristics. If teacher personality has a key influence on the teaching process this presumably comes about because of things which teachers with certain personalities do and say in the classroom. Personality cannot be described by observation but these manifestations can. It is not much help to tell a teacher who is experiencing difficulties that he or she has something wrong with their personality. It is much more helpful to be able to say that teachers who do not have these difficulties characteristically use specified behaviour and types of interactions and it is worth trying such approaches.

A second type of criticism relates to the fact that a number of studies of classrooms have used some form of grouping of teachers, often based on cluster analysis, as an analytical device. As we have seen, this is a form of data reduction which looks for structure in the variables on which the descriptions are based such that certain individuals can be grouped together. It serves the purpose of providing an economical description of large groups of individuals and also, in some cases, as the basis for comparisons of outcomes across the groups. In an attack on the Lancaster study of teaching style (Bennett, 1976), Barrow (1981) makes the astonishing claim that it is impossible *a priori* to describe teaching styles in terms of three clusters of teachers as is done in the research and suggests that it is equivalent to dividing teachers on the basis of eye colour.

While this extreme claim cannot be taken seriously some people may have reservations about describing people in terms of cluster membership and it is worth repeating what such an analysis means. (Although, as a matter of fact, teachers generally respond positively to the cluster descriptions contained in studies such as the Lancaster research and the ORACLE study.) What a cluster analysis does is to group together people who are very similar with regard to the variables of interest in order to simplify the process of description. It necessarily involves a trade-off of detailed accuracy for economy in description, although with large data sets the detailed accuracy is to some extent illusory as the information it provides is unmanageable. In the early stage of cluster analysis very little information is usually lost as the individuals grouped together are very similar or even identical with regard to the variables in the analysis. In the later stages it is probable that a good deal of information is lost as relatively dissimilar individuals are put together. However, this is an entirely empirical question. With some data sets dissimilar individuals may be put together when there are still a large number of clusters while with others the analysis may proceed to very few clusters while still keeping the groupings homogeneous. This can easily be determined in the analysis in the ways already described and cannot normally be known in advance. The fact that teaching is a complex activity does not mean that a small number of meaningful clusters may not accurately describe a group of teachers. As we have seen, all descriptions involve a process of abstraction of variables relevant for particular theoretical purposes and in some cases this may result in a small number of homogeneous clusters. The purpose for which the analysis is conducted will also determine the extent to which the researcher is prepared to accept relatively heterogeneous clusters.[2]

A third criticism, related to the two above, refers specifically to process-product analysis in classroom research. This is an analysis where observed processes in classrooms are related to outcomes in terms of pupil achievement or other measures of interest. It is, therefore, an analysis concerned with association and causality. The researcher is trying, first, to establish that certain processes are associated with higher or lower levels of the outcome variables and is then attempting to investigate patterns of causality in this relationship. Establishing causality with non-experimental data is notoriously problematic and the criticisms levelled against this kind of research have more in common with the cautions expressed by experienced researchers than do the other sorts of criticisms discussed above.

It is a basic axiom of social science that correlation does not establish causality. The fact that variable X is observed to correlate with variable Y does not mean that X causes Y. It may be that Y causes X or that they are jointly caused by a third variable or a combination of other variables. However, even to express the matter in these simple terms suggests the possibilities as well as the limitations of causal analysis. If a correlation can be consistently established between two variables and appropriate significance tests allow us to reject the possibility that it has come about by chance (Croll, 1984) then rejecting chance necessarily implies that it has come about as a result of some underlying mechanism operating causally. This mechanism may be operating through the effects of another variable including other variables which have not been included in the analysis but any considerations of this sort are necessarily concerned with causality. Spurious correlation is an instance of a causal mechanism as well as being a problem in causal analysis.

The strongest procedure for getting round the difficulties involved in sorting out the nature of the causal relationships between a set of variables is the experiment. Here, experimental controls establish that only random factors can complicate the causal relationship between the variables of interest and significance tests tell us the likelihood that this has happened. For many research problems in education experiments are impractical and causal processes are investigated through statistical controls. This is essentially a process of attempting to offer explanations for observed patterns of association between variables and testing these explanations against the data. For example, if research starts with the hypothesis that teachers using certain methods will achieve higher average class gains on a test than do teachers using other methods, the first test is to establish which teachers use the method and to compare their gains with other teachers. If their pupils have achieved higher gains then there is tentative support for the hypothesis. (Technically the hypothesis has survived the test.) However, the researcher will also want to investigate alternative explanations. Perhaps teachers change their methods in response to pupil success rather than the success being in response to the methods. This hypothesis can be tested by investigating the stability of teaching methods over time. Perhaps some other variable is responsible both for the different methods used by the successful teachers and for their pupils' success. For example, perhaps parental pressure or teacher experience influence both methods and success. This can be tested by controlling for these variables in some of the ways discussed in chapter 6. In introducing controls the researcher will want to investigate a variety of possible influences of other variables. It may be that teacher experience influences success and method independently, in which case the apparent correlation is spurious, but it may also be that it influences success via its influence on method in which case method can be seen as an intervening variable with a direct causal link with pupil gains (see Croll and Willcocks, 1980; and Galton and Croll, 1980 for instances of this sort of elaborated analysis).

There are three specific points of criticism of this procedure which should be considered briefly.

The first is the suggestion that a consideration of cause and effect cannot take place because it will never be complete for every individual to whom it is applied. This sort of argument claims that: '... who is to say that one or more of the children in the ORACLE survey were not materially affected in their performance by factors such as their liking for their teacher, the support they receive at home ... a nagging toothache ... their ability to read ....' (Barrow, 1984, p. 210).

It is clearly the case that causal explanation in social science cannot be complete because it can never offer a total explanation for individual characteristics. Most people would be rather relieved about this. But this in no way invalidates the conclusions of statistical generalizations which have a probabalistic relationship to any individual. The conclusion that a particular teaching method is more appropriate than another for teaching a particular curriculum area to children of a particular age is not invalidated by the fact that one of them had toothache. If it turns out that the method is regularly associated with toothache then this relationship should be included in the analysis.

A somewhat more sophisticated criticism is the claim that many other variables than those included in the analysis may be systematically related to the outcome variable. Clearly, a large number of variables may be related to teaching outcomes in a causal fashion and it is impractical to include them all in any particular research project. However, it is important to be clear about the implications of this. The fact that some other variable, which is not in the analysis, has a systematic effect on pupil gains in the curriculum area which forms the product measure in a piece of research does not in itself have any implications at all for the validity of an analysis which investigates the causal relationship between aspects of teaching method observed in the classroom and gains in this curriculum area. The effect of a third variable can only have a confounding effect on the analysis if it is systematically related to both of the original variables in a way that accounts for the observed pattern of association between them. A variable such as pupil ambition or parental support may well be related to the progress pupils make, but this is only relevant to an analysis of the relationship between progress and the kind of questions a teacher asks if ambition and support also influence the style of questioning.

This brings us to the third point which is that although researchers can bring into the analysis additional variables which may have a confounding influence, and test for such an influence, there may always be additional variables which they have not considered but which may have a confounding influence on those variables which are in the analysis. This is a logical limitation on the conclusions which can be drawn from this sort of research and emphasizes their provisional nature. It should be noted, however, that all scientific findings are provisional and that the progress of scientific enquiry involves a constant testing of our ideas and theories against data. The proper reaction to these limitations is to explore the possible forms of interrelationship between variables by constructing rival explanations for observed correlations and devizing ways of testing them. To say that this is pointless because it might all be due to some variable that no one has thought of is like rejecting a philosophical argument on the grounds that it might have a logical flaw that no one has yet spotted.

Systematic Observation and Other Research Methods

Systematic classroom observation is a specific research technique not a complete and self-contained approach to educational research. Most research programmes which use systematic observation also use other techniques and it is interesting to consider the interrelationship between systematic observation and other methodologies.

The most obvious and important of these is the relationship between systematic observation and qualitative or ethnographic research in classrooms. Systematic observation may draw on qualitative observation techniques for a number of reasons. When a researcher decides to investigate an aspect of classroom life it is unlikely that enough will be known about the area to be investigated for the researcher to simply sit down and design an observation schedule. Consequently, most studies using systematic observation are likely to start out with periods of time spent in classrooms in a less formal, more qualitative fashion. This period of informal observation is when the researcher can begin to get a feel for the aspects of the classroom that he or she wishes to investigate and can also identify appropriate observational variables and their definitions. This stage of the research may also be used to generate hypotheses which can be tested when the systematic observation data have been collected. In an earlier discussion we saw that one of the criticisms of systematic observation is that it is inflexible in operation. An initial period of informal observation can form part of the exploratory, creative, hypotheses generating stage of the research which is a necessary counterpart to the formal, rigorous testing stage.

As well as providing a preliminary sensitizing and developmental stage which precedes the systematic observation, a period of qualitative observation may also follow on from systematic observation. Having established statistical regularities by means of systematic observation it might then be valuable to investigate them further in a more naturalistic way to get more of a feel for the processes being described. In these ways it is possible to move both from qualitative to quantitative approaches in the early stages of a study and possibly also from quantitative to qualitative methods in the final stages.

The above discussion has dealt with the interrelationship from the point of view of an essentially quantitative study which may draw on more qualitative techniques when appropriate. However, it is also often appropriate to introduce systematic observation methods into studies which are principally qualitative in nature. It has already been mentioned that quasi-statistical statements frequently occur in qualitative research (usually, infrequent etc.). Such research can obviously be strengthened if quantitative data are gathered with regard to any important, essentially quantitative, generalizations of this kind. For example, ethnographic researchers working in a feminist tradition have suggested that boys receive more attention from teachers than girls in the same classroom (for example, Spender, 1981; Clarricotes, 1980; Stanworth, 1981). These assertions are about aspects of classroom life on which it is perfectly straightforward to produce statistical evidence based on systematic observation. Systematic studies which have taken up these points have basically confirmed the conclusions of these researchers although in slightly modified form (Croll, 1985). Other ethnographic researchers have suggested that lower-achieving children and children from disadvantaged backgrounds receive less attention from the teacher in primary schools than do other pupils (Rist, 1970; Sharp and Green, 1975). In this case the evidence of systematic observation shows that these claims do not stand up and that, to some extent, the reverse is the case (Galton, Simon and Croll, 1980; Croll, 1981; Croll and Moses, 1985).

A different use for systematic observation data within an essentially qualitative study is to use the systematic data as the basis for an exploration of aspects of individual characteristics of teachers and pupils. Delamont (1976) uses FIAC data as a starting point for a comparison of the teaching behaviour of two teachers but the main point of her analysis is the understanding, intentions and personalities of the two individuals. Systematic observation is not being used to check on qualitative assertions but as an initial reference point from which a qualitative analysis can be developed. This has something in common with the earlier suggestion that qualitative approaches might be used to throw further light on patterns of statistical regularities established by systematic means, but is within a context where the qualitative analysis is the centre of the exercise rather than being an additional feature.

The relationship between systematic and qualitative observation is an obvious one because it arises naturally from the fact that they both use observation as a data collection technique and do so in the same settings. Other research methods which may be used alongside systematic observation do not have this natural relationship with it but arise from the requirements of particular research projects. Process-product studies typically use tests or other assessment techniques to gather product data which can be set against the process data generated by systematic observation. Questionnaires or personal interviews may be used to gather attitudinal data or data on social background or other aspects of individual experience which can be used to test hypotheses about different behavioural characteristics of teachers or pupils with different social characteristics, attitudes and so on.

In such instances the other data collection methods are essentially separate sources of data about the individuals. They relate to different aspects of individual characteristics like social background and classroom interaction which it is hypothesized might be interrelated. For example, in the study reported in *Fifteen Thousand Hours* (Rutter *et al*, 1979) a great variety of sources of information were used in what was effectively a series of case-studies of twelve comprehensive schools. Systematic observation in classrooms was carried out alongside the collection of data by interviews and questionnaires and from school records. Aspects of classroom behaviour could then be correlated with measures such as pupil attitudes and examination pass rates.

A different approach to combining different data collection methods is to use different methods to provide information on the same characteristics of individuals. This procedure is called *triangulation* and is an attempt to describe a phenomenon from more than one perspective (see Denzin, 1978; Cohen and Manion, 1980, chapter 11). Using this approach a researcher might gather sociometric data from pupils by means of self-completion questionnaires and also gather observational data about patterns of pupil-pupil interaction. Similarly, the researcher might talk to pupils or teachers about how they see their behaviour and activities in class and also gather observational data on these activities. This is partly a data confirmation technique in which data are strengthened where the same results are produced by different procedures. However, it can also serve to give greater depth to the data and give the researcher a greater understanding of it. This approach is implicit in some of the ways of interrelating qualitative and quantitative observational methods discussed above.

Triangulation of this kind involves looking at the same individuals from more than one perspective. In the ORACLE research on primary classrooms, different perspectives on the classroom situation were gained by looking at the classroom from both the pupils' point of view and also from that of the teacher, and contrasting these with the sort of overview of classroom life which is available to the casual observer. This shows the assymetry in the teachers' and the pupils' views of the classroom and the way in which classroom life looks different from different perspectives which adds to our understanding of classroom processes.

Systematic Observation Research, Teachers and Teaching

A key issue for anyone involved in educational research is that of relevance. To what extent is the research which is being conducted relevant to the work of teachers and of other educationalists? Does it contribute to an improvement in education? Why should funding be found for it and why should teachers and schools cooperate in research and perhaps even engage in it themselves? A strong case in principle can be made for the relevance of systematic classroom observation based on its location within educational settings and its concern with on-going educational processes. On the face of it systematic observation looks relevant in a way that some other areas of educational research may not. There is undoubtedly something in this and some aspects of this immediate classroom relevance will be discussed below. However, the argument to be made here for the importance of systematic classroom observation and its relevance to teachers is a broader one which will emphasize what this approach has in common with other areas of empirical enquiry within education as well as what makes it distinctive.

Appropriate criteria for relevance of educational research go beyond a concern with the immediate improvement of classroom practice and embrace a wider concern with educational issues. Research may often be directed directly at classroom issues, contributing to the solution of a specific problem as experienced and defined by teachers, providing ways for teachers to engage in an on-going evaluation of their own and their pupils' work, comparing the effectiveness of different teaching strategies or patterns of classroom organization for specified purposes or outlining general principles for effective classroom teaching. But research can also be relevant to teachers through its relevance to education generally. Research can contribute to educational issues that must be resolved outside the classroom at the level of educational policy. Issues such as the educational consequences of different class sizes or of comprehensive reorganization are clearly relevant to teachers even though they are not always of immediate relevance to classroom practice.

Apparent relevance should also not be regarded as a restrictive condition on the validity of educational research. Research is concerned with description, explanation and understanding. It is motivated by a curiosity about educational processes and a desire to come to understand them better as well as by immediate problems and by the desire to improve education. This curiosity over educational processes is part of the relevance of educational research for teachers; teachers are not only involved in educational practice and committed to improving it, they are also interested in it. This interest may have practical payoffs for their work in the classroom and may help in the development of informed educational policies but it is also intrinsically rewarding. It is also the case that this open-ended approach to the relevance of educational research may lead to work that turns out to have practical relevance even where this relevance was not immediately apparent.

Teacher-as-Researcher

The model of the relationship between research and teaching which makes the closest and most necessary links between the two is that of the teacher-as-researcher. In this model the roles of teacher and researcher are identical and the teacher takes a research orientation towards his or her professional practice, preferably in collaboration with colleagues and possibly with the support of an outside 'facilitator'. The approach usually also incorporates action research. This approach was first articulated in Britain by Stenhouse (1975) and is seen as an aspect of the professional development of teachers (Elliott, 1980). Proponents of the approach have not generally been enthusiastic about systematic observation or indeed other quantitative methods but there is no reason why these methods should not be incorporated in teacher-as-researcher projects and a number of reasons why it may be appropriate.

The first of these is the point made earlier that a good many of the descriptions which arise from qualitative studies are of a quasi-statistical essentially quantitative kind and would be much strengthened if they were based on procedures which provided a firm basis for these statements.

The second argument refers not so much to the provision of results in quantitative form but to the advantages of using at least some very explicit categories and definitions in a research project. The rather private nature of teacher-as-researcher projects has been a problem for people working in this area who have often stressed the importance of publication as a way to make the exercise a genuine piece of research rather than just a self-critical approach to teaching (Elliott, 1983). The use of some of the sorts of explicit categories and variables which are necessitated by the use of systematic observation would help in this process of 'going public' and would help to establish greater comparability between different teacher-as-researcher enterprises and make for more cumulative outcomes from such studies.

The collaborative nature of many teacher-as-researcher projects makes the use of systematic observation techniques more practical than it would otherwise be. The use of systematic observation in one's own classroom is only possible either for short periods of time or with very simple schedules but groups of teachers working collaboratively can conduct observation in one another's classes.

The use of systematic observation by teachers using approaches based on behaviour modification with children in their classrooms can also be regarded as an example of the teacher-as-researcher although it may not be recognized as such by some proponents of the model. This is probably one of the most effective ways in which teachers can use research techniques in a limited and small-scale fashion to identify and describe classroom problems and to evaluate the effectiveness of their intervention strategies. Wheldall and Merrett

(1984) provide a number of examples of projects where teachers have carefully specified a problem of behaviour, devized observation procedures to monitor it and used these procedures to measure the impact of teaching approaches designed to reduce the incidence of the behaviour.

Large-Scale Classroom Surveys

A major function of research using systematic classroom observation has been to provide descriptions of pupil and teacher activities in classrooms based on large-scale surveys of substantial samples of classrooms and schools. The observation system developed by Flanders, FIAC, has generated data on many thousands of hours of pupil-teacher interaction and Hilsum and Cane's, *The Teacher's Day* study, described in chapter 2 and the associated secondary study (Hilsum and Strong, 1978) have provided a teacher's eye view of the school day based on days spent with hundreds of teachers. The ORACLE project also discussed in chapter 2 has provided information on patterns of teacher and pupil activities and teacher-pupil interaction in over a hundred primary school classrooms.

The value of such studies is partly that they provide us with a picture of what certain aspects of education are like. Teachers get a view of the educational system much wider than they could obtain from their own experience and one which abstracts certain elements for particular consideration in a way which we do not ordinarily do. It also provides other educationalists and people concerned with educational policy with an informed insight into the educational experience of pupils and teachers as well as describing different areas of the educational system for teachers whose personal experience is limited to other sectors. This is the kind of information which is vital to an informed discussion of educational issues and is an aspect of the professional relevance of research for teachers which goes beyond immediate classroom practice. From the teachers' point of view it can be regarded as an aspect of 'professional literacy', a knowledge and understanding of the world of education beyond personal experience, which is necessary to take an informed part in it.[3]

One function of such large-scale surveys is to make public and communicable what is often a very private and isolated activity. It has often been pointed out how infrequently teachers see other teachers in the classroom for any extended period (Galton, Simon and Croll, 1980; King, 1984). This isolation can mean that teachers sometimes have little sense of how their own classroom practice is related to that of other teachers, the extent to which their problems are general or are specific to them and the possibilities that alternative strategies may be operated successfully. Such large-scale surveys can present a reference point against which personal experience can be located and individual approaches better understood within the context of their typicality and uniqueness.

Large-scale surveys of this sort are not just, or even primarily, concerned to give a picture of average or typical teachers, pupils and classrooms. As the discussion in chapter 6 made clear, analysis strategies are just as much concerned to describe variety, possibly through cluster analysis or other grouping procedures as they are to describe typicality and can also describe individual cases. Such individual descriptions are given additional meaning if it is also possible to determine whether they are statistically unusual or typical.

It is certainly the case that the descriptions to arise from systematic observation lack the richness of qualitative descriptions but for many purposes this may not be a serious limitation. Teachers and even students can describe the richness and individual detail of the teaching situation from their own experience. What their experience cannot give them is the large-scale and comparative perspective on classrooms offered by systematic methods. Experience with both students and experienced teachers suggest that statistical generalizations about activity and interaction in classrooms is seen as very relevant, and that the typologies of patterns of teacher and pupil behaviour to arise from cluster analysis have an immediate resonance with their own experience.

Such surveys may also be relevant to educational policy and to the initial and in-service training of teachers. Much prescriptive writing in these areas is heavily based on empirical assumptions about the nature and consequences of teaching practices. Two opposing examples of such prescription are the Plowden Report on primary education and the Black Papers which presented a highly critical view of the work of teachers in the 1960s.

Although prescriptive in content, the Plowden Report (DES, 1967) rests heavily on the assumption that child-centred teaching approaches, relying heavily on individualized methods and an integrated approach to curriculum content, were widely used in primary schools and were successful and generally unproblematic. The Black Papers (Cox and Dyson, 1969a and 1969b) made a similar assumption about the extent of this informal approach to teaching but claimed that, as a result, schools had abandoned the basic skills along with discipline and control. In fact, as a number of empirical studies showed (Barker-Lunn, 1970; Bealing, 1972; Bennett, 1976), only a small minority of schools were using informal approaches and the emphasis on basic skills and good order was overwhelming, at least in the primary school. A later study using systematic observation confirmed the extent of an emphasis on the basic skills, orderly classrooms and teacher control (Galton, Simon and Croll, 1980). This study also showed some of the difficulties which can accompany attempts to use the methods advocated by Plowden, in particular the way in which a highly individualized approach to teaching did not seem to lead to the stimulating and challenging pupil-teacher interactions which were assumed to be its consequence in the Plowden Report. It was also suggested that a formal/informal dimension or dichotomy did not accord with the reality of primary classrooms. These studies cannot take the place of educational judgments in determining policy and the appropriate preparation for teachers but they are highly relevant to such judgments. Both the Plowden Report and the Black Papers have had a good deal of impact on education. This impact has, at least in part, come about because of a belief that the assumptions they made about what was happening in schools were correct. Once their empirical base has been shown to be faulty the strength of their prescriptions is very much reduced.

Systematic Observation and Effective Teaching

The final area to be considered, where the results of systematic observation may be relevant to teachers and others concerned with education, is with regard to what such research can tell us about effective teaching. Many studies using systematic observation, especially in the United States, have compared teaching approaches with regard to their effectiveness or have tried to isolate elements of teacher behaviour or class organization which make for more effective teaching. The only large-scale study of this kind based on systematic observation in Britain is the ORACLE research.

Many of these studies have dealt with the relationship between teaching approaches and pupil achievement, principally as measured by standardized achievement tests. However, this is not the only aspect of teaching effectiveness which has been the subject of study. Researchers such as Kounin (1970) have looked at the relationship between teaching approaches and effective classroom management and control and the *One in* Five study (Croll and Moses, 1985) addresses the problems teachers have in effective classroom management with children with special educational needs. A major British study, *Fifteen Thousand Hours* (Rutter *et al*, 1979) incorporated systematic observation in a multi-method study of comprehensive schools which related school and classroom processes to a variety of academic and social/behavioural outcomes of schooling. Some of the results of the American research, in particular the effectiveness of 'direct instruction' which emerges from these studies, is summarized by Brophy (1979).

The methodological issues which arise in conducting and interpreting research on the relationship between teaching behaviour and pupil outcomes has already been discussed. What is also of interest is the relevance of this research for teachers and for others concerned with education. What should be the relationship between the statistical generalizations generated by research and the individual and particularistic decisions teachers must make about their work in the classroom?

It is clear that research cannot be used in a straightforward way to tell teachers how to teach. This is both because the results of such researches are virtually always expressed in probabalistic terms (X is associated with Y, rather than X always leads to Y and nothing else does) and also because social research cannot make definite predictions about future behaviour; the fact that no one has ever been able to teach successfully in a particular way does not mean that it is impossible so to do. Nevertheless, a responsible teacher will want to be familiar with the results of research before making decisions about appropriate methods of teaching. We will need very good reasons to embark on a course of action which has in the past proved ineffective. It is also relevant that teachers do not in fact make totally individual decisions about their work. Teaching approaches are strongly constrained by decisions made by headteachers and education authority officers and advisers and also, in practice, by their preparation in institutions of teacher education. It may be argued that research results are even more relevant to those responsible for preparing teachers and for controlling the contexts in which they work than to classroom teachers themselves, as these people are inevitably working in terms of the sorts of generalizations which are also the concern of research on teacher effectiveness.

Process-product studies based on systematic observation in classrooms can result in limited generalizations such as saying that generally speaking children with learning difficulties spend more time on their work in a particular type of setting while this effect is less strong for other children (Croll and Moses, 1985), or wider generalizations such as saying that children taught by teachers adopting certain teaching styles make more progress in the basic skills than children taught by teachers using other approaches (Galton and Croll, 1980). If possible, the research should also attempt to identify what it is about these styles that produced these results. Such research findings make it possible to relate effectiveness to identifiable acts on the part of teachers and pupils. They are much more relevant to teachers than research which shows that more (or less) experienced teachers get better results or that children from certain social backgrounds perform poorly.

These statistical generalizations are a way of making publicly available the collective experience of members of the teaching profession. It is helpful to know that a majority of people using method X get above average results while only a minority of those using method Y do. For individual teachers, heads and advisers this provides a context for decisions about their own practice. For researchers it may lead to a study of successful users of method Y and unsuccessful users of method X or some other elaboration of the process of data collection and analysis to provide empirical tests for ideas about what goes on in classrooms.

Some Concluding Remarks

Throughout this book there has been an attempt to locate systematic classroom observation within both an educational and a methodological context. The problems and issues which arise in the use of systematic classroom observation relate to the educational questions to which this particular methodology is applied but also provide instances of wider questions in the methodology of social enquiry.

A distinctive feature of systematic observation which has been emphasized here is the importance of exact and explicit definitions as the basis for descriptions of educational situations (and, by extension, other social settings). It has been argued that the value of such an emphasis includes clarity and scientific rigour and the fact that research employing such exact definitions is cumulative and replicable. It has also been suggested that this clarity and exactness is of particular value to teachers and other educationalists who wish to draw upon the results of educational research. They can engage with research results on the basis of an explicit awareness of how they were arrived at and can make an informed judgment as to their relevance and value.

Another major feature of systematic classroom observation is that results are reported in quantitative terms. This should not be confused with a belief that descriptions of educational situations can be reduced to averages or that measures of quantity are the same thing as measures of importance. As has been emphasized throughout, statistical analysis is as much concerned with variation and differences as with similarity and averages, and judgments about the educational significance of research results are constrained by the statistical findings but are not determined by them.

This book has attempted to consider the issues, problems and possibilities in the application of a particular methodology to educational questions. It is not intended to be prescriptive and researchers faced with particular research problems may well decide to ignore some of the advice contained here. What is important is that they should do so with a self-critical knowledge of the consequences and implications of decisions about research methods and research design.

Notes

1 Providing exact statistical values also provides a safeguard for the reader against the tendency of some researchers to insert an unargued interpretive framework into an account of results. Research reports sometimes include phrases like 'as many as 30 per cent' or 'only 30 per cent' when criteria for regarding such values as high or low have not been established. If figures are given, alert readers can form their own views on the appropriate interpretation. Where only verbal indications are given the researcher's judgment about what counts as 'infrequent' or 'usually' is inextricably bound up with the evidence which the reader is offered.

2 It should also be pointed out that Barrow's critique of the Lancaster study is based upon a misreading. The researchers did not force all of the teachers in their study into one of three clusters. On the basis of a very large sample of teachers, twelve clusters were identified. Two of these were combined to form the informal grouping, two were combined to form the formal grouping and three were combined to form the mixed grouping. The teachers in the process-product stage of the research each came from one of these seven clusters.

3 I am grateful to Geoff Whitty of Bristol Polytechnic for suggesting the relationship between professional development and professional literacy. I am not of course suggesting that a familiarity with the results of systematic observation is the whole, or even the most important, part of professional literacy, nor that it only involves a concern with empirical research.

Suggestions for Further Reading

BENNETT, S.N., ANDREAE, J., HEGARTY, P. and WADE, B. (1980) *Open Plan Schools*, Windsor, NFER for the Schools Council. An account of a research project studying open plan primary schools. Much of the information is based on systematic observation.

BOYDELL, D. (1978) *The Primary Teacher in Action*, London, Open Books. A useful review of research on primary education which draws upon a number of observational studies.

BURGESS, R.G. (1984) *In the Field: An Introduction to Field Research*, London, Allen and Unwin. An introductory text on field research which provides guidance on data collection and analysis for researchers using qualitative methods. Many of the examples are based on the author's research in schools.

BURGESS, R.G. (Ed) (1985) *Field Methods in the Study of Education*, Lewes, Falmer Press, and BURGESS, R.G. (Ed) (1984) *The Research Process in Educational Settings: Ten Case Studies*, Lewes, Falmer Press. These collections of articles are concerned with qualitative research methods but include discussions on securing access to classrooms and schools and ethical issues in observational research which are of general relevance.

CHANAN, G. and DELAMONT, S. (Eds) (1975) *Frontiers of Classroom Research*, Windsor, NFER. A collection of articles, mostly dealing with classroom observation and including reviews of the field as well as examples of research using systematic observations and also qualitative observational methods.

COHEN, L. (1976) *Educational Research in Classrooms and Schools*, London, Harper and Row. A collection of procedures for use in educational research, including examples of systematic observation schedules.

CROLL, P. and MOSES, D. (1985) *One in Five: The Assessment and Incidence of Special Educational Needs*, London, Routledge and Kegan Paul. A research study of children with special educational needs in junior classrooms. Part of the research is based on extensive observation of children and teachers in classrooms using systematic observation techniques.

DELAMONT, S. (1983) *Interaction in the Classroom*, (2nd edn), London,

Methuen. An introduction to the study of classroom interaction which deals mainly with qualitative techniques but includes discussion of systematic observation.

FLANDERS, N. (1970) *Analyzing Teaching Behaviour*, New York, Addison Wesley. An extensive discussion of the methodology and uses of the Flanders Interaction Analysis Categories (FIAC). As well as providing a clear account of how the system is used, the book also shows how this apparently very simple system can be used as the basis for complex and sophisticated analyses of classroom interaction.

GALTON, M. (1978) *British Mirrors*, Leicester, School of Education, University of Leicester. An anthology of observation instruments which have been developed for use in British classrooms.

GALTON, M. and SIMON, B. (Eds) (1980) *Progress and Performance in the Primary Classroom*, London, Routledge and Kegan Paul. One of a series of books based on the ORACLE research programme. This volume reports on a process-product study in which teacher styles are established by means of systematic classroom observation and the progress of children taught by the teachers using the different styles are compared.

GALTON, M., SIMON, B. and CROLL, P. (1980) *Inside the Primary Classroom*, London, Routledge and Kegan Paul. The first volume in the series dealing with the ORACLE research project, a major British study using systematic observation in primary classrooms. This book deals with the methodology of the project and provides a descriptive account of patterns of teacher and pupil behaviour and interactions.

GALTUNG, J. (1970) *Theory and Methods of Social Research*, London, Allen and Unwin. This is one of the best accounts of the methodology of quantitative social science but is more suitable at an advanced level than as a basic introduction. It does not deal explicitly with systematic observation but is of value to anyone concerned with quantitative research.

HAMMERSLEY, M. and ATKINSON, P. (1983) *Ethnography: Principles in Practice*, London, Tavistock. A good introduction to the methodology of ethnographic research.

HILSUM, S. and CANE, B. (1971) *The Teacher's Day*, Windsor, NFER. The report of a large-scale research project describing the work of primary school teachers by means of systematic observation in which observers accompanied teachers throughout the school day. Includes a valuable discussion of methodology as well as an account of the results of the study.

HILSUM, S. and STRONG, C. (1978) *The Secondary Teacher's Day*, Windsor, NFER. A parallel study to *The Teacher's Day* focussing on secondary school teachers.

HOPKINS, D. (1985) *A Teacher's Guide to Classroom Research*, Milton Keynes, Open University Press. The best of the introductory books for teachers on classroom research. Includes a brief but clear section on systematic observation.

KERRY, T. and WRAGG, E.C. (1979) *Classroom Interaction Research*, Nottingham, University of Nottingham School of Education.

Pamphlet-length discussion in the Rediguide series. A useful introduction to research on classroom interaction but too brief to really do justice to the many research possibilities raised.

KOUNIN, J. (1970) *Discipline and Group Management in Classrooms*, New York, Holt, Rinehart and Winston. A book based on a major research programme in the United States which uses systematic observation to analyze effective classroom management procedures.

MCALEESE, R. and HAMILTON, D. (Eds) (1978) *Understanding Classroom Life*, Windsor, NFER. A collection of papers dealing with different aspects of classroom observation. Includes the important article by MCINTYRE and MACLEOD which discusses some of the criticisms which have been made of systematic classroom observation.

POWELL, J.L. (1985) *The Teachers Craft*, Edinburgh, Scottish Council for Research in Education. A study of teaching methods in Scottish primary schools. The data are based on direct observation but the observations result in global ratings of aspects of the teachers' work made at five points in the day. This is a rather different approach to classroom observation to the one presented in the present volume.

RUNCIMAN, W.G. (1983) *A Treatise on Social Theory Vol. 1*, Cambridge, Cambridge University Press. A major study of the methodology of the social sciences. Particularly valuable for the discussion of the relationship between understanding social actors' meanings and reporting social events.

SELLTITZ, C. *et al* (1965) *Research Methods in Social Relations*, London, Methuen. One of the best introductory texts on social research. There is a fourth edition by KIDDER (1981).

SIMON, A. and BOYER, G. (1970) *Mirrors for Behaviour* (2 vols) and (1974), *Mirrors for Behaviour III*, Philadelphia, Research for Better Schools Inc. Massive anthology of classroom observation systems, mainly developed in the United States.

SOLOMON, D. and KENDALL, A. (1979) *Children in Classrooms: An Investigation of Person-Environment Interaction*, New York, Praeger. An account of an American research study using a process-product design in which the measures of classroom process are based on systematic observation.

WHELDALL, K. and MERRETT, F. (1984) *Positive Teaching: the Behavioural Approach*, London, Allen and Unwin. An introduction to the use of behaviour modification techniques in the classroom. Contains examples and suggestions for the use of simple systematic observation procedures which help to understand problem behaviour in classrooms and monitor attempts at intervention.

WRAGG, E.C. (Ed) (1984) *Classroom Teaching Skills*, Beckenham, Croom Helm. Reports on the Teacher Education Project, a major study of teaching skills based on direct observation of secondary school lessons which included extensive use of systematic observation procedures.

References

AITKEN, M., BENNETT, S. and HESKETH, J. (1981), 'Teaching styles and pupil progress: A reanalysis', *British Journal of Educational Psychology*, 51.

ALTMAN, J. (1974), 'Observational sampling of behaviour; Sampling methods'. *Behaviour*, 49.

ASHTON, P. (1983) 'IT-INSET: A cooperative, school-based approach to teacher education', *Primary Education Review*, 16.

ASHTON, P., KNEEN, P., DAVIES, F. and HOLLEY, B.J. (1975) *The Aims of Primary Education*, London, Macmillan Education for the Schools Council.

ATKINSON, P. (1975) 'In cold blood: Bedside teaching in a medical school', in CHANAN, G. and DELAMONT, S. (Eds) *Frontiers of Classroom Research*, Windsor, NFER.

ATKINSON, P. and DELAMONT, S. (1980) 'Effective teaching: A comment', *British Journal of Teacher Education*, 6, 3.

BARKER-LUNN, J. (1970) *Streaming in the Primary School*, Windsor, NFER.

BARROW, R. (1981) *The Philosophy of Schooling*, Brighton, Wheatsheaf.

BARROW, R. (1984) *Giving Teaching Back to Teachers*, Brighton, Wheatsheaf.

BEALING, D. (1972) 'The organization of junior school classrooms', *Educational Research*, 14, 2.

BEATTY, J. and WOOLNOUGH, B. (1982) 'Practical work in 11–13 science', *British Educational Research Journal*, 8, 1.

BENNETT, S.N. (1976) *Teaching Styles and Pupil Progress*, London, Open Books.

BENNETT, S.N. and JORDAN, J. (1975), 'A typology of teaching styles in primary schools', *British Journal of Educational Psychology*, 45.

BENNETT, N., O'HARE, E. and LEE, J. (1983) 'Mixed age classes in primary schools', *British Educational Research Journal*, 9, 1.

BOYDELL, D. (1974) 'Teacher-pupil contact in junior classrooms', *British Journal of Educational Psychology*, 44.

BOYDELL, D. (1975) 'Pupil behaviour in junior classrooms', *British Journal of Educational Psychology*, 45.

BROPHY, J. (1979) 'Teacher behaviour and its effects', *Journal of Educational Psychology*, 71, 6.

BROWN, G. (1975) 'Micro-teaching: Research and developments', in CHANAN, G. and DELAMONT, S. (Eds) *Frontiers of Classroom Research*, Windsor, NFER.

BRYMAN, A. (1984) 'The debate about quantitative and qualitative research: A question of method or epistemology?' *British Journal of Sociology*, 35, 1.

BURGESS, R.G. (1984a) *In the Field: An Introduction to Field Research*, London, Allen and Unwin.

BURGESS, R.G. (1984b) 'The whole truth? Some ethical problems in the study of a comprehensive school', in BURGESS, R.G. (Ed) *Field Methods in the Study of Education*, Lewes, Falmer Press.

BURGESS, R.G. (Ed) (1986) *Key Variables in Social Investigation*, London, Routledge and Kegan Paul.

CHILD, D. (1970) *The Essentials of Factor Analysis*, London, Holt, Rinehart and Winston.

CLARRICOTES, K. (1980) 'The importance of being Ernest ... Emma ... Tom ... Jane: The perception and categorization of gender, conformity and gender deviation in primary schools', in DEEM, R. (Ed) *Schooling for Women's Work*. London, Routledge and Kegan Paul.

COHEN, L. (1976) *Educational Research in Classrooms and Schools*, London, Harper and Row.

COHEN, L. and MANION, L. (1980) *Research Methods in Education*, London, Croom Helm.

COLLINS, H.M. (1974) 'The TEA set: Tacit knowledge and scientific networks', *Science Studies*, 4.

COOK, T. and CAMPBELL, D. (1979) *Quasi-Experimentation*, Chicago, Rand McNally.

COX, C.B. and DYSON, A.E. (Eds) (1969a) *Fight for Education: A Black Paper*, Critical Quarterly Society.

COX, C.B. and DYSON, A.E. (Eds) (1969b) *Black Paper Two: The Crisis in Education*. Critical Quarterly Society.

CROLL, P. (1981) 'Social class, pupil achievement and classroom interaction', in SIMON, B. and WILLCOCKS, J. (Eds) *Research and Practice in the Primary Classroom*, London, Routledge and Kegan Paul.

CROLL, P. (1983) 'Transfer and pupil performance' in GALTON, M. and WILLCOCKS, J. (Eds) *Moving from the Primary Classroom*, London, Routledge and Kegan Paul.

CROLL, P. (1984) 'Statistical inference in educational research', *Educational Research*, 26, 3.

CROLL, P. (1985) 'Teacher interactions with individual male and female pupils in junior-age classrooms', *Educational Research*, 27, 3.

CROLL, P. and MOSES, D. (1985) *One in Five: The Assessment and Incidence of Special Educational Needs*, London, Routledge and Kegan Paul.

CROLL, P. and WILLCOCKS, J. (1980) 'Pupil behaviour and progress', in GALTON, M. and SIMON, B. (Eds) *Progress and Performance in the Primary Classroom*, London, Routledge and Kegan Paul.

DELAMONT, S. (1976) 'Beyond Flanders Fields', in STUBBS, M. and DELAMONT, S. (Eds) *Explorations in Classroom Observation*, Chichester, Wiley.

DELAMONT, S. (1983) *Interaction in the Classroom* (2nd edn), London, Methuen.

DELAMONT, S. (1984) 'The old girl network', in BURGESS, R.G. (Ed) *The Research Process in Educational Settings: Ten Case Studies*, Lewes, Falmer Press.

DELAMONT, S. and HAMILTON, D. (1984) 'Revisiting classroom research: A continuing cautionary tale', in DELAMONT, S. (Ed) *Readings on Interaction in the Classroom*, London, Methuen.

DENZIN, N. (1978) *The Research Act* (2nd edn) London, McGraw Hill.

DEPARTMENT OF EDUCATION AND SCIENCE (1967) *Children and Their Primary Schools* (The Plowden Report), London, HMSO.

DUNKERTON, J. and GUY, J. (1981) 'The science teaching observation schedule: Is it quantitative? *European Journal of Science Education*, 3, 3.

EGAN, K. (1983) *Education and Psychology*, New York, Teachers College Press.

EGGLESTON, J. and GALTON, M. (1981) 'Reply to the article by J. DUNKERTON and J.J. GUY', *European Journal of Science Education*, 3, 3.

EGGLESTON, J., GALTON, M. and JONES, M. (1975a) 'A conceptual map for interaction studies', in CHANAN, G. and DELAMONT, S. (Eds) *Frontiers of Classroom Research*, Windsor, NFER.

EGGLESTON, J., GALTON, M. and JONES, M. (1975b) *A Science Teaching Observation Schedule*, London, Macmillan.

ELLIOTT, J. (1980) 'Implications of classroom research for professional development', in HOYLE, E. and MEGARRY, J. (Eds) *Professional Development of Teachers; World Year Book of Education*, London, Kogan Page.

ELLIOTT, J. (1983) 'Self-evaluation, professional development and accountability' in GALTON, M. and MOON, B. (Eds) *Changing Schools, Changing Curriculum*, London, Harper and Row.

EVERITT, B. (1974) *Cluster Analysis*, London, Heinemann.

FLANDERS, N. (1970) *Analyzing Teaching Behaviour*, New York, Addison-Wesley.

FRICK, T. and SEMMEL, M. (1978) 'Observer agreement and reliabilities of classroom observational measures', *Review of Educational Research*, 48, 1.

FURLONG, V. and EDWARDS, A. (1977) 'Language in classroom interaction: Theory and data', *Educational Research*, 19, 2.

GALTON, M. (1978) *British Mirrors*, Leicester, School of Education, University of Leicester.

GALTON, M. (1979) 'Systematic classroom observation: British research', *Educational Research*, 21, 2.

GALTON, M. and CROLL, P. (1980) 'Pupil progress in basic skills', in GALTON, M. and SIMON, B. (Eds) *Progress and Performance in the Primary Classroom*, London, Routledge and Kegan Paul.

GALTON, M. and SIMON, B. (1980) (Eds) *Progress and Performance in the Primary Classroom*, London, Routledge and Kegan Paul.

GALTON, M., SIMON, B. and CROLL, P. (1980) *Inside the Primary Classroom*, London, Routledge and Kegan Paul.

GALTON, M. and WILLCOCKS, J. (1982) (Eds) *Moving from the Primary*

Classroom, London, Routledge and Kegan Paul.

GALTUNG, J. (1970) *Theory and Methods of Social Research*, London, Allen and Unwin.

GIESON, P. and SIROTNIK, K. (1979) 'The Methodology of Classroom Observation in A Study of Schooling', Los Angeles, (ERIC Document Reproduction Service No. ED 214 875)

GRAY, J. and SATTERLY, D. (1976) 'A chapter of errors: Teaching styles and pupil progress in retrospect', *Educational Research*, 19, 1.

GRAY, J. and SATTERLY, D. (1981) 'Formal or informal? A reassessment of the British evidence', *British Journal of Educational Psychology*, 51.

HAMILTON, D. and DELAMONT, S. (1974) 'Classroom research: A cautionary tale?' *Research in Education*, 11.

HAMMERSLEY, M. (1985) 'From ethnography to theory: A programme and paradigm in the sociology of education', *Sociology*, 19, 2.

HAMMERSLEY, M. and ATKINSON, P. (1983) *Ethnography: Principles in Practice*, London, Tavistock.

HARROP, L. (1979a) 'An examination of observer bias in a classroom behaviour modification experiment', *Educational Studies*, 5, 2.

HARROP, L. (1979b) 'Unreliability of classroom observation', *Educational Research*, 21, 3.

HILSUM, S. and CANE, B. (1971) *The Teacher's Day*, Windsor, NFER.

HILSUM, S. and STRONG, C. (1978) *The Secondary Teacher's Day*, Windsor, NFER.

HOINVILLE, G. and JOWELL, R. (1978) *Survey Research Practice*, London, Heinemann Educational Books.

HOPKINS, D. (1985) *A Teacher's Guide to Classroom Research*, Milton Keynes, Open University Press.

JASMAN, A. (1980) 'Training observers in the use of systematic observation techniques', Appendix 1 of GALTON, M., SIMON, B. and CROLL, P. *Inside the Primary Classroom*, London, Routledge and Kegan Paul.

JONATHON, R. (1981) 'Empirical research and educational theory', in SIMON, B. and WILLCOCKS, J. (Eds) *Research and Practice in the Primary Classroom*, London, Routledge and Kegan Paul.

KELLY, A. (1985) 'Traditionalists and trendies: Teachers' attitudes to educational issues', *British Educational Research Journal*, 11, 2.

KERRY, T. and WRAGG, E. (1979) *Classroom Interaction Research*, Nottingham, University of Nottingham School of Education (Rediguide 14).

KIDDER, L. *et al* (1981) *Research Methods in Social Relations* (4th edn.) New York, Holt, Rinehart and Winston.

KING, R. (1984) 'The man in the wendy house: Researching infants' schools', in BURGESS, R.G. (Ed) *The Research Process in Educational Settings: Ten Case Studies*, Lewes, Falmer Press.

KOUNIN, J. (1970) *Discipline and Group Management in Classrooms*, New York, Holt, Rinehart and Winston.

LEA, J. (1978) 'Non-work related activity in primary classrooms', MEd dissertation, University of Leicester.

McINTYRE, D. (1980) 'Systematic observation of classroom activities', *Educational Analysis*, 2, 2.

McINTYRE, D. and MacLEOD, G. (1978) 'The characteristics and uses of systematic observation', in McAleese, R. and Hamilton, D. (Eds) *Understanding Classroom Life*, Windsor, NFER.

McQuitty, L. (1957) 'Elementary linkage analysis for isolating orthogonal and oblique types and typal relevancies', *Educational and Psychological Measurement*, 17.

Medley, D. *et al* (1973) 'The personal record of school experiences (PROSE)', in Boyer, E. *et al* (Eds) *Measures of Maturation*, Philadelphia, Research for Better Schools Inc.

Medley, D. and Mitzel, H. (1963) 'Measuring classroom behaviour by systematic observation', in Gage, N. (Ed) *Handbook of Research on Teaching*, Chicago, Rand-McNally.

Moses, D. (1982) 'Special educational needs: The relationship between teacher assessment, test scores and classroom behaviour', *British Educational Research Journal*, 8, 2.

Neill, S. (1985) 'Should systematic observers investigate participants' views?' *Research Intelligence*, 19.

Nie, N. *et al* (1975) *Statistical Package for the Social Sciences*, New York, McGraw Hill.

Nie, N.H. *et al* (1983) *SPSS-X User's Guide*, New York, McGraw Hill.

Open University (1976) *Personality and Learning*, Course E201, Milton Keynes, Open University Press.

Page, E. (1975) 'Statistically recapturing the richness within the classroom', *Psychology in the Schools*, 12.

Popper, K. (1963) *Conjectures and Refutations*, London, Routledge and Kegan Paul.

Poppleton, P. (1975) 'The classroom setting as a unit of analysis in observation studies', in Chanan, G. and Delamont, S. (Eds) *Frontiers of Classroom Research*, Windsor, NFER.

Powell, J. (1975) 'A Scottish alternative to interaction analysis', in Chanan, G. and Delamont, S. (Eds) *Frontiers of Classroom Research*, Windsor, NFER.

Powell, J. *et al* (1977) 'Taking a closer look: Time sampling and measurement error', *Journal of Applied Behaviour Analysis*, 10, 2.

Presland, J. (1976) 'Modifying behaviour NOW', *Special Education Forward Trends*, 3.

Rist, R. (1970) 'Student social class and teacher expectations: The self-fulfilling prophecy in ghetto education', *Harvard Educational Review*, 40, 3.

Rosenshine, B. (1970) 'Some criteria for evaluating category systems', in Gallagher, J. (Ed) *Classroom Observation*, Chicago, Rand-McNally.

Roth, J. (1966) 'Hired hand research', *The American Sociologist*, 1, 4.

Runciman, W.G. (1983) *A Treatise on Social Theory, Vol. 1*, Cambridge, Cambridge University Press.

Rutter, M. *et al* (1979) *Fifteen Thousand Hours: Secondary Schools and Their Effects on Children*, London, Open Books.

Ryans, D. (1960) *Characteristics of Teachers*, Washington D.C., American Council on Education.

Samph, T. (1976) 'Observer effects on teacher verbal classroom behaviour', in Bennett, N. and McNamara, D. (Eds) *Focus on Teaching*, London,

Longman.

SATTERLY, D. (1981) *Assessment in Schools*, Oxford, Basil Blackwell.

SCOTT, W. (1955) 'Reliability of content analysis: The case of nominal scale coding', *Public Opinion Quarterly*, 19.

SELLTITZ, C. et al (1965) *Research Methods in Social Relations*, London, Methuen.

SHARP, R. and GREEN, A. (1975) *Education and Social Control*, London, Routledge and Kegan Paul.

SHIPMAN, M. (1985) 'Ethnography and educational policy making', in BURGESS, R.G. (Ed) *Field Methods in the Study of Education*, Lewes, Falmer Press.

SIMON, A. and BOYER, G. (1970) *Mirrors for Behaviour, Vols I and II*, Philadelphia, Research for Better Schools, Inc.

SIMON, A. and BOYER, G. (1974) *Mirrors for Behaviour, Vol III*, Philadelphia, Research for Better Schools Inc.

SIMON, B. and WILLCOCKS, J. (Eds) (1981) *Research and Practice in the Primary Classroom*, London, Routledge and Kegan Paul.

SIROTNIK, K. (1983) 'What you see is what you get', *Harvard Educational Review*, 53, 1.

SOLOMON, D. and KENDALL, A. (1979) *Children in Classrooms: An Investigation of Person-Environment Interaction*, New York, Praeger.

SPENDER, D. (1981) 'Women and educational research', *Research Intelligence*, April.

STANWORTH, M. (1981) *Gender and Schooling: A Study of Sexual Divisions in the Classroom*, London, Women's Research and Resources Centre.

STENHOUSE, L. (1975) *An Introduction to Curriculum Research and Development*, London, Heinemann.

WALKER, R. and ADELMAN, C. (1976) 'Strawberries', in STUBBS, M. and DELAMONT, S. (Eds) *Explorations in Classroom Observation*, Chichester, Wiley.

WELLS, G. (1981) *Learning Through Interaction*, Cambridge, Cambridge University Press.

WHELDALL, K. et al (1981) 'Rows versus tables: An example of the use of behavioural ecology in two classes of eleven year old children', *Educational Psychology*, 1, 2.

WHELDALL, K. and MERRETT, F. (1984) *Positive Teaching: The Behavioural Approach*, London, Allen and Unwin.

WILLCOCKS, J. (1983) 'Pupils in transition', in GALTON, M. and WILLCOCKS, J. (Eds) *Moving from the Primary Classroom*, London, Routledge and Kegan Paul.

WILLIAMS, H. et al (1980) *Precision Teaching: A Classroom Manual*, Coventry, School Psychological Service.

WILSON, J. (1972) *Philosophy and Educational Research*, Windsor, NFER.

WILSON, J. (1979) *Fantasy and Commonsense in Education*, Oxford, Martin Robertson.

WINER, B. (1971) *Statistical Principles in Experimental Design*, London, McGraw Hill.

WISHART, D. (1969) *Clustan 1A: User Manual*, Fife, University of St Andrews Computing Laboratories.

WRAGG, E.C. (1970) 'Interaction analysis as a feedback system for student teachers', *Education for Teaching*, 81.

WRAGG, E.C. (1973) 'A study of student teachers in the classroom', in CHANAN, G. (Ed) *Towards a Science of Teaching*, Windsor, NFER.

WRAGG, E.C. (1974) *Teaching Teaching*, London, David and Charles.

WRAGG, E.C. (1984) *Classroom Teaching Skills*, Beckenham, Croom Helm.

Index

Index

BANK MERGERS & ACQUISITIONS

The New York University Salomon Center Series on Financial Markets and Institutions

Volume 3

BANK MERGERS
& ACQUISITIONS

Edited by

YAKOV AMIHUD

and

GEOFFREY MILLER

KLUWER ACADEMIC PUBLISHERS
BOSTON / DORDRECHT / LONDON

A C.I.P. Catalogue record for this book is available from the Library of Congress.

ISBN 0-7923-9975-7

Published by Kluwer Academic Publishers,
P.O. Box 17, 3300 AA Dordrecht, The Netherlands.

Sold and distributed in the U.S.A. and Canada
by Kluwer Academic Publishers,
101 Philip Drive, Norwell, MA 02061, U.S.A.

In all other countries, sold and distributed
by Kluwer Academic Publishers,
P.O. Box 332, 3300 AH Dordrecht, The Netherlands.

Printed on acid-free paper

Table of contents

Introduction

The financial services industry in the United States and around the world is undergoing a radical transformation. Rapidly evolving technological changes, coupled with the enactment of the Riegle-Neal Interstate Banking and Branching Efficiency Act of 1994, have revolutionized American banking and triggered a wave of mergers and consolidations of a scope not seen since the Great Depression. Hostile acquisitions, once nearly unheard of in the U.S. banking industry, are no longer uncommon; the Wells Fargo acquisition of First Interstate is only one of the more visible of a series of hostile or semi-hostile bids.

Financial Institution mergers are rapidly becoming a global phenomenon. Japan witnessed the mega-merger of the Bank of Tokyo and Mitsubishi Bank, and over the next few years, there will undoubtedly be a number of important mergers of distressed financial institutions in that country. North American banking markets have been liberalized under NAFTA and subsequent Mexican legislation. In Europe, it is only a matter of time before major banks conduct full scale operations throughout the European Union.

These mergers are also instigated by the globalization of the financial services industry. As the playing arena is now the world financial market rather than the more narrowly defined and historically protected national markets, financial institutions must achieve a critical size in order to compete. Mergers of nationally important institutions help them compete effectively with large foreign competitors, whose penetration into the domestic markets is facilitated by new technologies and relaxed regulations.

Technological innovations and developments have greatly improved the operational efficiency of the financial services industry. Electronic home banking, improvements in communications and data processing technology, and the enormous opportunities offered by the Internet, generate economies of scale and scope in relevant financial markets. This improves the production function in the industry and increases the span of control and scope of operation in these organizations.

While these changes have been most pronounced in the commercial banking industry, they also have a profound impact on other financial institutions –

insurance firms, investment banks, and institutional investors. The structure of
the whole financial services industry is being transformed.

The papers in this volume bring together leading researchers in economics,
finance and law and high level practitioners to discuss these important issues.
Presented during a conference on mergers of financial institutions sponsored
by the NYU Stern School of Business Salomon Center, in cooperation with the
NYU Law School Center for the Study of Central Banks, these papers deal
with such important topics as:

- Changing Economies of Scale and Scope in Banking and Other Financial
  Markets
- The Efficiency and Value Effects of Bank Mergers and Acquisitions
- The Antitrust Implications of Financial Institution Mergers
- The Effect of the Regulatory Changes on the Structure of the Banking
  Industry
- The Effects of Bank Mergers on Bank Safety and Soundness
- Implications of Recent Developments on the Global Competitiveness of
  U.S. Firms
- The Law and Economics of Hostile Acquisitions of Financial Institutions

Part One of the book provides a general and theoretical background to the
topic of bank mergers and acquisitions.

Frederic Mishkin, in his paper "Bank Consolidation: A Central Banker's
Perspective," looks at why bank consolidation has been taking place in the
United States and what the structure of the banking industry might look like in
the future. Mishkin points to a fundamental puzzle that, in a sense, defines
the theme of this volume: for many years – between the 1930s and the 1980s –
the number of commercial banks in the United States was remarkably stable,
fluctuating between 13,000 and less than 15,000; yet since 1985 the number of
banks has dropped precipitously. Mishkin observes that part of the
consolidation movement might be explained by poor profitability, but not all:
since 1992 banks have been highly profitable, but the merger trend has
continued. Mishkin attributes the most recent phase of consolidation, in
part, to the effect of geographic deregulation which has enabled banks to
expand their activities across state lines. Writing from the perspective of a
central banker, Mishkin takes a generally favorable view of the bank
merger trend, subject the caveat that regulators would properly become
concerned if competitive pressures caused banks to take undue risks with
depositor funds.

Roy Smith and Ingo Walter analyze the topic from an international
perspective. They present empirical evidence regarding mergers and
acquisitions in the global financial services industry. They examine the deal-
flow during the eleven year period from 1985-1995, and generate a global
typology of intra- and inter-sectoral merger and acquisition transactions
among and between banks, insurance companies and securities firms. The
authors identify financial services as one of the most active industries involved

in the global mergers and acquisitions deal-flow. They also identify the areas of greatest merger and acquisition intensity within the world financial services industry. They assess the motivations for financial services merger and acquisitions transactions in the context of changed regulatory and competitive factors and evolution in management objectives, emphasizing the pursuit of greater operating efficiencies, enhanced economies of scale and scope, and great market power which executives and boards of directors believe has led (or will lead) to increased shareholder value and competitive performance.

William Emmons and Stuart Greenbaum's paper looks to the future. Their contribution, "Twin Information Revolution and the Future of Financial Intermediation," identifies two information-related trends that have dramatically altered our perceptions of financial intermediation in recent years: (1) an ongoing paradigm shift in financial-economic theory and regulation that focuses on the role of financial intermediaries in overcoming informational problems in financial contracting and transactions as their primary source of value creation, and (2) a protracted series of technology shocks with order-of-magnitude effects on the costs of transmitting and processing information (which the authors refer to as "digital information"). The authors take a generally sanguine view of the future of financial intermediation, predicting that the needs of previously unserved or underserved clienteles will be better met as these twin revolutions continue.

Emmons and Greenbaum distinguish between two logically distinct types of financial intermediaries, namely, brokers and qualitative asset transformers. The former's activities are characterized, in their view, by a simple matching of buyers and sellers, taking little or no direct financial risk in the transaction. This type of intermediary uses relatively large amounts of digital information and relatively small amounts of physical or financial capital. The falling cost of digital information inputs is a significant windfall for this type of intermediary, whose activities are predicted to expand. The qualitative asset transformer, on the other hand, is characterized by direct financial participation in a transaction. This type of financial intermediary uses digital information less intensively to produce credible information, so windfall gains from cheaper digital information are less significant.

Part Two of the book considers the effect of bank mergers on efficiency and shareholder wealth.

One of the puzzles associated with bank mergers is the lack of empirical evidence on benefits to the merging parties. Steven Pilloff and Anthony Santomero point out that the unprecedented level of consolidation in the banking industry has been associated with a belief that gains can accrue through expense reduction, increased market power, reduced earnings volatility, and scale and scope economies. However, a review of the literature suggests that the value gains that are alleged have not been verified by empirical findings. Furthermore, the market seems to be unable to predict the success of individual mergers. The authors address alternative explanations which attempt to reconcile the data with continued merger activity, and find that these explanations are rationalizations for the non existence of positive value outcomes, not alternative, testable theories. A recent new approach to the study of this issue is to understand individual cases, looking into the process of change for a particular merger. The focus is on the managerial process and the specific cost structure and efficiency gains. This idiosyncratic approach may be necessary because there may be no wide patterns that can be applied to all bank mergers. Although this approach seems potentially rewarding and revealing, what we will learn is still an open question.

Alan Berger examines efficiency effects of bank mergers in the 1990s. The data suggest that bank mergers increase profit efficiency relative to other banks, but have little effect on cost efficiency. However, efficiency gains are concentrated in mergers of small banks; in mergers of large banks, the evidence on such gains is insiginificant. These results are consistent with the findings of efficiency gains in mergers of small banks, documented by Boyd and Graham in this part of the book.

Berger finds that efficiency gains in bank mergers are found to be unrelated to whether the acquiring bank is more efficient than the acquired bank, but they are much more pronounced when the participating banks are relatively inefficient ex ante. This is consistent with a hypothesis that mergers may "wake up" inefficient management or are used as an excuse to implement unpleasant restructuring. The data suggest that part of the efficiency gain results from improved diversification of risks, which may allow consolidated banks to shift their output mixes from securities toward consumer loans and business loans, raising expected revenues.

In their study on the effects of bank mergers on efficiency and risk, John Boyd and Stanley Graham focus on small banks. They find that in mergers of small banks, there are significant gains in cost efficiency and profitability. This result departs from those of earlier studies that found no efficiency gains in bank mergers. A reason for the difference in results is that the bulk of the mergers in the industry is among large banks, where economies of scale are unlikely to be generated. Regarding the effect on risk, the consolidation in the banking industry may soften the effect of a future downturn in the industry, because banking firms may become better diversified, both in terms of product lines and geographically. Yet, there is no evidence that, ceteris paribus, large banks are less likely to fail than are small banks. Still, the creation of large banks by mergers may induce the federal government to intervene because of the "too big to fail" policy. Such a policy may exacerbate the results of a bank crisis because it may induce large banks to take unreasonable risks. Another concern with bank mergers is that they substantially increase concentration in the banking industry, especially at the state and national levels. This has not yet had a large effect on competition in banking because it has not noticeably affected the level of actual bank markets (MSAs and countries). Yet, the trend in the data suggests a reason for concern.

Sandra Chamberlain studies the effect of bank ownership changes on subsidiary-level earnings. Her study investigates whether mergers result in improved profitability of 180 bank subsidiaries acquired between 1981 and 1987. Her findings do not support the hypothesis that bank mergers improve bottom-line net income. Although net interest margins widen, and premises and salaries expenses are reduced in the post merger period, these gains are offset by increases in *other non-interest expenses*. Other non-interest expenses are an amalgamation of expense items such as management fees, directors fees, and data processing charges. Though subsidiary level call reports do not yield sufficient detail to isolate the cause of these increases, the finding points to a potentially fruitful area of future research. If increases in other non-interest expenses can also be detected at the consolidated bank holding company level, 10-k reports can be used to pinpoint why these expenses increase. The change in bank ownership is also associated with increases in loan loss provisions and losses from sales of securities in the year the merger is consummated, raising the possibility that ownership changes lead to changes in subsidiary-level earnings management.

Chamberlain conducts a sensitivity analysis to examines whether merger effects are constant across sample selection criteria. A key finding is that when the 1980's mergers of Texas banks are eliminated from the sample, the remaining sample mergers result in improved profit performance of acquired subsidiaries. Merger effects are also found to be sensitive to the size of the acquired organization. Acquisitions between banks of similar sizes are more likely to result in improved performance, than those between large and small institutions. These combined findings suggest that the success of mergers are partially determined by local regulatory and business factors. The sensitivity analysis questions the advisability of lumping diverse sets of mergers into an assumed homogeneous sample.

The evidence in the studies presented in this section shows that while there are some real gains in bank mergers, they appear to take place in mergers between small banks. This raises the question of what motivates the megamergers in the banking industry. Evidence on the real economic gains produced by such mergers is quite inconclusive.

Part Three of the book addresses issues of competitiveness and regulation in connection with financial institution mergers.

Jonathan Macey and Geoffrey Miller's paper, "Bank Mergers and American Bank Competitiveness," argues that the bank merger wave of the 1990s is a natural economic extension of the bank failure wave of the 1980s. Many of the bank failures of the 1980s were caused by changing technology that lowered demand for the services traditionally offered by banks, and inefficient legal rules that prevented banks from offering new services. The same factors led to the bank merger wave of the 1990s, according to these authors. Thus, bank mergers of the 1990s should be viewed as a low-cost substitute for the bank failures of the previous decade. The authors argue that these mergers will not solve bank's core business problems. Instead, such problems should be addressed by changes to the laws related to lender liability and bankruptcy, and by repeal of the rules that currently impair banks# ability to enter high-growth areas such as corporate finance.

Anthony Nanni addresses the bank merger wave from the perspective of a government antitrust regulator. In "Consolidation in the Banking Industry: An Antitrust Perspective," he describes the process of antitrust scrutiny of proposed bank mergers, with particular reference to the process of inter-agency coordination that produced specialized bank merger screening guidelines in 1995. Addressing the technological changes that are revolutionizing the industry, Nanni concludes that no fundamental reform of the existing process of antitrust merger analysis is warranted: in his view, the analysis is sufficiently flexible and robust that it can readily account for any change in market dynamics that may occur in the industry.

John Coates's paper, "Reassessing Risk-Based Capital in the 1990s: Encouraging Consolidation and Productivity," looks at bank capital regulation in light of the bank merger trend. After reviewing the theory behind the risk-based capital rules, Coates observes that the rules may become binding constraints on U.S. banks as a result of market forces that are pressuring banks to take steps that result in lower risk-based capital ratios. The paper argues against past and likely future proposals to raise capital minimums on the ground that higher ratios would interfere with the healthy, ongoing consolidation in the industry. Addressing the rules themselves, Coates argues that they perversely encourage the most risky type of bank growth (product innovation) while discouraging the least risky type of bank growth (acquisitions that produce greater geographic diversification). The author calls for a re-evaluation of the way in which the risk based capital rules apply to acquisitions, with a view toward better discriminating between risk-increasing and risk-decreasing transactions.

The final paper in this volume, Gregory Udell's analysis of "The Consolidation of the Banking Industry and Small Business Lending," is certainly one of the most important from a public policy standpoint. Critics of bank mergers often claim that the massive, nationwide institutions that are predicted to result from the consolidation trend will be less responsive to the needs of small business than were the smaller institutions that they replaced. To what extent is this claim borne out by the empirical evidence? Udell synthesizes the theoretical arguments that provide economic content to this popular view, and then reviews the extant empirical literature which generally provides support for the contention that larger banks, and the merger of larger banks, are associated with lower allocation of bank assets to small business lending. However, Udell cautions that the empirical evidence also suggests that increased lending by other banks in the local market, as well as other factors, may likely offset reductions in small business lending by the consolidating institutions.

The papers in this volume provide a valuable compendium of current research and policy analysis that should be of interest to anyone interested in the dramatic and far-reaching trend of consolidation that is now occurring in the financial services industry.

Yakov Amihud
Geoffrey Miller
New York, 1997

List of contributors

Yakov Amihud is Professor of Finance and Yanaichi Faculty Fellow at the Stern Schhol of business, New York University and was on the Faculty of Management, tel Aviv University. Received the BA degree from the Hebrew University and the MSc and PhD degrees from New York University. Editor and coeditor of *Exchange Rates and Corporate Performance* (Irwin, 1994), *Leveraged Management Buyouts* (Dow Jones-Irwin, 1989), and *Market Making and the Changing Structure of the Securities Industry* (Lexington, 1985). Author of more than seventy scholarly articles on topics including the effect of ownership and control in corporations on corporate finance policies, firms' dynamic pricing policies and macroeconomic policies, the effects of liquidity and trading mechanisms on stock and bond prices, and models of market-making and dealership in security markets

Allen N. Berger is Senior Economist at the Board of Governors of the Federal Reserve System and Senior Fellow at the Wharton Financial Institutions Center. Mr. Berger is co-editor of the *Journal of Money, Credit, and Banking*, an editor of the *Journal of Productivity Analysis,* and serves as associate editor of the *Journal of Banking and Finance* and the *Journal of financial Services Research.* He also serves on the board of directors of the Financial Management Association. He has co-organized research conferences at the Board of Governors, the Wharton School, and the Atlanta Federal Reserve Bank, and is co-editor of special issues of the *Journal of Banking and Finance, Journal of Money, Credit, and Banking,* and *European Journal of Operational Research.* Mr. Berger has published about 50 professional economics and finance articles, including papers in the *Journal of Political Economy, American Economic Review, Journal of Monetary Economics, Journal of Business,* and *Brookings Papers on Economic Activity.* His research covers a variety of topics related to financial institutions, including efficiency and productivity growth; capital; credit rationing and credit crunches; small business lending; the effects of bank mergers and market structure; and the economics of collateral, off-balance sheet activities, securitization, nationwide banking, market value accounting, and the payments system. He received his Ph.D. in Economics from the University of California, Berkeley in 1983, and his B.A. in Economics from Northwestern University in 1976.

John. H. Boyd received his PhD from the University of Pennsylvania. He has taught at Northwestern University (Kellogg School of Management). He has served as Senior Research Officer in the Research Department of the Federal Reserve Bank of Minneapolis. Currently he is Kappel Chair in Business and Government at the Carlson School of Management, University of Minnesota. He has served or is serving as consultant to the Federal Reserve Bank of Minneapolis, the U.S. Treasury Department, the World Bank, and the FDIC. He has published in *American Economic Review, Journal of Economic Theory, Economic Theory, Review of Finance & Statistics, Journal of Finance*, and *Journal of Monetary Economics.*

Sandra L. Chamberlain is an assistant professor of accounting at Santa Clara University. She received her B S in finance from the University of California, Berkeley in 1981 and worked for three years in commercial banking. Upon receipt of her PhD from the University of Chicago in 1991 she began her career as an assistant professor in accounting at the Wharton School. Chamberlain's research focuses on accounting and organizational design decisions in the financial services sector. Recent work studies the shareholder wealth effects of SFAS 115; the size and significance of exchange rate exposure in U.S. and Japanese banking companies, and merger effects in the insurance industry.

John C. Coates is a partner at the New York law firm of Wachtell, Lipton, Rosen & Katz, specializing in financial institution merger and acquisitions, and is an adjunct professor at New York University School of Law.

Stanley L. Graham. Economist. Research Department. Federal Reserve Bank of Minneapolis.

William R. Emmons conducts research in the areas of bank competition and regulation at the Federal Reserve Bank of St. Louis. Mr. Emmons holds a PhD degree in Finance from the Kellogg Graduate School of Managment of Northwestern University. Prior to joining the St. Louis Fed, Mr. Emmons taught at the Amos Tuck School of Business Administration, Dartmouth College. He currently serves as an Adjunct Professor of Finance at the Olin School of Business, Washington University in St. Louis.

Stuart I. Greenbaum was appointed dean of the John M. Olin School of Business at Washington University In July 1995. Before joining the Olin School, Dean Greenbaum spent twenty years at the Kellogg Graduate School of Management at Northwestern University where he was the

Director of the Banking Research Center and the Norman Strunk
Distinguished Professor of Financial Institutions. From 1988-92, he served
as Kellogg's Associate Dean for Academic Affairs. Before Northwestern,
Dean Greenbaum served as Chairman of the Economics Department at the
University of Kentucky, and on the staffs of the Comptroller of the
Currency and the Federal Reserve. Dean Greenbaum has published two
books and more than 75 articles in academic journals and other professional
media. He is founding editor of the *Journal of Financial Intermediation* and
has served on the editorial boards of eight other academic journals.

Jonathan R. Macey is the J. DuPratt White Professor of Law and Director of
the John M. Olin Program in Law and Economics at Cornell Law School.
He specializes in corporate law, banking regulation, law and economics, and
the economics of regulation. Recently he has served as Reporter for the
American Bar Association's Committee on Corporate Laws' Model
Business Corporation Act Revision Project, President of the Association of
American Law Schools' Section on Financial Institutions and Consumer
Financial Services, a member of the Board of Arbitrators of the National
Association of Securities Dealers, and a Member of the Executive
Committee of the Association of American Law Schools' Section on
Corporate Law. Professor Macey is the coauthor of a major treatise,
Banking Law and Regulation, published by Little, Brown and Company and
now in its second edition, and the author of over 100 scholarly articles and
numerous editorials in such publications as the *Wall Street Journal* and the
Los Angeles Times. Professor Macey specializes in comparative corporation
law and international banking. He has taught these subjects at major
universities throughout the world, including the University of Tokyo
Faculty of Law; the University of Toronto Faculty of Law; and the
Stockholm School of Economics, Department of Law. In the fall of 1993,
Professor macey was a Fellow in Banking Law Studies at the International
Centre for Economic Research (ICER) in Turin, Italy. In May 1995,
Professor Macey was awarded the Paul M. Bator Award for Excellence in
Teaching, Scholarship and Public Service by the Federalist Society for Law
and Public Policy Studies at the University of Chicago Law School, and in
October 1996, he was awarded a Ph.D. in Law *honoris causa* from the
Stockholm School of Economics.

Geoffrey P. Miller is Professor of Law at New York University Law School
and Director of the Law School's Center for the Study of Central Banks. He
attended Columbia University Law School, where he was Editor-in-Chief of
the Law Review, served as a judicial clerk to Judge Carl McGowan of the
U.S. Court of Appeals for the District of Columbia Circuit and to Justice
Byron White of the United States Supreme Court, and worked as an
attorney in the United States Department of Justice Office of Legal Counsel
and at a private law firm before entering law teaching. Prior to joining NYU

in 1995, Millers was the Kirkland & Ellis Professor at the University of Chicago Law School, where he served as Associate Dean, Director of the Program in Law and Economics, and Editor of the *Journal of Legal Studies*. He is author of more than sixty scholarly articles in the fields of corporate law, banking law, legal ethics, separation of powers, civil procedure, and law and economics, and has published *Banking Law and Regulation* (2d ed., Aspen Law and Business 1997) (with Jonathan R. Macey).

Frederic S. Mishkin is currently an Executive Vice President and Director of Research at the Federal Reserve Bank of New York. He is on leave from the Graduate School of Business, Columbia University where he is the A. Barton Hepburn Professor of Economics. He is also a Research Associate at the National Bureau of Economic Research. Since receiving his Ph.D. from the Massachusetts Institute of Technology in 1976, he has taught at the University of Chicago, Northwestern University, Princeton University and Columbia. Professor Mishkin's research focuses on monetary policy and its impact on financial markets and the aggregate economy. He is the author of *A Rational Expectations Approach to Macroeconometrics: Testing Policy Ineffectiveness and Efficient Markets Models* (Chicago: University of Chicago Press, 1983), *Money, Interest Rates, and Inflation* (Edward Elgar: London 1993), *The Economics of Money, Banking and Financial Markets*, 4th Edition (New York: HarperCollins 1995), *Financial Markets, Institutions and Money* (New York: HarperCollins 1995) and has published extensively in professional journals. In addition, Professor Mishkin has served on the editorial board of the *American Economic Review* and has been an associate editor at the *Journal of Business and Economic Statistics*. He is currently the editor of the *Federal Reserve Bank* of *New York Economic Policy Review* and is an associate editor at the *Journal of Applied Econometrics*, the *Journal of International Money and Finance*, the *Journal of Money, Credit and Banking*, and the *Journal of Economic Perspectives*. He has been an academic consultant to the Board of Governors of the Federal Reserve System, on the Academic Advisory Panel of the Federal Reserve Bank of New York and a visiting scholar at the Ministry of Finance in Japan and the Reserve Bank of Australia.

Anthony V. Nanni is the Chief of the Litigation I Section, Antitrust Division, U.S. Department of Justice. He graduated from Rensselaer Polytechnic Institute with a Bachelor of Electrical Engineering degree. He received a Juris Doctorate degree from Fordham Law School in New York. Mr. Nanni has been with the Antitrust Division for over 20 years. He began his career as a trial attorney with the New York Field Office where he prosecuted both civil and criminal antitrust matters for two years. He then became a Special Assistant to the Director of Operations in Washington and subsequently the Assistant Chief of the Trial Section. He became Chief of the Trial Section in 1979 and subsequently Chief of the Litigation I

Section following a reorganization within the Antitrust Division. Mr. Nanni has supervised numerous complex criminal antitrust prosecutions, as well as major civil challenges to mergers and acquisitions under Section 7 of the Clayton Act. Until a recent restructuring within the Antitrust Division, his Section had been responsible for the review of each bank merger transaction that occurred over the past 21/2 years.

Steven J. Pilloff is an economist with Board of Governors of the Federal Reserve System. He conducts research on such topics as bank consolidation. multimarket contact, and market competition. He attended the Wharton School of Busineess where he received his Ph.D. in finance in 1995. His research has been published in the Journal of Money, Credit, and Banking.

Anthony M. Santomero is a leading authority on financial institution risk management and financial structure and a recognized consultant to major financial institutions and regulatory agencies throughout North America, Europe and the Far East. His studies into the effects of capital regulation have influenced the way regulators around the world control the industry, and his examination of risk management systems continues to pioneer new approaches and techniques in this area as well. As a consultant for leading financial institutions in the U.S. and abroad, Dr. Santomero has addressed issues of financial risk management procedures, the pricing of risk of various kinds and credit risk evaluation and management. He has advised the Federal Reserve Board of Governors, the FDIC and the General Accounting Office on a wide range of issues relating to capital regulation and structural reform. Internationally, he has been a consultant to the European Economic Community in Brussels, the Inter-American Development Bank, the Kingdom of Sweden, the Ministry of Finance of Japan, the Treasury of New Zealand, the Bank of Israel, the National Housing Bank of India, the Saudi Arabian Monetary Agency, and the Capital Markets Board of Turkey. In addition, he currently serves as a permanent Advisor to the Swedish Central bank. Dr. Santomero serves on the Board of Directors of the Compass Capital Funds Group, the Zweig Fund, and the Zweig Total Return Fund. He has also served as U.S. representative on the steering committee of the European Finance Association. Dr. Santomero is associate editor of seven academic journals, including the *Journal of Money, Credit and Banking, Journal of Financial Services Research* and *Journal of Banking and Finance*. He has written more than 85 articles and monographs on financial sector regulation and economic performance, including one of the first studies to analyze the behavior of banks in Japan. Dr. Santomero received his AB in economics from Fordham University in 1968, his Ph.D. in economics from Brown in 1971, and has recently received an honorary doctorate from the Stockholm School of Economics in 1992.

Roy C. Smith has been on the faculty of the Stern School of Business at New

York University since September 1987 as a professor of finance and international business. Prior to assuming this appointment he was a General Partner of Goldman, Sachs & Co. specializing in international investment banking and corporate finance. Upon his retirement from the firm to join the faculty, he was the senior international partner. During his career at Goldman Sachs he set up and supervised the firm's business in Japan and the Far East, headed business development activities in Europe and the Middle East and served as President of Goldman Sachs International Corp, while resident in the firm's London office from 1980 to 1984. Mr Smith received his B.S. degree from the U.S. Naval Academy in 1960, and his M.B.A. degree from Harvard University in 1966 after which he joined Goldman, Sachs & Co. He is a frequent guest lecturer at other business schools in the U.S. and in Europe. Mr. Smith's principal areas of research include international banking and finance, global capital market activity, mergers and acquisitions, leveraged transactions, foreign investments, and finance in emerging markets and Eastern Europe. In addition to various articles in professional journals and op-ed pieces, he is the author of *The Global Bankers*, E.P. Dutton, 1989, *The Money Wars*, E.P. Dutton, 1990 and *Comeback: The Restoration of American Banking Power in the New World Economy*, Harvard Business School Press, 1993. He is also co-author with Ingo Walter of *Investment Banking in Europe: Restructuring in the 1990s,* Basil Blackwell, 1989, *Global Financial Services*, Harper and Row, 1990, and *Global Banking*, Oxford University Press, 1996 (forthcoming). Mr. Smith is currently a Limited Partner of Goldman, Sachs & Co., a former Director of Harsco Corporation and Tootal plc, a U.K. Corporation, and a founding partner of Large, Smith & Walter, a European financial services consulting company. He is also a Director of the Atlantic Council of the United States and a member of the Internal Research Council of the Center for Strategic and International Studies, Washington, D.C.

Gregory F. Udell is the Director of the William R. Berkley Center for Entrepreneurial Studies and an Associate Professor of Finance at the Leonard N. Stern School of Business of New York University. He received his undergraduate degree in economics from DePauw University and both his MBA and his Ph.D degrees in finance from Indiana University. Professor Udell has published numerous articles on financing small and mid-sized firms, on financial contracting and on financial intermediation in such journals as the *Journal of Political Economy*, the *Journal of Monetary Economics*, the *Journal of Business, Journal of Banking and Finance*, the *Journal of Money, Credit and Banking*, the *Economic Journal*, and the *Journal of Financial Intermediation*. He was co-editor of a special 1991 issue of the *Journal of Banking and Finance* on deposit insurance reform and has written several articles on the 1990's bank credit crunch. He is also co-author (with L. Ritter and W. Silber) of *Principles of Money, Banking and*

Financial Markets, 9th edition (forthcoming). He is currently an associate editor of the *Journal of Banking and Finance* and an associate editor of the *Journal of Money, Credit and Banking*. Prior to starting his academic career Professor Udell was a commercial loan officer in Chicago during the 1970s. More recently Professor Udell has been a visiting economist and consultant to the Board of Governors of the Federal Reserve System. He is co-author of a comprehensive Federal Reserve Board study of the market for privately placed debt – the first such study in nearly 25 years. Professor Udell joined the faculty of New York University in 1983.

Ingo Walter is the Charles Simon Professor of Applied Financial Economics at the Stern School of Business, New York University, and also serves as Director of the New York University Salomon Center, an independent academic research institute founded in 1972 to focus on financial institutions, instruments and markets. He also holds a joint appointment as Swiss Bank Corporation Professor of International Management, INSEAD, Fontainebleau, France. Prof. Walter received his A.B. and M.S. degrees from Lehigh University and his Ph.D. degree in 1966 from New York University. He taught at the University of Missouri – St. Louis from 1965 to 1970 and has been on the faculty at New York University since 1970. From 1971 to 1979 he was Associate Dean for Academic Affairs and subsequently served a number of terms as Chairman of International Business and Chairman of Finance. His joint appointment with INSEAD dates from 1985. Dr. Walter's principal areas of academic and consulting activity include international trade policy, international banking, environmental economics, and economics of multinational corporate operations. He has published papers in various professional journals in these fields and is the author or editor of 25 books, the most recent of which is *Global Banking* co authored with Prof. Roy C. Smith (New York: Oxford University Press, 1997). A new book entitled *Street Smarts: Leadership, Professional Conduct and Shareholder Value in the Securities Industry* (also with Roy Smith) will be published in 1997 by Harvard Business School Press. At present, his interests focus on competitive structure, conduct and performance in the international banking and financial services industry, as well as international trade and investment issues. He has served as a consultant to various government agencies, international institutions, banks and corporations, and has held a number of board memberships.

PART ONE

FREDERIC S. MISHKIN

1. Bank consolidation:
A central banker's perspective

ABSTRACT

This paper looks at why bank consolidation has been taking place in the United States and what the structure of the banking industry might look like in the future. It then discusses the implications of bank consolidation for the economy and the challenge it poses for central bankers.

From the 1930s until the 1980s, the number of commercial banks in the United States was remarkably stable, with the number of banks between the 13,000 and 15,000 level. Yet as Figure 1 shows, beginning in the mid-1980s, the number of commercial banks began to fall dramatically. Why has this dramatic decline taken place?

1. THE DECLINE IN THE NUMBER OF BANKS: THE INITIAL PHASE

The first phase in the decline in the number of banks occurred when the banking industry hit some hard times in the 1980s and early 1990s. In the United States the importance of commercial banks as a source of funds to nonfinancial borrowers has shrunk dramatically. As we can see in Figure 2, in 1980 commercial banks provided 33% of these funds; yet by 1996, their market share was down to near 25%. Another way of viewing the declining role of banking in traditional financial intermediation is to look at the size of banks' balance-sheet assets relative to those of other financial intermediaries (Table

Presented at the Conference on Mergers of Financial Institutions, New York University Salomon Center, Leonard N. Stern School of Business, October 11, 1996. I thank Larry Radecki and Philip Strahan for their assistance and helpful comments. Any views expressed in this paper are those of the author only and not those of Columbia University, the National Bureau of Economic Research, New York University, the Federal Reserve Bank of New York or the Federal Reserve System.

3

Y. Amihud and G. Miller (eds.), Bank Mergers & Acquisitions, 3–19
© 1998 Kluwer Academic Publishers. Printed in the Netherlands.

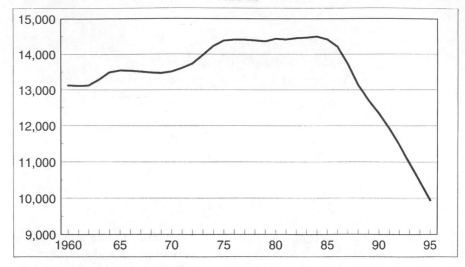

Figure 1–1. Number of Commercial Banks in the U.S.
Source: Federal Deposit Insurance Corporation, Statistics on Banking.
Note: Number of insured commercial banks and trust companies in the U.S. or its Territories and Possessions.

1). Commercial banks' share of total financial intermediary assets has fallen from around the 40% range in the 1960-80 period to below 30% by the beginning of 1996.

Clearly, the traditional financial intermediation role of banking, in which banks make loans that are funded with deposits, is no longer as important in our financial system. The reason for the decline in the traditional financial intermediation role of banking is that fundamental economic forces have been producing financial innovations which have been eroding the profitability of traditional banking activities. Financial innovations have caused banks to suffer declines in their cost advantages in acquiring funds, that is, on the liabilities side of their balance sheet, and have also caused banks to lose income advantages on the assets side of their balance sheet.

Decline in Cost Advantages in Acquiring Funds

Until 1980, banks were subject to deposit rate ceilings that restricted them from paying any interest on checkable deposits and (under Regulation Q) limited them to paying a maximum interest rate of a little over 5% on time deposits. Until the 1960s, these restrictions worked to the banks' advantage because their major source of funds was checkable deposits (over 60%) and the zero interest cost on these deposits meant that the banks had a very low cost of funds. Unfortunately, this cost advantage for banks did not last. The rise in inflation from the late 1960s on led to higher interest rates, which made

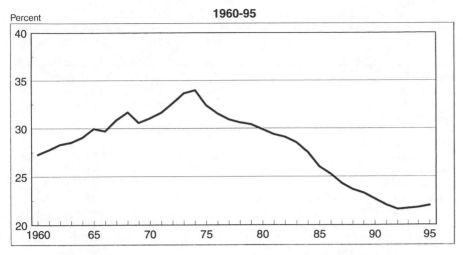

Percent   **1960-95**

Figure 1–2. Commercial Banks' Share of Total Nonfinancial Borrowing
Source: Board of Governors of the Federal Reserve System, Flow of Funds Accounts.
Note: The share is the ratio of the total credit market assets held by U.S. Commercial Banks to total credit market debt owed by domestic nonfinancial sectors.

investors more sensitive to yield differentials on different assets. The result was a process of disintermediation in which households and businesses began to take their money out of banks, with their low interest rates on both checkable and time deposits, and began to seek out higher-yielding investments.

At the same time, attempts to get around deposit rate ceilings and reserve requirements led to the financial innovation of money market mutual funds, which put the banks at an even further disadvantage because depositors could now obtain a high-yielding substitute for a savings account. One manifestation of these changes in the financial system was that the low-cost source of funds, checkable deposits, declined dramatically in importance for banks, falling from over 60% of bank liabilities to around 20% today.

The growing difficulty for banks in raising funds led to their supporting legislation in the 1980s that eliminated Regulation Q ceilings on time deposit interest rates and allowed checkable deposits like NOW accounts that paid interest. Although these changes in regulation helped make banks more competitive in their quest for funds, it also meant that their cost of acquiring funds had risen substantially, thereby reducing their earlier cost advantage over other financial institutions.

Decline in Income Advantages on Uses of Funds

The loss of cost advantages on the liabilities side of the balance sheet for American banks was one reason that they became less competitive, but they were also hit by a decline in income advantages on the assets side from

Table 1–1. Relative Shares of Total Financial Intermediary Assets 1960-95

	1960	1970	1980	1990	1995
			(Percent)		
Insurance companies					
Life insurance	19.2	14.9	11.4	12.4	12.8
Other insurance	4.4	3.8	4.5	4.8	4.6
Pension funds					
Private	6.8	9.2	12.4	14.6	16.2
Public (state and local					
government)	3.3	4.5	4.8	7.4	8.5
Finance companies	4.8	5.3	5.4	6.0	5.3
Mutual funds					
Stock and bond	3.9	3.9	1.7	6.0	12.1
Money market	0.0	0.0	1.9	4.5	4.6
Depository institutions (banks)					
Commercial banks	38.0	38.4	36.5	30.2	27.7
Savings and loans and					
mutual savings	18.6	18.8	19.5	12.3	6.3
Credit unions	1.0	1.3	1.7	2.0	1.9
Total	100	100	100	100	100

Source: Board of Governors of the Federal Reserve System, Flow of Funds Accounts.
Note: The share is the percentage of the intermediary's total financial assets relative to the sum of total financial assets for all categories listed. The percentages do not add to 100 due to rounding.

financial innovations such as junk bonds and securitization and the rise of the commercial paper market.

Improvements in information technology have made it easier for firms to issue securities directly to the public. This has meant that instead of going to banks to finance short-term credit needs, many of the banks' best business customers now find it cheaper to go to the commercial paper market for funds instead. The loss of this competitive advantage for banks is evident in the fact that before 1970, the amount of nonfinancial commercial paper was less than 5% of commercial and industrial bank loans, whereas this percentage has grown to over 20% today.

In addition, this growth in the commercial paper market has allowed finance companies, which depend primarily on commercial paper to acquire funds, to expand their operations at the expense of banks. Finance companies, which lend to many of the same businesses that borrow from banks, have increased their market share relative to banks: before 1980 finance company loans to business were around 30% of commercial and industrial loans, whereas currently they account for over 60%.

The rise of the junk bond market has also eaten into banks' loan business. Improvements in information technology have made it easier for corporations to sell their bonds to the public directly, thereby bypassing banks. Although

Fortune 500 companies started taking this route in the 1970s, now lower-quality corporate borrowers are using banks less often because they have access to the junk bond market.

Improvements in computer technology are another source of banks' loss of income advantages in the use of their funds. Low cost computers have promoted securitization, whereby illiquid financial assets such as bank loans or mortgages can be bundled together cheaply and transformed into marketable securities where their interest and principal payments can be passed through to third parties. Computers also have enabled other financial institutions to originate loans because they can now accurately evaluate credit risk with statistical methods. As a result, banks no longer have the same advantage in making loans when default risk can be easily evaluated with computers. Without their former advantages, banks have lost loan business to other financial institutions even though the banks themselves are involved in the process of securitization.

The Impact of the Decline in the Profitability of Traditional Banking

The decline in cost advantages in acquiring funds and income advantages on the uses of funds was one source of the decline from 1980 to 1992 in bank profitability, both in terms of return on assets and return on equity, that we see in Figure 3. In any industry a decline in profitability usually results in exit from

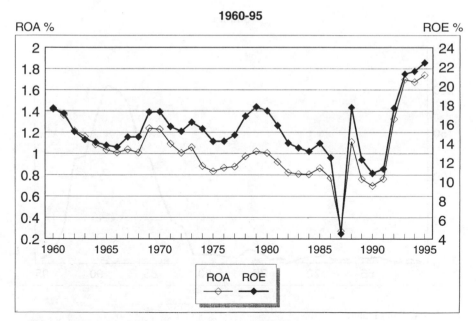

Figure 1–3. Return on Assets and Equity for Commercial Banks
Source: Federal Deposit Insurance Corporation, Statistics on Banking.

the industry (often by business failures) and a shrinkage of market share. This is exactly what occurred in the banking industry: as we have seen in Figure 1 and Table 1 market share declined precipitously, while bank failures were running at a rate of over one hundred per year in the 1985-1992 period (Figure 4). Bank failures are part of the story explaining the decline in the number of commercial banks, but are by no means the whole story. From 1985 to 1992, when bank failures were running at a high rate, the number of banks declined by about 3,000 while the number of failures added up to around 1,300, less than half of the decline.

Another explanation of the decline in the number of banks is that in an attempt to survive and maintain adequate profit levels, banks needed to develop more cost-effective structures to deliver their services. Bank consolidation is a natural way of achieving gains in efficiency and it provides an explanation for the additional decline in the number of banks in the 1985-92 period.

Banks also could attempt to maintain their profitability by expanding into new, riskier, areas of lending. For example, U.S. banks increased their risk-taking by placing a greater percentage of their total funds in commercial real estate loans, traditionally a riskier type of loan. In addition, they increased lending for corporate takeovers and leveraged buyouts, which are highly-leveraged transactions loans. The decline in the profitability of banks' traditional business may thus have helped lead to the large loan losses in the

1960-95

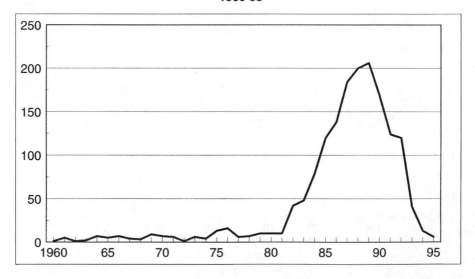

Figure 1–4. Bank Failures
Sources: Federal Deposit Insurance Corporation, 1994 Annual Report, and Quarterly Banking Profile.
Note: Number of failed FDIC-insured and Bank Insurance Fund-Member Depository Institutions.

late 1980s and early 1990s, which were an important source of the decline in bank profits (Figure 3) and bank failures (Figure 4).[1]

An alternative way banks sought to maintain former profit levels is to pursue new, off-balance sheet, activities that are more profitable. As we see in Figure 5, U.S. commercial banks did begin this process starting in the early 1980's, nearly doubling the share of their income coming from off-balance sheet, noninterest-income, activities by the 1990s.[2] If profitability in these new activities required larger banking units, this would have been a further impetus to bank consolidation in this period.

2. THE DECLINE IN THE NUMBER OF BANKS: THE NEXT PHASE

The next phase in bank consolidation cannot be explained by poor profitability. As we can see in Figure 2, since 1992 the banking industry has returned to health, with record profits being reported. Yet in the period from 1992 to 1996, despite the turnaround, the number of commercial banks declined by a little over 1,500; of these, less than 200 were bank failures (less than 15 percent of the decline) and most failures were of small banks.

The continued need for more cost-effective distribution networks and banks' new nontraditional activities have maintained the incentive for banks to form larger units, through both mergers of banks held by the same holding company and through mergers of the holding companies themselves. This

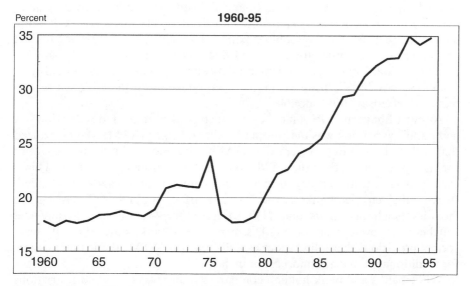

Figure 1–5. Share of Noninterest Income in Total Income for Commercial Banks
Source: Federal Deposit Insurance Corporation, Statistics in Banking.
Note: The share is the ratio of total noninterested income to the sum of net interest income and total noninterest income.

process has been stimulated by deregulation of restrictions on both interstate banking as well as deregulation of within-state branching.

As of the middle of the 1970s, banks faced limits on geographic expansion. The McFadden Act of 1927 prohibited national banks from branching across state lines, while the Douglas Amendment to the 1956 Bank Holding Company Act prevented bank holding companies from acquiring out-of-state banks unless the target bank's state explicitly allowed such acquisitions by statute. Since none did as of the mid-70s, bank holding companies were effectively prohibited from operating across state lines. Similarly, about two-thirds of the states had laws that limited or prohibited branch banking.[3] Most of these states, however, permitted bank holding companies to own a controlling interest in several banks even if intrastate branching was not permitted. Thus, even if banks could only operate in one city or county, bank holding companies could still reap the risk-reducing benefits of diversification and cost-reducing benefits of scale economies by owning banks throughout a state.

Two important developments enhanced bank holding companies' ability to expand geographically. First, the Garn, St Germain Act of 1982 amended the Bank Holding Company Act to permit bank holding companies to purchase failing out-of-state banks. As a consequence, bank holding companies headquartered in New York, Ohio, North Carolina, Michigan and California gained entry into the Texas market by purchasing failing institutions. The result was that some bank holding companies were able to operate across state lines.

Second, bank holding companies began avoiding interstate banking and branching restrictions by exploiting a provision of the Bank Holding Company Act which defined a bank as a financial institution that accepts demand deposits *and* makes commercial and industrial (C&I) loans. Bank holding companies realized that they could expand across state lines by opening limited service banks that either took demand deposits but made no C&I loans, or made C&I loans but took no demand deposits. The Competitive Equality in Banking Act of 1987, however, placed a moratorium on these limited service banks, thus closing this loophole.

Another financial development that helped banks get around restrictions on geographic expansion was the automatic teller machine (ATM). Banks realized that if they did not own or rent the ATM but instead paid a fee to the owner for each transaction, then the ATM would not be considered a branch. This is exactly what the regulatory agencies and courts in most states concluded. Because they enabled banks to widen their markets, a number of these shared facilities (such as Cirrus and NYCE) have been established nationwide. Furthermore, even when an ATM is owned by a bank, states typically have special provisions that allow wider establishment of ATMs than is permissible for traditional "brick and mortar" branches.

While banks and bank holding companies found ways to avoid restrictions on expansion across state lines, some were still unable to achieve their aims. Many banking companies, particularly large, expansion-minded bank holding companies, therefore argued that these restrictions ought to be dismantled.

While some banks – mainly the smaller ones – benefitted from these restrictions, their resistance to deregulation began to weaken as it became increasingly clear that bank holding companies were finding ways to get around the laws.[4] Moreover, the banking industry as a whole began to face increasing competitive pressures from nonbank financial companies not subject to geographical restrictions. In some states, for example, thrifts were permitted to branch while banks were not.

The views of other interested parties, such as businesses relying on local banks for credit and households relying on local banks for transaction services, also played a role in shaping the political forces leading to deregulation. For instance, middle-market and large borrowers may have pushed for deregulation as a way to encourage the expansion of large banks, who were more able to provide the wide array of services demanded by larger firms. On the other hand, small firms, traditionally served by small banks, may have had less at stake in the deregulation debate.

As a result of these pressures, states began to relax their restrictions on branching. Typically, a state would first permit its banks to branch statewide only by purchasing existing banks or their branches. In this way the incumbent banks, potentially threatened by increased competition, could at least sell out to the new entrants. Only later did most states permit *de novo* branching statewide.

The particular factors leading to branching deregulation differed across states. For instance, the Pennsylvania legislature faced lobbying pressure from large bank holding companies such as Mellon Bancorp, which argued that "they needed powers to meet challenges from national financial institutions and to bolster themselves to compete in an anticipated era of interstate banking."[5] In six states the relaxation of branching restrictions was initiated by a national bank regulator, the Office of the Comptroller of the Currency (OCC). Based on a provision of the National Bank Act of 1864, the OCC ruled that national banks could branch to the same extent as thrifts.[6] After the OCC ruling was upheld by the courts, state-chartered banks asked for and won similar rights. By the early 1990s, almost all states permitted relatively unrestricted statewide branching.

The process of interstate banking deregulation followed a similar pattern. In 1975 Maine enacted the first interstate banking legislation which allowed out-of-state bank holding companies to purchase Maine banks. Again, by forcing out-of-state bank holding companies to buy their way into the market, incumbent banks in Maine could reap the benefits of selling out to the highest bidder. In 1982, Massachusetts enacted a regional compact with other New England states to allow interstate banking. Some states relaxed restrictions on interstate banking to encourage economic activity. South Dakota, for instance, permitted out-of-state bank holding companies to set up two limited-service *de novo* banks to encourage entry by credit card banks. During the middle of the 1980s, many other regional compacts were adopted until, by the early 1990s, almost all states allowed some form of interstate banking.

While similar forces that led states to deregulate branching also led them to deregulate interstate banking restrictions, increased financial distress experienced by the banking industry in the 1980s probably provided further motivation. Proponents of interstate banking would be supported by nonbank business interests that feared that they would be harmed by weak or failing local banks. Moreover, by entering an interstate banking arrangement, a state could increase the potential number of bank holding companies which could acquire its weak or failing banks, thereby reducing the cost of recapitalizing its banking system.[7]

With barriers to interstate banking and branching breaking down in the 1980s, banks and bank holding companies recognized that they could gain the benefits of diversification because they would now be able to make loans in many states rather than just one. This gave them the advantage that if one state's economy was weak, another in which they operated might be strong, thus decreasing the likelihood that loans in different states would default at the same time. In addition, allowing bank holding companies to own banks in multiple states meant that they could take advantage of economies of scale, both by increasing their size through out-of-state acquisitions and by merging the banks operating in the same state into a single bank with many branches. Another result of the loosening of restrictions on interstate banking is the development of a new class of institutions, the so-called *superregionals* such as Nationsbank and BancOne, which are bank holding companies that have begun to rival the money centers in size but whose headquarters are not in one of the money center cities (New York, Chicago and San Francisco).

Banking consolidation has been given further stimulus by the passage of the 1994 Riegle-Neal Interstate Banking and Branching Efficiency Act (IBBEA). This law expands the regional compacts to the entire nation, thereby overturning the McFadden Act and the Douglas Amendment to the Bank Holding Company Act. Moreover, IBBEA allows interstate *branching* by allowing bank holding companies to merge banks they own in separate states into a single bank with branches in different states beginning June 1, 1997. States do have the option of allowing interstate branching to occur earlier than this date, and several have done so, while they may also opt out of interstate branching, a choice only Texas has made.

3. What will the structure of the U.S. banking industry look like in the future?

With true nationwide banking becoming a reality, the benefits of bank con-solidation for the banking industry have increased substantially, thus driving the next phase of mergers and acquisitions and accelerating the decline in the number of commercial banks. Great changes are occurring in the structure of this industry and the natural question arises: What will the industry look like in say ten years or so?

One view is that the industry will consolidate to only a couple of hundred commercial banks. A more extreme view is that industry will look like that of Canada or the United Kingdom with a few large banks dominating the industry. Research on this question, however, comes up with a different answer. The structure of the U.S. banking industry will still be unique, but not as unique as it once was. Most experts see the bank consolidation surge as settling down with the U.S. banking industry having several thousand, rather than several hundred banks. One simple way of seeing why the number of banks will continue to be substantial is to recognize that California, which has unrestricted branching throughout the state, has close to 400 commercial banks. Blowing up the number of banks by the share of banking assets in California relative to the whole country, produces an estimate of the number of banks with unrestricted nationwide branching on the order of 4,000. More sophisticated research suggests that the number of banks in the U.S. will probably be somewhat smaller than this, but not by much.[8]

Banking consolidation will not only result in a smaller number of banks, but as the recent merger between Chase Manhattan Bank and Chemical Bank suggests, a shift in assets from smaller banks to larger banks as well. Within ten years, the share of bank assets in banks with less than $100 million in assets is expected to halve, while the amount at the so-called megabanks, those with over $100 billion in assets, is expected to more than double.[9]

Important developments in the banking industry that will affect the course of consolidation are the major changes that are occurring in retail distribution networks as a result of the ability to provide low-cost remote delivery of banking services using modern computer technology. The largest retail banks are restructuring by developing electronic channels to deliver retail banking services to the household sector, such as phone centers, and home banking using PCs, and ATMs. Bank of America, for example, has indicated that in 1995 it conducted twice as many ATM transactions with its customer base than it did with face-to-face transactions at its branches.[10] Banks are also using technology to develop new designs for branch offices, such as supermarket (or in-store) branches and one-stop financial centers.

The effect of these developments on bank consolidation cuts both ways. Some of them yield cost advantages to larger banks and therefore will further encourage bank consolidation. For example, since there are a very limited number of large supermarket chains in any state or metropolitan area (usually two or three) and alliances are typically exclusive, small banks may not be able to develop supermarket branches. Indeed, so far, supermarket branches have been set up between the largest players, both supermarkets and banks, in a geographic area.

On the other hand, over time banks have been switching to electronic, shared distribution channels which provide opportunities for small banking institutions. In operation now are national and regional ATM networks and credit card networks organized by Visa and MasterCard. It is likely that home banking will not only be available from individual banks, but also from software firms, regional ATM networks, national credit card associations like Visa and MasterCard and consortiums of banks. As in the case of ATM networks, these electronic distribution channels will not be owned and operated by individual banks but by combination of banks or third parties. The growing use of shared distribution networks thus means that economies of scale may be available to small banks, and this decrease the incentives for bank consolidation.

New branch designs and electronic delivery channels therefore introduce considerable uncertainty into projections of consolidation trends in the banking industry. Econometric studies of the economies of scale and scope use data from an era when banks had an extensive network of traditional branch offices and most transactions were conducted face-to-face with branch personnel. If in the future banks shed many of their branches for electronic delivery systems or switch to a new low-cost type of branch offices, the findings of these studies may not give reliable indications of economies of scale in banking, from which we infer the minimum size needed for a bank to be viable, the number of banks that will be in operation, and the concentration of assets among the largest. Furthermore, currently it is hard to predict which new technologies in financial services will be cost effective for banks and widely accepted by the public. Banks are exploring many different new ideas, and which will come to dominate the industry is far from clear.

Thus the brave new world of retail banking that is currently under development makes predicting how much bank consolidation will take place in the United States in the future highly speculative. What does seem clear, however, is that the number of banks twenty years from now is likely to be less than half the quantity today, but is also likely to be substantially greater than the couple of hundred found in some countries.

4. Is bank consolidation and nationwide banking a good thing?

Advocates of nationwide banking believe that it will produce more efficient banks and a healthier banking system less prone to bank failures. However, critics of bank consolidation and nationwide banking fear that it will eliminate small (community) banks and that this will result in less lending to small businesses. In addition, they worry that a few banks will come to dominate the industry, making the banking business less competitive.

I am skeptical of the above criticisms of bank consolidation. As we have seen above, research indicates that even after bank consolidation is completed, the U.S. will still have plenty of banks. Furthermore, megabanks will not dominate the banking industry. Research such as that by Berger et al (1995) suggest that there will be more than ten banks with assets over $100 billion, and their share of bank assets will be less than 50%. The banking industry will thus remain highly competitive, probably even more so than now since banks which have been protected from competition from out-of-state banks will now have to compete vigorously with out-of-state banks to stay in business.

It also does not look as though community banks will disappear. When New York State liberalized branching laws in 1962, there were fears that community banks upstate would be driven from the market by the big New York City banks. Not only did this not happen, but some of the big boys found that the small banks were able to run rings around them in their local markets. Similarly, California, which has had unrestricted statewide branching for a long time, continues to have a vibrant set of community banks. Community banks are likely to remain viable because they serve a niche in the market which larger banks cannot fill: some segments of the public are willing to pay more for dealing with a small local institution that has a personal touch with the customer, and, furthermore, community banks may have better information about small businesses which gives them inherent advantages in small business lending.

As an economist, it is hard not to see some important benefits of bank consolidation and nationwide banking. The elimination of geographic restrictions on banking will increase competition and drive inefficient banks out of business, thus raising the efficiency of the banking sector. The move to larger banking organizations also means that there will be some increase in efficiency because of economies of scale. Indeed, some of the new distribution networks mentioned in the previous section may be particularly efficient if they are spread nationwide, and the elimination of geographic restrictions will allow banks to take full advantage of these new technologies.

Even more important from the perspective of a central banker who has to worry about banking and financial crises, the increased diversification of banks' loan portfolios may lower the probability of a banking crisis in the future. One of the recent features in the banking crisis in the United States was that bank failures were often concentrated in states with weak economies. For example, after the decline in oil prices in 1986, all the major commercial banks in Texas, which had been very profitable, found themselves in trouble. At that time, banks in New England were doing fine. However, when the 1990-91 recession hit New England very hard, it was the turn of the New England banks to start failing. With nationwide banking, a bank could make loans in both New England and Texas, and would thus be less likely to fail because when the loans were going sour in one location, they would likely be doing well in the other. Thus nationwide banking is a major step toward creating a healthier banking system that is less prone to banking crises.

One potential negative to bank consolidation is that it might lead to a reduction in bank lending to small businesses because of the reduction in assets at small banks. Small banks specialize in small business lending because restrictions on the fraction of their capital that can be lent to any one borrower necessarily mean that they cannot make large loans, which is what is often required by big businesses. The fear is that an acquisition of a small bank by a larger bank will result in a decline in lending to small businesses because the large bank will pay less attention to this kind of lending. Because small businesses may be particularly dependent on bank lending to finance their activities, the reduction in small business lending to banks could hurt the efficiency of the economy.[11]

The evidence on whether bank consolidation will lead to a reduction in small business lending is however quite mixed. The fact that large banks have a smaller fraction of their business devoted to small business lending does not mean that when they acquire smaller banks they will reduce this lending if it is profitable. Some research finds that small bank lending is unlikely to be reduced as a result of bank consolidation while other research comes to the opposite conclusion.[12] However, even researchers who point out that bank lending to small business might decline are not sure that this would reduce economic efficiency. The restrictions on competition in the past which helped many small banks stay in business may have produced more small business lending than is socially optimal. The implicit subsidy to small banks from the restrictions on competition might have been passed onto some small businesses who would not have obtained loans otherwise.

A second possible negative to bank consolidation is that the rush of banks to expand into new geographic markets might lead them into increased risk taking which might lead to bank failures. Particularly worrisome would be banks that take on excessive risks by expanding extremely rapidly through acquisitions without having the managerial capital to manage this expansion successfully. Although a central banker needs to worry about this possibility, the job of our prudential supervisors is to prevent this occurrence.

In the past, much of bank supervision focused on assessment of the quality of the bank's balance sheet at a point in time whether it complies with capital requirements and restrictions on asset holdings. Although the traditional focus is important for reducing excessive risk-taking by banks, it is no longer felt to be adequate in today's world in which financial innovation has produced new markets and instruments which make it easy for banks and their employees to make huge bets both easily and quickly. In this new financial environment, a bank that is quite healthy at a particular point in time can be driven into insolvency extremely rapidly from trading losses, as has been forcefully demonstrated by the failure of Barings in 1995. Thus bank supervision which focuses only on a bank's position at a point in time, may not be effective in indicating whether a bank will in fact be taking on excessive risk in the near future.

This change in the financial environment for banking institutions has resulted in a major shift in thinking about the bank supervisory process both in the United States and throughout the world. Bank examiners are now placing far greater emphasis on evaluating the soundness of bank's management processes with regard to controlling risk. This shift in thinking was reflected in a new focus on risk management in the Federal Reserve System's 1993 guidance to examiners on trading and derivatives activities. The focus was expanded and formalized in the Trading Activities Manual issued early in 1994, which provided bank examiners with tools to evaluate risk management systems. In late 1995, the Federal Reserve and the Comptroller of the Currency announced that they would be assessing risk management processes at the banks they supervise. Now bank examiners separately evaluate risk management which feeds into the overall management rating as part of the CAMEL system. Four elements of sound risk management are assessed to come up with the risk management rating: 1) The quality of oversight provided by the board of directors and senior management, 2) the adequacy of policies and limits for all activities that present significant risks, 3) the quality of the risk measurement and monitoring systems, and 4) the adequacy of internal controls to prevent fraud or unauthorized activities on the part of employees. With this new focus of bank supervision on evaluating the soundness of bank management processes, bank supervisors can help prevent the dangers of banks expanding too rapidly without the proper management expertise in place.

5. CONCLUSION

Bank consolidation is the result of fundamental economic forces which have increased competition and improved the efficiency of our financial system. Thus, it would be problematic for central bankers to stand in the way of the bank consolidation trend. Furthermore, because nationwide banking and bank consolidation will increase diversification of banks' portfolios, it makes it less likely that we will have bank collapses of the type that occurred in Texas in the mid 1980s and New England in the early 1990s. The increased diversification resulting from bank consolidation should therefore make for a healthier banking system which is less prone to banking crises.

Nevertheless, bank consolidation and the increasingly competitive environment which the banking system finds itself in does present central bankers with some challenges. Central bankers need to be vigilant to make sure that bank consolidation does not result in excessive risk taking by banks which seek out excessive growth through bank acquisitions or unhealthy concentrations in certain activities. As we are well aware, banks have made mistakes in the past, such as their excessive exposure in commercial real estate lending in the 1980s, and they may make mistakes in the future. Although we need to carefully monitor banks in order to spot whether they are taking on excessive risks in the course of consolidating and restructuring, it does not make sense for us to micromanage the strategic plans for banks. Banks know how to run their own businesses better than we do, and it would be highly undesirable if the regulatory/supervisory process ended up stifling the creativity and drive for efficiency that the capitalist system generates in the financial sector.

One result of bank consolidation is that it will lead to more very large banks. The presence of larger banks does present a challenge because the failure of a very large bank may put substantial strain on the banking system.

The problem of the danger from the failure of a very large bank has been with us for a long time, and bank consolidation does not present us with a new problem. The presence of very large banks in the past and the possibility for greater numbers of them in the future means that supervision of these institutions to ensure that they are healthy and are not engaging in excessive risk taking is extremely important. This is a job that we would have to do even in the absence of bank consolidation, but it is likely to be even more imperative in the future.

With the appropriate bank supervision, bank consolidation and the increasingly competitive environment of the banking industry will promote economic efficiency and benefit both consumers and businesses.

NOTES

1. U.S. banks have an incentive to take additional risk because of federal deposit insurance. Insured depositors have little incentive to monitor banks and to penalize them for taking too much risk. This moral hazard problem was compounded by the *de facto* "too-big-to-fail" policy for large banks. Although the 1991 Federal Deposit Insurance Corporation Improvement Act (FDICIA) has a least-cost resolution provision that makes it harder to bail out large depositors, there is an exception to the provision whereby a bank would be in effect declared too-big-to-fail so that all depositors would be fully protected if two-thirds majority of both the Board of Governors of the Federal Reserve System and the Directors of the FDIC as well as the secretary of the Treasury agreed. Thus, the moral hazard problem created by too-big-to-fail has been reduced but not entirely eliminated by the 1991 FDICIA legislation.
2. Note that some off-balance sheet activities such as loan commitments and letters of credit which produce fee income can be classified as traditional banking business. The data in Figure 3 therefore overstate somewhat non-traditional banking business.
3. For a description of the history of branching and interstate banking laws, see Kane (1996).
4. Flannery (1984) found that unit banks' profits were enhanced by branching restrictions.
5. *Wall Street Journal*, 3/5/82.
6. Banks achieved the right to branch statewide in this way in Texas, Florida, Mississippi, Tennessee, Louisiana and New Mexico. For descriptions of the OCC decision and its court challenges, see "Texas Get Statewide Branching," *American Banker*, 6/27/88 and "National Banks Can Branch Statewide in Mississippi," *Banking Expansion Reporter*, 3/2/87.
7. For a more detailed description of interstate banking restrictions and the deregulation process during the 1980s, see Savage (1993).

REFERENCES

Amel, Dean F., "Trends in the Structure of Federally-Insured Depository Institutions: 1984-94," Federal Reserve Bulletin, January 1996, 1-15.

Berger, Allen N., Anil K Kashyap and Joseph M. Scalise, "The Transformation of the U.S. Banking System: What a Long Strange Trip it's Been," *Brookings Papers on Economic Activity* 2:1995, 55-218.

Cole, Rebel A. and John D. Wolken, "Financial Services used by Small Businesses: Evidence from the 1993 Survey of Small Business Finances," *Federal Reserve Bulletin*, July 1995, 629-667.

Flannery, Mark J., "The Social Costs of Unit Banking Restrictions," Journal of Monetary Economics 13:1984, 237-249.

Kane, Edward J., "De Jure Interstate Banking: Why Only Now?" Journal of Money, Credit and Banking 28(2), May 1996, 141-161.

Peek, Joe and Eric Rosengren, "Small Business Credit Availability: How Important is the Size of the Lender?" In Anthony Saunders and Ingo Walter, eds., Universal Banking: Financial System Design Reconsidered, Burr Ridge, Illinois: Irwin Publishing (forthcoming).

Savage, Donald, "Interstate Banking: A Status Report," *Federal Reserve Bulletin,* December 1993, 1075-89.

Strahan, Philip E. and James Weston, "Small Business Lending and Bank Consolidation: Is there Cause for Concern?" Federal Reserve Bank of New York, *Current Issues in Economic and Finance*, March 1996, 1-6.

ROY C. SMITH AND INGO WALTER[1]

2. Global patterns of mergers and acquisition activity in the financial service industry

ABSTRACT

This paper analyzes empirical evidence regarding mergers and acquisitions in the global financial services industry. It examines the global deal-flow during the eleven-year period 1985-95 and generates a global typology of intra- and inter-sectoral M&A transactions among and between banks, insurance companies and securities firms. From these data it identifies financial services as one of the most active industries involved in the global M&A deal-flow. It also identifies the areas of greatest M&A intensity within the world financial services industry. The paper then assesses the motivations for financial services M&A transactions in the context of changed regulatory and competitive factors and evolution in management objectives emphasizing the pursuit of greater operating efficiencies, enhanced economies of scale and scope and greater market power which executives and boards of directors believe has led (or will lead) to increased shareholder value and competitive performance.

1. INTRODUCTION

Recent years have seen what is arguably the most intensive period of reorganization in the history of the financial services industry. This has been caused by a decade of institutional failure and underperformance in banking, savings and other types of financial services all around the world. It has been accelerated by enhanced capital market capacity that has encouraged extensive global merger and acquisitions (M&A) activity across a wide spectrum of industries. Failures of institutions in the banking, savings and loan, mortgage and consumer finance, insurance, and securities industries in a number of countries have been the result, directly and indirectly, of extensive deregulation, intensified disintermediation, interest rate volatility and asset deflation, much greater competition for funds and transactions, and in many cases management mistakes. These problems have resulted in extensive inter-vention (rescues) by regulators and taxpayers, and greater shareholder activism

21

Y. Amihud and G. Miller (eds.), Bank Mergers & Acquisitions, 21–36
© 1998 Kluwer Academic Publishers. Printed in the Netherlands.

and opportunism at a time of substandard performance on the part of many financial services firms.

Consolidation, especially in U.S. commercial banking, has been considerable – with the number of banks being reduced by one-third from nearly 15,000 to under 10,000 over the decade 1985-95. What is less visible, however, may be the intensity of financial services industry reorganizations relative to the degree of reorganization in other sectors of the economy, and the extensive parallel activity that has taken place in the financial services industries in Europe and Japan for substantially the same reasons.

These events have taken place during a time of far-reaching globalization of capital markets, with greatly increased volumes of financial activity made possible by the need to finance government deficits, technological developments, financial innovation and competitive opportunities. An environment for funding and executing large merger and acquisition transactions arose. As a result, a growing volume of M&A deals developed during the 1980s, some of them hostile, resulting in a significant restructuring of industrial companies in the United States. This wave of activity spread to Europe at the end of the 1980s, making possible transactions that could not have been completed only a few years before. [Walter and Smith, 1990] At the same time, banks and other financial services firms discovered that they were no longer protected from such activity by their regulators – and no longer able to repel takeover attempts effortlessly – so they became subject to much the same market pressures that characterized industry in general. As a result, a world-wide, market-driven period of consolidation and restructuring in financial services began.

Despite market conditions and the critical need for economic restructuring in financial services, however, these developments might not have occurred if two major regulatory developments not taken place at about the same time. The adoption of the BIS accords in 1986 by the central banks of the leading industrial countries provided an approach to assuring safety for banking systems by applying standards of risk-adjusted minimum capital adequacy ratios. This enabled regulators to shift their emphasis from maintaining stability and safety – at whatever cost to efficiency and competitiveness – to higher levels of banking performance and providing adequate market returns to investors. The second major regulatory shift occurred when the European Union finalized its Second Banking Directive in 1987, which provided for a single banking license for the conduct of business throughout the EU – subject to home country supervision – as well as the acceptance of universal banking principles by all member countries and the ability of non-European firms to participate in the new marketplace through an EU-licensed subsidiary subject to reciprocity understandings. These developments in Europe accelerated regulatory shifts towards universal banking in the United States and Japan as well, and creating both strategic difficulties and strategic opportunities for many. [Smith, 1993; Saunders & Walter, 1995; Smith & Walter, 1997].

2. INDUSTRIAL RESTRUCTURING THOUGH MERGERS AND ACQUISITIONS

During the eleven years from 1985 through 1995, more than $4.5 trillion in M&A transactions were completed.[2] This total comprised approximately 58,000 reported transactions in the United States, Europe and the rest of the world, and represented the largest nominal volume of M&A transactions in history – although probably not the largest relative to global economic activity. About 47% of the value of the 1985-95 transactions-flow was accounted for entirely in the United States, which had experienced three prior merger booms in the Twentieth Century. Another 14% of the deal-flow was accounted for by cross-border transactions in which one party was from the United States, usually the seller. And 39% of the transactions by value (46% by number of deals) were entirely outside the United States (i.e., neither buyer nor seller were U.S.-based companies). During this eleven-year period, the total volume of global transactions increased four-fold (in dollar-value terms). However, the non-U.S. component grew over ten-fold, reflecting the fact that Europe, in particular, was experiencing its first major M&A boom as a result of a variety of factors including extensive deregulation and increased competition in the EU as a result of the Single Market Act, improved capital market capacity, privatizations, global convergence of attitudes regarding corporate governance, performance and shareholder value, and increasing know-how and ease of execution of corporate restructurings through market-driven M&A transactions. [Walter & Smith, 1990; Smith, 1993] The relevant data are contained in Exhibit 1.

During the eleven year period 1985-1995, firms in the financial service industry[3] participated extensively in M&A transactions, accounting for more than 44% of the total and aggregating almost $2 trillion in announced values.4 They represented 42% of the U.S. domestic total and almost half of the total transaction volume outside the United States.

In the United States, financial services was the most active industry in terms of sellers, and second by buyers of all sectors involved in M&A transactions during the period. In Europe, it was the second most active industry in terms of both buyers and sellers. In short, the intensity of financial services M&A transactions increased significantly, especially outside the United States. Mergers were big during the past decade, and financial services mergers were a major reason why.

Exhibit 2 provides a summary geographic profile of global M&A activity in the financial services sector during this period.

These data do not include some of the world's largest banking mergers, such as Bank of Tokyo and Mitsubishi Bank, Chemical Bank and Chase Manhattan, and First Interstate and Wells Fargo in the United States, or Banque Indosuez and Credit Agricole in France – all of which occurred after the end of 1995.

Exhebit 1. Completed Global M&A Transactions 1985-1995($ billions – thousands of transactions)

	1985		1995		11 Years 1985-1995	
	$ Value (%)	# (%)	$ Value (%)	# (%)	$ Value (%)	# (%)
US Domestic						
All Industries	192.5 (82.5)	0.8 (72.7)	389.2 (46.9)	6.5 (40.1)	2,129.1 (47.3)	24.2 (41.9)
All Financial Services	*47.9 (82.3)*	*0.7 (77.7)*	196.5 (49.9)	2.5 (41.7)	904.3 (46.1)	17.1 (45.1)
US Cross-Border						
All Industries	15.7 (6.8)	0.1 (0.9)	109.6 (13.2)	1.8 (1.1)	618.8 (13.8)	6.4 (11.1)
All Financial Services	*6.3 (10.8)*	*0.1 (8.6)*	20.1 (5.1)	0.3 (5.0)	271.6 (13.9)	2.8 (7.4)
Non-US						
All Industries	24.8 (10.7)	0.2 (1.8)	330.4 (39.8)	7.9 (48.8)	1,751.1 (38.9)	27.2 (47.0)
All Financial Services	*4.0 (6.9)*	*0.1 (8.6)*	176.9 (45.0)	3.2 (53.3)	785.1 (40.0)	18.0 (47.5)
Total						
All Industries	233.0 (100.0)	1.1 (100.0)	829.2 (100.0)	16.2 (100.0)	4,499.0 (100.0)	57.8 (100.0)
All Financial Services	*58.2 (100.0)*	*0.9 (100.0)*	393.5 (100.0)	6.0 (100.0)	1,961.0 (100.0)	37.9 (100.0)

Data: Securities Data Corporation. Author calculations.

Exhibit 2. Intensity of Financial Services M&A Activity

Dollar Value of Financial Services Industry as a %	1985	1995	11 Years
U.S. domestic as percent of global total	24.9	41.6	40.6
U.S. cross-border as percent of global total	15.9	78.3	49.4
Non-U.S. as percent of global total	16.1	52.1	42.8
Financial Services as percent of global M&A activity	25.0	50.7	42.1

Data: Securities Data Corporation

3. THE DYNAMICS OF M&A ACTIVITY IN FINANCIAL SERVICES

Strategic restructuring in the financial services industry may reflect many different types of transactions, each of which represents a different approach. First, domestic banks may acquire other domestic banks – such as the aforementioned Chemical Banking Corp. acquisition of Chase Manhattan in the United States (technically a merger) and Mitsubishi Bank's combination with Bank of Tokyo, or Credit Suisse's acquisition of Swiss Volksbank. Or the emphasis could be on acquiring a foreign bank through a cross-border M&A deal such as the Hong Kong and Shanghai Banking Corporation's acquisition of Midland Bank of the U.K. The same intra-sector domestic or cross-border acquisitions may occur in insurance, such as the French AXA group's acquisition of a controlling interest in Equitable Life in the United States. Or it may occur in the securities industry, as developed domestically in a major way after a spate of deregulation during the 1970s in the U.S. and during the 1980s in the U.K. (such as Morgan Stanley's 1997 merger with Dean Witter) – and more recently on a cross-border basis in the case of Merrill Lynch's 1995 takeover of Smith New Court in London. Finally, cross-sector domestic or foreign acquisitions may take place bi-directionally between banks and insurance companies, banks and securities firms, or securities firms and insurance companies. Recent examples include Swiss Bank Corporation's acquisition of S.G. Warburg & Co., Internationale Nederlanden Groep's acquisition of Barings PLC, and Travelers Group's acquisitions of Smith Barney and Shearson Lehman Brothers.

These transactions are generally motivated by strategic considerations, and sometimes the strategy proves to be unsuccessful. When this turns out to be the case, divestitures take place. Among the more prominent of these are included American Express' sale of its Trade Development Bank and the Shearson Lehman businesses, and General Electric's sale of Kidder Peabody.

Financial Services Subgroups

Financial services M&A activities involve an array of industry subgroups and are carried out in many countries and across borders. We have separated the deal-flow associated with just three groups – commercial banking, securities, and insurance – from the global financial services industry M&A totals. Together, these three subgroups represented over 25% of the total value of M&A transactions during 1985-1995.[5] Exhibit 3 presents the composition of the transactions from this sample, and demonstrates the predominance of transactions in the banking sector, where industry consolidation has been pervasive.

Intra-sector Transactions. During the eleven-year period, there were $417 billion of completed M&A transactions in this sample. Of these transactions, 59.5% represented banks acquiring other banks (average transaction size, $51.2 million), with about 60% of the activity occurring in the United States. The second largest component was insurance companies acquiring other insurance companies (average deal size $95 million) comprising 22.8% of the total. Intra-banking and intra-insurance deals therefore accounted for more than 80% of all transactions for these three financial services industry segments – presumably reflecting the relative size of the two groups. Probably for the same reason, transactions among securities broker-dealers were small by comparison, representing only 3.5% of the total (average deal size $26.3 million). Almost 70% of the value of transactions within the securities industry occurred in the United States and the United Kingdom, the only countries with significant numbers of independent broker-dealers.

Exhibit 3. Selected Financial Services M&A Deal-Flow, 1985-1995
($ millions and number of transactions)

	Target Institutions			
Acquiring Institution	Commercial Banks	Securities Firms	Insurance Cos.	Total Buyers
Commercial Banks	306,331 (5,416)	15,934 (331)	15,329 (137)	337,594 (5,884)
Securitis Firms	8,047 (139)	19,772 (692)	5,462 (49)	33,281 (817)
Insurance Cos.	17,322 (137)	4,421 (100)	107,151 (1,337)	128,894 (1,573)
Total Sellers	331,700 (5,691)	40,127 (1,060)	127,942 (1,523)	449,769 (8,274)

Data: Securities Data Corporation.

Cross-border intra-sector transactions were concentrated in foreign acquisitions of U.S. and U.K. banks, German and British acquisitions of insurance companies abroad, and foreign purchases of U.K merchant banks. Banks acquiring foreign insurance companies occurred mainly in emerging market countries, especially as part of the debt-for-equity swap transactions that occurred in the 1980s.

Inter-sector transactions. In terms of inter-sector deal-flow, the largest transaction volume was between banks and insurance companies, representing 7.2% of the total. Almost all of these transactions were in Europe, where banking/insurance combinations are permitted (they were not in the United States and Japan). There were slightly more insurance company purchases of banks (125 deals valued at $16 billion, averaging $128 million in size) than banks purchasing insurance companies (110 transactions valued at $14 billion, averaging $127 million in size). There were, however, 298 bank purchases of securities firms, mostly in advanced countries (valued at $12 billion, averaging $40.3 million in size) and 128 transactions representing securities firms buying banks ($7.7 billion, averaging $60.2 million in size), mostly in emerging-market countries and often involving control groups acquiring state-owned banks that were privatized.

Partial stakes and alliances. The data also reveal that about 15% of the M&A deal-flow involved partial ownership stakes (as opposed to 100% control), mainly in emerging market countries. This pattern reflects a long-standing practice in banking to participate in "strategic alliances," although for larger institutions such alliances have usually been unrewarding and have often been unwound after a time. Nonetheless, the data indicate that 68% of the deals where banks acquired stakes in insurance companies and 53% of the deals where banks acquired stakes in securities firms involved partial control. In the case of securities firms acquiring banks, partial stakes represented 70% of the deal-flow.

Hostile deals. The data also indicate a relatively minor role in financial service transactions of hostile deals – that is, deals which (however they eventually end-up) were initially met by a non-friendly response from the board of directors of the target institution. Altogether, about 9% of the intra-bank deals were hostile in 1985-1995, with almost all of this volume originating in the United States and France. Since 1994, however, hostile attempts have made noteworthy appearances in the Unites States (Wells Fargo and First Interstate, for example). Also, banks and insurance companies that were thought to be underperforming by key shareholders have triggered pressures to merge. For example, Chase Manhattan was under shareholder pressure prior to merging with Chemical Banking Corporation, and Kemper fought off GE Capital before being acquired by Zurich Insurance. Hostile activity has even appeared in one of the most unlikely places of all, Switzerland, where a dissident shareholder attempted to change the board of directors of the Union Bank of Switzerland. This effort was ultimately unsuccessful, but close enough to extract a number of important concessions.

The share of hostile transactions within the insurance sector was only 16%, but over 42% of that deal-flow involved partial ownership positions. Within the securities industry, 32% of the deals were hostile and 40% involved partial ownership positions. Overall, it appears that, for the most part, the role of hostile transactions in the financial services sector is quite limited, while the role of partial stakes is high as compared with global M&A transactions in the non-financial sector. [Smith and Walter, 1997] This may be partially explained by the role of regulatory approvals in this sector, the importance of human resources who may well leave in the event of a hostile takeover, and the perceived value of strategic alliances cemented by stakeholdings in achieving management objectives without attaining full control.

4. DRIVING FORCES

Some of our earlier work has helped us understand the motivations for underlying global M&A activity in the past. An analysis of the merger boom in the United States in the 1980s, together with the three prior merger booms earlier in the century [Smith, 1990] indicates that while no single cause for surges in M&A activity has been identified, merger booms do tend to develop during times when four conditions apply: (1) there are significant changes in government regulatory or economic policies; (2) There is solid economic or technological rationale for the restructuring; (3) Companies are undervalued relative to their replacement values; and (4) Strong "bull" markets exist in which transactions can be financed.

Boom conditions in Europe. Our analysis of the early days of the first-ever merger boom in Europe [Smith & Walter, 1990] indicates that all of these conditions applied after the middle 1980s. It was clear that the passage of the EU's Single Market Act and a more market-oriented economic philosophy – reflected in significant changes in government economic policies – was likely to increase competition within most European industries and require all companies to rethink their overall competitive effectiveness, their strategic objectives, and their exposure to risk. This corporate repositioning was a strong motivation, in many cases, for rapid reorganizations through the markets. And as financial market depth increased, corporations began to rely on it for restructuring purposes. For their part, having been reorganized in many cases by regulatory changes in the mid-1980s, the markets were able to supply the financial capacity needed to make the M&A transactions possible.

Special conditions in financial services. Among all of the industries in the U.S. and Europe that have undergone restructuring during the past decade, the financial services sector has been clearly in the lead. In addition to the factors mentioned above, the industry has experienced several important developments not shared by nonfinancial industries:

● **Major financial losses were incurred in banking and insurance all around the world** from asset-liability mismatching, and adverse credit exposures on loan positions that had grown rapidly as a result of intensified competition and gaps in risk-management capability. A significant part of these losses can be attributed to out-of-date managements attempting to cope with a surge of unusually aggressive rivalry among banks during a period of high interest rate volatility. The carnage was especially severe in those countries in which the banks boldly attempted to stake-out market leadership positions for the future and failed (Japan, the United States, the United Kingdom, France, and Scandinavia). One consequence was that large part of national banking systems had to be rescued or reorganized in order to save them, and this resulted in major management changes and strategic rethinking.

- **A massive shift in wholesale finance from bank-based to market-based financing facilities** as capital markets grew and became deeper and more efficient on a globalized basis, and as bank lending became increasingly uncompetitive. Many key business areas in banks and insurance became obsolete.
- **Increased competition for deposits from nonbanking suppliers** such as mutual funds, even as many banks remained in the grip of out-of-date regulatory constraints that did not apply to the new competitors.
- **Rapidly changing technology** that increased the speed of product and process innovation and stimulated the willingness of traditional clients to shop around.
- **Regulatory conditions blocked important financial institutions from responding** in a timely or preemptive way to the many changes in their business. Besides applying entry and operating restrictions to foreign-based players, many regulators tolerated a certain amount of anti-competitive or cartel-like behavior on the part of domestic institutions. For years, regulators understood that a well-protected industry may not be efficient from the standpoint of the customer, but it tends to be a safe industry, and therefore not a problem for the regulators. Thus they were reluctant to change things if making banks more competitive also meant they might be riskier. Still, in time the regulatory blanket was lifted and replaced by new regimes that were more sympathetic to enhanced competitive performance, but also tougher on performance that was not up to solvency standards. For at least a decade, what banks in particular could do and not do was in continuous state of change.

Induced strategic changes. In response to these conditions, many banks adopted strategic changes designed to meet them. These were both offensive and defensive in character. Among the offensive strategies were those of several U.S. banks such as Bank of America, NationsBank, Wells Fargo, First Union, BancOne and Key Bank, which relied on superior management to be able to realize significant market-share opportunities by rapidly increasing their size and reach. Two American banks, JP Morgan and Bankers Trust, sold branches or reconfigured their business in order to become specialists in wholesale finance, securities and risk management. Still others, like Citibank, streamlined themselves to focus on consumer finance. Many peripheral activities were hived-off in the process. In Canada, the major banks all acquired securities firms. Other offensive strategies were seen in Europe where large banks such as Crédit Lyonnais strove to gain leading market shares in the new, integrated European banking market by acquiring banks in other countries – ultimately with little success and at enormous cost to the French taxpayer. Some banks preferred strategic alliances or minority ownership positions with banks in other countries, such as Santander-Royal Bank of Scotland and Dresdner Bank-BNP. Other banks, like Deutsche Bank, Swiss Bank Corp., UBS, the Dutch banking-insurance group ING as well as Dresdner Bank focused on cross-border acquisitions in non-lending sectors such as securities and asset management, especially in the U.K. where all but two major merchant banks and brokers have been sold or linked to foreign firms seeking to build up their capital market activities..

Insurance attracted several banks as well, especially Deutsche Bank (which started its own life insurance subsidiary) and Lloyds Bank of the U.K. Internationale Nederlanden Groep (ING) was created out of the merger of a large insurance company with the third largest commercial bank and the postal savings system, and has since acquired Baring Brothers in the U.K. The Travelers Group in the U.S., once a premier insurance company, was aggressively remade by new management into a financial services holding company specializing in insurance, asset management and securities brokerage.

Other strategies have been more defensive in nature, and emphasized profit and market-share protection by increasing the size of the franchise and the capital base, more than creating new revenues from different activities or client groups. Among these were the aforementioned mergers that appeared in the United States, the Netherlands, Finland, Italy, Sweden, Switzerland, and perhaps most recently and visibly in Japan, where some of the world's largest banks (Mitsubishi Tokyo, Dai-Ichi Kangyo, Sakura, Asahi) have been assembled by merger, apparently at the suggestion or encouragement of the Ministry of Finance. In the United States, domestic banking merger transactions were motivated by mainly cost-cutting (profit enhancing) opportunities and a belief in economies of scale, and elsewhere by the massing-together of branches, customers and capital so as to create an impregnable force in the home market.

Speed of change. We now know that not all of these strategies – especially those based on acquisitions – have been successful in the financial services sector. But the changes in the financial services industry were so considerable during this period that virtually all of the major institutions adjusted their strategies as a result. The virtue of change by acquisition was usually the speed with which it could be done, as compared to a much slower do-it-yourself approach. Part of the appeal of speed lay in the publicrelations component. Management could persuade others that motion was progress, and wait for the market to reward the motion – if not ultimately the strategy.

Synergies and economies. Economies of scope and scale may be significantly restrained by regulatory restrictions in a particular market, indicating the importance of the impact of competitive distortions on horizontal integration. Within this context, various motivations have been identified as to why financial services firms engage in M&A transactions. [Hawawini and Swary, 1990] These include:

- **Accessing information and proprietary technologies** (know-how) in possession of by the target firm.
- **Increasing market power** by raising market share to widen cost-price margins, including the ability to carry out large transactions that otherwise would require participation by other firms.
- **Reduce unit costs** and increase operating efficiency by eliminating redundant facilities and personnel, as well as improve the quality of management, including hostile takeovers to improve incumbent under-performing management.
- **Achieve economies of scale** by creating a combined institution of larger size capable of achieving lower unit-costs of producing financial services.
- **Achieve economies of scope**, or synergies with the target firm.
- **Achieve diversification** and greater earnings stability.
- **Achieve certain tax benefits**.
- **Satisfy management's goals,** when its hubris and self aggrandizement may be driven by a utility function that is quite different from that of shareholders.

Not every M&A transaction is motivated by all of these factors, but most are motivated by some. Whether or not these objectives are realized, and over how long a time-period, determines whether or not an individual transaction eventually succeeds from the perspective of shareholder value.

5. ACHIEVEMENT OF ECONOMIES OF SCALE AND SCOPE

From a strategic perspective, one of the main reasons for M&A activity in the financial services industry is capturing significant economies of scale and scope, both domestically and internationally. Whether such economies exist in financial services – a question that is at the heart of strategic and regulatory discussions about optimum firm size and structure in the financial services sector – can be approached by comparing the performance of large and diverse firms with smaller and more narrowly-focused ones.

Economies of scale. In an information- and distribution-intensive industry with high fixed costs, such as financial services, there should be ample potential for scale economies – as well as for diseconomies attributable to administrative overhead, agency problems and other cost factors once very large size is reached.

Economies of scope. As in the case of economies of scale, there should be ample potential for economies and diseconomies of scope in the financial services sector, which may arise either through supply- or demand-side linkages.

On the supply side, they relate to cost savings through sharing of overheads and improving technology through joint production of similar services, with diseconomies arising from such factors as inertia and lack of responsiveness and creativity that may come with increased firm size and bureaucratization, "turf" and profit-attribution conflicts that increase costs or erode product quality in meeting client needs, or cultural differences across the organization that inhibit seamless delivery of a broad range of financial services.

On the demand side, economies of scope (cross-selling) arise when the all-in cost to the buyer of multiple financial services from a single supplier – including the price of the service, plus information, search, monitoring, contracting and other transaction costs – is less than the costs of purchasing them from separate suppliers by virtue of lower non-price costs. Demand-related diseconomies of scope could arise through conflicts of interest encountered by the multi-product financial firm that may cause it to act against the interests of the client in sale of one service in order to facilitate sale of another, or information disclosure considered inimical to the client's interests.

Empirical findings. Individually or in combination, economies (dis-economies) of scale and scope may be passed along to the buyer in the form of lower (higher) prices resulting in a gain (loss) of market share, or absorbed by the supplier to increase (decrease) profitability. They should be directly observable in cost functions of suppliers and aggregate performance measures. Studies of scale and scope economies in financial services are unusually problematic. The nature of the empirical tests used, the form of the cost function, the existence of unique optimum output levels, and the optimizing behavior of financial firms all present conceptual difficulties. Limited availability and conformity of data present empirical problems. And the conclusions of any study that has detected (or failed to detect) economies of scale and/or scope in a sample selection of financial institutions does not necessarily have general applicability.

Estimated banking cost functions form the basis most empirical tests of economies of scope and scale in financial services. Past empirical studies of this subject have included Benston [1982], Berger [1987], Fields & Murphy [1989], Gillian et al. [1984], Goldstein [1987], Kim [1986] Kolari & Zardhooki [1987], Lawrence [1989], Mester [1987, 1990], Murray & White [1983], Noulas et al [1990], Shaffer [1988], and Yoshika & Nakajima [1987]. In 14 of the 19 studies, economies of scale were found to apply, at least to very small banks. Only one study, focusing on Canadian insurance agencies [Kellner & Mathewson, 1983] actually rejected the proposition that scale economies exist. Various studies found the point of increasing marginal costs to be anywhere between $25 million and $60 billion in assets. Most concluded that the point of inflection was well below $100 million in asset size. Most also concluded that some diseconomies of scope are found across all banks.

A more recent study [Saunders and Walter, 1994) presents two sets of empirical tests on data taken from the world's 200 largest banks during the

1980s. First, evidence is found – using data from the 1980s – that very large banks have grown more slowly than the smaller among the large banks. Second, positive economies of scale and negative-cost (supply-side) economies of scope appear to have been the rule for large banks.

In most national markets for financial services, suppliers have shown a tendency towards oligopoly but are prevented from developing into full monopolies. Internationally, there are relatively few cases where foreign-based financial institutions have made significant inroads into domestic markets. This suggests that gains to scale may be fully utilized in domestic markets, but may be prevented from being utilized in international markets. By looking only at the large banks across many countries, full utilization of economies of scale seems not to have been exploited in the past. If this is true, considerable consolidation of banking worldwide may follow international liberalization of markets for financial services. Such consolidation, in turn, may be limited by diseconomies of scale which, empirical evidence suggests, set in among the largest of the large banks.

With regard to diseconomies of scope found in the empirical research, the 1980s was a period during which institutions wishing to diversify away from purely commercial banking activities incurred considerable costs in expanding the range of their activities, either by acquisition or otherwise. If this diversification effort involved significant sunk costs – while expenses on the accounting statements during the period under study – to effect future penetration of fee-earning service markets, then we would expect to see particularly strong evidence of diseconomies of scale in non-interest-related activities and diseconomies of scope between lending and non-interest-related activities reversed in future periods. If the banks' investment in staff, training, and systems bear returns in future periods commensurate with these expenditures – and if those banks that offer non-traditional banking services unprofitably retreat from the field – then neutrality or positive economies of scope may well exist.

It is also reasonable to conclude that some demand-related scope economies are realizable. Hence, if there are zero supply diseconomies of scope (as there appear to be for the large banks included in empirical studies) one would expect demand-related economies of scope to dominate. Several authors have found very large disparities in efficiency among banks of similar size – difference in so-called x-efficiency – suggesting that the way banks are run is far more important that their size or the selection of businesses that they pursue. [Berger, Hancock and Humphrey, 1993; and Berger, Hunter and Timme, 1993]

Pricing factors. A healthy bank typically will be acquired at a premium above its book (or liquidation) value. The premium reflects the value of the goodwill of the franchise being acquired and other intangibles. But it also represents the value to the acquirer of the opportunity to manage the acquired business, and the opportunity to realize potential economies of scale and scope. Presumably the acquired institution would be managed differently so as to create the incremental value needed to reimburse the shareholder of the acquiring institution for the willingness to pay the premium in the first place. Adding new customers, offering more services, eliminating redundancies and lowering costs can accomplish this, although to do so often means sudden layoffs of large numbers of personnel, an action that is not possible in all countries. Historically, bank acquisitions have occurred at price to book value ratios of about 2.0, sometimes as high as 3.0 or even more. In eight of the eleven years of our study, however, the average price to book ratio for the U.S. banking industry acquisitions was lower than 2.0, averaging 1.5 and ranging from 1.1 in 1990 and 1.8 in 1985. In two years, the price to book ratio exceeded 2.0 – in 1986 it was 2.8 and in 1993 in was 3.2. Price does matter, although perhaps it matters more to economists and shareholders than to managers of the acquiring institutions. However strategically attractive, at the wrong price an acquisition will fail to accomplish its objectives.

Shareholder responses. If a strategic change does not produce economies of scale and/or scope or greater x-efficiency – reflected in greater profits for the same assets and/or greater penetration of the market – then what is its value? Avoiding an acquisition attempt from a better-managed suitor who will pay a premium price for the enterprise does not seem as acceptable today to shareholders as it did in the past. In a world of more open and efficient markets for shares in financial institutions, shareholders increasingly tend to have the final say about the future of enterprises. They will buy or sell shares based on what they think about plans and capabilities of firms and their managements. Today, at least in the United States, shareholders have been rewarding acquirers and those being acquired alike. Those attempting bold new actions are being rewarded, although some may be seen to fail in the future and lose their investors' support.

6. Conclusions

The global financial services industry has been buffeted by changes emanating from powerful internal and external forces over the past decade, and is reacting by reorganization, consolidation and streamlining. Much of the transformation of the industry is occurring in the M&A market, which permits major strategic plans to be initiated and executed quickly. The intensity of the transformation is greatest in the United States, where the markets are reasonably efficient and pressures for change from shareholder groups can be strong. But parallel activity is clearly visible as well in most OECD countries – even in Japan, which traditionally had a low level of M&A transactions, and in certain emerging market countries. During the eleven-year period under study – and continuing since – the global financial services industry has been in the grip of a global mergers and acquisition boom which is likely to continue for some time to come. The task of reorganizing twenty or thirty thousand banks around the world is a formidable one that will require years. As financial markets become still more "seamless," the M&A volume presented here may well be just the beginning. Furthermore, some of the evidence from the past, such as the limited role of hostile transactions and the extensive role of minority stakeholdings, are likely to evolve rather differently in the future.

What is less clear is the structures into which the industry will ultimately itself. Competitive considerations are dominant for now, and financial services firms know they must change significantly to become more competitive, sell out to someone else if they cannot, or gradually wither away. Major banking, securities and insurance franchises worry about being displaced by competition from outside their specific sector or by powerful new entrants from abroad. They also know they must achieve returns on their capital that are fully consistent with the risks they run and at least equal to returns available elsewhere in the economy for comparable risks. Various strategies have thus emerged, both offensive and defensive, specialized and universal, cross-sectoral and global. All of them seek economies of scale and of scope that may be hard to find given contradictory and incomplete empirical evidence as to how prevalent they actually are. In any case, strategy isn't everything. Implementation is at least as important.

There are less defensible reasons for M&A transactions in the financial services industry as well, some of which may eventually place firms in conflict with shareholders (e.g., aggressive overbidding), antitrust authorities, and bank regulators. As abuses occur, however, countervailing regulatory or corporate-governance actions tend to develop. Managers ignore these countervailing actions at their own peril. Equally important will be the market's reaction to those whose strategies succeed and those whose don't.

NOTES

1. Paper presented at the Conference on Financial Institution Mergers, NYU Salomon Center, October 11, 1996.
2. Data for this paper is from the merger and acquisition database of Securities Data Corporation.
3. The SDC financial services "industry" grouping includes commercial banks and bank holding companies; savings institutions; credit institutions; real estate, mortgage bankers and brokers; investment and commodity firms; dealers and exchanges; insurance companies; and other financial organizations.
4. The data are for completed transactions only, recorded at their date of announcement.
5. The database captures all announced and completed deals.

REFERENCES

Benston, George, "Universal Banking," *Journal of Economic Perspectives*, Volume 8, Number 3, Summer 1994.

Benston, George, G. Hanweck and D. Humphrey, "Scale Economies in Banking," *Journal of Money, Credit and Banking*, 14, 1982.

Berger, Allen N., Diana Hancock and David B. Humphrey, "Bank Efficiency Derived from the Profit Function," *Journal of Banking and Finance*, April 1993.

Berger, Allen N., G. Hanweck, and D. Humphrey, "Competitive Viability in Banking," *Journal of Monetary Economics*, 20, 1987.

Berger, Allen N., William C. Hunter and Stephen J. Timme, "The Efficiency of Financial Institutions: A Review of Research Past, Present and Future," *Journal of Banking and Finance*, April 1993.

Clark, Jeffrey A., "Economies of Scale and Scope at Depository Financial Institutions: a Review of the Literature," Federal Reserve Board of Kansas City Review, October 1988.

Fields, Joseph A. and Neil B. Murphy, "An Analysis of Efficiency in the Delivery of Financial Services: The Case of Life Insurance Agencies," *Journal of Financial Services Research*, 2, 1989.

Gilligan, Thomas and Michael Smirlock, "An Empirical Study of Joint Production and Scale Economies in Commercial Banking," *Journal of Banking and Finance*, 8, 1984.

Gilligan, Thomas, Michael Smirlock and William Marshall, "Scale and Scope Economies in the Multi-Product Banking Firm," *Journal of Monetary Economics*, 13, 1984.

Goldstein, Steven, James McNulty, and James Verbrugge, "Scale Economies in the Savings and Loan Industry Before Diversification," *Journal of Economics and Business*, 1987.

Hawawini, Gabriel and Itzhak Swary, "Mergers and Acquisitions in the U.S. Banking Industry" (Amsterdam: North Holland, 1990).

Kellner, S. and G Frank Mathewson, "Entry, Size Distribution, Scale and Scope Economies in the Life Insurance Industry," *Journal of Business*, 1983.

Kim, H. Youn, "Economies of Scale and Scope in Multiproduct Financial Institutions," *Journal of Money, Credit and Banking*, 18, 1986.

Kolari, James and Asghar Zardhooki, "Bank Cost Structure and Performance" (Lexington, Mass.: Heath Lexington, 1987).

Lawrence, Colin, "Banking Costs, Generalized Functional Forms, and Estimation of Economies of Scale and Scope," *Journal of Money, Credit and Banking*, Vol. 21, No. 3, 1989.

Mester, Loretta, "A Multiproduct Cost Study of Savings and Loans," *Journal of Finance*, 42, 1987.

Mester, Loretta, "Traditional and Nontraditional Banking: an Information Theoretic Approach," Federal Reserve Board Working Paper, No. 90-3, February 1990.

Murray, John D. and Robert S. White, "Economies of Scale and Economies of Scope in Multiproduct Financial Institutions," *Journal of Finance*, June 1983.

Noulas, Athanasios G., Subhash C. Ray and Stephen M. Miller, "Returns to Scale and Input Substitution for Large U.S. Banks," *Journal of Money, Credit and Banking*, Vol. 22, 1990.

Saunders, Anthony and Ingo Walter, *Universal Banking in the United States* (New York: Oxford University Press, 1994).

Shaffer, Sherrill, "A Restricted Cost Study of 100 Large Banks," Federal Reserve Bank of New York Working Paper, 1988.

Smith, Roy C. and Ingo Walter, Global Banking (New York: Oxford University Press, 1997).

Smith, Roy C., *Comeback-The Restoration of American Banking Power* (Cambridge, Harvard Business School Press, 1993)

Smith, Roy C., *Money Wars*, (New York, E.P. Dutton, 1990)

Tschoegl, Adrian E. , "Size, Growth and Transnationality among the World's Largest Banks," *Journal of Business*, Vol. 56, No. 2, 1983.

Walter, Ingo, *Global Competition in Financial Services* (Cambridge: Ballinger-Harper & Row, 1988).

Walter, Ingo, and Smith Roy C., *Investment Banking in Europe* (Oxford, Basil Blackwood, 1990)

Yoshioka, Kanji and Takanobu Nakajima, "Economies of Scale in Japan's Banking Industry," Bank of Japan Monetary and Economic Studies, September 1987.

WILLIAM R. EMMONS AND STUART I. GREENBAUM

3. Twin information revolutions and the future of financial intermediation

This thing [technology] is like a tidal wave.
If you fail in the game, you're going to be dead.

Hugh McColl, Chairman and
C.E.O.of Nationsbank Corp.,
in the *Wall Street Journal*,
July 25, 1996, p. A1.

Two information-related trends have dramatically altered our perceptions of financial intermediation in recent years. These trends are:
(1) an ongoing paradigm shift in financial-economic theory and regulation that focuses on the role of financial intermediaries in overcoming informational problems in financial contracting and transactions as their primary source of value creation, and
(2) a protracted series of technology shocks with order-of-magnitude effects on the costs of transmitting and processing information.

This paper explores selected implications of these "twin information revolutions." In particular, we provide tentative answers to the following questions:

- If overcoming informational problems is the *raison d'Être* of financial intermediation, does the falling cost of information transmission and processing portend the demise of financial intermediaries?
- Will the clienteles served by financial intermediaries continue to shift over time?
- Why have public financial markets in which financial intermediaries play predominantly a broker's role increased in importance relative to private markets in which intermediaries act as principals?
- What are the structural, regulatory, and welfare implications of the likely evolution of financial intermediation?

While we believe, as do many others, that the decline in information costs will continue to perturb and reshape financial intermediation in the years to come, we do not believe the more dire predictions of demise of financial intermediaries as we know them. Survival of traditional financial intermediation follows as an implication of the twin information revolutions noted above. Falling costs of transmitting and processing data will vastly

The views expressed in this paper are those of the authors and not those of the Federal Reserve Bank of St. Louis or of the Federal Reserve System.

Y. Amihud and G. Miller (eds.), Bank Mergers & Acquisitions, 37–56
© *1998 Kluwer Academic Publishers. Printed in the Netherlands.*

reduce the economic value that financial intermediaries can produce through the mere processing of data, as in the clearing of payment instructions or scoring of standard credit risks, for example. For non-standard or opaque risks and transactions, however, there will be a continuing demand for differentiated, branded, and credible information production, the hallmark of financial intermediaries. However, new classes of customers will migrate from unserved and underserved to served, as better-served customers migrate to public markets. This segué of classes of customers will pose new risk management challenges for financial intermediaries.

An analysis of the twin information revolutions noted here deepens our understanding of the shifting clienteles served by financial intermediaries, on the one hand, and the vastly expanded role of direct contracting in public financial markets observed in recent years, on the other. Traditional on-balance sheet financial intermediaries employ physical, financial, and human capital to compensate for scarce and imperfect information about counterparties and market risks. The declining real cost of obtaining and processing data means that brokers using public markets rather than their own balance sheets can effectively compete for certain standard financial transactions without the dedicated physical, financial, and human capital resources of traditional financial intermediaries. The result is that capital-intensive intermediaries will lose the customer segments that can be adequately served by increased disclosure and standardized risk analysis. These customers will migrate to public financial markets where financial intermediaries' role is primarily that of a broker requiring relatively little human and especially financial capital.

At the other extreme of the traditional on-balance-sheet financial intermediary's clienteles – those customers most difficult to analyze, price, and monitor – the falling cost of information opens up new opportunities. More data and standardized analytical techniques can be brought to bear on these risks, improving the quality of the credible information produced while lowering its cost. The result is an expansion of the potential customer base into the ranks of the previously unserved or underserved.

The effects of falling information costs on scale and scope economies are less clear, although we believe they do *not* point toward large-scale consolidation or conglomeration of the financial-intermediation sector. Economies of large-scale information processing are more pronounced as a result of the information-processing revolution, since marginal costs have fallen faster than fixed costs, leading to larger minimum efficient scale. This might lead one to expect consolidation into fewer, larger financial firms whatever their type (on-balance-sheet asset transformer or broker). On the other hand, the growing trend of functional disintermediation – outsourcing – demonstrates that specialist non-intermediary firms can effectively capture scale economies for resale to small and specialized financial intermediaries, contributing to their continued viability. Similarly, economies of scope might appear to be more easily captured by diversified financial intermediaries with improved information-processing capabilities; but the users of financial services – intermediaries' ultimate customers – are also better able to manage multiple intermediary relationships. In sum, there is no clear impetus for large-scale consolidation or conglomeration in the financial-intermediary sector. At the same time, there are no compelling reasons why the optimal scale and scope of intermediaries will diminish greatly, given that there are still fixed capital and production requirements in the technology of financial intermediation.

The implications of the twin information revolutions for the regulation of financial intermediation also are far from certain. If regulation continues to be primarily institution-based, we would expect the overall regulatory burden to be roughly proportional to the size of the regulated subsectors. Although we do not believe the subsectors that have traditionally been heavily regulated – for example, banking and insurance – will necessarily decline in relation to the size of the economy, we do foresee a decline in their importance relative to the scope of financial intermediation activity as a whole, including also brokerage services in public financial markets. Therefore, our baseline expectation is for a steady or perhaps slightly declining regulatory burdern.

There are two countervailing risks, however. Financial activity that occurs in public markets is typically harder to regulate, since the contracts traded in markets are flexible and even the jurisdiction of trading activity is a matter of negotiation between the trading parties. If the scope of financial-market regulation were to be expanded to compensate for any possible shrinkage of the regulated subsectors, the burden of regulation might not decline and could even increase. At the same time, there is a compelling need for governments to restructure and sharpen the regulation that protects the public's underwriting of guarantees provided to financial intermediaries. More effective regulation is needed because the ability of financial intermediaries to exploit underpriced options will increase. On the one hand, the number of nimble players in public markets will increase, while on the other hand, banks, insurance companies, and other traditional on-balance-sheet intermediaries will become more opaque, increasing the risk that public guarantees will be mispriced.

The paper proceeds in five sections. Section I briefly outlines the "twin information revolutions" noted above. Section II provides a simple framework for understanding the implications of the twin information revolutions. Section III applies the framework to analyze why financial intermediaries' clienteles have shifted and why direct contracting by ultimate counterparties in public financial markets has increased at the expense of intermediated contracting via private markets. Section IV explores the structural, regulatory, and welfare implications of the trends we identify in financial intermediation. Finally, Section V concludes.

1. THE TWIN INFORMATION REVOLUTIONS

A. The information revolution in the theory of financial intermediation

Traditional explanations of financial intermediaries focused on the technical conveniences and mechanical functions of firms that interposed themselves between the ultimate buyers and sellers of financial claims (Tobin, 1992, p. 80). These functions included risk-pooling, -reduction, and -allocation; maturity shifting; enhancing the liquidity of and fractionating financial claims. Very little explicit importance was attached to the information-processing tasks undertaken by financial intermediaries, although there was certainly an implicit understanding that sorting, monitoring, and controlling of one or both counterparties in a transaction was essential to the "gatekeeper" role played by banks and other financial institutions (Schumpeter [1911], 1934, pp. 72-74).

The information revolution in the theory of financial intermediation involves a recognition that informational and contracting problems are a major source of value creation by financial intermediaries.[1] While the existence of informational frictions – difficulties in contracting and transacting that would diminish or vanish altogether if everyone had perfect information – is a profound insight of this theoretical paradigm, a second implication of the revolution in information theory may be just as important for providing clues to the future of financial intermediation. This secondary insight is that the mere availability of data is not the same thing as having economically useful information.[2] Thus, the modern information-based theory of financial intermediation implies that one must account for qualitative distinctions according to the source and nature of the information transmitted and received.

All financial intermediaries process risk and information. Nevertheless, it is useful to distinguish between two broad categories according to the type of risk-processing performed (see Greenbaum and Thakor, 1995, Chapter 2). Brokerage is a function performed by financial intermediaries that process information but largely avoid directly absorbing financial risk; the risks they face relate instead to the marketability of the information they produce and to the potential loss of reputation they could suffer if a client becomes dissatisfied. The financial services that correspond to our notion of the brokerage function include transactions services, provision of financial advice, screening and certification, origination and issuance of securities for borrowing firms, securing other types of funding and trust services. These firms may not require as much specialized human capital nor as large a quantity of financial capital as some other types of financial intermediaries.

Qualitative asset transformers, on the other hand, are financial intermediaries that process information and also absorb financial risk by acting as a principal in financial transactions. (The risks of producing worthless information and of exposing the firm's reputation to harm are also relevant for the qualitative asset transformer, of course.) The financial services encompassed by the qualitative asset-transformation function include monitoring of borrowers, provision of management expertise as in a venture-capital firm, provision of financial guarantees, and liquidity provision or enhancement.

The usefulness of financial intermediaries that perform pure brokerage functions can be described in terms of searching an informational grid for a given piece of information. The larger the grid or the more difficult it is to recognize the object of search, the more valuable is the broker for given costs of information collection. Qualitative asset transformers, in addition to searching for information, also provide valuable risk-intermediation services to the extent that they are able to offer contracts that are preferable to direct contracting in financial markets for one or more of the ultimate counterparties to a transaction.

B. The information revolution in data processing and communications

The second "information revolution" influencing financial intermediation is being driven by the falling cost of transmitting and processing data, or "digital information." Advances in computer hardware and software, tele-communications, and in the physical networks that support data communication and processing have combined with dramatic steps toward deregulation and restructuring across a wide spectrum of industries to drive the marginal costs of communicating and processing digital information toward zero. The technology shocks implied by the computing and tele-communications revolutions radically alter the relative marginal factor productivities of the inputs used by financial intermediaries, namely, data, capital resources, and labor. This basic fact is the driving force in our analysis of financial intermediation.

2. FINANCIAL INTERMEDIARIES AS PRODUCERS OF CREDIBLE INFORMATION

We posit two distinctive technologies for producing "credible information" from three types of inputs, namely, capital, labor, and "digital information," or data. To qualify as output of credible information, the information produced by a financial intermediary must either serve as a basis for profitable principal transactions by the intermediary itself or be sold to others; in other words, it must pass a market test. The output is calibrated according to the "opacity" or "information intensity" of the various customer segments in the economy. For example, opacity might be related empirically to the risk premium that a given customer would be required to pay to borrow on an unsecured basis.

The two technologies for producing credible information correspond to our notions of brokerage and qualitative asset transformation. A broker produces credible information as output according to the production function

$$Y^B = f(L,I)$$

and an asset-transforming financial intermediary produces credible output according to

$$Y^{AT} = g(K,L,I)$$

where f and g are increasing and concave functions in each of the inputs used and are subject to decreasing returns to scale. We will think of K as a vector of capital resources dedicated to credible-information production, encompassing physical capital such as bricks and mortar as well as financial capital, each measured in appropriate units.[3] Note that the use of physcial and financial capital inputs is the distinguishing feature of asset-transforming financial intermediaries. The labor input, L, represents both skilled and unskilled labor services employed by the firm, measured as a vector of person-hours at each skill level. Finally, digital information or data, I, is publicly available information the reliability of which does not depend on who sends it. This input is measured in physical units such as bits.

The value of Y_j that we apply to a financial intermediary, j, is the most opaque customer segment served by that firm. We will think of customer opacity as a one-dimensional scale along which all potential customers are sorted, as in Figure 3–1:

Transparent...Translucent...Opaque

| 1 | 2 | 3 | 4 | 5 | 6 | 7 |

Figure 3–1. Opacity of customer segment[4]

This representation of the financial firm's output is meant to suggest only that serving more opaque customers requires the use of more inputs, in general. The key property of financial intermediaries' production function is that the inputs are, to some extent, substitutable for each other.

A profit-maximizing financial intermediary's problem is to minimize the total cost of producing a given output of credible information, Y0. The cost function for an asset-transforming intermdiary is

$$C^{AT} = \Phi + w_K K^{AT} + w_L L^{AT} + w_I I^{AT}$$

where Φ is the fixed cost associated with maintaining significant capital resources, and w_K, w_L, and w_I are the unit prices of the inputs K, L, and I (w_K and w_L are vectors of capital and labor costs corresponding to the different types of capital and labor noted above). The input prices are strictly positive and are determined in the economy as a whole. They are taken as given by each competitive financial intermediary. The fixed cost, Φ, is unique to the asset-transforming intermediary and is the cost component generated by the existence of capital resources. In contrast to the term $w_K K^{AT}$, which is the *flow* cost of capital services, Φ is invariant to the level of output and corresponds to the cost of maintaining the *stock* of capital. Thus, Φ corresponds in our setup to the upkeep and depreciation of physical capital and to the "maintenance costs" of financial capital, which include expenses like regulatory compliance costs.

The cost function for a brokerage intermediary is

$$C^B = w_L L^B + w_I I^B$$

where the terms are defined as above. The key difference in the cost function of the broker is the absence of either fixed or variable costs associated with capital inputs.

Our two main static results relate to the boundaries of financial-intermediary activity. The first describes the limit of financial intermediation, in general.

Result 1: Rationing. There exists $\bar{Y} < \infty$ such that financial intermediaries will not serve any customer segments that require credible information greater than $\bar{Y}$. That is, all customer segments in the set $Y > \bar{Y}$ are rationed, *i.e.*, are either unserved or are underserved.

Intuition. The result follows from the assumption of increasing concave production functions and strictly positive factor prices. Since $f_{ii} < 0$ and $g_{ii} < 0$ for all factor inputs i, there must exist a $\bar{Y}_i$ such that $f_i = w_i$ and $g_i = w_i$ for each factor. The smallest of all the $\bar{Y}_i$ is the output level, $\bar{Y}$, beyond which financial intermediaries are unprofitable.

Stated differently, the intuition behind this result is simply that, with diminishing marginal returns to greater inputs of capital, labor, and digital information, there is an upper bound on the information opacity that can be profitably served by a financial intermediary. Beyond some point, limited economic resources are more profitably deployed elsewhere in the economy.

In terms of the ordinal scale of customer-segment opacity described above, this result implies that the scale can be constructed such that one or more (non-empty) segments are left unserved or underserved by financial intermediaries. For example, if $\bar{Y}$ lies between customer segments five and six, we would represent the extent of financial intermediation as in Figure 3–2.

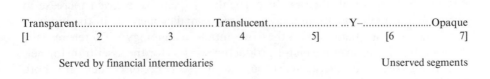

Transparent..Translucent........................ ...Y–.......................Opaque
[1   2   3   4   5]   [6   7]

       Served by financial intermediaries   Unserved segments

Figure 3–2. Opacity of customer segment

The second result describes the nature of the boundary between customer segments served by asset-transforming financial intermediaries – "private markets" – and those segments served in public markets by brokerage-type financial intermediaries.

Result 2: Public/private market boundary. There exists a $\underline{Y}$, $0<\underline{Y}<\bar{Y}<\infty$, such that the average cost of serving a customer segment below this level is greater in private than in public markets and the reverse is true above this level. That is, brokers serve any customer segments that require credible information less than $\underline{Y}$, while qualitative asset transformers serve only customer segments that require credible information greater than $\underline{Y}$.

Intuition. The proof consists of showing that the average cost curve of a broker is flatter than that of an asset-transforming financial intermediary and that they intersect at an output level $\underline{Y}$. This point characterizes the boundary between public and private markets, as indicated in Figure 3–3.

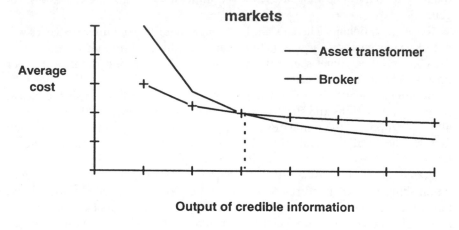

Figure 3–3. The boundary between public and private markets

The total and average cost curves of an asset-transforming intermediary lie above those of a broker at very low outputs of credible information since the asset transformer incurs fixed costs, $\Phi>0$. At the other extreme, the situation is reversed. This is because the asset transformer's higher fixed costs become insignificant while its average variable costs are lower for any level of output. Lower average variable costs for the asset transformer follow from diminishing marginal returns of all factors. In particular, to achieve a given increase in output, the three-input technology requires a smaller increase in the input of any one factor than does the two-input technology. Therefore, the deterioration in the average factor productivity is less for the asset transformer.

Finally, the two average-cost curves intersect because they are both continuous. That is, there must exist a Y such that both types of financial intermediary make the same profit on that customer segment. All customer segments in the set $Y \leq \underline{Y}$ are served in public markets by brokers, while customers for whom $Y > \underline{Y}$ are either served in private markets (*via* asset transformers) or not at all.

The intuition behind this result is that very transparent clienteles can be served profitably by using relatively less capital (literally none in our stylized example) to facilitate direct trade with ultimate counter parties. Meanwhile, more opaque clienteles can best be served by financial intermediaries that enhance basic data with dedicated physical and financial capital resources.

Why would a financial intermediary acquire specialized capital inputs if these are not strictly necessary to produce credible information? The concept of "information reusability" (Chan, Greenbaum, and Thakor, 1986) refers to the ability of a financial intermediary to extract rents in one financial transaction on the basis of proprietary information obtained in a prior transaction with the same or a different but similar customer (Chan, Greenbaum, and Thakor, 1986; Rajan, 1992; Boot, Greenbaum, and Thakor, 1993). The existence of reusable information in the hands of an incumbent intermediary constitutes a barrier to entry for a potential competitor. To compete on an equal footing, this newcomer would need to procure the information for itself.

For example, if $\underline{Y}$ lies between customer segments two and three, we would represent the extent of financial intermediation as in Figure 3–4.

Transparent.................... $\underline{Y}$ ....Translucent.................... ....$\overline{Y}$........................Opaque

[1	2]	[3	4	5]	[6	7]

| Public markets | | Private markets | | Unserved | |
| Brokers | | Asset transformers | | | |

Figure *3–4*. Opacity of customer segment

We have argued that profit-maximizing asset-transforming financial intermediaries will ration some customers at the opaque end of the informational spectrum, while these intermediaries will be unable to profitably serve some clienteles at the transparent end of the spectrum, where brokers facilitate trade in public markets. Given this static characterization, we now examine the comparative-static effects of falling digital-information costs on the extent of rationing by financial intermediaries and on the public/private market boundary.

3. SHIFTING INTERMEDIARY CLIENTELES AND THE EXPANSION
OF PUBLIC MARKETS

Falling digital-information costs have profoundly affected the nature and scope of financial intermediation. This section highlights two of these effects, namely: (1) a secular expansion of the customer base served by asset-transforming financial intermediaries toward more information-intensive (opaque) and previously unserved or underserved segments, and (2) the simultaneous expansion of public markets serviced by brokerage-type financial intermediaries at the expense of asset-transforming intermediaries in private markets. In terms of the ordinal scale presented above that ranks customer segments according to their information opacity, asset-transforming financial intermediaries have unambiguously shifted to the right as a result of lower digital-information input costs. While public markets and therefore brokers have increased in importance and the number of unserved customer segments has decreased, it is not at all clear whether private markets and asset transformers have increased or decreased in absolute size, profitability, or scope. This is because previously unserved clienteles have, to some extent at least, replaced the customer segments lost to public markets.

Evidence that asset-transforming financial intermediaries have increasingly served more opaque customer groups is abundant. Banks have increased their lending over the last several decades to developing-country borrowers, lower-rated businesses, and consumers with sub-prime credit characteristics. Insurance companies have pushed into riskier investment categories. Investment banks have become involved in junk bonds, bridge loans, and private banking to even the moderately wealthy.

In terms of our model of the asset-transforming financial intermediary, the declining unit cost of digital information induces a greater input of this factor, in turn increasing the output of credible information that is possible. In other words, some of the clienteles for whom credible-information production was prohibitively costly can now be served at acceptable cost, as the following result shows.[5]

Result 3: Falling digital information costs decrease rationing. Suppose that financial intermediaries ration all customer segments with information opacity $Y > \bar{Y}$ when the unit cost of digital information is w_I (see Result 1). Now suppose that the unit cost of digital information falls to $w_I' < w_I$. Then there exists a $\bar{Y}'$, $\bar{Y} < \bar{Y}' < \infty$, such that financial intermediaries will not serve any customer segments that require credible information greater than $\bar{Y}'$, but can serve segments with $Y \le \bar{Y}'$. Thus, now only the customer segments in the set $Y > \bar{Y}'$ are rationed.

Intuition. We start by assuming the existence of a level of rationing defined by $\bar{Y}$ when the unit cost of digital information is w_I such that customer segments with information opacity $Y > \bar{Y}$ are not served (Result 1). The result follows by noting that a fall in the cost of one factor input induces profit-maximizing intermediaries to increase the amount of that input used until the equality among all marginal factor productivities is re-established. With unchanged technologies, this increased input of the now cheaper factor unambiguously raises output for both types of intermediary. As before, the fact that $f_{ii}<0$ and $g_{ii}<0$ for all factor inputs i means that there must exist a $\overline{Y_i}'$ such that $f_i = w_i$ and $g_i = w_i$ for each factor. The smallest of all the $\overline{Y_i}'$ is the output level, $\overline{Y}'$, beyond which financial intermediaries are unprofitable. It must be true that $\overline{Y}<\overline{Y}'<\infty$, that is, that the customer segments rationed out of the market are fewer than before the digital-information cost fell.

In terms of the ordinal scale discussed above, falling digital-information costs shift to the right the boundary between customer segments served by financial intermediaries and those left unserved, as shown in Figure 3–5.

Transparent....................$\underline{Y}$........................Translucent...................$\overline{Y}$............ ..$\overline{Y}'$......Opaque

[1   2]   [3   4   5   6]   [7]

Public markets   Private markets   Unserved
Brokers   Asset transformers

Figure 3–5. Opacity of customer segment

A rapid shift toward more opaque customer segments has necessitated processing of new and less familiar risks by existing financial intermediaries. One result has been increased fragility of many institutions as their dedicated human-capital resources, such as specialized corporate lenders, have been prematurely depreciated. A declining credit standing for many opaque financial intermediaries bears witness to this transition cost (see Figure 3–6).

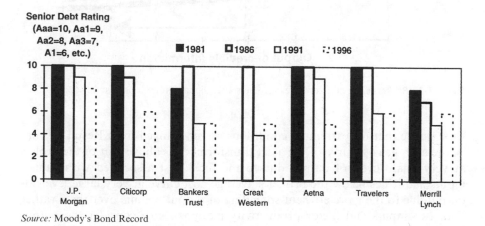

Source: Moody's Bond Record

Figure 3–6. Bond ratings of opaque financial institutions, 1961-96

The asset-transforming financial intermediary's gain in market share due to its ability to profitably service previously unserved clienteles is offset by a loss of market share to public markets, however, as the next result makes clear. The intuition for this result is that the brokerage technology uses the now cheaper digital-information inputs more intensively than does asset transformation, so the productivity of brokerage in public markets increases more than does asset transformation in private markets.

Result 4: Falling digital information costs shift the public/private market boundary. There exists a $\underline{Y}>0$ such that the average cost of serving a customer segment below this level is greater in private than in public markets (Result 2). Now suppose the unit cost of digital information falls to $w_I'<w_I$. Then there exists a $\underline{Y}'$, where $\underline{Y}'>\underline{Y}>0$, such that the average cost of serving a customer segment below $\underline{Y}'$ is greater in private than in public markets and the reverse is true above this point. Therefore, the public market expands at the expense of private markets.

Intuition. The argument is that the intersection of the average-cost curves of asset-transforming financial intermediaries and brokers occurs further to the right (at a greater level of output, Y) after the cost of digital information falls (Figure 3–7).

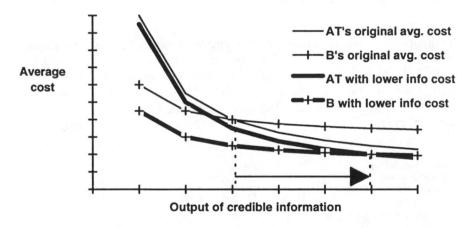

Figure 3–7. Brokers serve more opaque customers after digital-information cost falls

First notice that the extremum conditions are unchanged from Result 2. That is, the average cost curve of the asset transformer lies above that of the broker at very small levels of output due to the fixed cost associated with capital inputs and it lies below the broker's average cost curve at very large levels of output due to the more efficient spreading of output volume over three rather than two inputs and factor productivity margins. Now consider the output level $\underline{Y}$ at which the average cost curves of the two types of intermediaries are equal under the original cost of digital information, w_I. Since the broker must produce the same output with only two inputs, rather than the asset transformer's three inputs, each of the inputs is used relatively more intensively by the broker. In particular, $I^B > I^{AT}$ for any fixed level of output.

Any given reduction in the unit cost of input I therefore results in a larger reduction in total and average costs for the broker for unchanged inputs and output than is true for the asset transformer. That is, the broker's average cost is lower at the output level $\underline{Y}$ than is the asset transformer's average cost. Since the asset transformer's average cost curve is steeper than the broker's and the extremum conditions are the same as in Result 2, the new intersection of the average cost curves, $\underline{Y'}$, must lie to the right of the old intersection, or $\underline{Y'} > \underline{Y} > 0$, after each type of intermediary re-optimizes its supply schedule over all output levels. The boundary between public and private markets shifts to the right, meaning that some customer segments that were formerly served by asset-transforming intermediaries are now served by brokers.

In terms of the ordinal scale used above, falling digital-information costs shift the boundary to the right between customer segments served by public and private markets (see Figure 3–8).

| Transparent.............$\underline{Y}$.................$\underline{Y'}$.....Translucent.................. ... $\overline{Y}$............ .. $\overline{Y'}$... Opaque |

| [1 | 2 | 3] | [4 | 5 | 6] | [7] |

Public markets   Private markets   Unserved
Brokers   Asset transformers

Figure 3–8. Opacity of customer segment

For example, corporate borrowers that previously used bank loans to manage liquidity shift to commercial paper and note-issuance facilities; other borrowers that relied on traditional mortgages, term loans, or private placements shift toward securitized offerings that rely directly on the public capital market. Although many of the same financial intermediaries may be involved, the nature of their involvement shifts from acting as principal to that of a brokering agent.

In sum, the unambiguous effects of falling digital-information costs are twofold: the extent of rationing by financial intermediaries declines, while the extent of the public market and the role of brokerage-type financial intermediaries increases. The net effect of these changes on the market share and profitability of asset-transforming financial intermediaries remains ambiguous, in principle. The next section explores some of the collateral implications of the scenario sketched above.

4. STRUCTURAL, REGULATORY, AND WELFARE IMPLICATIONS

As noted by Coase (1937) and echoed by Merton and Bodie (1995), the net effects of technological change (or changing factor input prices generally) on the optimal scale and scope of firms and on the industrial organization of an affected sector may be ambiguous, in principle. Coase concluded that

> ... most inventions will change both the costs of organizing [a firm] and the costs of using the price mechanism [for trading in markets]. In such cases, whether the invention tends to make firms larger or smaller will depend on the relative effect on these two sets of costs. (Ronald H. Coase, "The Nature of the Firm," (1937), note 31.)

Merton and Bodie apply a functional perspective on financial intermediation to reach a similar conclusion:

> Whether the financial services industry becomes more concentrated or more diffuse in this scenario [in which aggregate trading volume expands secularly, and trading is increasingly dominated by institutions] is ambiguous. The central functions of information and transactions processing would seem to favor economies of scale.... On the other hand, expansion in the types of organized trading markets, reductions in transactions costs, and continued improvements in information processing and telecommunications technologies will all make it easier for a greater variety of firms to serve the financial services functions. (Robert C. Merton and Zvi Bodie, "A Conceptual Framework for Analyzing the Financial Environment," (1995), p. 25.)

Our analysis may therefore help to clarify what appears to many to be a fundamental ambiguity regarding the outlook for financial intermediation. We are able to do this by disaggregating the sector into its two logically distinct functional components, namely, brokerage and qualitative asset transformation. By doing so, we are able to analyze the effects of falling digital-information costs on each subsector individually. While some observers, such as Allen and Santomero (1996), hint at our general conclusion that the financial-intermediation sector as a whole must expand as a result of technological developments in recent years, they are unable to shed light upon the causal connection running from falling digital-information costs to increased financial intermediation.[6] They thus do not identify the glacial shift that is occurring *within* the financial-intermediation sector itself.

The declining importance in the U.S. of opaque financial intermediaries and the simultaneous ascendance by more transparent intermediaries has been evident for many years. What is new in recent years is merely the speed with which this restructuring of the financial-intermediary sector has been occurring (see Figure 3–9).

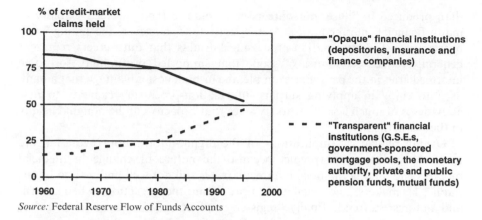

Source: Federal Reserve Flow of Funds Accounts

Figure 3–9. The decline of "opaque" financial institutions, 1960-95

Our framework leads us to predict that scale and scope economies will become more important for some financial intermediaries but not for all. In particular, intermediaries that carry out brokerage functions will become larger and more diverse, although these diverse activities will all share the characteristics of brokerage. This result follows from the fact that brokerage-type intermediaries use digital information relatively intensively to produce credible information. Falling digital-information costs represent a significant windfall for firms engaging in these activities, leading them to expand. Evidence that these trends are already in place comes both from the aggregate financial-asset data above and from the anecdotal evidence of recent expansion of online stockbrokers and mutual-fund distributors, electronic banking and personal-finance providers, securitizers of various sorts, and mass-distribution insurance companies, to name but a few.

Qualitative asset transformers, on the other hand, benefit relatively less than do brokers from falling digital-information costs. As outlined in previous sections, the focus of asset-transformation services is of necessity being shifted away from the more transparent clienteles that have become prey for brokers in public markets and toward more opaque customer segments that were previously unserved. The ambiguous effect on scale, scope, and profitability identified by Coase, Merton and Bodie, and others properly applies to this subsector only.

Asset-transforming financial intermediaries also face competitive pressures from non-intermediary firms offering outsourcing of various operations. Functional disintermediation represents a threat to the continued institutional viability of opaque intermediaries that is focused not at the boundaries of traditional intermediary activity but at the very core of their operations. Of course, Coase's dictum that "inventions" cut both ways applies here, as well. By allowing scale economies and technical expertise to be bought in rather than produced in-house, outsourcers contribute to the continued viability of many financial intermediaries. At the same time, however, the falling entry barriers into the information-processing business that outsourcers represent generally reduce economies of scope that supported profitability for some intermediaries in the past. For example, the in-built cost advantage that a bank used to enjoy in applying surplus information-processing capacity to new activities is of much less value today since that capacity can be bought cheaply in the market.

Overall regulatory implications of the digital-information revolution are particularly difficult to predict because the nature of change in financial markets and among financial intermediaries is still not well understood by the public, lawmakers, and regulators. Forecasting their reactions when current and unforeseen trends finally "register on their radar screens" is therefore fraught with non-economic risks. If traditional rationales for financial regulation remain intact, including a large concern for systemic and macro-economic risks, then institution-based oversight and regulation will continue to predominate. Since the most intrusive regulation has focused on opaque financial intermediaries, their declining relative importance would translate into a declining regulatory burden.

One implication that follows logically from falling information costs is the declining ability of public regulators to limit the private value derived from public guarantees. Falling information costs have lowered barriers to entry in much of financial intermediation. Lower entry barriers translate into greater competition, which, in turn, squeezes the rents that intermediaries might expect to earn. As is now well-recognized, positive rents are *necessary* for implementing incentive-compatible regulation designed to limit the cost of government safety nets and guarantees (Chan, Greenbaum, and Thakor, 1992). Thus, falling information costs translate into an increased exposure of the public purse to exploitation by financial intermediaries in the absence of reform of extant guarantees.

If consumer protection and other aspects of social policy grow in political importance, however, the shifting composition of the intermediary sector will be less important. In fact, the shift toward larger public markets and a more opaque clientele for asset-transforming financial intermediaries would make consumer-protection and similar mandates more difficult to carry out. This is due in part to the ease of entry and exit by participants in markets and also to the ease of shifting the jurisdiction of such activity. It may also be more difficult to deliver regulatory benefits to the more opaque customer segments that are an increasing part of financial intermediaries' clienteles.

The net welfare effects of the digital-information revolution are unambiguously positive, at least in the long run. The extent of financial intermediation has increased, as previously unserved and underserved clienteles are drawn into the market. The shifting composition of the financial-intermediary sector reflects the free interplay of supply and demand factors and therefore must represent a more desirable distribution of activity and resources than that which preceded it. The only wild card in the scenario is the possible infringement of the financial marketplace by overzealous and relatively ineffective regulation. This risk appears remote, however, as the process of financial innovation that has already occurred has not evoked any sizable backlash among politically influential clienteles.

5. CONCLUSIONS

We conclude on the basis of an analysis of the "twin information revolutions" affecting financial intermediation that the total amount of financial intermediation will increase in the economy. The information revolution in the theory of financial intermediation reveals that intermediaries are viable because they transform raw data, or digital information, into branded and reliable, or credible, information. A straightforward implication of this insight is that falling digital-information costs – the outcome of the second information revolution – reduce the real cost of producing credible information. These twin information revolutions lead us to predict that a greater amount of financial intermediation will occur in the economy. This, in turn, raises economic welfare unambiguously, at least in the long run after transitional costs diminish.

Looking beneath the surface, we see quite different implications of the digital-information revolution for the two major types of financial intermediaries. Qualitative asset-transforming intermediaries may or may not increase in proportion to the economy, but they will of necessity serve a more opaque clientele, on average. Intuitively, this shift among the clienteles served by banks, insurance and finance companies, and other asset transformers, results from their attempt to exploit their comparative advantage in producing credible information with a technology including relatively large amounts of human, reputational, and financial capital.

Brokerage-type intermediaries operating in public markets, on the other hand, will almost certainly expand in relation to the level of economic activity generally, as has been the case for many years. The relatively transparent and standard risks that can be served more profitably by brokers in public markets than by asset transformers in private markets have increased in number because falling digital-information costs represent a significant windfall to brokers. The broker's production function for producing credible information relies heavily on digital information, so its reduced cost greatly increases the broker's productivity.

We do not foresee dramatic implications for the structure of the financial-intermedation sector emanating from changed scale and scope economies. Although brokerage is likely to reflect the economies of large scale evident in the information-processing business generally due to its massive digital-information inputs, there is little reason to believe that asset-transforming financial intermediaries will become much larger as a result of falling information costs. The rising tide of functional disintermediation (outsourcing) in fact points in the opposite direction, toward a reduction in the minimum efficient scale and scope of the asset-transforming financial intermediary. Specialist providers (including brokers) will displace conglomerates.

The economic burden imposed by regulation of financial intermediaries could (and we believe will) decrease as a result of the twin information revolutions. Intuitively, financial regulation either for consumer-protection purposes or to protect the public purse's exposure to government guarantees will become more difficult (less "productive"). The rational response would be to decrease the amount of regulation attempted along with circumscribing the extent of public guarantees. Whether this in fact occurs depends on the policy process, which we are loath to predict.

SUMMARY

Two information-related trends will continue to shape financial intermediation. The information revolution in the theory of financial intermediation, which recognizes that overcoming informational and contracting problems is a major source of value creation, implies that intermediaries exist to produce "credible information" for sale to others or for own-account trading and investment. The second information revolution is symbolized by the falling cost of transmitting and processing data (what we term "digital information"). Since digital information is a key input into the production of credible information, the real input costs of financial intermediation will fall and output will rise. Previously unserved or underserved clienteles will be better served.

We distinguish between two logically distinct types of financial intermediaries, namely, brokers and qualitative asset transformers. The former's activities are characterized by a simple matching of buyers and sellers, taking little or no direct financial risk in the transaction. This type of intermediary uses relatively large amounts of digital information and relatively small amounts of physical or financial capital. The falling cost of digital-information inputs is a significant windfall for this type of intermediary, whose activities will expand. The qualitative asset transformer, on the other hand, is characterized by direct financial participation in a transaction. This type of financial intermediary uses digital-information less intensively to produce credible information, so windfall gains from cheaper digital information are less significant. Therefore, asset transformers lose relatively transparent clienteles to brokers, while gaining more opaque and previously unserved or underserved clienteles.

NOTES

1 A representative list of papers developing this view includes Leland and Pyle (1977), Campbell and Krakaw (1980), Diamond (1984), Ramakrishnan and Thakor (1984), Millon and Thakor (1985), Fama (1985), Chan, Greenbaum, and Thakor (1986), Boyd and Prescott (1986), and Allen (1990). Bhattacharya and Thakor (1993) and Greenbaum and Thakor (1995) provide comprehensive overviews of the information-theoretic approach to financial intermediation.
2 Merton (1987) makes a similar point by drawing a distinction between companies producing information through public disclosure and investors actually assimilating it. Our distinction between data and information describes the process by which financial intermediaries transform data into information as it flows from the ultimate producer to the ultimate buyer.
3 Of course, we are not suggesting that brokers operate without any physical or financial capital, but merely that these inputs are not as central to the brokerage function as to the asset-transformation function.
4 The terms "transparent," "translucent," and "opaque" are from Ross (1989, p. 542).
5 See Berlin and Mester (1992) on the cross-sectional value to borrowers of intensive monitoring and renegotiation provided by banks.
6 Allen and Santomero conclude (1996, p. 25): "Transaction costs have fallen and information has become cheaper and more available. However, these changes have not coincided with a reduction in intermediation. In fact, quite the reverse has happened. Intermediaries have become more important in traditional markets.... We have argued that participation costs are crucial to understanding the current activities of intermediaries and in particular their focus on risk management."

REFERENCES

Allen, Franklin, "The Market for Information and the Origin of Financial Intermediation," *Journal of Financial Intermediation* 1 (1990), pp. 3-30.
Allen, Franklin and Anthony M. Santomero, "The Theory of Financial Intermediation," Wharton Working Paper 96-32, August 1996.
Berlin, Mitchell and Loretta J. Mester, "Debt Covenants and Renegotiation," *Journal of Financial Intermediation* 2 (1992), pp. 95-133.
Bhattacharya, Sudipto and Anjan V. Thakor, "Contemporary Banking Theory," *Journal of Financial Intermediation* 3 (1993), pp. 2-50.
Boot, Arnoud W.A., Greenbaum, Stuart I. and Anjan V. Thakor, "Reputation and Discretion in Financial Contracting," *American Economic Review* 83 (1993), pp. 1165-1183.
Boyd, John H. and Edward C. Prescott, "Financial Intermediary Coalitions," *Journal of Economic Theory* 38 (1986), pp. 211-232.
Campbell, Tim S. and William A. Krakaw, "Information Production, Market Signalling, and the Theory of Financial Intermediation," *Journal of Finance* 54 (1980), pp. 863-882.
Chan, Yuk-Shee, Greenbaum, Stuart I. and Anjan V. Thakor, "Information Reusability, Competition, and Bank Asset Quality," *Journal of Banking and Finance* 10 (1986), pp. 243-253.
Chan, Yuk-Shee, Greenbaum, Stuart I. and Anjan V. Thakor, "Is Fairly Priced Deposit Insurance Possible?" *Journal of Finance* 47 (1992), pp. 227-246.
Coase, Ronald H., "The Nature of the Firm," *Economica* 4 (1937), pp. 386-405.
Diamond, Douglas W., "Financial Intermediation and Delegated Monitoring," *Review of Economic Studies* 51 (1984), pp. 393-414.
Fama, Eugene F., "What's Different About Banks," *Journal of Monetary Economics* 15 (1985), pp. 29-39.
Greenbaum, Stuart I. and Anjan V. Thakor, *Contemporary Financial Intermediation* (Fort Worth: The Dryden Press, 1995).

Leland, Hayne and David Pyle, "Information Asymmetries, Financial Structure, and Financial Intermediation," *Journal of Finance* 32 (1977) pp. 371-387.

Merton, Robert C., "A Simple Model of Capital Market Equilibrium with Incomplete Information," *Journal of Finance* 42 (1987), pp. 483-510.

Merton, Robert C. and Zvi Bodie, "A Conceptual Framework for Analyzing the Financial Environment," Chapter 1 in *The Global Financial System* (Boston: Harvard Business School Press, 1995), pp. 3-31.

Millon, Marcia and Anjan V. Thakor, "Moral Hazard and Information Sharing," *Journal of Finance* 40 (1985), pp. 1403-1422.

Rajan, Raghuram, "Insiders and Outsiders: The Choice Between Informed and Arm's- Length Debt," *Journal of Finance* 47 (1992), pp. 1367-1400.

Ramakrishnan, R.T.S. and Anjan V. Thakor, "Information Reliability and a Theory of Financial Intermediation," *Review of Economic Studies* 51 (1984), pp. 415-432.

Ross, Stephen A., "Institutional Markets, Financial Marketing, and Financial Innovation," *Journal of Finance* 44 (1989), pp. 541-556.

Schumpeter, Joseph A., *The Theory of Economic Development*, 1911, translated from the German by R. Opie (Cambridge, Mass: Harvard University Press, 1934).

Tobin, James, "Financial Intermediaries," in Peter Newman, Murray Milgate, and John Eatwell, editors, *The New Palgrave Dictionary of Money and Finance* (London: MacMillan Press, 1992), pp. 77-85.

PART TWO

STEVEN J. PILOFF AND ANTHONY M. SANTOMERO

4. The value effects of bank mergers and acquisitions

ABSTRACT

The banking industry has experienced an unprecedented level of consolidation on a belief that gains can accrue through expense reduction, increased market power, reduced earnings volatility, and scale and scope economies. A review of the literature suggests that the value gains that are alleged have not been verified. The paper then seeks to address alternative explanations and reconcile the data with continued merger activity. In general, we find these explanations are rationalizations for the non existence of positive value outcomes, not alternative, testable theories. Recently, a new thread of the literature has developed which seeks to understand individual cases, looking into the process of change for a particular merger. This approach seems potentially rewarding and revealing, but what we will learn is still an open question.

1. INTRODUCTION

Over the past decade, the banking industry has experienced an unprecedented level of consolidation as mergers and acquisitions among large financial institutions have taken place at record levels.[1] In the last three years alone more than 1500 mergers have occurred in the US market. To a large extent, this consolidation is based on a belief that gains can accrue through expense reduction, increased market power, reduced earnings volatility, and scale and scope economies. Whether or not bank mergers actually achieve the expected performance gains is the critical question. If consolidation does, in fact, lead to value gains, then shareholder wealth can be increased. On the other hand, if consolidating entities does not lead to the promised positive effects, then mergers may lead to a less profitable and valuable banking industry.

A reading of the literature suggests that the value gains that are alleged to

---

The views expressed do not necessarily reflect those of the Board of Governors or its staff.

Y. Amihud and G. Miller (eds.), Bank Mergers & Acquisitions, 59–78
© *1998 Kluwer Academic Publishers. Printed in the Netherlands.*

accrue to the large and growing wave of merger and acquisition activity have not been verified. This has left the research community in a quandary. Has the industry followed a path of massive restructuring on a misguided belief of value gains? Is management in this sector just incompetent? Or, are they merely lying to shareholders about the effect of their activity on shareholder value?

The present paper seeks to address these alternative explanations and reconcile the data with the empirical reality of continued merger and acquisition activity. It is not easy. The banking industry is following a path of widespread consolidation even while academics seek answers to why it is going on. The literature in the area is rich in terms of data and variation of techniques employed. But, the results are disappointing in that they leave the reader with no greater understanding of why banks are merging, or which banks are merging, or when this transformation of the industry will stop.

In this paper we begin with a review of this literature on the effects of merger and acquisition activity. Then we attempt to put it in context, and finally, we try to learn from the experience. We argue that the literature, in fact, has done a good job in researching the question at hand. It is just that we do not understand the answer. Gains by many measures are either small or non-existent. The researchers in this field try to explain away the overwhelming message of the literature. In general, these explanations are rationalizations for the non existence of positive value outcomes from the previously reviewed literature. They are not alternative, testable theories, in and of themselves. In fact, these rationalizations can be seen as attempts to defend the approaches taken in the literature from professional economists or bankers who do not find the results credible. But, recently, a new thread of the literature has developed which we find somewhat more promising. The recent interest in understanding individual cases, looking into the process of change for a particular merger and the realized outcome from the event, seems potentially rewarding and revealing. Where these case studies will lead, and what we will learn that can be generalized is still an open question.

Our review of the subject proceeds as follows. In Section 2, we begin with a synopsis of the benefits that are supposed to accrue to a merger transaction. Section 3 outlines the major empirical methodologies used to investigate and measure these alleged gains. This is followed by a discussion of the findings reported in the major studies in the area, although we have, no doubt, left out a few. As noted above, the results obtained are overwhelmingly unsupportive of the value effects. Both accounting and event studies offer no evidence of value gains. The average merger has either no effect on total firm value, or a slightly negative one. The reasons offered for these (non)results are enumerated and critiqued in Section 5, which we appropriately refer to as rationalizations. Then, in Section 6, we present a discussion of the newly emerging case approach. We attempt to explain why this research procedure is being employed and present both sides of the issue of whether such field studies will yield results. We end with Section 7, where our final thoughts are offered.

2. TRADITIONAL VIEWS OF THE VALUE OF MERGERS AND ACQUISITIONS

Merger and acquisition activity results in overall benefits to shareholders when the consolidated post-merger firm is more valuable than the simple sum of the two separate pre-merger firms. The primary cause of this gain in value is supposed to be the performance improvement following the merger. The search for post-merger performance gains has focused on improvements in any one of the following areas, namely efficiency improvements, increased market power, or heightened diversification.

Several types of efficiency gains may flow from merger and acquisition activity. Of these, increased cost efficiency is most commonly mentioned. Many mergers have been motivated by a belief that a significant quantity of redundant operating costs could be eliminated through the consolidation of activities. For example, Wells Fargo estimated annual cost savings of $1 billion from its 1996 acquisition of First Interstate.[2]

Consolidation enables costs to be lowered if scale or scope economies can be achieved. Larger institutions may be more efficient if redundant facilities and personnel are eliminated within the post-merger organization. Moreover, costs may be lowered if one bank can offer several products at a lower cost than separate banks each providing individual products. Cost efficiency may also be improved through merger activity if the management of the acquiring institution is more skilled at holding down expenses for any level of activity than that of the target.

Bank merger and acquisition activity may also encourage improved revenue efficiency in a manner analogous to cost efficiency. Some recent deals, such as the proposed acquisition of Boatmen's Bancshares by NationsBank, have been motivated by potential gains in this area.[3] According to this view, scale economies may enable larger banks to offer more products and services, and scope economies may allow providers of multiple products and services to increase the market share of targeted customer activity. Additionally, acquiring management may raise revenues by implementing superior pricing strategies, offering more lucrative product mixes, or incorporating sophisticated sales and marketing programs. Banks may also generate greater revenue by cross-selling various products of each merger partner to customers of the other partner. The result is supposed to be higher revenue without the commensurate costs, i.e., improved profit efficiency. The latter term in general refers to the ability of profits to improve from any of the sources noted above, cost economies, scope economies or marketing efficiency. In a sense, it represents the total efficiency gains from the merger without specific reference to the separately titled efficiency improvement areas.

Merger-related gains may also stem from increased market power. Deals among banks with substantial geographic overlap reduce the number of firms in markets in which both organizations compete. A related effect of in-market mergers is that the market share of the surviving organization in these markets is raised. These changes in market structure make the affected markets more vulnerable to reduced competition. The increased market power of the surviving organization may enable it to earn higher profits by raising loan rates and lowering deposit rates.

It should be noted that antitrust policies of the Federal Reserve and Department of Justice are designed to prohibit mergers with substantially anti-competitive effects. However, to the extent that a local market can be exploited by a merger which results in substantial market power, the potential gain could be significant.

Finally, mergers may enhance value by raising the level of bank diversification. Consolidation may increase diversification by either broadening the geographic reach of an institution or increasing the breadth of the products and services offered. Moreover, the simple addition of newly acquired assets and deposits facilitates diversification by increasing the number of bank customers.

Greater diversification provides value by stabilizing returns. Lower volatility may raise shareholder wealth in several ways. First, the expected value of bankruptcy costs may be reduced. Second, if firms face a convex tax schedule, then expected taxes paid may fall, raising expected net income.[4] Third, earnings from lines of business where customers value bank stability may be increased. Finally, levels of certain risky, yet profitable, activities such as lending may be increased without additional capital being necessary.[5]

Any one of these reasons for gains from mergers is sufficient, and different ones presumably are relevant in different circumstances. Not all mergers are expected to result in cost efficiencies, nor does each one result in higher revenue and/or diversification gains. However, for any specific merger to create value, at least one of these gains appears to be necessary to achieve it. A casual review of the press suggests most mergers assert cost advantages, while revenue and diversification gains are less often mentioned. When firms of dissimilar franchise merge, on the other hand, revenue efficiency or diversification are often the indicated reasons. Participants in in-market mergers trumpet cost efficiencies, while others allege market power outcomes. In the U.S., the geographic expansion of the franchise of major super regionals, by contrast, often speaks of the transference of best practice in production and the stability of a large geographic distribution channel.

Whether any of these gains are obtained is another matter. Bankers, and their investment bankers can allege all sorts of benefits. The key issue for the researchers in the area is whether or not these gains are observable. To address this issue, the literature has examined mergers in several different, but hopefully complementary ways. It is to this area that we now turn.

3. TRADITIONAL APPROACHES TO TESTING THE EFFECTS OF CONSOLIDATION

Most academic studies follow one of two approaches to estimate and evaluate the significance of merger-related gains.[6] The first compares the pre-merger and post-merger performance of institutions using accounting data to determine whether consolidation leads to changes in reported costs, revenue or profit figures. The strengths of this approach are that accounting performance can be directly measured and the data used are both easily obtained and well understood. The approach is also fairly straightforward. Data from both the pre-merger and post-merger period are used in the analysis and evaluated for evidence of a change in the performance around the merger activity. Proponents of this methodology argue that accounting data measure actual performance conditions, not investor expectations, and are therefore likely to be somewhat more reliable than the second approach which uses equity returns.

However, studies of accounting data have several drawbacks. Although accounting data are designed to measure actual performance, they may be inaccurate in an economic sense. Data are based on historical figures and often neglect current market values. In addition, measured changes between the pre-merger and post-merger period may not be solely due to the merger. Other events may have occurred during the period that is being investigated which may more accurately account for the observable performance changes. Failing to account for such extraneous events may lead to improper conclusions regarding merger-related changes.

The second approach to analyzing merger benefits evaluates the stock market reaction to merger announcements. Proponents of this approach argue that in as much as it relies on market data rather than accounting figures, it more accurately conveys the implied value of merging two independent entities. In essence, they argue that accounting data are unreliable and the market's reaction is likely to be a better indicator of the real economic effects of the announced deal. Most studies examine the abnormal returns of acquirers and targets separately, but several papers analyze the total change in shareholder wealth. In such cases, the value-weighted sum of acquirer and target abnormal returns is the appropriate measure of overall gains stemming from merger and acquisition activity. This measure quantifies the value creation that the market believes the merger will provide. Studies of the abnormal returns experienced by individual merger parties can not differentiate between the effect on value of consolidation and the effect of the wealth transfer embodied in the purchase price.

As with any approach, market price studies themselves are not perfect. They have their share of detractors who focus most often on the timing of the analysis. While abnormal return studies, which use market prices, have the benefit of not relying on potentially misleading accounting data, most studies only measure returns during a short period around the merger announcement. The analysis is, therefore, based solely on market expectations of unrealized events. Studying abnormal returns during the post merger period, however, has its own set of problems. The interpretation of the few studies of abnormal returns that extend into the post-merger period is unclear. Observed returns may be attributable to expected bank performance or to other factors which may be unrelated to the merger transaction under investigation.

In all studies, it is unclear what event period is most preferred. How many days before the announcement are necessary to capture the effect of information leakage without including too much unrelated noise? How many days after the announcement are appropriate to enable the market to fully trade on information regarding the proposed transaction? If the event period is important, results may be influenced substantially by the window selected for analysis.

Another potential shortcoming of abnormal return studies is that samples tend to be small. By definition, sample mergers must involve publicly traded institutions. However, relatively few banks have traded equity, so only a small portion of all bank mergers can be included in studies of abnormal returns.

Recently, a third approach has emerged in the literature which incorporates and extends the two basic methods of analysis. Several papers not only analyze the relationship between mergers activity and both changes in accounting figures and stock market returns, but go a step further. These studies measure the correlation between changes in accounting data and abnormal returns. In so doing, the ability of the market to accurately forecast subsequent performance changes is examined. The extended analysis addresses the question of whether the market is able to differentiate among mergers that ultimately achieve improved performance and those that fail to achieve gains.

4. A REVIEW OF THE PUBLISHED LITERATURE

Before examining the applications of the three approaches enumerated above, a practical issue arises, namely, what should be the level of the analysis. Two primary approaches to defining mergers exist in the literature. Mergers are defined at the bank level and at the holding company level. A bank-level merger occurs when previously distinct banks are consolidated into one institution. Consolidations of individual banks under the same holding company are often included in samples of mergers defined this way. Analyzing mergers at the bank level is appealing for several reasons. Not only have there been a great number of mergers at this level, but, because the FDIC Report of Income and Report of Condition (call report) measure performance at the bank level, data are easily obtained for these types of mergers. However, studying bank-level mergers centers the study on the impact of changing organizational structure. It does not clearly assess the gains brought about by new ownership which economists general view as the centerpiece of the analysis of mergers and acquisitions. Therefore, most studies focus on mergers of holding companies. A merger at the holding company level is defined by a change in ownership of a subsidiary bank or a group of subsidiary banks. This type of merger is viewed in the same manner regardless of whether the newly acquired banks are consolidated into a single institution or continue to operate as separate entities under new ownership. By construction, analysis of this type of merger is particularly useful in examining the effect of changes in ownership.

A large portion of the empirical work examining the benefits of mergers focuses on changes in cost efficiency using available accounting data. Berger and Humphrey (1992), for example, examine mergers occurring in the 1980s that involved banking organizations with at least $1 billion in assets. The results of their paper are based on data aggregated to the holding company level, using frontier methodology and the relative industry rankings of banks participating in mergers. Frontier methodology involves econometrically estimating an efficient cost frontier for a cross-section of banks. For a given institution, the deviation between its actual costs and the minimum cost point on the frontier corresponding to an institution similar to the bank in question measures X-efficiency. The authors find that, on average, mergers led to no significant gains in X-efficiency.[7] Berger and Humphrey also conclude that the amount of market overlap and the difference between acquirer and target X-efficiency did not affect post-merger efficiency gains. In addition to testing X-efficiency, they also analyze return on assets and total costs to assets and reach a similar conclusion: no average gains and no relation between gains and the relative performance of acquirers and targets. Non-interest costs yield significant results, but the findings are opposite of expectations that the operations of an inefficient target purchased by an efficient acquirer should be improved.

Akhavein, Berger, and Humphrey (1997) analyze changes in profitability experienced in the same set of large mergers as examined by Berger and Humphrey. They find that banking organizations significantly improved their profit efficiency ranking after mergers. However, rankings based on more traditional ROA and ROE measures that exclude loan loss provisions and taxes from net income did not change significantly following consolidation.

DeYoung (1993) also utilizes frontier methodology to examine cost efficiency and reaches similar conclusions as Berger and Humphrey. Cost benefits from mergers did not exist for 348 bank-level mergers taking place in 1986 and 1987. In addition to the lack of average efficiency gains, improvements were unrelated to the difference between acquirer and target efficiency. However, DeYoung does find that when both the acquirer and target were poor performers, mergers resulted in improved cost efficiency.

In addition to frontier methodology, the literature contains several papers that solely employ standard corporate finance measures to analyze the effect of mergers on performance. For example, Srinivasan and Wall (1992) examine all commercial bank and bank holding company mergers occurring between 1982 and 1986. They find that mergers did not reduce non-interest expenses. Srinivasan (1992) reaches a similar conclusion.

Both of these studies focus solely on non-interest expenses resulting in an incomplete picture of the cost savings associated with mergers. In order to gain a complete view of bank costs, the total of interest and non-interest expenses must be examined. Various funding and investment strategies have different impacts on the two cost components. For example, an increase in purchased funds raises interest costs, but lowers non-interest costs. Therefore, to avoid attributing efficiency gains to changes in funding methods or investment choices, total costs must be evaluated.[8]

Toward this end, Rhoades (1993) conducts a thorough examination of in-market mergers taking place between 1981 and 1986. He regresses the change in several performance measures on control variables and a dummy variable differentiating banks that engaged in an in-market merger from those that did not. Rhoades also conducts several logit analyses where the dependent variables measure whether the efficiency quartile of a bank increased, decreased, or remained unchanged. In both sets of tests, cost reductions and efficiency gains were not significantly related to horizontal mergers.

The 1993 study is the most recent of a number of studies on the subject by this author. In an earlier study, Rhoades (1987) examines the impact of mergers on the ratios of net income before extraordinary items to assets and non-interest expenses to assets. He runs probit analyses in which a dummy variable distinguishing non-acquired banks from banks acquired by multibank holding companies is the dependent variable. Performance measures and several control variables serve as the independent variables. Rhoades finds that neither income nor non-interest expenses were affected by merger activity. In Rhoades (1990), a similar study to Rhoades (1993) is conducted with 13 acquisitions involving billion dollar banks. Consistent with his other work, Rhoades finds no performance effect due to mergers.

The work of Linder and Crane (1992) is also noteworthy. They analyze the operating performance of 47 bank-level intrastate mergers that took place in New England between 1982 and 1987. Of the 47 mergers in the sample, 25 were consolidations of bank subsidiaries owned by the same holding company. The authors aggregate acquirer and target data one year before the merger and compare it to performance one and two years after consolidation. The performance of merged banks is adjusted by the performance of all non-merging banks in the same state as the merging entities. The results indicate that mergers did not result in improved operating income, as measured by net interest income plus net non-interest income to assets.

Several studies find evidence of merger gains, but the results of these studies must be scrutinized carefully. Spindt and Tarhan (1993) find gains in their sample of 192 commercial bank mergers completed in 1986. Non-parametric tests comparing the performance changes of merged banks with a group of matched pairs indicate that mergers led to operating improvements. The results, however, may be due primarily to economies of scale. The existing evidence in the literature suggests that scale economies do exist for institutions holding less than $100 million in assets.[9] Spindt and Tarhan's results are based on a sample that is dominated by mergers involving banks of this size. Because the results may be driven by economies of scale at small institutions, it is unclear whether their findings are relevant to large mergers – the transactions most severely transforming the banking industry.

Chamberlain (1992) demonstrates the importance that sample selection can have in influencing the results of a merger study. Her sample consists of 180 bank subsidiaries that were acquired by bank holding companies between 1981 and 1987. The unit of analysis is the individual target bank that experienced a change in ownership, but was not consolidated into another bank. For each merger, matched pair analysis is conducted. Pre-merger and post-merger performance of the acquired bank are compared to those of a non-acquired bank from the same area and of similar size and leverage. While Chamberlain finds evidence of overall gains when Texas mergers are omitted from the sample, the full sample yields no evidence of gains.

Turning to studies of stock market reactions to merger announcements, researchers also generally fail to find total gains from consolidation. Most abnormal return studies typically analyze target and acquirer returns separately. However, in order to measure the overall anticipated gains resulting from a merger, the value-weighted average of bidder and target abnormal returns must be analyzed. Most research on abnormal returns does not do this.

Hannan and Wolken (1989) conduct a study of the value-weighted abnormal returns experienced in 43 deals announced between 1982 and 1987. The authors find that, on average, total shareholder value was not significantly affected by the announcement of the deal. The authors do, however, find that one determinant, target capitalization, cross-sectionally influenced expected synergistic gains. Target capital was negatively related to the change in total value.

Houston and Ryngaert (1994) examine abnormal returns from four days before the target was initially declared a takeover candidate (by any bank) to the announcement day. In their sample of 153 mergers announced between 1985 and 1991, acquirers suffered a loss in value and targets enjoyed a gain. However, there was no significant aggregate effect on the overall value of the two organizations. The amount of value that was created was highest when acquirers were strong pre-merger performers and when substantial overlap existed. This relationship of value creation with the degree of overlap is consistent with the market expecting mergers best-suited for improved efficiency and/or increased market power to experience the greatest level of post-merger benefits.

Madura and Wiant (1994) study abnormal returns of acquirers over a lengthy period following the merger announcement. They find that average cumulative abnormal returns of acquirers in a sample of 152 deals taking place between 1983 and 1987 were negative during the 36-month period following the merger announcement. Moreover, abnormal returns were negative in nearly every month. Acquirer losses around the time of the announcement may reflect a loss of wealth from an overly generous acquisition price. Negative abnormal returns in months after the announcement, however, are not likely to be due to the price. They seem more attributable to either the merger achieving fewer benefits than projected, or the market revising downward its expectations for the merger.

The only serious study of the European market on this issue is the recent work by Cybo-Ottone and Murgia (1996). In it they analyze 26 mergers of

European financial services firms (not just banks) taking place between 1988 and 1995 in 13 European banking markets. Their results are qualitatively similar to much of the analysis conducted on American banking organizations. Average abnormal returns of targets were significantly positive and those of acquirers were essentially zero. This pattern suggests that there was a transfer of wealth from acquirers to targets. Also comparable to mergers of American banks, the change in overall value of European financial firms at the time of the announcement was small and not significant. This pattern continued for at least a year. In the year following the merger, (excluding the first 10 days after the announcement), the combined value of the acquirer and target did not change significantly.

The findings of Zhang (1995) on U.S. data contradict those of most abnormal return studies. Among a sample of 107 mergers taking place between 1980 and 1990, the author finds that mergers led to a significant increase in overall value. Although both merger partners experienced an increase in share price around the merger announcement, target shareholders benefited much more on a percentage basis than the acquiring shareholders. Cross-sectional results suggest that increases in value were smallest when improved efficiency and increased market power were expected to have their greatest potential impact. Changes in value decreased as targets got larger relative to acquirers and as the amount of geographic overlap between acquirers and targets increased. The latter finding is consistent with diversification creating value.

Recently, several papers incorporate both approaches in the literature. The first of these studies is conducted by Cornett and Tehranian (1992) and examines 30 large holding company mergers occurring between 1982 and 1987. The authors find that profitability, as measured by cash flow returns on the market value of assets, improved significantly after the merger. This finding, however, must be viewed closely for several reasons. First, cash flow returns may be a poor measure of bank operating income. This measure includes provisions, a large non-cash expense for many banks during the sample period. Second, the market value of assets may be an inappropriate measure for standardizing income. It is defined primarily from the liability side of the balance sheet as the market value of common stock plus the book value of long-term debt and preferred stock less cash. Given the nature of banks as financial intermediaries, it is unclear why deposits are not included in this liability-based definition. The appropriateness of subtracting cash holdings is also debatable. Cornett and Tehranian find that net income to assets, a more traditional measure of bank profitability, does not change by a significant amount.

In addition, the findings of Cornett and Tehranian may also be partially driven by adjusting performance by an improper benchmark. The authors use, as their peer group, a sample of banks located throughout the country that were traded on either the NYSE or AMEX and that did not merge during the sample period. This comparison set of banking organizations may not be relevant to the sample institutions which had significantly different regional characteristics. This problem is accentuated by a set of sample observations which has a number of questionable deals.[10] As a result, Cornett and Tehranian's findings of post-merger improvements relative to a benchmark may be due to the unique data used for the study.

Cornett and Tehranian also examine value-weighted abnormal returns around the time of the merger announcement. They find that the market responded to announced deals by raising the combined value of the merger partners. The authors also find that changes in several performance measures, including cash flow returns on the market value of assets, were positively correlated with value-weighted abnormal returns. These relationships suggest that the market may have been able to accurately forecast the eventual benefits of individual mergers. Net income to total assets is not one of the variables that was correlated to value-weighted abnormal returns, however.

Pilloff (1996), like Cornett and Tehranian, combines both approaches found in the literature to analyze a sample of 48 mergers of publicly traded banking organizations that merged between 1982 and 1991. His study improves upon Cornett and Tehranian by addressing many of the problems in that paper. First, results are based on traditional measures of performance that are appropriate for a study of banking organizations. Second, the performance of merging banks is compared to a more accurate benchmark that controls for geographic location. Third, and perhaps most importantly, the merger sample is larger with substantially fewer observations that are poorly suited for analysis.

Pilloff obtains results that are consistent with the bulk of the merger literature. In general, mergers were not associated with any significant change in performance, suggesting that managers were unable to generate benefits from deals on average. Moreover, the mean overall change in shareholder value was also quite small.

Although there was no average change in either operating performance or shareholder value, there was a great deal of variation among banks. Some mergers proceeded successfully and others resulted in failure. Likewise, the dispersion of changes in market values indicates that investors expected some mergers to increase and others to decrease firm value. A particularly important result of this paper is that merger-related changes in performance were found to be unrelated to changes in market value at the time of merger announcement. Investors recognized that although the mergers would not create benefits on average, some would result in better performance and some would lead to worse performance. However, the market was unable to distinguish between the two types of deals at the time the mergers were initially announced.

In summary, most studies fail to find a positive relationship between merger activity and gains in either performance or stockholder wealth. This conclusion of no economic benefits holds across a wide variety of methodologies, samples, and levels of analysis, (individual bank or bank holding company). Moreover, there appears to be no relationship between changes in value at announcement and subsequent outcomes. Although Cornett and Tehranian find the existence of a relationship, Pilloff provides stronger evidence for nonexistence.

5. EXPLANATIONS AND RATIONALIZATIONS

The general findings of the merger literature raises the question of why bank consolidation has been and continues to be so prevalent, when gains are not observable on average. Moreover, equity returns indicate that they have been difficult, if not impossible, to accurately forecast. Several answers to this question have been offered. The first of these is the most straightforward. The argument goes that the nature of the data may obscure the true economic impact of mergers.

There are a number of arguments offered in this regard. It is often contended that the lack of market data biases studies of accounting data. It is also argued that perhaps the post-merger time period is insufficiently long to capture the gains. Consolidation includes well-known transition costs, which may disguise operating gains achieved shortly after merger completion. Moreover, many performance gains may take time to either be achieved or be reflected in financial reports.[11] Extending the post-merger period does not alleviate the issue, because this solution includes its own problems. Beyond a certain point, the analysis of the merged firm relative to some peer control group relates less to the merger itself than to the idiosyncratic circumstances of each market or firm-specific strategy. There is a limit to the extent that the merger can be held accountable for the firm's relative performance.

Studies of abnormal returns are also not immune from these data problems. In these studies, the time period under consideration is typically short, but the exact interval is uncertain. With firms engaged in discussions prior to announcement and investors speculating on potential acquisition targets, the researcher is frequently unsure about the exact period to analyze. In truth, the correct timing is likely to be deal-dependent and probably requires careful analysis in each and every case. However, to do so somewhat vitiates the benefits of a broad based cross-section analysis. The researcher hopes to gain some insight into the average benefits by looking at a large number of such events. If the time period of analysis varies across the transactions investigated, the standardization is lost. So, researchers have tended to examine fixed pre- and post-merger time periods for purposes of gaining insight on market value effects.

There is another issue that frequently comes up when critiquing the empirical studies, some selection bias. Researchers often examine mergers in a way that excludes relevant data points in an effort to obtain a clean data set. Typically, only deals that involve banks that engaged in no other major merger activity during the period surrounding the deal of interest are studied. Deals by banks that either had multiple mergers in the same year or engaged in several deals over a given time period are often excluded from analysis. Requirements like these omit the very firms that are most relevant to analysis of consolidation. For example, banks such as Nations Bank and Bank One, just to name two, have been active acquirers, and are reputed to be especially efficient in the integration process. However, these very firms are often excluded from the samples investigated due to the selection criteria listed above. The consequence may be a sample that biases results. These firms may be active participants that achieve substantial gains. Their elimination may lead to the no-gain results reported above. At the very least, their omission from many of the samples may exclude interesting data from the analysis.

Is this list of data problems sufficiently severe to lead one to discount the entire literature? We think not. While there are always data problems in every field, it is hard for us to imagine that the results reported above by so many different researchers can be dismissed because of data impurities. While these problems should clearly be of concern and the effect of sample bias and timing needs ongoing scrutiny, it seems unlikely that those technical features alone can reverse the overwhelming quantity of evidence against gains in performance and value.

Other researchers seem to concur with the conclusion that data problems are not masking real gains, and have recently offered stories to explain the inconsistency of the empirical evidence with the ongoing wave of bank mergers. The explanations center on two allegations concerning managerial behavior. The first of these explanations is managerial hubris. In short, managers have an unrealistic view of their skill and talent, leading them to believe that they are capable of obtaining gains from the acquisition of another institution. However, in truth, they are no more capable than others. Therefore, ex post results do not lead to superior performance.[12] The argument, then, comes down to the contention that ex ante expectations of performance gains systematically exceed ex post performance. Variability in realized gains are not attributable to differences in managerial skill, but to unpredictable noise in the integration process. This rationalization of the empirical results is appealing, at least to the research community that studies, but does not operate within, the banking industry. The argument states that the research is correct and the managers are systematically incorrect.

However, the managerial hubris argument is a bit incredulous. It is based upon a view that managers are systematically blind to the reality of the situation, and that they do not observe the actual outcomes of their past actions or the actions of their peers. Further, it contends that shareholders and boards are oblivious to the reality of the situation and allow management to engage in activity that systematically has no positive shareholder value. This story might work for a one-time event, as in an industry where mergers and acquisitions are rare. In such circumstances, the truth of the situation is not apparent until after the action and there is no way to develop reasonable expectations of the ex post earnings effects. These conditions do not seem consistent, however, with the U.S. banking market. With the number of mergers totaling 420 in 1995, 564 in 1994 and 477 in 1993[13], it is hard to believe that shareholders are unaware of the consequences of managerial action in this area or the likely outcome of the next acquisition.

In addition, it is not at all clear why managerial hubris in the mergers and acquisitions area should be any greater than in other areas of bank activity. Perhaps managers have over-inflated egos and unrealistic views of their own talents. However, elsewhere in finance we presume that reality impinges upon delusion and markets have a way of sorting these things out. Why is it the case that this does not occur here? The literature is silent on this point.

A second rationalization offered for the absence of observed gains in the literature centers around agency problems. It is well known that there is a general lack of alignment between the interests of shareholders and managers. This point has received considerable attention in the recent corporate finance literature.[14] To many, the recent wave of mergers in the banking industry is one more piece of evidence of this phenomenon. According to this view, mergers are in the best interest of managers but not necessarily shareholders. The former engage in the activity to increase their own power and remuneration, which are both assumed to be related to institutional scale. However, this behavior comes at the expense of the shareholders of the acquiring institutions who, in general, overpay for such acquisitions and suffer dilution, if not decline, in firm value itself. Managers in the acquired institution seem oblivious to the issue of agency problems. They seem able to exploit the interests of the acquiring manager by obtaining systematic gains to shareholders of acquired firms even while they are displaced in the process.

Some may appropriately object to this characterization of acquired firm managers. They seem more than capable of obtaining golden parachutes and lucrative buyout agreements. However, the evidence is that, on average, they negotiate a price which increases shareholder value, even while the acquiring management is following another agenda of self-interest.

This contrast between the managerial behavior of acquired and acquiring firms is problematic. It seems that if manager behavior is driven by self-interest, rather than purely increasing market value, then the behavior of managers on both sides of the negotiation should be explainable using the same paradigm. This is indeed possible. Perhaps the gains from mergers are a reality. However, the side payments to the two groups of managers completely exhaust them, resulting in a neutral effect on value and reported performance measures. This would be consistent with the data and the allegations of an agency problem. Continuing management, according to this view, obtains the gains associated with running a larger organization, such as greater power, prestige and remuneration, while departing management receives the present value of their gain in terms of a buyout compensation package. The mystery is why the costs of such a transaction are born by the acquiring organization, rather than split by the two groups of shareholders. Perhaps there is a "winners' curse", where acquiring firms bid up the price of other firms who are willing to sell out. However, this theory has not been investigated empirically, and the differential returns accruing to acquirer and acquired firm shareholders remains a puzzle.

In light of our inability to explain the results reported above using conventional economic arguments some recent researchers have attempted to investigate the effect of merger activity using a different approach. They propose investigating merger events with close scrutiny of managerial process and the extent to which plans are both put in place and accomplished. This approach, while still in a nascent state, argues that the performance gains that can be forthcoming from merger activity are often unique to a specific merger and difficult to estimate or even see using the standard cross-section tools heretofore employed. Rather, to understand and obtain estimates of the value gains requires case by case examination of merger activity. This has led to a growing number of case-specific studies which have tried to analyze specific mergers and document the outcomes and their associated efficiency gains or, in some cases, losses.

At the core of this examination of merger results is a view that it is difficult to go from the specific to the general. It argues that averages obscure the fact that many good mergers occur, which add efficiency gains, and that can be explained on a case by case basis. And, there are still others where gains, while potentially sizable, never accrue to the surviving firm's shareholder. In the latter case, the management may never follow through with plans to downsize operations or eliminate excess capacity, or does not fully exploit the merger's potential. Yet, from a technical point of view the efficiency gains are both feasible and estimable. Researchers pursuing this line of investigation hope to obtain results on managerial best practice by examining events on a case by case basis. They look for estimates of pure efficiency gains and a better understanding of why the standard cross-section analysis does not systematically find evidence of performance gains.

6. THE MANAGERIAL PROCESS OR FOLLOW THROUGH APPROACH

Economists are understandably suspect of an examination of empirical regularities that begins with an assertion that every case is unique. Nonetheless, the reality is that existing explanations of the data seem hard-pressed to explain the ongoing and substantial merger activity in the banking sector. It does seem that the research in this area is somehow missing an important factor in this ongoing trend. Whether the managerial process studies can unearth new insights or result in mere rationalizations for the fact that traditional empirical approaches are incapable of revealing performance gains is still open to question. But certain facts suggest that this approach to understanding the effect of mergers warrants at least some consideration.

It is a well-documented fact that the variability of efficiency across banks of a specific size and product mix is far greater than any variation in efficiency that has been associated with either scale or scope.[15] Accordingly, there seems to exist an opportunity for revenue enhancement as well as cost efficiency gains from the merger of firms with different efficiency levels. In fact, the data reported by Berger and Humphrey (1992) suggest that on average acquiring firms are more efficient than acquired institutions. Yet, the data show no evidence of across-the-board ex post efficiency gains.

The goal of this new field based research is to investigate why these efficiency gains do not materialize in the average merger data by closely examining mergers on a case by case basis. According to this approach, one needs to examine each merger to estimate the gains or losses associated with different parts of the merger process in order to understand the gain or loss from the entire merger transaction. These studies investigate the fixed costs associated with the transition to a merged entity, the time and the effort needed to downsize, restructure and close redundant production facilities, and management's attention to aggressively slashing expenses. They seek to understand where merged institutions quickly align their practices to least cost procedures and where they do not. They separately estimate transition costs, and gains from long term operating efficiency accruing to the combined organization. In fact, one of the goals of these studies is to separate these two features of any merger. They also study the process and timing issues surrounding the convergence to a single operating environment, as it is well known that the gains from the mergers materialize more quickly when the process of transition is completed early.[16]

At the very least, these studies may help provide an explanation for the observed cross section behavior reported in Section 4 above. In addition, by concentrating on a wider array of data, institutional detail and idiosyncratic evidence surrounding the process, they may offer new insight to the research community.

Doubters may argue that this procedure is too idiosyncratic. By moving to the specific from the general, broad patterns are lost. However, as has been reported above, there are no broad patterns! This type of investigation may permit some to emerge. It may also be suggested that this approach is nothing more than documenting the reasons for the failure of the average merger. However, it is important to understand that the focus of the hubris and the agency stories is that gains in fact do not exist. In the present context, the argument is quite different. Gains may exist, but they require specific know how and process talent to be achieved. The focus is on why some firms succeed while others fail, and it attempts to document the causes of these differences. As such, it is quite a different approach than the ones enumerated above. If successful, the literature may emerge from this exercise with a better understanding of both the merger process and the difficulties it encounters. In any case, it seems worthy of investigation.

Thus far there are three studies of which we are aware, of this case by case approach. The first reported by Calomiris and Karcuki (1996) examines nine bank merger cases. The second is a broad-based study at Wharton, including work by Frei, Harker and Hunter (1995) and Singh and Zollo. In both cases, the studies are on-going and results are scarce. The last is an on-going effort at the Fed, in which a similar project will produce results of nine in-depth analyses and, hopefully, lessons learned from the exercise.

While each of these studies is far from definitive and some have not even been formally released, the expectation is that they will begin to provide insights into the drivers of efficiency gains and obstacles to achieving them. Already, participants in such studies have suggested that process design and merger planning play a large role in the short and intermediate term benefits from mergers, (Frei, Harker and Hunter (1995), Frei and Harker (1996)). Each case study provides an insight into the reasons for the empirical outcome, not merely a rationalization of them. Whether they will truly provide fundamental economic insights is still an open question. However, as noted by Akhavein, Berger and Humphrey (1997), the data on X-efficiency suggests that many banks have cost levels that are 20% to 25% above those using best practice. Understanding firms' practices in merger consolidation may illustrate where gains are, which firms have exploited them, and by extension which managers have superior abilities in this area. At this point, however, it is only a hope.

7. SUMMARY AND CONCLUSIONS

The literature on the value of bank mergers and acquisitions presents a clear paradox. Empirical evidence indicates clearly that on average there is no statistically significant gain in value or performance from merger activity. On average, acquired firm shareholders gain at the expense of the acquiring firm. This is documented over the course of many studies covering different time periods and different locations. It is true whether one looks at accounting data or the market value of equity. Even more disturbing is that the market is unable to accurately forecast the ultimate success of individual mergers, as indicated by the absence of any correlation between changes in accounting-based performance measures and stock market returns around the merger announcement. Yet, mergers continue. Indeed the merger wave that has swept the U.S. shows no sign of abating and there is increasing evidence of a similar move in Europe.

How can these facts be reconciled? The answers that appear in the literature are reasonable enough and follow a predictable path. Maybe the empirical work is wrong. But, this does not seem likely because there have been many studies by many authors with incredibly robust results.

Maybe managers are suffering from self-delusion? But, it is hard to believe that a massive restructuring of the world financial structure is occurring because of a misguided view of one's own managerial talent.

Maybe managers are lying, telling the shareholders that they are creating value but merely expanding their own power base and compensation? But, here too, it seems incredulous to argue that major institutions have engaged in massive acquisition plans with the blessing of shareholders that gain no value from the exercise.

The truth may be that we do not understand what exactly is going on in the process of industry consolidation. The efforts that have recently begun to examine the managerial process and follow through that is associated with a specific merger deal may help shed some light on the matter. The key question is: can we explain the process and the recent expanded activity level from investigating merger deals on a case by case basis? Can this process lead us to an appreciation of the potential efficiency gains, and why they do not on average appear in the data that most economists examine? While we are not convinced, it appears a productive path to pursue, at least for a while.

NOTES

1 Throughout this paper, the terms "merger" and "acquisition" are used interchangeably.
2 Barton Crockett, "First Bank Claims Wells Overstates Deal Savings," American Banker (November 20, 1995).
3 Kenneth Cline, "NationsBank Sees Boatmen's Revenue Potential," American Banker (September 26, 1996).
4 See Santomero (1995) for a discussion of the benefits of diversification on shareholder value. This area of risk management has grown substantially as this review will illustrate.
5 This is a key rationalization in favor of a move toward universal banking. See Saunders and Walters (1994).
6 Rhoades (1994) provides an excellent discussion not only of the two approaches, but of many of the studies conducted from 1980 to 1993 that adopt them.
7 See Berger, Hunter, and Timme (1993) for an excellent discussion on the topic of financial institution efficiency.
8 The problems with ignoring total expenses and only analyzing non-interest costs are discussed in Berger and Humphrey (1992).
9 For good surveys of the literature on economies of scale, see Clark (1988) or Humphrey (1990).
10 See Piloff (1996) for a detailed discussion of this problem.
11 Discussions with a number of bank consultants and analysts indicated that as much as one half to three quarters of all merger-related cost savings should be achieved within a year.
12 See Roll (1986) for a further discussion
13 "Mergers and Acquisitions Roundup", American Banker (1996)
14 The obvious strategy point here is Fama (1980), but some more recent references include Morck, Shleifer, and Vishny (1990).
15 See Berger, Hanweck and Humphrey (1987), Berger and Humphrey (1991), Berger, Humphrey and Timme (1993) or Berger and Humphrey (1994) for a discussion of the overwhelming evidence.
16 Frei, Harker and Hunter (1995).

REFERENCES

Akhavein, J., A. Berger and D. Humphrey, "The Effects of Megamergers on Efficiency and Prices: Evidence from a Bank Profit Function," *Review of Industrial Organization* 12, forthcoming, 1997.
Amel, D., "State Laws Affecting Commercial Bank Branching, Multibank Holding Company

Expansion, and Interstate Banking," Working Paper, Board of Governors of the Federal System, 1991.

American Banker, "Mergers and Acquisitions Roundup," January 29, 1996.

Beatty, R., A. Santomero, and M. Smirlock, "Bank Merger Premiums: Analysis and Evidence," *Monographs in Finance and Economics*, Salomon Brothers Center, New York University, 1987.

Berger A., D. Hancock, and D. Humphrey, "Bank Efficiency Derived from the Profit Function," *Journal of Banking and Finance* 17 (2-3): 317-47, April 1993.

Berger, A., G. Hanweck and D. Humphrey, "Competitive Viability in Banking: Scale and Scope and Product Mix Economies," *Journal of Monetary Economics* 20 (3): 501-20, December 1987.

Berger, A. and D. Humphrey, "Bank Scale Economies, Mergers, Concentration and Efficiency: The U.S. Experience," Working Paper 94-25, Wharton Financial Institutions Center, University of Pennsylvania, 1994.

Berger, A. and D. Humphrey, "The Dominance of Inefficiencies over Scale and Product Mix Economies in Banking," *Journal of Monetary Economics* 28 (1): 117-48, August 1991.

Berger, A. and D. Humphrey, "Megamergers in Banking and the Use of Cost Efficiency as an Antitrust Defense," *The Antitrust Bulletin* 37 (3): 541-600, Fall 1992.

Berger, A., W. C. Hunter and S. G. Timme, "The Efficiency of Financial Institutions: A Review and Preview of Research Past, Present, and Future," *Journal of Banking and Finance* 17 (2-3): 221-249, April 1993.

Calomiris, C. and J. Karenski, "The Bank Merger Wave of the 1990s: Nine Case Studies," University of Illinois, 1996.

Chamberlain, Sandra L., "The Effect of Bank Ownership Changes on Subsidiary-Level Earnings," *Bank Mergers and Acquisitions*, Kluwer, forthcoming 1997.

Clark, Jeffrey A., "Economies of Scale and Scope at Depository Financial Institutions: A Review of the Literature," *Economic Review*, Federal Reserve Bank of Kansas City, 73 (8): 16-33, 1988.

Cline, Kenneth, "Nations Bank Sees Boatmen's Revenue Potential" *American Banker*, September 25, 1996.

Cornett, Marcia Millon and Hassan Tehranian, "Changes in Corporate Performance Associated with Bank Acquisitions," *Journal of Financial Economics* 31(2): 211-234, April 1992.

Crockett, Barton "First Bank Claims Wells Overstated Deal Savings", *American Banker*, November 20, 1995.

Cybo-Ottone, Alberto and Maurizio Murgia, "Mergers and Acquisitions in the European Banking Market," Working Paper, University of Pavia, Italy, 1996.

DeYoung, Robert, "Determinants of Cost Efficiencies in Bank Mergers," Working Paper 93-1, Office of the Comptroller of the Currency, 1993.

Fama, Eugene, "Agency Problems and the Theory of the Firm," *The Journal of Political Economy* 88 (2): 288-307, April 1980.

Frei, Frances and Patrick Harker, "Measuring the Efficiency of Service Delivery Processes: With Application to Retail Banking," Working Paper 96-31, Wharton Financial Institutions Center, University of Pennsylvania, 1996.

Frei, Frances, Patrick Harker and Larry Hunter, "Performance in Consumer Financial Services Organizations: Framework and Results from the Pilot Study," Working Paper 95-03, Wharton Financial Institutions Center, University of Pennsylvania, 1995.

Hannan, Timothy H. and John D. Wolken, "Returns to Bidders and Targets in the Acquisition Process: Evidence from the Banking Industry," *Journal of Financial Services Research* 3 (1): 5-16, October 1989.

Hawawini, Gabriel and Itzhak Swary, *Mergers and Acquisitions in the U.S. Banking Industry: Evidence from the Capital Markets*, Elsevier Science Publishers B.V., Amsterdam, the Netherlands, 1990.

Healy, Paul M., Krishna G. Palepu and Richard S. Ruback, "Does Corporate Performance Improve After Mergers?" *Journal of Financial Economics*, 31 (2): 135-175, April 1992.

Houston, Joel F. and Michael D. Ryngaert, "The Overall Gains from Large Bank Mergers," *Journal of Banking and Finance* 18 (6): 1155-1176, December 1994.

Humphrey, David B., "Why Do Estimates of Bank Scale Economies Differ?" Federal Reserve Bank of Richmond, *Economic Review* 76 (5): 38-50, September/October 1990.

Linder, Jane C. and Dwight B. Crane, "Bank Mergers: Integration and Profitability," *Journal of Financial Services Research* 7(1): 35-55, January 1993.

Madura, J. and K. J. Wiant, "Long-Term Valuation Effects of Bank Acquisitions," *Journal of Banking and Finance* 18(6): 1135-1154, December 1994.

Morck, R., A. Shleifer and R.Vishny, "Do Managerial Objectives Drive Bad Acquisitions?" *Journal of Finance* 45 (1): 31-48, March 1990.

Piloff, Steven J., "Performance Changes and Shareholder Wealth Creation Associated with Mergers of Publicly Traded Banking Institutions," *Journal of Money, Credit and Banking* 28: 294-310, 1996.

Rhoades, Stephen A, "The Efficiency Effects of Bank Mergers: Rationale for Case Study Approach and Preliminary Findings," Proceedings of a Conference on Bank Structure and Competition, Federal Reserve Bank of Chicago, 1993.

Rhoades, Stephen A., "The Operating Performance of Acquired Firms in Banking," in Wills, Caswell, Culbertson eds.: *Issues after a Century of Federal Competition Policy*, Lexington Books, Lexington, MA, 1987.

Rhoades, Stephen A., "Billion Dollar Bank Acquisitions: A Note on the Performance Effects", Mimeo, Board of Governors of the Federal Reserve System, 1990.

Rhoades, Stephen A., "Efficiency Effects of Horizontal (In-Market) Bank Mergers," *Journal of Banking and Finance* 17 (2-3): 411-422, April 1993.

Rhoades, Stephen A., "A Summary of Merger Performance Studies in Banking, 1980-1993, and an Assessment of the 'Operating Performance' and 'Event Study' Methodologies," *The Federal Reserve Bulletin* 80 (7): 588-590, July 1994.

Roll, Richard, "The Hubris Hypothesis of Corporate Takeovers," *Journal of Business*, 59 (2), Part 1: 197-216, April 1986.

Santomero, Anthony M., "Financial Risk Management: The Whys And Hows," *Financial Markets, Instruments and Institutions* 4 (5): 1-14, 1995.

Saunders, Anthony, and Ingo Walters, *Universal Banking in the US: What Could We Gain? What Could We Lose?*, Oxford University Press, 1994.

Spindt, Paul A. and Vefa Tarham, "The Impact of Mergers on Bank Operating Performance," Working Paper, Tulane University, 1993.

Srinivasan, Aruna, "Are There Cost Savings from Bank Mergers?" Federal Reserve Bank of Atlanta, *Economic Review* 77(2): 17-28, March/April 1992.

Srinivasan, Aruna and Larry D. Wall, "Cost Savings Associated with Bank Mergers," Working Paper 92-2, Federal Reserve Bank of Atlanta, 1992.

Zhang, Hao, "Wealth Effects of U.S. Bank Takeovers," *Applied Financial Economics* (55) 5: 329-336, October 1995.

ALLEN N. BERGER

5. The efficiency effects of bank mergers and acquisition: A preliminary look at the 1990s data

ABSTRACT

We estimate the cost, standard profit, and alternative profit efficiency effects of bank mergers of the 1990s. The data suggest that on average, bank mergers increase profit efficiency relative to other banks, but have little effect on cost efficiency. Efficiency gains are much more pronounced when the participating banks are relatively inefficient ex ante, consistent with an hypothesis that mergers may "wake up" inefficient management or are used as an excuse to implement unpleasant restructuring. The data suggest that part of the efficiency gains result from improved diversification of risks, which may allow consolidated banks to shift their output mixes from securities toward loans, raising expected revenues.

1. INTRODUCTION

Over the past five years, there has been a substantial research effort into the question of whether mergers and acquisitions (M&As) in the banking industry improve the efficiency of the consolidating firms.[1] Most of the research has focused on cost efficiency, or whether mergers reduce costs per unit of output for a given set of output quantities and input prices. However, some recent research has begun using profit efficiency, which includes the cost efficiency effects of M&As and also incorporates the revenue effects of the changes in output that occur after a merger. We will argue below that analysis of profit efficiency is more appropriate for the evaluation of M&As than cost efficiency because outputs typically *do* change substantially subsequent to a merger.

There are likely two main reasons for the research emphasis on the

The views expressed do not necessarily reflect those of the Board of Governors or its staff. The author thanks Yakov Amihud and Geoffrey Miller for organizing the conference, allowing me to present the paper, and providing helpful editorial advice, Katherine Schipper for very useful discussant's comments, Joel Houston, Dave Humphrey, Steve Rhoades, and the participants in the NYU Conference on Mergers of Financial Institutions for beneficial suggestions, and Seth Bonime for outstanding research assistance.

Y. Amihud and G. Miller (eds.), Bank Mergers & Acquisitions, 79–111
© *1998 Kluwer Academic Publishers. Printed in the Netherlands.*

efficiency effects of M&As. First, the literature is catching up with reality. The U.S. banking industry has been consolidating at a rapid rate over the 1980s and first half of the 1990s, largely due to the reduction of geographic barriers to branching and holding company affiliation imposed by the states, particularly the lifting of interstate barriers. Since the beginning of the 1980s, the number of independent banking organizations – top-tier holding companies plus unaffiliated banks – has shrunk by over one-third, from more than 12,000 to fewer than 8,000, and more than a quarter of the industry is now owned by holding companies headquartered in another state (see Berger, Kashyap, and Scalise 1995). The consolidation of the industry is likely to continue under the Riegle-Neal Interstate Banking and Branching Efficiency Act of 1994, which allows interstate branching into almost every state as of June 1, 1997.

The second reason for the recent research effort into the efficiency effects of M&As is that it is part of a general boom in the study of the efficiency of financial institutions. Berger and Humphrey (1997) documented 130 studies that measured the X-efficiency or frontier efficiency of financial institutions. Incredibly, 116 of these studies were dated 1992 or later.[2] This burgeoning literature is due in part to the ready availability of new efficiency measurement techniques and software that can be easily applied to the regulatory data provided by financial institutions. However, perhaps more important in the development of this research agenda is the recognition that efficiency information can be very usefully employed to study questions of public policy, to address research issues, and to improve managerial performance. Most of the efficiency studies over the past five years have not just measured efficiency, but have endeavored to determine the underlying causes and determinants of efficiency, including the effects of changes in corporate control like M&As.

X-efficiency estimation is particularly important to the study of bank M&As because it is the only way of which we are aware to determine whether these mergers may be in the public interest. A merger may have social value added if it improves cost efficiency by allowing the same outputs to be produced while employing a smaller value of inputs or if it improves profit efficiency by increasing the value of output produced more than the value of inputs employed. Such efficiency gains, if they occur, would have to be weighed against any social losses that may occur from an increase in the exercise of market power that might be brought about by an increase in market share or concentration associated with the M&A.

In principle, antitrust authorities could trade off between the social benefits of any expected improvements in firm efficiency and the social losses from any expected increase in the exercise of market power in setting bank prices for deposits, loans, or other services.[3] X-efficiency analysis can help by providing general information as to whether bank mergers do or do not improve efficiency. Moreover, efficiency analysis can be used to help discover specific information about the ex ante conditions that predict whether a particular merger is likely to yield significant efficiency gains that might then be traded off against predicted increases in the exercise of market power. In addition, X-efficiency analysis may be useful in measuring the change in the exercise of market power associated with mergers. Market power is generally measured using price or profit data, which depend upon both market power and efficiency. Therefore, to obtain a clean measure of the impact of M&As on the use of market power, it is necessary to control for the simultaneous effects of the change in efficiency.[4]

Perhaps most important, without measuring X-efficiency, we know of no way to distinguish improvements in efficiency from increases in the exercise of market power from M&As. Many studies have examined simple cost and profit ratios from before and after M&As, but such ratios incorporate both improvements in efficiency from input or output quantity changes and increases in the exercise of market power in setting prices. That is, costs may decrease because the consolidated bank is able to produce the same amount of output with fewer inputs or because the increase in local market concentration allows it to pay depositors lower rates. Similarly, revenues may increase because a higher valued product mix is being produced with the same inputs or because the consolidated bank is able to raise loan rates by virtue of an increase in market concentration and market power. In either case, a simple cost or profitability ratio cannot disentangle the socially beneficial effects of an increase in efficiency from the socially costly effects of the exercise of market power in pricing.

Other studies have estimated the effects of M&As or M&A announcements on the value of the banking firm through event studies and similar methods. However, as was the case for the simple cost and profit ratios, there is no way to determine whether the value of the firm increases because it has become more efficient or because it is able to exercise more market power. Markets assign equal value to increases in profitability from efficiency and market power. Only X-efficiency analysis, which examines the effects of changes in quantities, holding prices constant statistically, can determine whether there has been an increase in social value added.

The main purpose of this paper is to extend the past efficiency analysis of M&As to take a preliminary look at the 1990s data. We use data from the 1990-1995 interval to analyze the effects of mergers of U.S. banks over 1991-1994. To be comprehensive, we employ three separate X-efficiency concepts – cost efficiency, standard profit efficiency, and alternative profit efficiency. Only one prior study to our knowledge has examined the profit efficiency effects of any type of M&A, and this was limited to bank "megamergers" of the 1980s between banking organizations with assets over $1 billion (Akhavein, Berger, and Humphrey 1997).

By contrast, we shift the focus to the 1990s, and examine bank mergers of all sizes. We examine mergers in which two or more bank charters are combined during a single year into a consolidated bank. In many cases, these mergers are the consequences of holding company acquisitions in the same year or in the past few years. However, we exclude from consideration holding company acquisitions in which the banks retain separate charters, as these consolidations are likely to have different effects.

We measure whether the mergers on average improve the three types of efficiency, and also try to determine if there are any reliable ex ante conditions that might help predict which types of M&As are most likely to be successful in improving efficiency. We also test several hypotheses about which of these ex ante conditions predicts improvements in performance from M&As. The results are compared with some of the earlier findings that used data from the 1980s, which typically found little or no cost efficiency gains on average associated with M&As, but did find profit efficiency improvement in the one study of this topic.

The new information from the 1990s may yield particularly useful insights because there are several reasons to suspect that the efficiency effects of M&As in the 1990s may differ from those of the 1980s. As discussed below, changes in the goals of M&A participants, the removal of regulatory restrictions, differences in market conditions, and innovations in technology and applied finance may tend to predict more efficiency improvements on average for mergers of the 1990s than for those of the 1980s.

The remainder of the paper is organized as follows. Section II gives a brief summary of prior research on merger efficiency. Section III summarizes our methodology in measuring the three types of efficiency. Section IV gives our empirical results which include 1) the estimated cost, standard profit, and alternative profit efficiency effects of the mergers of the 1990s; 2) an analysis of how some of these efficiency gains might be manifested; 3) a regression analysis of some ex ante factors that may predict these efficiency effects; and 4) some results from prior studies of mergers of the 1980s using similar methodologies for comparison purposes. Section V concludes.

2. Brief Review of the Recent Bank Merger Efficiency Literature

The literature suggests that there is a substantial potential for efficiency improvements from mergers of banking organizations. On the cost side, the literature generally finds that average X-inefficiencies are on the order of about 20% to 25% of costs in the banking industry, although more recent estimates are often slightly below this range (see Berger and Humphrey 1997). This suggests that cost efficiency could be considerably improved by M&As in which relatively efficient banks acquire relatively inefficient banks and spread their superior management talent over more resources.[5] There may be additional potential for cost efficiency improvement when the merging banks are in the same local markets. This could occur by consolidating back-office operations, such as payments clearing, data processing, and accounting into the more efficient bank's operations center, and by eliminating duplicate branch offices, tellers, and mid-level management.

On the revenue side, there is potential for better diversification of risks through M&As. Putting together the loan portfolios of two different banks may improve diversification owing to wider coverage of geographic areas, industries, types of loans (e.g., commercial, real estate, consumer, municipal), and maturity structures. Although geographical diversification is likely the most important, these other types of diversification benefits can occur even in mergers of banks in the same local market. The improved diversification of risks would allow banks to shift from securities to loans and take on additional credit risks and earn higher expected returns for the same amount of equity and overall risk. That is, greater diversification would allow banks to shift into a higher revenue product mix – since loans have a higher expected return than securities – without the market requiring additional capital or higher interest rates on uninsured debt (see Benston, Hunter, and Wall 1995, Hughes, Lang, Mester, and Moon 1996, Akhavein, Berger, and Humphrey 1997, Demsetz and Strahan 1997).

Given that the potential for efficiency improvements from bank mergers has been fairly well established, the important question is whether this potential is achieved in practice. We argue that efficiency analysis is needed to determine whether consolidated banks actually do make improvements such as bringing the acquired portion of the consolidated entity up to the acquired's efficiency standard, enhance the performance of back-office and branching operations, and take advantage of diversification gains by shifting their portfolios into higher-expected-revenue investments. Importantly, measured efficiency changes also take into account any managerial diseconomies that may be engendered by a merger – such as difficulties in monitoring a larger firm, problems in integrating data processing systems, or conflicts in corporate culture – that may offset any of the other improvements in performance that occur following M&As.

Most of the merger cost studies have compared simple cost ratios – such as costs per dollar of assets – before and after M&As (e.g., Rhoades 1986,1990, Srinivasin 1992, Srinivasin and Wall 1992, Linder and Crane 1992, Pilloff 1996). As discussed earlier, these studies do not control for input prices, and so a reduction in costs per unit of output or assets could reflect lower interest expenses due to an increased exercise of market power in setting deposit interest rates. There are some studies which examine operating cost ratios that exclude interest expenses, and so would not be subject to this problem (e.g., Cornett and Tehranian, 1992, Linder and Crane 1992, Srinivasin, 1992, Srinivasan and Wall 1992). However, by excluding more than half of all banking costs, such studies are subject to some potentially more serious difficulties. In particular, these studies may be biased toward showing benefits from mergers. As banks merge and grow larger, they often tend to substitute interest cost-intensive purchased funds for operating cost-intensive core deposits, which would tend to make the operating cost ratio lower even if there is no decrease in total costs.

Another difficulty with cost ratios is that they do not account for the multiproduct nature of banking. Banks produce different output mixes that have very different costs of production. For example, the production of commercial loan outputs requires costly research and monitoring expenses in addition to the costs of raising the investable funds, whereas producing Treasury securities in the bank's portfolios requires little more than just the costs of raising the funds. The use of cost-to-asset ratios implicitly assumes that $1 of assets in either category should entail the same costs.[6]

Other studies used X-efficiency methods that employ cost functions to control for input prices, outputs, and other factors, to measure the efficiency effects of M&As (e.g., Berger and Humphrey 1992, Fixler and Zieschang 1993, Rhoades 1993, DeYoung 1997, Peristiani 1997). These studies control for prices, and so disentangle efficiency changes from the market power changes which may be incorporated into prices. These studies also account for the fact that different product mixes may have different costs by specifying multiple outputs. X-efficiency studies also typically include other control variables for the economic environment of the bank.

Of course, X-efficiency studies are not completely without sin, either. These studies (including the present study) typically treat prices as exogenous despite the possibility that the firm's efficiency or market power may affect the prices it pays on deposits or receives on loans. To the extent that prices are endogenous to the firm's actions, this may bias the coefficients of the cost or profit functions, which would affect the residuals used to measure X-efficiency. In addition, these efficiency residuals embody all the misspecifications of the cost or profit function, such as excluded variables, misspecifications of functional form, and errors in measuring the cost or profit dependent variable. As argued below, however, we consider X-efficiency measurement to be the lesser of evils.

Despite the differences in approach between the X-efficiency studies and the cost ratio studies, both come to essentially the same conclusion. There appears to be little or no improvement in cost efficiency on average from the mergers of the 1980s, with changes in efficiency or costs on the order of 5% or less. If there were technological gains on average from consolidating branches, computer operations, payments processing, etc., these may have been offset by managerial difficulties in monitoring the larger organizations, conflicts in corporate culture, or problems in integrating systems.[7]

Despite appearances, these academic findings do *not* necessarily conflict with consultant studies which forecast considerable cost savings from large bank mergers. As discussed in detail in Berger and Humphrey (1992), the academics and consultants tend to state their findings in different terms that may make their results appear inconsistent. However, when the assumptions and results of these two types of studies are expressed in the same fashion, they are generally consistent with each other. For example, Berger and Humphrey (1992) showed that a consultant claim of savings of 30% of the acquired bank's noninterest expenses might be about 3% of the consolidated bank's total expenses, within the range found by academic studies. This is because the acquired bank might be about 1/3 as large as the consolidated bank, and noninterest expenses might be about 30% of total expenses (based on the interest rates of the 1980s), giving 30% • (1/3) • .3 = 3%.

Moreover, the cost efficiency improvements that did occur were not very well predicted by ex ante factors thought to improve efficiency (relative efficiencies of merging banks, degree of market overlap, etc.). From a public policy viewpoint, this finding implies that it would be very difficult to trade off the expected social benefits of cost efficiency gains from M&As against the expected social losses from any greater exercise of market power in setting bank prices. To use such a trade off in antitrust policy, the efficiency gains would need to be shown to be fairly likely to occur based on ex ante information.

We argue here that analysis of profit efficiency is more appropriate than the analysis of cost efficiency to the study of M&As because it includes the revenue effects of changes in output that typically occur after mergers. Profit X-efficiency is a more general concept that includes the cost X-efficiency effects of the merger plus any revenue and cost effects of changes in output. The social value added that may be considered for trading off against social losses from the exercise of market power should include both cost and revenue effects. That is, the social value added includes *both* the change in the value of real resources consumed, which is represented by the change in costs for given input prices, and the change in the real value of output produced, which is represented by the change in revenues for given output prices. The only way we know of to measure this is through evaluating profit efficiency.[8]

A number of studies have compared simple pre- and post-merger profitability ratios, such as the return on assets (ROA) or return on equity (ROE) based on accounting values. The results of these ratio analyses are mixed. Some found improved profitability ratios associated with bank mergers (e.g., Cornett and Tehranian 1992, Spindt and Tarhan 1992), although others found no improvement in these ratios (e.g., Berger and Humphrey 1992, Linder and Crane 1992, Pilloff 1996, Akhavein, Berger, and Humphrey 1997, Chamberlain 1997).

Several studies have employed event study or other techniques to look at the effects of M&As on market values of the merger partners, rather than using accounting data from balance sheets. As was the case for the profitability ratios, the results are mixed. Some event studies found increases in the combined value for the acquiring and acquired banking organizations (Cornett and Tehranian 1992, Zhang, 1995). Other studies found no improvement in the total combined market value of the consolidating banks associated with merger announcements (e.g., Hannan and Wolken 1989, Houston and Ryngaert 1994, Pilloff 1996). The latter studies found that the market usually bids down the equity value of acquiring banks and bids up the value of the acquired banks, so the change in the combined equity value is usually not significantly different from zero. In addition, the post-merger performance improvement of merged firms has been found to be insignificantly related to the equity market's response to merger announcements (Pilloff 1996).

An important caveat to the event study findings is that the market price reaction may include factors other than just the value created or destroyed by the merger itself. For example, the method of financing chosen for the merger may influence the prices of the merger partners. For example, if new equity is issued, the value of the acquiring bank may decline because of an adverse selection problem that is not created by the merger itself. If this occurs, there might be a net increase in value created by M&As that is obscured by the adverse selection problem which brings the net change in the total value of the consolidating firms to zero. Event studies are also subject to other well known caveats, such as whether some of the information may have been leaked to market participants substantially before the public announcements.[9]

The profitability ratio and market value analyses both have methodological drawbacks that are similar to those of the cost ratio studies. The most important problem is that without controls for the prices of loans and deposits, there is no way to determine the source of any profitability change. The ROA and ROE ratios might increase because of an improvement in profit efficiency (an increase in social value added) or an greater exercise of market power (higher loan prices or lower deposit prices) associated with mergers. These two sources of profitability changes cannot be disentangled without a profit efficiency analysis. Similarly, merger event studies and other studies which use market equity values rather than accounting data, cannot differentiate between expectations of efficiency gains and expectations of market power gains from mergers, since markets evaluate expected gains in profitability from all sources equally.

The one prior study of the profit efficiency effects of bank M&As found a substantial increase in profit efficiency on average from bank megamergers of the 1980s (Akhavein, Berger, and Humphrey 1997). They found that merging banks were able to increase revenues without much change in costs or equity by shifting their output mixes from securities toward loans. This raises profit efficiency because issuing loans creates more value than purchasing securities. This shift in mix may occur because merging banks have improved diversification of risks (better coverage of geographic areas, industries, types of loans, and maturity structures) that allow higher loan/asset ratios with about the same or lower equity ratios and costs of uninsured debt, supporting a *Diversification Hypothesis* of bank mergers. Also supporting the *Diversification Hypothesis* are 1) the finding by Benston, Hunter, and Wall (1995) that acquiring banks tend to bid more to acquire safer banks; 2) the finding by Demsetz and Strahan (1997) that larger bank holding companies are better diversified than smaller ones and are able to hold lower capital ratios and higher loan ratios; and 3) the finding by Hughes, Lang, Mester, and Moon (1996) that larger banking organizations are able to shift the risk-expected return frontier upward so that a higher expected return can be earned for the same amount of risk. As noted above, there may diversification benefits even from mergers of banks in the same local market which specialize in different types of loans, etc.

Other recent literature on the effects of mergers and acquisitions on lending is mixed. The usual findings are that mergers between small banks may tend to increase lending to small businesses, but mergers involving larger banks generally decreases this type of lending or leaves it constant (Keeton 1996, 1997, Peek and Rosengren 1996, 1998, Strahan and Weston 1996, 1998, Berger, Saunders, Scalise, and Udell 1997, Craig and Santos, 1997). Lending to large businesses, which has not been studied as much, appears to increase with mergers and acquisitions (Berger, Saunders, Scalise, and Udell 1997).

There has been very little academic study of the market power effects of M&As on bank prices. Several studies found that higher levels of local market concentration are associated with lower deposit rates and higher loan rates (e.g., Berger and Hannan 1989,1997, Hannan 1991). However, such studies neglect the many differences between the dynamic effects of M&As on performance and the static equilibrium relationships between market structure and performance. One study did find that M&As that violate the Justice Department guidelines for banks (local market Herfindahl over 1800, increase of over 200) sometimes substantially reduce the deposit rates paid by rival banks in the affected markets, consistent with market power effects of M&As (Hannan and Prager, 1996). However, this study did not control for the efficiency effects of mergers, which may affect prices. One other study did use efficiency and found only minuscule effects of price changes relative to efficiency changes (Akhavein, Berger, and Humphrey 1997). However, that study did not have accurate survey prices, but rather used balance sheet ratios to construct estimated prices.

3. THE MEASUREMENT OF EFFICIENCY

To evaluate whether and by how much bank M&As affect efficiency, we estimate the efficiency of virtually all U.S. banks annually over the period 1990-1995, whether or not they were involved in mergers. For each merger from 1991 through 1994, we calculate the improvement in efficiency associated with the merger as the efficiency rank of the consolidated bank averaged over the available merger-free years after the merger less the weighted average rank of the acquiring and acquired banks over the available merger-free years before the merger (weights based on gross total assets). In all cases, the efficiency rank is calculated relative to the peer group of all banks without mergers over the same years. In this way, we control for any industry-wide changes in costs or profits that may occur and keep the data consistent and comparable over time.

We estimate three types of X-efficiency – cost efficiency, standard profit efficiency, and alternative profit efficiency. See Berger and Mester (1997) for a detailed discussion of these three efficiency concepts. Briefly, cost efficiency takes outputs as given and determines how close the firm is to the minimum costs that a best-practice bank would have for producing the same output facing the same input prices and other conditions. Cost efficiency excludes consideration of how banks might improve their output mix to raise revenues after a merger.

Standard profit efficiency includes revenues as well as costs and measures how close the firm is to earning the maximum profits that a best-practice firm would earn under the same circumstances. Standard profit efficiency allows output to vary, and so incorporates errors in choosing outputs as well as inputs. This concept also holds output prices constant statistically, so that increases in output prices that reflect greater exercise of market power have little effect on measured standard profit efficiency. These treatments of output errors and market power considerations make standard profit efficiency our preferred method of evaluating the efficiency effects of mergers.

Alternative profit efficiency measures the degree to which profits are maximized, as does standard profit efficiency, but takes outputs as given as does cost efficiency. Alternative profit efficiency is relevant when some of the assumptions underlying cost and standard profit efficiency are violated. For example, alternative profit efficiency may be useful if there are substantial unmeasured differences in product quality – such as variations in the amount of service provided to depositors or differences in the average duration of loans. If it costs more to provide higher quality deposit services or to raise longer-term funds to duration-match longer-term loans, and the banks that provide these types of services charge higher prices that fully compensate for the extra costs, then such firms may be incorrectly measured as inefficient by cost or standard profit efficiency methods. Alternative profit efficiency may help mitigate this problem by including the extra revenues of these high quality banks (unlike cost efficiency) and by allowing this revenue to be earned through higher prices (unlike standard profit efficiency which hold prices constant statistically). This may be particularly important for studying the efficiency effects of mergers, since the quality of service may change after merger, such as may occur if the average distance of depositors to their nearest bank branch or ATM changes.[10]

Alternative profit efficiency also has some limitations for merger analysis. One obvious limitation is that this concept cannot distinguish well between efficiency and market power, since output prices are not statistically controlled for when estimating alternative profit efficiency. Banks that gain market power in setting output prices will generally be measured as improving their alternative profit efficiency, but this comes at the expense of their customers and does not represent an increase in social value added. As well, alternative profit efficiency may fail to capture improvements in the bank's choice of output bundle, since output quantities are held constant statistically. As shown in prior research and extended here below, banks tend to change their outputs in a systematic way after mergers – shifting from securities toward loans. For these reasons, we employ alternative profit efficiency primarily as a check on the other two methods.

The cost and profit function specifications are the same as those in Berger and Mester (1997), although the efficiency ranks that are derived from the cost and profit functions are somewhat different. We estimate cost, standard profit, and alternative profit functions separately for each year, 1990-1995, allowing the coefficients for each year to differ to reflect changes in technology, regulation, and market environment.

Table 1 gives the definitions of all the variables used in the cost and profit functions, as well as their sample means and standard deviations for 1995. The variable input prices w are the interest rates on purchased funds and core deposits and the price of labor. The variable outputs y include consumer loans, business loans, and securities. We specify off-balance sheet activities, physical capital, and financial equity capital as fixed netputs z. We include the nonperforming loan to total loan ratio for the state in which the bank is located STNPL to account for lending conditions.

We specify the Fourier-flexible functional form, which is a global approximation that includes a standard translog plus Fourier trigonometric terms, and has been shown in a number of research papers to fit the data better than local translog approximation. (McAllister and McManus 1993, Mitchell and Onvural 1996, Berger and DeYoung 1997, Berger, Leusner, and Mingo 1997, Berger and Mester 1997, Berger, Cummins, and Weiss 1997). For the cost function we specify:

$$
\begin{aligned}
\ln(C/w_3z_3) = \ & \alpha + \Sigma_{i=1}^{2} \beta_i \ln(w_i/w_3) + \tfrac{1}{2} \Sigma_{i=1}^{2} \Sigma_{j=1}^{2} \beta_{ij} \ln(w_i/w_3) \ln(w_j/w_3) \\
& + \Sigma_{k=1}^{3} \gamma_k \ln(y_k/z_3) + \tfrac{1}{2} \Sigma_{k=1}^{3} \Sigma_{m=1}^{3} \gamma_{km} \ln(y_k/z_3) \ln(y_m/z_3) \\
& + \Sigma_{r=1}^{2} \delta_r \ln(z_r/z_3) + \tfrac{1}{2} \Sigma_{r=1}^{2} \Sigma_{s=1}^{2} \delta_{rs} \ln(z_r/z_3) \ln(z_s/z_3) \\
& + \Sigma_{r=1}^{2} \Sigma_{k=1}^{3} \eta_{ik} \ln(w_i/w_3) \ln(y_k/z_3) \\
& + \Sigma_{i=1}^{2} \Sigma_{r=1}^{2} \rho_{ir} \ln(w_i/w_3) \ln(z_r/z_3) \\
& + \Sigma_{k=1}^{3} \Sigma_{r=1}^{2} \tau_{kr} \ln(y_k/z_3) \ln(z_r/z_3) \\
& + \Sigma_{n=1}^{7} [\phi_n \cos(x_n) + \omega_n \sin(x_n)] \\
& + \Sigma_{n=1}^{7} \Sigma_{q=n}^{7} [\phi_{nq} \cos(x_n+x_q) + \omega_{nq} \sin(x_n+x_q)] \\
& + \Sigma_{n=1}^{7} [\phi_{nnn} \cos(x_n+x_n+x_n) + \omega_{nnn} \sin(x_n+x_n+x_n)] \\
& + \upsilon_1 \ln(STNPL) + \tfrac{1}{2} \upsilon_{11} \ln(STNPL) \ln(STNPL) \\
& + \ln u_C + \ln \epsilon_C, \qquad\qquad\qquad (1)
\end{aligned}
$$

where $\ln u_C$ is an inefficiency factor that may raise costs above the 'best-practice' level and $\ln \epsilon_C$ represents random error. The values of (y_k/z_3), (z_r/z_3), and STNPL variables have 1 added for every firm in order to avoid taking the natural log of zero. The x_n terms are rescaled values of the $\ln(w_i/w_3)$, $\ln(y_k/z_3)$, and $\ln(z_r/z_3)$ terms, so that they fit in the $[0,2\pi]$ interval.[11]

The standard and alternative profit functions use essentially the same specification with a few changes. First, the dependent variable for the profit functions replace $\ln(C/w_3z_3)$ with $\ln[(\pi/w_3z_3) + |(\pi/w_3z_3)^{min}| + 1]$, where π is profits and $|(\pi/w_3z_3)^{min}|$ indicates the absolute value of the minimum value of (π/w_3z_3) over all banks for the same year. This assures that the natural log is taken of a positive number, since the minimum profits are typically negative. For the alternative profit function, this is the only change in specification (other than relabelling the composite error term as $\ln u_{a\pi} + \ln \epsilon_{a\pi}$), since the exogenous variables are identical to those for the cost function. For the

Table 5–1. Variables Employed in Measuring Cost, Standard Profit, and Alternative Profit Efficiency – Means and Standard Deviations for 1995 only (All financial variables measured in 1000's of constant 1994 dollars)

Symbol	Definition	Mean	Std Dev
	Dependent Variables		
C	Total operating plus interest costs	13,466	105,671
π	Profits	8,628	66,767
	Variable Input Prices		
w_1	Price of purchased funds (jumbo CDs, foreign deposits, federal funds purchased, all other liabilities except core deposits).	.0410	.0111
w_2	Price of core deposits (domestic transactions accounts, time and savings)	.0284	.0081
w_3	Price of labor (1000's of constant dollars per employee)	32.5	6.8
	Variable Output Quantities (Cost and Alternative Profit Functions Only)		
y_1	Consumer loans (installment and credit card and related plans)	38,179	298,130
	Variable Output Quantities (Cost and Alternative Profit Functions Only)		
y_2	Business loans (all other loans)	164,952	1,489,552
y_3	Securities (all non-loan financial assets, i.e., Gross Total Assets - y_1 - y_2 - z_2)	114,916	838,231
	Variable Output Prices (Standard Profit Function Only)		
p_1	Price of consumer loans	.0926	.0329
p_2	Price of business loans	.0898	.0126
p_3	Price of securities	.0468	.0087
	Fixed Netput Quantities		
z_1	Off-balance sheet activities (commitments, letters of credit, derivatives, etc.) measured using Basle Accord risk weights to be credit risk equivalent to loans.	26,367	445,427
z_2	Physical capital (premises and other fixed assets)	4,818	38,909
z_3	Financial equity capital	26,686	184,880

Table 5–1. (continued)

Symbol	Definition	Mean	Std Dev
	Environmental Variable		
STNPL	State average of nonperforming loans (past due at least 90 days or on nonaccrual basis) divided by total loans.	.0220	.0043
Num. observations, cost and alternative profit regressions, 1995		9,002	
Num. observations, standard profit regressions, 1995		8,378	

Notes: All stock values are real quantities as of the December call report and all prices are flows over the year divided by these stocks.
Because the price data are subject to error from this procedure, we eliminate observations in which the prices on assets and liabilities (which are interest rates) are more than 2.5 standard deviations from the mean value for that year. Similarly, we eliminate observations in which liability and asset rates are more than .10 above and more than .50 above the one-year Treasury rate, respectively. The standard profit function uses fewer observations because these procedures eliminated some output price data. We also eliminated observations in which equity was below 1% of gross total assets because the data for such banks are suspicious.
All of the continuous variables that can take on the value 0 have 1 added before taking logs in specifying the cost and profit regressions. This applies to the y's, z's, and STNPL. For p, an additional adjustment was made because profits can take on negative values (see text).

standard profit function, the terms containing the variable output quantities $\ln(y_k/z_3)$ and their x_n, terms are replaced by corresponding output price terms $\ln(p_k/w_3)$ and their x_n terms.

As shown, all of the cost, profit, input price, and output price terms – including the Fourier terms for prices before transformation – are normalized by the last input price w_3 in order to enforce linear homogeneity in prices on the model. We also normalize all cost, profit, variable output quantities, and fixed netput quantities by the last fixed netput z_3, equity capital. This helps keep heteroskedasticity in check and helps reduce a scale bias in the standard profit function in which large banks will tend to have higher profits in part because they were able to gain size that small banks cannot achieve in the short term. Normalization by equity makes the dependent variable essentially the bank's return on equity or ROE (normalized by prices and with a constant added), or a measure of how well the bank is utilizing its scarce financial capital.

There are a number of methods for measuring X-efficiency from cost and profit functions like the one shown in equation (1) which differ primarily in how they disentangle the inefficiency factor $\ln u$ from the random error $\ln \varepsilon$. The stochastic frontier approach treats $\ln u + \ln \varepsilon$ as a composed error in which the inefficiencies $\ln u$ are assumed to follow a specific asymmetric distribution, usually the half-normal, and the random errors $\ln \varepsilon$ are assumed to follow a specific symmetric distribution, usually the normal. In contrast, the distribution-free approach assumes that the efficiency of each firm is stable over time, whereas random error tends to average out to zero over time. The estimate of lnu for each firm in a panel data set is then determined as the difference between its average residual and the average residuals of the firms on the best-practice frontier, with some truncation often performed to account for the failure of the random error to average out to zero fully.

As will be shown, our method of determining efficiency ranks is generally consistent with both the stochastic frontier and distribution-free approaches. We choose to focus on the efficiency ranks of merging banks before and after the M&As relative to their peer groups which had data available for the same years. That is, we measure how the efficiency ranks of merging banks relative to all contemporaneous banks improves from before the merger to after the merger. We prefer the improvement in efficiency rank to the improvement in efficiency level for this application because efficiency levels in different time periods may not be comparable. That is, mergers that took place in 1991 may have experienced a larger or smaller improvement in the level of efficiency than 1994 mergers simply because the distribution of efficiencies may be more or less dispersed in the periods surrounding the earlier merger date. The use of rank generally neutralizes this problem by focusing on the relative point in the efficiency distribution, rather than the dispersion of the distribution. Importantly, the use of rank is preferred because it indicates the position of the merging bank relative to the appropriate peer group of banks at the same time, because it is neutral with respect to changes in the dispersion of costs and profits that occur over time (due to the interest rate cycle, macroeconomic cycle, etc.), and because improvements in rank reflect changes in performance relative to banks with similar efficiency, rather than changes relative to the efficient frontier which may be virtually unattainable for some banks.

Efficiency rank is measured on a uniform scale between 0 and 1 and gives the proportion of peer group with efficiency below that of the merging bank. Thus, a bank in any given year with efficiency better than 80% of the banks in the same year is assigned a rank of .80. We compute the efficiency ranks based on the cost and profit function residuals. For example, a bank with a cost function residual that is below 80% of the residuals for that year is assigned a rank of .80. This is exactly the same rank that would be assigned by the stochastic frontier approach, no matter what distributional assumptions were imposed on the lnu and lnε terms. This is because the stochastic frontier approach forms the expectation of the inefficiency term lnu on the observed residual (i.e., it uses lnû = Ê[lnu | lnu + lnε]), which ranks the efficiencies in the same order as the residuals no matter what distributions are imposed on lnu and lnε. This procedure also yields the same ordering as the distribution-free approach if it were applied to a single year, which bases efficiency estimates on the average residual of each bank, which would be the current residual in this special case.[12] As noted above, we take the average rank before and after the M&A over all available years with clean data from the 1990s that are undisturbed by other mergers. This averaging over time of the ranks is fairly consistent with the averaging over time of the residuals in the distribution-free approach.

As noted above, a "sin" of X-efficiency studies like this one is that we treat deposit prices as exogenous in all of our estimations and we treat loan prices as exogenous in the standard profit function model. This could create biased coefficients of the cost and profit regression equations because these prices may be affected by firm efficiency or market power. This may also create bias in the efficiency ranks if efficiency is correlated with prices, although this bias is expected to be relatively small. This is because the efficiency ranks are the ranks of the residuals of the regression equations, and the same biased coefficients are employed to measure the residuals for every firm. A potentially more serious problem with our X-efficiency ranks is that the residuals embody all the misspecifications of the cost or profit function (excluded variables, mis-specifications of form, measurement error). For example, a firm that has relatively high costs because of an excluded variable (e.g., low average account size) may be inadvertently measured as inefficient. Despite these potential problems of bias and error, we consider our choice of X-efficiency to be a lesser evil than ignoring prices, output mixes, and other control variables entirely, as typically occurs in studies using cost and profit ratios, or event studies and similar methods. That is, we believe that neglecting to specify prices, product mix, and other control variables creates much larger problems of misspecification than putting in these variables. We also try and mitigate the potential problems of using X-efficiency by measuring and comparing three types of X-efficiency (two of which do not specify output prices), by using the global Fourier-flexible functional form, and by including a number of control variables (such as state nonperforming loans, equity capital, etc.) to try to leave as little error as possible in the cost and profit function residuals.

4. EMPIRICAL RESULTS

As noted above, in this section we give our estimated bank merger efficiency effects for the 1990s, compare them to the results from the 1980s, test for how the efficiency improvements are manifested, and try to find ex ante factors to predict these improvements.

Merger Efficiency Effects for the 1990s Versus the 1980s

In Table 2, we show the improvement in efficiency ranks from megamergers of the 1980s, taken from Berger and Humphrey (1992) and Akhavein, Berger, and Humphrey (1997). These papers applied similar methodology to that employed here using data from a different era. The cost, standard profit, and alternative profit efficiencies shown are based on a common data set of M&As in which both parties had assets exceeding $1 billion, so the differences among these 1980s results should reflect differences in efficiency concept, rather than differences in the data set. The pre-merger rank is the weighted average of the ranks of the merging banks in the years before merging, using the assets in the year immediately prior to the merger for the relative weights. As shown, there

Table 5–2. Changes in Efficiency Associated with Megamergers of the 1980s[a]

	Pre-Merger Rank	Post-Merger Rank	Improvement
Cost Efficiency Rank	N/A	N/A	.05
Standard Profit Efficiency Rank	.74	.90	.16**
Alternative Profit Efficiency Rank	.77	.90	.13**

Number of Observations: 57

*(**) For improvement column only, figure is significantly different from zero at the 5% (1%) level, two-sided.

[a] Megamergers of the 1980s include all bank and holding company mergers and acquisitions in which both partners had over $ 1 billion in total banking assets in current dollars before the merger

Notes: Efficiency rank is measured on a uniform scale between 0 and 1 and gives the proportion of peer group with efficiency below that of the merging bank.
For this table, the pre-merger period for the acquiring bank and the acquired bank(s) were based on all the years going back in time prior to the merger until either another megamerger involving that bank or the year 1980 was reached. Similarly, the post-merger period for the consolidated bank was based on all the megamerger-free years going forward unless 1990 was reached.
The efficiency ranks shown in this table are measured against all other banks with at least $1 billion in assets at some time over the 1980s that existed and had no megamergers over same time period as the bank being compared.
Pre-Merger Efficiency Rank is the weighted average of the efficiency ranks for the merging banks (weights are proportional to the banking assets of the organizations).
Improvement equals Post-Merger Efficiency Rank minus Pre-Merger Efficiency Rank.
Cost efficiency results are taken from Berger and Humphrey (1992) and profit efficiency results are from Akhavein, Berger, and Humphrey (1997).

were large, statistically significant improvements in the ranks of both types of profit efficiency, but the improvement in cost efficiency rank was smaller and not statistically significant.

Table 3 shows comparable data for bank mergers of the 1990s, as well as other information. There were 639 mergers from 1991 through 1994. Cost and alternative profit efficiencies are calculated for all 639 mergers, but standard profit efficiency is measured for only 546 mergers because one or more of the output prices of the banks involved in 93 of the mergers were judged to be insufficiently accurate and therefore were excluded from standard profit efficiency calculations (see notes to Table 1).

Each merger defined here is a melding of a surviving bank (which kept its charter) and all the banks it absorbed during the year (which lost their charters). As shown, the average number of banks per merger is 2.36, meaning that on average surviving banks absorbed 1.36 other banks during the year. In the cases of multiple acquisitions, all of the summary statistics regarding the acquired bank in a merger will refer to either a weighted average or total of these acquired banks, essentially treating these banks as a single acquired entity.[13] As noted above, many of these mergers follow holding company acquisitions in the same year or in the immediately prior few years.[14] However, we exclude from the analysis bank holding company acquisitions which do not result in the banks being merged, i.e., in which the banks retain their same

Table 5-3. Mergers of the 1990s[a]

	Number of Mergers	Banks per Merger	W_1	EFF_1	W_2	EFF_2	Pre-Merger Rank	Post-Merger Rank	Improvement		
									All Mergers	Top Half[b]	Bottom Half[b]
Cost Efficiency Rank											
Megamergers[c]	68	2.80	.836	.477	.164	.556	.489	.491	.002	-.089*	.092*
Minimergers[d]	334	2.19	.641	.521	.359	.399	.495	.501	.006	-.048**	.061**
All Mergers	639	2.36	.702	.521	.298	.454	.509	.514	.005	-.057**	.066**
Standard Profit Efficiency Rank											
Megamergers[c]	65	2.79	.833	.470	.167	.528	.490	.513	.023	-.089*	.131**
Minimergers[d]	270	2.16	.646	.518	.354	.492	.511	.545	.034*	-.018	.085**
All Mergers	546	2.34	.708	.505	.292	.507	.507	.545	.038**	-.043**	.118**
Alternative Profit Efficiency Rank											
Megamergers[c]	68	2.80	.836	.340	.164	.396	.339	.436	.097**	-.013	.206**
Minimergers[d]	334	2.19	.641	.566	.359	.551	.564	.524	-.039*	-.130**	.051**
All Mergers	639	2.36	.702	.425	.298	.519	.441	.485	.044**	-.081**	.169**

*(**) For improvement section only, figure is significantly different from zero at the 5% (1%) level, two-sided.

[a] Mergers of the 1990s include mergers and acquisitions between 1991 and 1994; efficiency data is from 1990 through 1995.

[b] Mergers are divided into Top Half and Bottom Half based on their Pre-Merger Rank.

[c] Megamergers of the 1990s include all mergers and acquisitions in which both the acquirer's gross total assets and the total of the acquired banks' gross total assets were over $1 billion in 1986 dollars before the merger.

[d] Minimergers of the 1990s include all mergers and acquisitions in which both the acquirer's gross total assets and the total of the acquired banks' gross total assets were under $100 million in 1986 dollars before the merger.

Notes: Efficiency rank is measured on a uniform scale between 0 and 1 and gives the proportion of peer group with efficiency below that of the merging bank. For this and all following tables, the pre-merger period for the acquiring bank and the acquired bank(s) were based on all the years going back in time prior to the merger until either another merger involving that bank or the year 1990 was reached. Similarly, the post-merger period for the consolidated bank was based on all the merger-free years going forward unless 1995 was reached.

Efficiency ranks were measured in each year by comparing cost or profit function residuals against those of all other banks that existed and had no mergers in the same year. EFF_1 is the pre-merger efficiency rank of the acquiring bank, and W_1 is the proportion of the pro forma bank's gross total assets held by the acquirer before the merger. EFF_2 is the weighted average of the acquired banks' efficiency ranks (weights are proportional to the gross total assets of the banks), and $W_2 = 1 - W_1$ is the proportion of the pro forma bank's gross total assets held by the acquired banks. Pre-Merger Rank is the weighted average of the efficiency ranks for the merging banks, i.e. $W_1 * EFF_1 + W_2 * EFF_2$, and the efficiency ranks shown in this table and thereafter are averages of these individual-year ranks over the merger-free years before or after a merger.

charters. It is likely that these holding company acquisitions would have different effects from bank-level mergers.[15]

Importantly, this distinction between bank mergers and holding company acquisitions differs from the treatment of the 1980s mergers in earlier studies reported in Table 2. These other studies included holding company acquisitions because these studies were focused on megamergers (both parties with assets over $1 billion), most of which are holding company acquisitions. The current paper has a broader focus on mergers of all sizes, but the limitation that we do exclude the large holding company acquisitions should be noted here.

To be comparable with the earlier studies, we break out the results separately for megamergers, which are defined as both the acquiring and acquired having over $1 billion in assets measured in constant 1986 dollars. We also show findings for "minimergers," defined here to be when both parties have real 1986 assets of below $100 million. As discussed above in the literature review, mergers of small banks have been found to have different effects on small business lending than other mergers, and changes in lending may be an important way in which standard profit efficiency may change after a merger. Interestingly, more than half of the mergers during this time period were minimergers (334 of 639), although the megamergers involve many more dollars of assets changing hands.

The next set of columns in Table 3 show the proportions of pre-merger assets of the pro forma bank held by the acquiring bank W_1 and acquired bank or banks W_2 ($W_1 + W_2 = 1$). These columns also show the pre-merger efficiency ranks of the acquiring and acquired banks, EFF_1 and EFF_2, respectively, and the combined pre-merger rank, which equals $W_1 \cdot EFF_1 + W_2 \cdot EFF_2$.[16] The efficiency ranks of the acquiring banks and acquired banks both have averages close to .50, the average for all banks together. An exception is alternative profit efficiency of banks involved in megamergers, which have relatively low efficiency ex ante by this measure. The ex ante conditions for the 1990s mergers tend to differ from earlier finding based on 1980s mergers, in which acquiring banks were usually found to be much more efficient than both acquired banks and the population of banks as a whole. This suggests that some of the motivations behind mergers may have changed in the 1990s or that the same types of banks are merging and something has changed to affect their measured efficiencies.

The next columns in Table 3 show the post-merger efficiency ranks and the improvements in rank. Similar to the results of studies employing the 1980s data, we find no economically or statistically significant improvement on average in cost efficiency, but both types of profit efficiency improve by a few percent and are statistically significant. The only exception is that the alternative profit efficiency rank for minimergers declines on average.

The most interesting results in Table 3, however, are in the last two columns, which break up the efficiency improvements into two halves which depend on the weighted average pre-merger efficiency rank of the participants. As shown in the last column, mergers in which ex ante efficiency was below the median had efficiency increases on average in all 9 cases, and all 9 are statistically significant. In some cases, the measured improvements are quite dramatic – up to 20.6% in efficiency rank – depending on the type of merger and the efficiency concept employed. There is similar consistency for mergers in which pre-merger efficiency ranks were above the median. In all 9 cases, these mergers reduced measured efficiency rank on average, and the decline is statistically significant in all but two cases. Thus, it appears that mergers are generally associated with efficiency improvements when there is more room for improvement, and vice versa when there is more room for efficiency decline.

These results give preliminary evidence that low pre-merger efficiency might be used as an ex ante condition for when mergers are likely to raise efficiency and possibly offset any social losses from increased exercise of market power in setting prices. This will be investigated further in a regression analysis below where we break out the pre-merger efficiencies and other variables by individual banks and test some hypotheses about what predicts merger efficiency improvements.

How Efficiency Gains are Manifested – Tests of the Diversification Hypothesis

In the findings thus far, our preferred measure of efficiency improvement – the change in standard profit efficiency rank – is the most consistent in terms of showing overall improvement from mergers, although all three efficiency measures show significant improvement for banks with relatively poor efficiencies ex ante. The literature showed qualitatively similar results using 1980s data, which suggested that bank mergers significantly raised profit efficiency, but not cost efficiency on average. We investigate how standard profit efficiency gains might be manifested or why standard profit efficiency might have improved more than the other measures of efficiency and performance improvement.

Specifically, we provide tests of the *Diversification Hypothesis* described above. Under this hypothesis, improved diversification of the loan portfolio owing to broader coverage of geographic areas, industries, loan types, or maturity structures might allow consolidated banks to shift their output mixes from lower-yielding securities toward higher-yielding loans without raising their costs of funding. That is, a better diversified bank can absorb the risks of more loans without any increase in equity capital or any increase in the cost of uninsured bank debt because the diversification helps protect the equity and debt holders from risk. A shift from securities to loans under the *Diversification Hypothesis* would improve the standard profit efficiency rank on average by increasing revenues for a given set of output prices. However, this revenue improvement would not affect cost efficiency, because cost efficiency excludes revenues entirely. The improvement would only affect alternative profit efficiency to the extent that outputs specified in the alternative profit function are imperfect in controlling for changes in product mix.

Table 4 shows the tests of the *Diversification Hypothesis*, which look at the

Table 5-4. Tests of the Diversification Hypothesis: Changes in Bank Activity Associated with Mergers of the 1990s

	Megamergers			Minimergers			All Mergers		
	Pre-Merger Rank	Post-Merger Rank	Change	Pre-Merger Rank	Post-Merger Rank	Change	Pre-Merger Rank	Post-Merger Rank	Change
Total Loans/GTA	.628	.633	.006	.456	.516	.060**	.519	.572	.053**
GTA/Equity	.690	.741	.051	.516	.564	.048**	.569	.609	.041**
Total Loans/Equity	.690	.744	.054*	.480	.549	.069**	.553	.615	.062**
Consumer Loans/GTA	.591	.679	.087**	.425	.446	.021*	.487	.529	.042**
Business Loans/GTA	.585	.534	-.051*	.487	.544	.057**	.521	.555	.034**
Consumer Loans/Equity	.650	.732	.082**	.441	.471	.030**	.513	.560	.048**
Business Loans/Equity	.662	.671	.009	.498	.568	.070**	.552	.603	.051**
Securities/GTA	.371	.369	-.001	.542	.481	.061**	.480	.427	-.054**
Securities/Equity	.519	.550	.031	.553	.531	-.021	.531	.511	-.021*
Purchased Funds/GTA	.697	.828	.131**	.446	.508	.062**	.512	.587	.074**
Purchased Funds/Equity	.736	.853	.117**	.458	.534	.076**	.537	.616	.079**
Purchased Funds Price	.836	.481	-.355**	.641	.467	-.174**	.702	.486	-.216**
No.\ of Obs.	68	68	68	334	334	334	639	639	639

*(**) For Change columns only, figure significantly different from zero at the 5% (1%) level, two-sided.

Notes: GTA indicates gross total assets (including loan loss reserves).

The definitions of consumer loans, business loans, securities, and purchased funds are all shown in Table 1 above.

changes in the ranks of a number of financial ratios from pre-merger to post-merger. Focusing first on the All Mergers columns at the far right of the table, we find that all 12 ratios move in the direction suggested by the *Diversification Hypothesis*, and all 12 are statistically significant. Moving down the last column, banks that merge tend to increase their proportions of loans in the asset portfolio, and have more assets and loans per dollar of equity. These results suggest that merging banks are able to shift toward loans without the capital market requiring more equity, consistent with a more diversified loan portfolio. The next six rows show that relative to the peer group, merging banks shift into both consumer loans and business loans and out of securities. The last three rows show that merging banks are able to raise additional uninsured purchased funds, and that they buy these funds at reduced rates. It appears mergers allow the participants to move from paying relatively high rates for purchased funds to about average rates, and to buy more of these funds, consistent with capital markets evaluating these banks as safer.

The signs of the rank changes for minimergers are all consistent with these findings, but the megamergers have a few exceptions. It appears that large merging banks do have more loans and assets per dollar of equity, they do switch into consumer loans, and they do buy more purchased funds and pay less for them post-merger. However, large merging banks do not appear to shift from securities into business loans.[17]

Overall, the results in Table 4 are quite consistent with the implications of the *Diversification Hypothesis*, and they suggest that it is important to use the standard profit efficiency concept as at least one of the tools employed when evaluating the implications of bank mergers. The cost efficiency concept and the simple cost ratio analyses described above do not measure the improvement in the value of output produced from the very significant changes in product mix that occur after merger. The alternative profit efficiency concept only measures the increase in value due to shifts that are not accounted for in the output measures in alternative profit function. The profitability ratio analyses and event studies and other methods using market values may include this change implicitly in the value of output produced, but they do not explicitly separate it out from the changes in earnings or expected earnings from increases in the exercise of market power in setting prices.

Ex Ante Conditions That Help Predict Merger Efficiency Improvements

Table 5 shows our analysis of ex ante variables that may be used to predict merger efficiency improvements. As noted above, if expected improvements in efficiency are to be used as an argument to offset any potential increases in the exercise of market power, the efficiency gains would have to be fairly predictable based on ex ante information. The dependent variables in Table 5 are the rank efficiency improvements for the individual mergers which were summarized in average form in Table 3 above, and the exogenous variables are all based on information available the year before the merger. Similar

Table 5–5. Ex Ante Sources of Merger-Related Changes in Efficiency

	1980s Mergers[a]		1990s Mergers								
	Cost	Std. π	Cost Efficiency			Std. π Efficiency			Alt. π Efficiency		
	Mega	Mega	Mega	Min	All	Mega	Mini	All	Mega	Mini	All
Intercept	.408	.87**	.147	.209	-.057	$\lbrace$.111	-.691**	-.292	-.602	-.331	-.144
$W_2 (EFF_1-EFF_2)$	-.133	.48**	.780	-.429**	-.154	-.434	-.331	.015	1.870*	-.396*	.009
$W_1 (EFF_1)$	N/A	-.63**	-.407*	-.160	-.290**	-.485**	-.119	-.399**	-.839**	-.287**	-.523**
$\partial Imp/\partial EFF_1$	N/A	-.40[b]	-.212	-.257**	-.249**	-.477**	-.194**	-.278**	-.395**	-.326**	-.365**
$W_2 (EFF_2)$	N/A	-.17	-.479	-.671**	.550**	-.766	-.990**	-.574**	.537	-1.062**	-.808**
$\partial Imp/\partial EFF_2$	N/A	-.18[b]	-.206*	-.087*	-.118**	-.055	-.233**	-.172**	-.218	-.239**	-.244**
W_2	N/A	-.25	.536	.363**	.250*	.211	.570**	.147	-.642	.543**	.179
OVERLAP	-.056	-.04	-.053	.013	.019	-.032	-.051	-.032	.101	.022	.011
STINCOME	N/A	-.11	-.763	-.353	-.129	.971	.284	.470	1.428	.921	.706
HERF	-.196	-.17	.760	-.110	-.086	.916	.317	.321*	.137	-.054	.023
SHARE	1.274	.09	-.973	.180	.122	-.454	-.251	-.167	.344	.160	.125
RETAIL	.041	-.16**	.406	-.229	.163	-.167	.868***	.537**	.527	.476	.409*
SCALE	-.503	-.18	-.350	.071	.074*	.416	.068	.087	.530	-.041	.071
Adjusted R^2	.134	.80	.162	.108	.122	.176	.145	.162	.229	.190	.253
No. of Obs.	57	57	68	334	639	65	270	546	68	334	639

*(**) Figure is significantly different from zero at the 5% (1%) level, two-sided.

[a] 1980s cost efficiency results are taken from Berger and Humphrey (1992) and 1980s profit efficiency results are from Akhavein, Berger, and Humphrey (1997).

[b] Tests of statistical significance were not given for the partial derivatives in Akhavein, Berger, and Humphrey (1997).

Notes: EFF_1, EFF_2, W_1, and W_2 are as defined in Table 3. $\partial Imp/\partial EFF_1$ and $\partial Imp/\partial EFF_2$ are the derivatives of the efficiency improvements with respect to EFF_1 and EFF_2, respectively, derived from the coefficients of the $W_2 (EFF_1-EFF_2)$ $W_1 (EFF_1)$, and $W_2 (EFF_2)$ regressors, and evaluated at the means of W_1 and W'_2. The control variables are as follows. OVERLAP is the proportion of the deposits of the merging banks that are in the same local market; STINCOME is the growth rate of state personal income; HERF and SHARE are the weighted average of the Herfindahl indices and market shares of the merging firms across their local markets; RETAIL is the deposit/asset ratio, measuring the degree of retail business focus of the merging banks; and SIZE is the weighted average of the size ranks of the merging banks.

regressions taken from the earlier studies using the 1980s data for megamergers are shown for comparison as well.

Two main hypotheses are tested in Table 5. Under the *Relative Efficiency Hypothesis*, the difference in efficiency between the acquiring bank and the acquired bank is important in determining merger efficiency gains. It is assumed that the acquiring bank tends to bring the efficiency of the acquired bank towards its own level by spreading its managerial expertise and policies and procedures over the resources formerly controlled by the acquired bank. Under this hypothesis, larger merger efficiency gains are predicted to the extent that EFF_1 is greater than EFF_2, and larger merger efficiency losses are predicted to the extent that EFF_2 exceeds EFF_1. This hypothesis is tested using the variable $W_2(EFF_1 - EFF_2)$, the difference in efficiency between the acquirer and the acquired banks. The W_2 weight is included to account for the proportion of the consolidated firm over which the change in efficiency would be implemented. A positive coefficient on this variable would be consistent with the management of the consolidated bank bringing the acquired portion of the bank toward the ex ante efficiency rank of the acquired portion.[18]

Under the *Low Efficiency Hypothesis*, an important ex ante condition is that either or preferably both the acquiring and acquired banks be inefficient prior to merger. Although this hypothesis might at first appear counterintuitive, we have already shown some evidence supporting it. The results in Table 3 above suggested that the efficiency of the merging firms tended to improve more when the weighted average of the pre-merger efficiencies was below the median.

The *Low Efficiency Hypothesis* is actually quite intuitive. The merger event itself may have the effect of "waking up" management to the need for improvement or may be used as an excuse to implement substantial unpleasant restructuring ("rightsizing") needed to improve efficiency that might otherwise create substantial morale problems. The efficiency improvement is expected to be greater, the more room there is to improve – i.e., the lower are the ex ante efficiency ranks of the participants. To test this hypothesis, we specify the variables $W_1(EFF_1)$ and $W_2(EFF_2)$, the pre-merger efficiencies of both the acquiring and acquired banks. The weights are needed because the larger is the share of one of the banks, the more its efficiency improvement will affect the efficiency of the consolidated bank. This hypothesis predicts that the coefficients of $W_1(EFF_1)$ and $W_2(EFF_2)$ will both be negative, as both parts of the consolidated bank can be "awakened" or "restructured" to improve efficiency.

Although the *Low Efficiency Hypothesis* is stated here in terms of bank mergers, it should be recognized that these are not the only events that could trigger such an improvement in efficiency. Other changes in corporate control – such as a replacement of senior or junior management, acquisition or spinoff of a nonbank activity, or purchase or sale of a number of branches – could in principle yield similar results. It is also possible that existing management could make substantial improvements with any change in corporate control, which could yield similar results. That is, if a firm is operating far below its potential, there are a number of ways to get management and/or employees to accept the changes necessary to effect a significant movement toward the efficient frontier, of which bank mergers is but one possibility.

Note that both the *Relative Efficiency Hypothesis* and the *Low Efficiency Hypothesis* can be true to some extent simultaneously. It is possible that the management of the acquiring bank implements its policies and procedures throughout the consolidated bank, which pulls the efficiency of the acquired portion of the consolidated bank toward the ex ante rank of the acquiring bank more, the greater is the weighted difference in efficiency ranks $W_2(EFF_1 - EFF_2)$. At the same time, the management might systematically begin "rightsizing" the staff throughout the consolidated bank, cutting more staff proportionately more in the least productive departments. This would yield greater efficiency improvements, the lower are the ex ante efficiency variables $W_1(EFF_1)$ and $W_2(EFF_2)$.

We also show in the table the derivatives of the efficiency improvements with respect to EFF_1 and EFF_2, $\partial Imp/\partial EFF_1$ and $\partial Imp/\partial EFF_2$, respectively, which are derived from the coefficients of the $W_2(EFF_1 - EFF_2)$, $W_1(EFF_1)$, and $W_2(EFF_2)$ regressors, and evaluated at the means of W_1 and W_2. As discussed below, these derivatives give the net effects of the ex ante efficiencies that may be useful in evaluating the types of M&As that improve efficiency.

Briefly, the other variables in these regressions are W_2, the relative size of the acquired bank, in order to control for potential differences between "mergers of equals" and other mergers; OVERLAP, the proportion of the deposits of the merging banks that are in the same local market; STINCOME, the growth rate of state personal income; HERF and SHARE, the weighted average of the Herfindahl indices and market shares of the merging firms across their local markets; RETAIL, the deposit/asset ratio, measuring the degree of retail business focus of the merging banks; and SIZE, the weighted average of the size ranks of the merging banks.

Turning to the results in Table 5, the coefficients of $W_2(EFF_1 - EFF_2)$ are not very consistent, being negative in 5 of 9 cases for the mergers of the 1990s. The two uses of this variable employing 1980s data are shown in the table as also having conflicting signs on the coefficients, although one is for cost efficiency and the other is for standard profit efficiency, which need not be consistent. It does not appear to be important that the acquiring bank be more efficient than the acquired bank for the merger to increase efficiency. These data do not support the *Relative Efficiency Hypothesis*.

In contrast, the data do appear to support the *Low Efficiency Hypothesis*. For $W_1(EFF_1)$, the coefficients are negative in 9 of 9 cases, and 7 of the 9 coefficients are statistically significant. The coefficient of this variable was also negative and statistically significant in the one test of it using the 1980s data. Similarly, the coefficients of $W_2(EFF_2)$ are negative in 8 of 9 cases, with 6 of the coefficients significantly negative and the lone positive coefficient statistically insignificant. These variables also had negative coefficients in the one study that tested them using 1980s data.

The derivatives of the improvements with respect to EFF_1 and EFF_2, $\partial Imp/\partial EFF_1$ and $\partial Imp/\partial EFF_2$, also provide useful summaries that help disentangle the effects of the relative and absolute efficiencies in the regressions. The effects of EFF_1 are negative in all 9 cases, and significant at the 1% level in 8 of the 9 cases. The mean value is -.306, suggesting that if the pre-merger efficiency rank of the acquiring bank is 10% lower, the improvement in rank subsequent to the merger is expected to be about 3% higher on average. Similarly, $\partial Imp/\partial EFF_2$ is always negative and is statistically significant in most cases. The mean value is -.175, so that a 10% lower pre-merger efficiency rank of the acquiring bank predicts a bit less than a 2% greater improvement for the consolidated bank after the merger on average.

Thus, the results are consistent with the *Low Efficiency Hypothesis* – it appears to be better for merger efficiency improvements that *both* the acquiring and acquired banks be relatively inefficient prior to merger, particularly the acquiring bank. This may "wake up" the consolidated bank to restructure itself or give management an excuse on which to blame the restructuring.

As a caveat, we note that the coefficients from our regressions and the derivatives formed from them essentially represent only the average results over our sample period over the ranges of the data that are observed. These findings would not necessarily apply to observations that are outside the observed range or even to observations that are within the observed range but are well away from the bulk of the data. For example, our result that it is better for efficiency improvement that the acquired bank be more inefficient might not hold for very inefficient acquirers, but such banks are rarely in the position of acquiring other banks. Similarly, the prediction model may not hold for future observations, as the conditions that predict merger success may change over time. We have seen some differences between the mergers of the 1980s and the 1990s to date, although for the most part the findings are qualitatively consistent.

Most of the control variables in these equations tend to have contradictory signs, and little in the way of conclusive information can be drawn from them. Nonetheless, two findings bear notice. First, the coefficients on OVERLAP are mutually inconsistent and are not significant in any cases, mirroring previous results. These findings suggest that if there are technological economies from merging banks in the same local market by consolidating branches or back-office operations, these may be offset by managerial difficulties in the merged institution or by diseconomies elsewhere in the merged banks. Second, the coefficients of the RETAIL variable in the profit efficiency regressions, along with results cited above, suggest that small, retail deposit-oriented banks may be able to improve profit efficiency more from mergers than other banks. The increased lending resulting from minimergers shown in Table 3, as well as the result from the extant literature that these types of mergers tend to increase small business lending, suggest that mergers of small banks may greatly facilitate the lending function of these banks and improve their revenues.

Finally, we address the policy question of whether the efficiency improvements that occur from bank mergers can be sufficiently well predicted using ex ante information to be useful for antitrust policy purposes. The relatively low adjusted R^2s on the 1990s regressions shown in Table 5 – between about 10% and 30% – suggest that the ex ante conditions specified here do not explain most of what makes for a successful, efficiency-increasing merger. Similarly, only between 1 and 4 of the 10 slope coefficients in each of these regressions are statistically significant, with many of the control variables having signs contradicting expectations. Therefore, in most cases, it would be difficult to predict that an efficiency increase was very likely.

However, there still may be individual cases in which merger success could be said to be quite likely. For example, the coefficients reported in Table 5 suggest that a minimerger between two retail-oriented small banks in which the acquired bank had a large share of the pro forma bank and was very inefficient ex ante (i.e., high RETAIL, high W_2, low EFF_2) may be very likely to create an increase in standard profit efficiency rank that could be traded off against a potential increase in the exercise of market power in setting prices.

5. CONCLUSIONS

This paper extends the literature on the efficiency effects of bank mergers using data from the 1990s, estimating the cost efficiency, standard profit efficiency, and alternative profit efficiency implications of these mergers. The analysis of these types of X-efficiency is the only way of which we are aware to determine whether these mergers are in the public interest. This is because it is the only way to separate the increases in social value added owing to improvements in efficiency from the increases in the private value of the firms owing to better opportunities to exercise market power in setting prices. We also analyze how some of the efficiency gains might be manifested, examine whether merger efficiency gains might be predictable from ex ante information that is available to antitrust authorities, and test some hypotheses about the conditions that are likely to bring about efficiency gains. In addition, we compare our results to some similar analyses of 1980s data to see whether the efficiency effects of mergers or the conditions underlying successful mergers may have changed over time.

Our findings suggest that bank mergers appear to yield statistically significant increases of a few percent in profit efficiency rank on average relative to other banks, but very little change in cost efficiency rank. A rather striking result is how much these findings are affected by the ex ante efficiencies of participating banks. When the merging banks are below median efficiency, the average improvement in efficiency rank is substantial – between about 5% and 21% – and is statistically significant for all three types of efficiency applied to the megamerger, minimerger, and all merger categories.

Similarly, efficiency rank tends to decline significantly after mergers for banks that were relatively efficient ex ante.

In part, the increase in profit efficiency may be manifested in a portfolio shift from securities into consumer loans and business loans. The data are consistent with a *Diversification Hypothesis* in which the improved diversification of risks associated with the merger from an improved mix of geographic areas, industries, loan types, or maturity structures might allow consolidated banks to shift their output mixes from securities toward both consumer loans and business loans, raising expected revenues. The greater diversification protects the shareholders and uninsured creditors, so there need be no increase in equity capital or rise in the costs of uninsured purchased funds. A number of tests of the *Diversification Hypothesis* using changes in the ranks of various financial ratios are consistent with this hypothesis, with only a few exceptions for megamergers.

We also examine how well merger efficiency improvements can be predicted using information available before the merger, since efficiency gains would have to be fairly predictable based on ex ante information if they are to be employed as an argument to offset any potential increases in the exercise of market power in setting prices. We test two main hypotheses in this regard. The data are *not* generally consistent with the *Relative Efficiency Hypothesis*, under which it is important that the acquiring bank be more efficient than the acquired bank so that superior management abilities and policies and procedures may be spread over more resources. However, the data are consistent with the *Low Efficiency Hypothesis*, under which greater merger efficiency gains are predicted if either or both of the participating banks are less efficient than other banks before the merger. The data predict larger ex post efficiency improvements when the efficiency of either the acquiring bank or acquired bank is less efficient ex ante. Thus, mergers may "wake up" inefficient management to the need for improvement or may be used as an excuse to implement substantial unpleasant restructuring might otherwise be difficult to implement. We acknowledge, however, that the *Low Efficiency Hypothesis* allows for the possibility that such restructurings do not necessarily require bank mergers to occur, but rather may be precipitated by other changes in corporate control or occur through a change in the orientation of existing management.

The data suggest that for antitrust policy purposes, a reasonably certain gain in efficiency – which might be used to offset social losses from any increased exercise of market power in setting prices – *cannot* be predicted from the ex ante information in most cases. The adjusted R^2s of between about 10% and 30% suggest that we simply do not know in advance exactly which mergers will improve efficiency and by how much. However, there may be some cases – particularly for mergers of relatively inefficient small banks – where substantial merger efficiency gains may be very likely to occur. In these cases, prospective social value added gains from likely efficiency improvements might be traded off against prospective social losses from any likely increase in the exercise of market power in setting prices.

Some comparisons of these results with those from efficiency studies employing data from the 1980s suggest that the merger efficiency findings from the two eras are qualitatively consistent. The profit efficiency comparisons are of necessity relatively limited because there is only one prior study of the profit efficiency effects of mergers, and that study employed a much more limited data set in terms of numbers of mergers and sizes of the banks involved. The main findings of no significant improvements on average in cost efficiency rank, significant improvements on average in profit efficiency rank, shifts from securities to loans that raise expected revenues, and greater improvements in efficiency when ex ante efficiencies are relatively low are consistent over the two decades.

Where the findings from the two decades appear to differ qualitatively is in the ex ante conditions under which the mergers typically take place. The efficiency ranks of the acquiring banks and acquired banks in the 1990s appear to be close to each other on average and close to the average efficiency for nonmerging banks. In contrast, the literature found that in the mergers of the 1980s, acquiring banks were typically found to be much more efficient than both acquired banks and nonmerging banks. This suggests that some of the motivations behind mergers may have changed in the 1990s or that something in the cost and profit functions differs between the 1980s and 1990s.

There are several reasons to suspect that both of these possibilities may be correct to some degree and explain the differences in ex ante efficiencies. Consistent with a change in merger motives, many of the merger participants in the 1980s focused on expanding their geographic bases to gain strategic long-run advantage by getting footholds in new locations, rather than on reducing costs or raising profits in the short term. Merger participants in the 1990s appear to be more focused on cutting costs quickly through mergers – for example, they often announce goals for employee layoffs, branch closings, and total cost savings in advance of the mergers. In addition, the removal of more geographic restrictions on bank branching and holding company expansion in the late 1980s and early 1990s may have removed some of the costs of merging and becoming larger. Consistent with a change in cost and profit functions, there have been many changes in the economic environment of the 1990s that may have affected the costs and profits of different types of banks differently. For example, low market interest rates in the 1990s may affect the measured efficiency of different types of banks differently because of their dependence on market-sensitive funds. In addition, improvements in technology and applied finance may have reduced costs more for some banks than others, which could increase or decrease the relative efficiencies of acquiring banks, acquired banks, and nonmerging banks in the 1990s.[19]

We close with a reminder of our caveat that these findings do not necessarily apply to observations that are outside the observed range of our data set or even outside the thick part of our data set. In addition, the Lucas Critique applies. If antitrust policy were to change to give more weight to the efficiency effects of mergers, it is possible that different types of mergers would be attempted with different efficiency consequences.

NOTES

1 For convenience, we use the terms merger, acquisition, merger and acquisition, and M&A interchangeably throughout the paper.

2 For convenience, we use the terms X-efficiency and frontier efficiency interchangeably. The term X-efficiency as it is currently used – including in the efficiency measures in this paper – incorporates both deviations from the best-practice cost or profit frontier (technical inefficiencies) and errors in responding to relative prices in choosing inputs or outputs (allocative inefficiency). This represents an expansion of the original X-efficiency concept of Leibenstein (1966), particularly its application to profits as well as costs.

3 In practice, current antitrust policy relies heavily on the use of the ex ante information on the Herfindahl index of concentration and market share for predicting market power problems, and considers firm efficiency only under limited circumstances. See U.S. Department of Justice and Federal Trade Commission (1992). The Department of Justice and the U.S. banking agencies more recently identified simple screens and other information that would allow applicants to identify proposed mergers that clearly do not have significant adverse effects on competition and therefore would be very unlikely to be challenged by these authorities (See Working Group Statement, 1995). Again, efficiency is not considered in these simplified guidelines.

4 An additional, likely more important problem with measuring the effects of market power is that M&As that are expected to result in the exercise of significant market power in pricing are simply not approved by the U.S. Justice Department and the relevant banking agencies. Thus, the most significant potential exercises of market power are typically not observed, making it difficult to estimate market power effects and their causes.

5 The merger literature confirms the potential for cost efficiency gains. Berger and Humphrey (1992) found that acquiring banks were substantially more cost X-efficient than the banks they acquired on average. Savage (1991) and Shaffer (1993) showed by simulation methods that large cost X-efficiency gains were possible if the best practice banks were to merge with and reform the practices of the least efficient banks. Altunbas, Maude, and Molyneux (1995) similarly showed that substantial potential for improvement was possible in mergers between UK banks and building societies.

6 Additional difficulties with using cost ratios are detailed in Berger and Humphrey (1992).

7 Some slightly different and interesting results were found by Vander Vennet (1996), who studied domestic and international mergers of credit institutions in the EC over 1988-1993. The M&As were divided into several groups and some (particularly international mergers) tended to improve cost efficiency), whereas other types tended to decrease cost efficiency.

8 See Berger, Hancock, and Humphrey (1993) for a more general discussion of profit efficiency and its advantages.

9 See Houston and Ryngaert (1996,1997) for more discussion and empirical results. See Rhoades (1994) and Pilloff and Santomero (1997) for more complete summaries of the literature on the value and performance effects of bank M&As.

10 Service quality could either increase or decrease following M&As. Depositors would presumably get access to a larger network of branches and ATMs, but their most convenient office may be closed. It is often found that banks shrink after merger. For example, after the 1986 Wells Fargo-Crocker merger, Wells Fargo's consolidated assets were 10.75 percent lower in real terms in 1987 than were the combined assets of the two banks in 1985 (see Berger and Humphrey 1992). Part of the shrinkage in some of the mergers may have occurred because either small depositors or small business borrowers perceived a reduction in the value of services provided.

11 We cut 10% off of each end of the $[0,2\pi]$ interval so that the x_n span $[.1 \bullet 2\pi,.9 \bullet 2\pi]$ to reduce approximation problems near the endpoints. The formula for x_n is $.2\pi - \mu \bullet a + \mu \bullet Var$, where [a,b] is the range of the variable being transformed Var, and $\mu \equiv (.9 \bullet 2\pi - .1 \bullet 2\pi)/(b-a)$. We limit the third-order Fourier terms to include just the interactions of the own terms because of computational limitations. The model as shown includes 122 net free parameters after imposing symmetry. We exclude consideration of factor share equations embodying Shephard's Lemma restrictions because this would impose the assumption of no allocative inefficiencies, and we want to capture allocative inefficiencies in our efficiency ranks.

12 These statements hold precisely in the case of cost efficiency. For profit efficiency, there is a chance that our method would yield slightly different rankings from the other approaches. This is because profits are not exactly multiplicative in u, so that the profit efficiency may vary slightly depending upon the exogenous variables in the profit function as well as on the estimate of lnu. See Berger and Mester (1997).

13 Thus, when we calculate the pre-merger efficiency of acquired banks (EFF_2), we measure the weight of the acquired bank relative to the total pro forma bank (W_2), and we decide whether the event is a megamerger, minimerger, or neither, we always consider the weighted assets or total assets across all the acquired banks. These terms will be defined momentarily.

14 For example, Berger, Saunders, Scalise, and Udell (1997) found that 41.3% of all bank-level mergers were between banks that had been holding company affiliates as of the end of the prior year. Moreover, when banks were acquired by a new top-tier BHC and were not merged with another bank in the same year, they were merged with another bank affiliate in the 3 years after acquisition 23.7% of the time.

15 Berger, Saunders, Scalise, and Udell (1997) found that holding company acquisitions and bank-level mergers had very different effects on bank lending, supporting this conclusion.

16 The weights and other pre-merger comparisons are all based on the pro forma bank, which simply adds together the balance sheets of the participating banks in the year prior to merger. The purpose is to limit the explanatory variables in the analysis to information that is available prior to the merger.

17 This last result may be in part an artifact of our statistical procedure, which ranks banks involved in megamergers against peer groups which include all banks with data at the same time, rather than just other large banks. Thus, if all large banks – merging and nonmerging – are following a different lending trend than other banks, this may be attributed to megamergers in our procedure. When we tried replaced the population ranks of banks involved in megamergers with ranks based only on large banks (not shown), most of the changes became much smaller, including the Business Loans/GTA change, which became -.011 (not significant). Interestingly, however, the change in the rank of Purchased Funds Price is still large and significant, supporting a decline in risk associated with megamergers.

18 More precisely, under the Relative Efficiency Hypothesis, the coefficient on $W_2(EFF_1 - EFF_2)$ is expected to be in the interval (0,1]. This coefficient may be interpreted as the portion of the way that the rank of the acquired portion of the bank has been brought toward the ex ante efficiency rank of the acquired bank.

19 See Calomiris and Karceski (1995) and Pilloff and Santomero (1997) for discussion of case studies that made shed light of changes in the motivations for mergers in the 1990s, and see Berger and Mester (1997) for more discussion of changes in the cost and profit functions in the 1990s.

REFERENCES

Akhavein, Jalal D., Allen N. Berger, and David B. Humphrey (1997) "The Effects of Megamergers on Efficiency and Prices: Evidence from a Bank Profit Function," *Review of Industrial Organization*, 12 (February): 95-139.

Altunbas, Yener, David Maude, and Phil Molyneux, (1995) "Efficiency and Mergers in the UK (Retail) Banking Market," working paper, Bank of England.

Benston, George J., William C. Hunter, and Larry D. Wall (1995) "Motivations for Bank Mergers and Acquisitions: Enhancing the Deposit Insurance Put Option versus Earnings Diversification," *Journal of Money, Credit, and Banking*, 27, 777-788.

Berger, Allen N., J. David Cummins, and Mary A. Weiss (1997) "The Coexistence of Multiple Distribution Systems for Financial Services: The Case of Property-Liability Insurance," *Journal of Business* 70.

Berger, Allen N., and Robert DeYoung (1997) "Problem Loans and Cost Efficiency in Commercial Banks," *Journal of Banking and Finance* 21, (June): 849-870.

Berger, Allen N., Diana Hancock, and David B. Humphrey (1993) "Bank Efficiency Derived from the Profit Function," *Journal of Banking and Finance*, 17, 317-47.

Berger, Allen N., and Timothy H. Hannan (1989) "The Price-Concentration Relationship in Banking," *Review of Economics and Statistics*, 71, 291-299.

Berger, Allen N., and Timothy H. Hannan (1997) "Using Measures of Firm Efficiency to Distinguish among Alternative Explanations of the Structure-Performance Relationship," *Managerial Finance*, 23: 6-31.

Berger, Allen N., and David B. Humphrey (1992) "Megamergers in Banking and the Use of Cost Efficiency as an Antitrust Defense," *Antitrust Bulletin*, 37, 541-600.

Berger, Allen N., and David B. Humphrey (1997) "Efficiency of Financial Institutions: International Survey and Directions for Future Research," *European Journal of Operational Research* 98: 175-212.

Berger, Allen N., Anil K Kashyap, and Joseph M. Scalise (1995) "The Transformation of the U.S. Banking Industry: What A Long, Strange Trip It's Been," *Brookings Papers on Economic Activity* 2: 55-218.

Berger, Allen N., John H. Leusner, and John J. Mingo, (1997) "The Efficiency of Bank Branches," *Journal of Monetary Economics*, 40.

Berger, Allen N., and Loretta J. Mester (1997) "Beyond the Black Box: What Explains Differences in the Efficiencies of Financial Institutions?", *Journal of Banking and Finance*, 21.

Berger, Allen N., Anthony Saunders, Joseph M. Scalise, and Gregory F. Udell (1997) "The Effects of Bank Mergers and Acquisitions on Small Business Lending," Working Paper, Board of Governors of the Federal Reserve System, Washington, DC, May.

Calomiris, Charles W., and Jason Karceski, Editors (1995) *The Bank Merger Wave of the 1990s: Nine Case Studies*, Office for Banking Research, University of Illinois, Urbana-Champaign.

Chamberlain, Sandra L. (1997) "The Effect of Bank Ownership Changes on Subsidiary-Level Earnings," this volume.

Cornett, Marcia M., and Hasan Tehranian (1992) "Changes in Corporate Performance Associated with Bank Acquisitions," *Journal of Financial Economics*, 31, 211-34.

Craig, Ben R., and João Cabral dos Santos (1997) "Banking Consolidation: Impact on Small Business Lending," working paper, Federal Reserve Bank of Cleveland (February).

Demsetz, Rebecca S., and Philip E. Strahan (1997) "Diversification, Size, and Risk at Bank Holding Companies," *Journal of Money, Credit, and Banking*, 29.

DeYoung, Robert (1997) "Bank Mergers, X-Efficiency, and the Market for Corporate Control," *Managerial Finance*, 23, 32-47.

Fixler, Dennis J., and Kimberly D. Zieschang (1993) "An Index Number Approach to Measuring Bank Efficiency: An Application to Mergers," *Journal of Banking and Finance*, 17, 437-50.

Hannan, Timothy H. (1991) "Bank Commercial Loan Markets and the Role of Market Structure: Evidence from Surveys of Commercial Lending," *Journal of Banking and Finance*, 15, 133-149.

Hannan, Timothy H., and Robin A. Prager (1996) "Do Substantial Horizontal Mergers Generate Significant Price Effects? Evidence from the Banking Industry," Working Paper, Board of Governors of the Federal Reserve System, Washington, DC.

Houston, Joel F., and Michael D. Ryngaert (1994) "The Overall Gains from Large Bank Mergers," *Journal of Banking and Finance*, 18, 1155-76.

Houston, Joel F., and Michael D. Ryngaert (1996) "The Value Added by Bank Acquisitions: Lessons from Wells Fargo's Acquisition of First Interstate," *Journal of Applied Corporate Finance*, 9, 74-82.

Houston, Joel F., and Michael D. Ryngaert (1997) "Equity Issuance and Adverse Selection: A Direct Test Using Conditional Stock Offers," *Journal of Finance*, 52.

Hughes, Joseph P., William Lang, Loretta J. Mester, Choon-Geol Moon (1996) "Efficient Banking Under Interstate Branching," *Journal of Money, Credit and Banking*, 28: 1045-71.

Keeton, William R. (1996) "Do Bank Mergers Reduce Lending to Businesses and Farmers? New Evidence from Tenth District States," Federal Reserve Bank of Kansas City *Economic Review* 81 (3): 63-75.

Keeton, William R. (1997) "The Effects of Mergers on Farm and Business Lending at Small Banks: New Evidence from Tenth District States," working paper, Federal Reserve Bank of Kansas City (February).

Linder, Jane C., and Dwight B. Crane (1992) "Bank Mergers: Integration and Profitability," *Journal of Financial Services Research*, 7, 35-55.

McAllister, Patrick H., and Douglas A. McManus (1993) "Resolving the Scale Efficiency Puzzle in Banking," *Journal of Banking and Finance*, 17 (April): 389-405.

Mitchell, Karlyn, and Nur M. Onvural (1996) "Economies of Scale and Scope at Large Commercial Banks: Evidence from the Fourier Flexible Functional Form," *Journal of Money, Credit, and Banking*, 28: 178-199.

Peek, Joe, and Eric S. Rosengren (1996) "Small Business Credit Availability: How Important is Size of Lender?" edited by Anthony Saunders and Ingo Walter, *Financial System Design: The Case for Universal Banking*, Burr Ridge, IL, Irwin Publishing: 628-55.

Peek, Joe, and Eric S. Rosengren (1998) "Bank Consolidation and Small Business Lending: It's Not Just Bank Size That Matters," *Journal of Banking and Finance* 22 (January).

Peristiani, Stavros (1997) "Do Mergers Improve the X-Efficiency and Scale Efficiency of U.S. Banks? Evidence from the 1980s," *Journal of Money, Credit, and Banking*, 29.

Pilloff, Steven J. (1996) "Performance Changes and Shareholder Wealth Creation Associated with Mergers of Publicly Traded Banking Institutions," *Journal of Money, Credit, and Banking*, 28, 294-310.

Pilloff, Steven J., and Anthony M. Santomero (1997) "The Value Effects of Bank Mergers and Acquisitions," this volume.

Rhoades, Stephen A. (1986) The Operating Performance of Acquired Firms in Banking Before and After Acquisition, Staff Economic Studies 149, Board of Governors of the Federal Reserve System, Washington, DC.

Rhoades, Stephen A. (1990) "Billion Dollar Bank Acquisitions: A Note on the Performance Effects," Working Paper, Board of Governors of the Federal Reserve System, Washington, DC.

Rhoades, Stephen A. (1993) "The Efficiency Effects of Horizontal Bank Mergers," *Journal of Banking and Finance*, 17, 411-22.

Rhoades, Stephen A. (1994) A Summary of Merger Performance Studies in Banking, 1980-1993, and an Assessment of the "Operating Performance" and "Event Study" Methodologies, Staff Economic Studies 167, Board of Governors of the Federal Reserve System, Washington, DC.

Savage, Donald T. (1991) "Mergers, Branch Closings, and Cost Savings," Working Paper, Board of Governors of the Federal Reserve System, Washington, DC.

Shaffer, Sherrill (1993) "Can Megamergers Improve Bank Efficiency?" *Journal of Banking and Finance*, 17, 423-36.

Spindt, Paul A., and Vefa Tarhan (1992) "Are There Synergies in Bank Mergers?," Working Paper, Tulane University, New Orleans, LA.

Srinivasan, Aruna (1992) "Are There Cost Savings from Bank Mergers?" Federal Reserve Bank of Atlanta *Economic Review*, 17-28.

Srinivasan, Aruna, and Larry D. Wall (1992) "Cost Savings Associated with Bank Mergers," Working Paper, Federal Reserve Bank of Atlanta, Atlanta GA.

Strahan, Philip E., and James Weston (1996) "Small Business Lending and Bank Consolidation: Is There Cause for Concern?" *Current Issues in Economics and Finance* 2, Federal Reserve Bank of New York Working Paper, (March).

Strahan, Philip E., and James Weston (1998) "Small Business Lending and the Changing Structure of the Banking Industry," *Journal of Banking and Finance* 22 (January).

U.S. Department of Justice and Federal Trade Commission (1992) "Horizontal Merger Guidelines".

Working Group Statement (1995) "Bank Merger Competitive Review," (February).

Vander Vennet, Rudi (1996) "The Effect of Mergers and Acquisitions on the Efficiency and Profitability of EC Credit Institutions," *Journal of Banking and Finance,* 20, 1531-58.

Zhang, Hao (1995) "Wealth Effects of U.S. Bank Takeovers," *Applied Financial Economics*, 55, 329-36.

JOHN H. BOYD AND STANLEY L. GRAHAM

6.   Consolidation in U.S. banking: Implications for efficiency and risk

1. INTRODUCTION

We don't really know why the U.S. banking industry is consolidating rapidly, as it has been doing for the last decade or so. After a large number of studies on the topic including this one, what seems clear is that consolidation is not producing significant efficiencies – at least not on average. Other dimensions of the consolidation trend – such as its heavy concentration in large banks – are just as poorly understood. Given this ignorance as to the "why" of consolidation, it is extremely risky to predict its future effects. Based on past experience and data, at least, we can conclude the following.

First. Consolidation is having a minimal effect on the efficiency of the banking industry. For some reason, the lion's share of mergers has occurred among relatively large banks, which have the least potential for efficiency gains due to economies of scale. New empirical work presented in this study finds that when small banks do merge, the average result is significant gains in cost efficiency and profitability. This finding seems quite robust and is consistent with predictions of the empirical literature on economies of scale in banking. However, small bank mergers are simply too infrequent – and involve too small a share of industry assets – to have any significant effect on overall industry performance.

Second. The consolidation trend has increased concentration in the banking industry very substantially at the state and national levels. However, at the level of actual bank markets (counties, SMAs and so on) it has not had a large effect – at least not yet. Thus, assuming that the traditional measures of banking market structure are the correct ones, consolidation has not yet had a

*Boyd, Federal Reserve Bank of Minneapolis and Carlson School, University of Minnesota; Graham, Federal Reserve Bank of Minneapolis. We thank Alan Berger for assistance with the data; Yakov Amihud and Greg Udell for helpful comments on an earlier draft. We thank Jody Fahland for excellent word processing, editorial inputs, and psychological support; Gary Barger, Yanat Chhith, and Jason Schmidt for computational assistance. The views expressed herein are those of the authors and not necessarily those of the Federal Reserve Bank of Minneapolis or the Federal Reserve System.

Y. Amihud and G. Miller (eds.), Bank Mergers & Acquisitions, 113–135
© 1998 Kluwer Academic Publishers. Printed in the Netherlands.

great effect on competition in banking. To the extent that it has, however, the effect has surely been detrimental. From an antitrust perspective, this trend is reason for concern.

Third. Recent years have witnessed an extremely profitable banking industry; but, there is no reason to believe that consolidation is causing this enviable profits record, or vice versa. In such an environment, the efficiency and risk effects of consolidation are difficult to ferret out. The next major downturn in the banking industry, whenever that is, will provide the test. On the one hand, consolidation should in principle result in banking firms that are better diversified, both in terms of products lines and geographically. On the other hand, there is no evidence that, ceteris paribus, large banks are less likely to fail than are small banks. Recent events in France and Japan clearly demonstrate that even the largest banks can get into dire trouble.

Fourth. What is most troubling about the consolidation trend, is its implications for the policy of "Too Big to Fail" (TBTF). Whether officially stated policy (as in the U.S.) or not, such a policy exists. Government claims to the contrary are time-inconsistent, and resultantly are discounted by the marketplace. TBTF conveys an unfair, unintended competitive advantage upon large banks, since it defacto insures their liabilities at no cost. In addition, it is a source of moral hazard, beyond the moral hazard produced by deposit insurance systems. The more concentrated a banking industry, the more of its firms that fall into the TBTF category; thus, the more subject it is to such distortions. And, the risk of TBTF government bailouts is commensurately greater. These disadvantages could be offset by significant efficiency advantages to a banking industry composed of large banks. Unfortunately, these other advantages do not appear to exist, except for scale economies resulting from the consolidation of very small banks.

2. RECENT DEVELOPMENTS: THE CONSOLIDATION PHENOMENON

As shown in Figure 1 and Table 1 the number of new bank charters exceeded exits via merger and failure between 1975 and 1984. In 1984 the number of banks and trust companies in the country peaked at 14,496. Between 1984 and 1994 new charters declined, failures jumped sharply, and the rate of mergers increased almost monotonically. As a result, the number of banks in the United States fell to 10,451 in 1994, or about 28 percent from the peak in 1984. Exit via failure was primarily due to the hard times the industry experienced from 1987 to 1991. However, the rate of new entry remained extremely low by historical standards after 1991, and the merger rate remained high during the 1990s. Over the five-year period 1990 to 1994, on average 460 banks were merged out of existence in each year.

Table 2 shows that the large decline in the number of firms has not been confined to commercial banks; it has similarly affected the savings and loan industry. Indeed, over the period 1985-94, while the number of banks declined

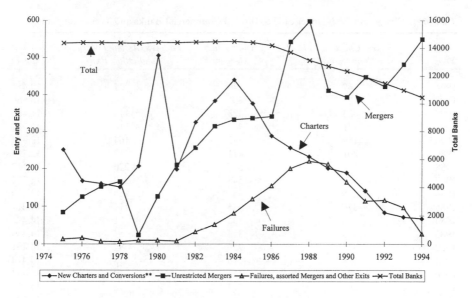

Figure 6–1. U.S. Insured commercial Banks and Trust Companies: Entry and Exit, 1975-1994.

by about 28 percent, the number of thrift institutions declined by more than 40 percent. Part of this thrift contraction is a hangover from the inherited problems of the "thrift crisis." However, thrift institutions, with their large bases of retail deposit customers, have also made attractive acquisition candidates for commercial banks. In this sense, consolidation in banking has extended even beyond the commercial banking industry.

2a. Merger Activity By Size of Bank

Table 3 shows the rate of merger activity by commercial banks over the period 1980–94, by size class. The left-hand panel in this table shows the number of acquisitions by size class of *acquiring* banks. Not surprisingly, large banks were by far the most active buyers. Out of 6,347 total acquisitions, 3,072 (about 48 percent) were done by banks over $1 billion in assets.[1]

The column labelled "Percent of Banks in Size Class," shows the number of acquirers in size class, divided by the total number of banks that were of that size at the end of 1980. Thus, this column represents the number of acquisitions relative to firms in the class; or, roughly speaking, the "rate of acquisitions" by size-class of bank.[2] For example, banks in the smallest size-class ($0-$10 million) did 27 acquisitions over the sample period. There were 2,811 firms of this size in 1980 resulting in a computed merger rate of (27/2,811) = 1.0 percent. The merger rate increases monotonically and rapidly with size class. For the largest size class, (over $5 billion), the merger rate was 5,665 percent. In other words, the average bank in this group acquired about 57 banks over

Table 6–1. Changes in the Number of U.S. Insured Commercial Banks and Trust Companies*

Year	New Charters and Conversions**	Unassisted Mergers	Failures, Assisted Mergers and Other Exit	Total Banks
1994	67	549	27	10,451
1993	71	481	96	10,960
1992	83	428	116	11,466
1991	141	447	114	11,927
1990	189	393	164	12,347
1989	201	411	212	12,715
1988	232	598	220	13,137
1987	256	543	200	13,723
1986	288	341	154	14,210
1985	376	336	119	14,417
1984	440	332	81	14,496
1983	383	314	51	14,469
1982	325	256	32	14,451
1981	198	210	8	14,414
1980	206	126	10	14,434
1979	207	224	10	14,364
1978	151	165	6	14,391
1977	160	152	7	14,411
1976	167	125	16	14,410
1975	251	84	13	14,384

Source: FDIC *Statistics on Banking: Historical 1934-94* Vol. I.
**Conversions are primarily thrift institutions converting to a commercial banking charter.

the 1980–94 period. Clearly, the largest banks did a hugely disproportionate amount of the buying.

This may seem to fit the conventional "big fish eating small fish" stereotype of acquisitions. However, as shown in the right-hand panel in Table 3, the stereotype is not exactly accurate in this instance. The right panel is the same as the left, except that merger activity is measured in terms of *acquired* – as opposed to acquiring – banks. By number of acquisitions, most of the activity involved small- and middle-sized banks, those with total assets of $500 million or less. Out of 6,347 total mergers over the sample period, 6,038 (or about 95 percent) involved acquired banks in this size range. However, the acquisition rate by size of the acquired bank is almost monotonically increasing in size. In the smallest size category, the ratio of acquired banks to number of banks in size class is 16 percent. In the largest size class, the ratio of acquired banks to banks in size class is more than 117 percent.

Table 4 gives a different perspective on this phenomenon. This table shows the total dollar value of *acquired* bank assets over the 1980–94 period, by the size class of the acquired bank. In these computations, we assume that all banks in a class have total assets exactly at the midpoint of their class range. This presents an obvious problem for the largest, open-ended size class which

Table 6–2. Change in the Number of Banks and Thrift Institutions, 1985–94*

Year	Commercial Banks	% Change	Thrifts**	% Change
1994	10,451	-4.64	2,152	-4.86
1993	10,960	-4.41	2,262	-5.36
1992	11,466	-3.86	2,390	-6.68
1991	11,927	-3.40	2,561	-9.02
1990	12,347	-2.89	2,815	-8.81
1989	12,715	-3.21	3,087	-10.21
1988	13,137	-4.27	3,438	-5.08
1987	13,723	-3.43	3,622	-1.50
1986	14,210	-1.44	3,677	1.41
1985	14,417		3,626	

Cumulative Change 1985–1994: Banks: -27.5%
                              Thrifts: -40.6%

Source: FDIC *Statistics on Banking: Historical 1934-94* Vol. I
**Thrifts include savings and loan associations, mutual savings banks, building and loan societies, and so on; credit unions are not included.

has no midpoint. Therefore, in case A we assume that all acquired banks in this class have total assets of exactly $5 billion – the most conservative assumption possible. In case B, we assume that they have total assets of $10 billion – still conservative, we think. As shown in Table 4, the results are not particularly sensitive to this assumption.[3]

What Table 4 shows is that, in terms of assets redeployed within the banking industry, the merger phenomenon was *heavily concentrated among banks which were relatively large in the first place.* Even under the most conservative assumption possible, about 85 percent of acquired assets were acquired from

Table 6–3. Bank Merger Activity by Size Class of Bank, 1980–1994*

Size Class of ACQUIRERS (Assets)**	Number of Acquisitions	Percent of Banks in Size Class	Size Class of ACQUIRED (Assets)**	Number of Acquisitions	Percent of Bank in Size Class
$0–10M:	27	1.0 %	$0–10M:	450	16.0 %
$10–25M:	240	5.1	$10–25M:	1,450	31.1
$25–50M:	541	15.2	$25–50M:	1,519	42.8
$50–100M:	687	34.8	$50–100M:	1,312	66.5
$100–500M:	1,273	93.9	$100–500M:	1,307	96.4
$500M–1B:	507	314.9	$500M–1B:	141	87.6
$1B–5B:	1,429	893.1	$1B–5B:	134	83.7
$ > 5B:	1,643	5665.5	$ > 5B:	34	117.2
Total:	*6,347*		*Total:*	*6,347*	

Sources: Rhoades, 1996. FDIC *Statistics on Banking*, 1980.
**M = $million, B = $billion.

Table 6–4. Dollar Value of Acquired Bank Asset by Size Class of Acquired Bank, 1980–94

Largest Size Class Assumption*	Size Class	Midpoint ($ Miilion)	Assumed Midpoint*	Number of Acquisitions	Dollar Value of Assets in Size Class ($ Billion)
	$0–10M	5		450	2.0
	$10M–25M	17.5		1,450	25.0
	$25M–50M	37.5		1,519	57.0
	$50M–100M	75.0		1,312	98.0
	$100M–500M	300.0		1,307	392.0
	$500M–$1B	750.0		141	106.0
	$1B–$5B	3,000.0		134	402.0
A:	> $5B	n.a.	5,000	34	170.0
B:	> $5B	n.a.	10,000	34	340.0

Total Acquired Assets (Assumption A):	1,252.0
Total Acquired Assets (Assumption B):	1,422.0
Percent of Acquired Assets > $100M (Assumption A):	85.0%
Percent of Acquired Assets > $100M (Assumption B):	87.0%

* Under assumption A, banks in the largest class are assumed to have total assets of $5 billion. Under assumption B, they are assumed to have $10 billion.

banks in the "over $100 million" category; about 54 percent were acquired from banks in the "over $500 million" category.

We believe this fact has important implications for the bank merger phenomenon, and how one tries to understand it. Very briefly, it is among the smaller banks that one would expect, a priori, to find significant scale economies after merger. To be sure, a substantial portion of small banks were acquired during 1980–94. For example, about 51 percent of dollar assets of banks in the "$100 million or less" class were acquired.[4] However, as shown in Table 4, no more than 15 percent of all acquired assets were of banks in the "$100 million and under" class, where efficiency gains are likely (and this estimate is biased on the high side).

We shall return to this issue, since it prompts us to investigate the efficiency gains resulting from mergers of very small banks. Before turning to our own empirical work, we first review some theory. In Section III which follows, we analyze the theoretical arguments as to why consolidation might, a priori, be expected to affect the performance of the banking industry.

3. THE ECONOMIC LOGIC: WHY CONSOLIDATION COULD AFFECT PERFORMANCE

In this section we review the economic arguments as to why consolidation might be expected to affect the performance of the banking industry. We consider three main arguments. The first is that there is excess capacity in banking and, resultantly, that consolidation is a useful way of mobilizing resources to other sectors of the economy. The second argument is that consolidation increases concentration in bank markets, and permits banks to earn increased monopoly rents. Although this may not be a socially optimal outcome, it would surely affect the profitability of the industry. The third argument is that there are economies of scale in banking; by increasing the average size of firms in the industry, consolidation may allow banks to operate more efficiently. In this context, several measures of efficiency have been considered in the literature: profits, operating costs, and risk exposure.

3a. Excess Capacity in Banking

It has been widely believed that banking is a declining industry, faced with reduced demand for the intermediation services it produces. In support of this view, economists have relied on data which show banks with a declining share of intermediated savings instruments (for example, deposits), loans, and total savings of the consumer sector. Most often, these data are from the Federal Reserve's Flow-of-Funds Accounts; and indeed, they do show a marked decline in commercial banks' share beginning, roughly, in the early 1980s. However, recent research (Boyd and Gertler 1995) suggests that the banking industry is not actually declining in any meaningful economic sense; rather, the nature of its intermediation activity is just changing.

It is true that banks have lost loan market share to nonbank lenders and have lost deposit market share to money market mutual funds and others. However, these measures are based on balance sheet data and ignore the rapid growth of new bank product lines which do not appear on balance sheets. These include financial guarantees of different kinds, a variety of products based on derivative securities, consulting, funds management, investment banking, and so on. Figure 2 below is an update of one provided by Boyd and Gertler. It shows that noninterest income (from off-balance-sheet sources) has more than doubled from about 0.75 percent of total assets in 1980 to 1.9 percent in 1994. None of this explosive growth in off-balance sheet activity is captured in the traditional market share measures.

Boyd and Gertler noted a second reason why market share computations based on Flow-of-Funds data have been misleading. Economists at the New York Fed (McCauley and Seth 1992) documented that official numbers on banks' commercial lending substantially underestimated the true totals. Although the Fed now reports commercial loan data which avoid this problem, lending totals were substantially under-reported in the late 1980s and early 1990s.[5]

Boyd and Gertler reconstructed banks' share of total financial intermediation, correcting for the understatement of commercial lending. They also employed several different methods to capitalize noninterest income – in effect turning that income into "balance sheet equivalent" assets. Figure 3 shows an updated version of their market share computations. The

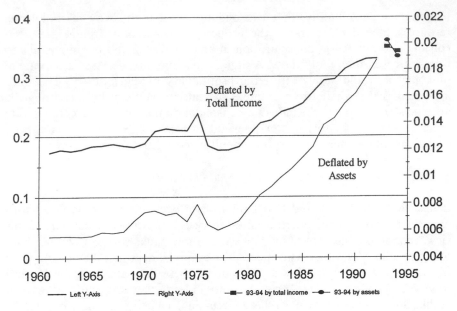

Figure 6–2. Trends in Non-Interest Income of Banks.

unadjusted bank share clearly peaked in about 1975 and declined continuously and substantially after that. The adjusted share computations (labelled "NIC-2" and "Basle Adjusted") also show some evidence of decline after 1975, but that decline is very slight and not statistically significant. Construction of the adjusted share measures is fully explained in Boyd and Gertler, op. cit. and will not be discussed here. It is worth noting, however, that of the two adjusted share measures the larger "NIC-2" measure is preferred.

When these adjustments are made, the conventional view simply does not appear to be right. Banks' share of financial intermediation in the United States has been roughly constant over the last four decades. In sum, banking doesn't need mergers as a means to shift resources out of a declining industry. Thus, there's no reason to view this as a desirable feature of consolidation, or one that would be beneficial to the banking industry.[6]

3b. Increasing Concentration in Banking

Banking concentration has risen substantially in the past decade. At the metropolitan area (MSA) level, the average share of total domestic commercial bank deposits held by the three largest banking organizations increased from 66.4 percent to 67.5 percent between 1980 and 1992. At the state level, the average share held by the three largest banking organizations rose from 29.9 percent to 38.6 percent between 1984 and 1994. And, at the national level, the

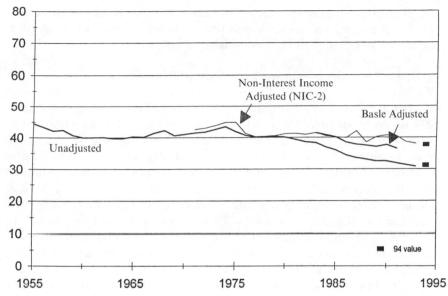

The Basle Adjusted Series employs balance sheet equivalents used by the regulator authorities in calculating capital requirements for off balance sheet risk exposures. The NIC-2 Adjusted Series capitalizes non-interest income (at the same rate as that earned on balance sheet assets), The Basle adjustment is "to small" for our purpose, since many off balance sheet activities are not included. See Boyd and Gertler (1993) for details.

Figure 6–3. Commercial Banks' Share of FInancial Intermediation, Unadjusted and Adjusted.

share held by the 100 largest banking organizations rose from 50.8 percent to 66.1 percent over the same period (Amel 1996, Savage 1993).

There is ample reason to believe that increasing concentration in bank markets, holding other factors constant, is associated with increasing bank profitability. A large number of studies have found that, when concentration rises in bank markets, loan rates tend to rise and deposit rates tend to fall. These findings suggest an increased ability to earn monopoly rents (which may or may not be accompanied by scale efficiencies). Interestingly, a recent study by Berger and Hannan (1995) finds that as concentration increases, banks actually become *less* efficient, in the sense that operating costs rise with no accompanying increase in services provided. One possible explanation for this finding is that bank managers use their rent-earning ability in pursuit of the "quiet life." That is, the ability to earn some rents permits them to operate less efficiently than they would otherwise do, with less managerial effort, more consumption of perquisites, and so on.

We have no idea how much of the recent increase in concentration in bank markets is due to merger activity, and how much is due to other developments. However, it seems that the net effect on bank profitability cannot have been large, at least not yet. That's because the increase in measured concentration at the actual bank market level (counties or MSAs) has not been too great. Thus, to the extent that these traditional definitions of bank markets are correct, we would not expect a large boost to bank profits. From an antitrust perspective, however, the trends in these data are still cause for concern.[7]

3c. Economies of Scale in Banking

There is a large empirical literature on cost economies of scale in banking, which is nicely summarized in Berger, Hunter, and Timme (1993). The consensus of this research is that, in terms of production costs, there are marked economies of scale for firms in this industry, but only up to a fairly modest size. After that, further increases in scale appear to have very limited effects on production efficiency. There is some disagreement as to the point at which the efficiency curve flattens, and estimates have ranged anywhere from $25 million to $500 million in assets. There is also some disagreement as to what happens beyond that point, with some researchers finding cost-efficiency gains over a very long output range (Shaffer 1993) and others actually finding diseconomies of scale for sufficiently large output levels. Still, the consensus seems to be that after a relatively modest scale is achieved, there are neither great advantages nor disadvantages to getting bigger.[8]

An alternative to the statistical cost approach is to examine the market prices of bank equities (or Tobin's q), on the grounds that significant scale economies should be reflected in them. Unfortunately, meaningful equity prices are only available for a few hundred banks in the United States, generally the largest ones. One study which takes this approach is Boyd and Runkle (1993). Over the size range they considered, they found no evidence of cost efficiencies of scale. However, there was evidence of risk efficiencies – in the sense that portfolio diversification seemed to improve with size of bank. However, Boyd and Runkle also found that as size increased, average profitability systematically fell and leverage increased. The combined net effect of the three factors was that large banks were no less likely to fail than were smaller ones. That finding logically leads us to a third and different way of looking at economies of scale in banking.

Scale and Failure Rates

From a policy perspective, the "bottom-bottom line" in size-performance comparisons is failure rates. After all, it is bank failures which result in costs to the deposit insurer or even, possibly, in negative externalities for the macro economy. Some years ago we (Boyd and Graham 1991), published numbers on U.S. bank failure rates by size, which were different from the official numbers released at that time. Specifically, we defined as "failed" any bank officially listed as failed, plus any bank which had received an infusion of government funds (in any form). Continental Illinois was a highly visible institution which fell into the second category. Table 5 recomputes and updates those numbers through 1994. Given the fortunate fact that failures of banks in the billion-dollar-plus category are relatively few, we can only meaningfully construct two

Table 6–5. Failure Rate Among "Small" and "Large" Banks As a Percentage of All U.S. Banks of Each Size 1971–94

	Asset Size of Banks	
Time Period	"Small" (< $1 Bil.)	"Large" (> $1 Bil.)
1971–78	.41 %	2.38 %
1979–86	3.15	3.79
1987–94	9.30	7.91
1971–94	12.00	17.00

Note: Banks include commercial banks and savings banks insured by the FDIC and, since 1990, by the BIF. For each size class, percentages are based on the cumulative number of failures and the average annual number of banks over the time period specified. The number of large savings banks since 1991 is estimated. The number of failures refers to banks and not to banking firms. For a list of large banks that failed during 1971–94, see Appendix A.

size categories: below $1 billion in assets, and above $1 billion in assets. Since there is some judgment involved in classifying an institution as failed and in dating that occurrence, we have listed all the large banks so-classified in Appendix A. In reading Table 5 it is important to be aware that the numerator is *cumulative* failures over the period; these are not annual rates.

We have divided the data into three time intervals: 1971–78, 1979–86, and 1987–94. In the first two sub-periods, the large bank failure rate was higher than the small bank failure rate, and significantly so in 1971–78. The last period, 1987–94, included some of the worst years for banking since the Great Depression. These numbers clearly show it. For small banks the cumulative failure rate nearly tripled and for large ones it nearly doubled. In this last subperiod, the large bank failure rate was somewhat lower than that for small banks. Over the entire period, 1971–94, however, the small banks did somewhat better than the large ones, with a cumulative total failure rate of 12 percent versus 17 percent.

These numbers suggest to us that there's no evidence, based on recent U.S. experience, that large banks are less likely to fail than are small ones. Too, they underscore the importance of what one defines as a "bank failure."

Summary

We have reviewed three economic arguments as to why consolidation in banking might be expected, a priori, to favorably affect industry performance. The first argument is that banking is a declining industry, which would benefit from a mobilization of resources to other economic sectors. We reject this argument on the grounds that the data, when correctly analyzed, do not suggest that banking is declining. A second argument is that consolidation will increase concentration and rent-earning in banking – thus benefiting banks if not society. Although this argument is surely correct, we find that (so far) the average rise in concentration in bank markets has not been enough to greatly affect profits. A third argument is that there are economies of scale which will be realized when banks merge. The existing literature, however, suggests that such cost efficiencies will generally be confined to mergers involving small banks. Finally, there is some evidence that large banks are benefited by better diversified asset holdings, which could represent a different form of scale economy in banking. However, if such an advantage exists, it simply does not show up in the data on failure rates of large versus small banks.

4. STUDIES EVALUATING THE EFFICIENCIES FROM BANK MERGERS

In this section we review previous studies of the efficiencies resulting from bank mergers. First, we look at the "event test" literature; then we turn to operating performance studies.

4a. Event Test Studies

A large number of studies (nicely reviewed in Rhoades 1994) have employed the event test methodology to examine the gains from bank mergers. This methodology has been widely employed in the finance literature, is well understood, and will not be reviewed here. In essence the idea is that equity markets are speedy and efficient aggregators of information. Immediately upon the announcement of a bank merger, therefore, stock prices should reflect the market's best prediction of the effect of that merger. Positive (negative) abnormal returns signal good (bad) predictions.

The results of such tests are best described as "mixed," but in general they do not suggest the existence of significant efficiency gains in bank mergers. Although the shares of the target firm frequently exhibit positive abnormal returns, shares of the acquirer frequently exhibit negative ones. Thus the total, combined wealth effect to both parties is generally small and of ambiguous sign. In any "event," there are several reasons to view the findings of this literature with caution. For one thing, the results seem to depend substantially on technical details such as the length of the "event window." For another, meaningful price data only exist for bank holding companies whose shares are actively, publicly traded. There are just two or three hundred such firms in the United States; thus sample sizes are necessarily small, and restricted to mergers involving only the largest banks.

4b. Operating Performance Studies

Numerous studies have examined the effects of bank mergers on bank operating efficiency and profitability (also reviewed in Rhoades 1994). The results generally suggest that mergers do not improve cost efficiency or profitability. Rhoades identifies 19 such studies published between 1980 and 1993. The typical methodology used in these studies is to compare the performance of merging banks before and after merger to a control group of nonmerging banks. The studies encompass a large range of performance variables. The most frequently used are the noninterest expense-to-asset ratio as a measure of cost efficiency, and the net income-to-asset (ROA) and/or net income-to-equity (ROE) ratios as measures of profitability. Most of the studies evaluated efficiency differences by comparing selected expense ratios across banks, but a few studies estimated translog production functions to measure X-efficiency and scale efficiency. The studies varied in the length of time over which the comparisons were made, ranging from five years prior to the merger to eight years after. Several studies analyzed performance differences of large bank mergers, but only one study examined small bank mergers, and that one involved failing banks.

The results of these studies generally suggest that the efficiency and profitability of merger banks relative to nonmerger banks do not improve after the merger. Only two studies with a sample size greater than one (Linder and Crane 1993, Spong and Shoenhair 1992) reported a relative improvement with respect to efficiency. However, none of the studies that used total expenses as a measure of efficiency found a relative improvement after merger. Only four studies (Spindt and Tarhan 1991, Cornett and Tehranian 1992, Rose 1992, Perestiani 1993) reported a relative improvement in the ROA or ROE measures of profitability after merger. However, no study showed a relative improvement in both the ROE and ROA, or in both the efficiency measure and a profitability measure.

5. ECONOMIC EFFECTS OF MERGERS OF SMALL BANKS

Empirical studies of scale economies in banking have generally concluded that significant inefficiencies exist at the low end of the size spectrum. A logical way to test this result is to examine changes in efficiency that have occurred as a result of small-bank mergers. Empirical studies of efficiencies in bank mergers have either examined large-bank mergers or have not focused on size at all. We are not aware of any studies that look specifically at small-bank mergers with this objective in mind.[9]

We examined the effects of small-bank mergers that occurred in 1989, 1990, and 1991, restricting our sample to mergers of independent banks where the surviving bank had total deposits of $400 million or less. Our definition of an independent bank merger excluded: 1) a consolidation of banks belonging to the same bank holding company or chain; 2) a merger where the surviving bank belonged to a multibank holding company and the surviving bank held only a small proportion of the holding company's deposits; and 3) a merger where either partner was a failed bank. We deleted a surviving bank from the sample in the year that it failed, became a target bank in a merger, or was

Table 6–6. Merging Banks by Combined Deposit Size for Year of Merger

Deposit Size ($ Million)	Year of Merger			
	1989	*1990*	*1991*	*Total*
0–25	3	4	4	11
25–50	15	5	5	25
50–100	17	20	14	51
100–200	13	9	16	38
200–300	4	8	10	22
300–400	1	4	5	10
Total	*53*	*50*	*54*	*157*

acquired by a large multibank holding company. A surviving bank that was involved as a survivor in mergers in more than one year was counted only once in the sample – in the year of its most recent merger. This set of restrictions yielded a sample of 157 mergers (53 in 1989, 50 in 1990, and 54 in 1991). Survivor banks are listed in Appendix B and Table 6 shows the size distribution of the sample.

We tested the efficiency results by comparing performance variables in the year preceding the merger with each of the three years following the merger, excluding the merger year itself. For the year before the merger we simply consolidated the target and survivor banks. We employed three performance measures: the ratio of net income to total assets (ROA), the ratio of noninterest expenses to total assets (NIE/A), and the ratio of total expense to assets (NIEE/A). All three measures are net of goodwill amortization to reflect the argument that the premium paid in a bank merger is independent of operating efficiency.

5a. Empirical Findings

Table 7 shows performance measures for our sample of small banks, before and after merger. Medians are reported since the means are heavily influenced by one or a few outliers. This table turns the sample bank medians into "performance relatives," dividing each of them by the industry average for all banks with assets of less than $1 billion in that year. Of course, this procedure accounts for time trends in the industry data. All the entries in the ROA panel are greater than 1.0 and all those in the expense ratio panels are less than 1.0 – reflecting a strong performance of the median sample bank relative to the industry. Before-and-after merger comparisons are unambiguously favorable with the NIE/A measure, which is always lower after merger than it is before. The comparisons are also favorable with the NIEE/A measure, showing

Table 6–7. Performance of Small Merging Banks Relative to Performance of All Small Banks for Mergers Consummated in 1989–91

	Ratio of Merging Banks (Median) to All Banks (Aggregate)			
	Year Preceding Merger	Years Following Merger		
Year of Merger		First	Second	Third
Return on Assets (ROA) Merger				
1989	1.32	1.47	1.38	1.14
1990	1.15	1.30	1.13	1.03
1991	1.24	1.09	1.12	1.03
Noninterest Expense/Total Assets (NIE/A)				
1989	.92	.89	.84	.83
1990	.94	.92	.92	.88
1991	.95	.92	.84	.91
(Interest Expense ⏐ Noninterest Expense)/ Total Assets (NIEE/A)				
1989	.98	.97	.95	.98
1990	.97	.86	.99	.97
1991	.99	.98	.93	.96

Note: Mergering banks have combined total deposits of $400 million or less. "All banks" are those with total assets less than $1 billion.

improvement (or no change) in eight out of nine cases. However, before-and-after comparisons are ambiguous with the ROA measure. For some reason, 1989 mergers did quite well, 1991 mergers did badly, and 1990 mergers were somewhere in the middle.

Multivariate Regressions
Table 8 shows the results of multivariate tests in which the three performance variables, ROA, NIE/A and NIEE/A are regressed on different sets of explanatory variables. All of these tests include year dummy variables to represent time effects, and individual firm dummy variables to represent firm effects. For brevity, the firm dummies are not included in Table 8, since there are 156 of them. Sample means, medians and correlations, as well as all variable definitions, are shown in Table 8D.

Table 8A shows regressions in which the three performance measures are regressed on a dummy variable for whether the bank is merged or not at the time of the observation (MERGED). Also included is a measure of bank size (LSIZE): the natural log of consolidated assets in the year of merger. Finally, there is an interaction term between size and the merger status dummy variable (LSIZEDUM). The results in panel A are similar with all three dependent

Table 6–8A. Regression Equations: Linear Interaction Effects

1. Dependent Variable ROA

Observations	615
R-squared	.594
Durbin-Watson Statistic	2.22

Variable	Coeff	T-Stat
1. MERGED	.0442	5.31
2. Y88	.0012	.47
3. Y89	.0008	.33
4. Y90	-.0014	.89
5. Y91	-.0007	.54
6. Y92	.0001	.07
7. Y93	-.0007	.63
8. LSIZE	.0005	1.40
9. LSIZEDUM	-.0036	5.10

2. Dependent Variable NIE/A

Observations	615
R-squared	.813
Durbin-Watson Statistic	1.91

Variable	Coeff	T-Stat
1. MERGED	-.0320	4.29
2. Y88	-.0034	1.47
3. Y89	-.0034	1.65
4. Y90	-.0020	1.46
5. Y91	-.0015	1.28
6. Y92	-.0001	.14
7. Y93	.0002	.17
8. LSIZE	.0023	7.15
9. LSIZEDUM	.0026	4.22

3. Dependent Variable NIEE/A

Observations	614
R-squared	.787
Durbin-Watson Statistic	2.13

Variable	Coeff	T-Stat
1. MERGED	-.0380	3.63
2. Y88	.0083	2.57
3. Y89	.0193	6.62
4. Y90	.0201	10.31
5. Y91	.0128	7.67
6. Y92	.0067	4.73
7. Y93	.0006	.44
8. LSIZE	.0057	11.46
9. LSIZEDUM	.0028	3.18

variables. Being merged "helps" in the sense of increasing ROA, and decreasing the expense measures, NIE/A and NIEE/A. The coefficients on these dummy variables are significantly different from zero at (at least) the 90 percent confidence level. However, in each case the interaction term enters with the opposite sign of the merged dummy, and is also highly significant.

These regressions clearly suggest that there can be efficiency gains to merging, but these depend on the size of banks involved. In essence, the smaller the banks the greater the merger benefit. However, these results also have the implication that above a certain size of merging firms, the ceteris paribus effect of merging is to *decrease* profitability and increase expenses. This turning point falls within the range of our sample data; for example when ROA is the dependent variable it occurs when total assets of the merging firms are about $238 million. We do not take this result too seriously, however, since it is not borne out by the regressions that follow.

The regressions presented in Table 8B are quadratic in both bank size, and in the relation between size and merger status. Specifically, these regressions include separate terms for bank size (SIZE), size squared (SIZESQ), the merger status dummy (MERGED), a linear merger-size interaction term (SIZEDUM), and a merger-size squared interaction effect (SIZESQDUM). The idea is to try to separate the *direct effect* of size on bank performance from the effects of merging on bank performance. As we have just seen, the effects of merging may also depend on the size of the merging firms. And we know from previous research that there is a strong direct relation between size and performance, which is likely to be nonlinear (Boyd and Gertler, 1993).

In two of three cases the results in Table 8B are consistent with the expectation of a nonlinear direct relation between size and performance. When NIE/A and NIEE/A are the dependent variables, SIZE and SIZESQ enter with opposite signs and are highly significant. This underscores the importance of controlling for these direct size effects. In all three regressions, the merger status dummy variable (MERGED) is highly significant and, as in Table 8A, indicates efficiency gains from mergers. However, the interrelationship between merger benefit and size of bank has now become less obvious. In fact, when NIE/A and NIEE/A are the dependent variables, there is no evidence of a significant interaction effect. When ROA is dependent, the linear interaction term SIZEDUM is negative and significant, as it was in Table 8A.

The results in Table 8B must be interpreted with considerable caution, given the large number of correlated explanatory variables included. However, these results are strongly suggestive of two conclusions. First, whether or not the sample banks are merged, there are strong direct effects of size on performance. This is not surprising given the findings of earlier studies. Second, controlling for these direct effects *does not* eliminate the beneficial effect of mergers on costs and profitability. This is an important robustness check on the merger benefit suggested by the regressions in Table 8A.

Table 8C contains a third and final set of regressions, the results of which are generally consistent with the others. In Table 8C the merger status

Table 6–8B. Regression Equations: Quadratic Effects

1. **Dependent Variable ROA**

	Observations	615
	R-squared	.596
	Durbin-Watson Statistic	2.21

Variable	Coeff	T-Stat
1. MERGED	1.002e-002	4.97
2. Y88	3.252e-003	1.34
3. Y89	2.415e-003	1.10
4. Y90	-3.492e-004	.24
5. Y91	-1.081e-005	.01
6. Y92	6.371e-004	.58
7. Y93	-3.060e-004	.27
8. SIZE	2.534e-005	.24
9. SIZEDUM	-6.081e-005	3.05
10. SIZESQ	-1.888e-007	.29
11. SIZESQDUM	8.165e-008	1.62

2. **Dependent Variable NIE/A**

	Observations	615
	R-squared	.815
	Durbin-Watson Statistic	1.88

Variable	Coeff	T-Stat
1. MERGED	-3.470e-003	1.93
2. Y88	-1.964e-003	.91
3. Y89	-2.023e-003	1.03
4. Y90	-1.006e-003	.77
5. Y91	-6.992e-004	.60
6. Y92	6.277e-004	.64
7. Y93	8.213e-004	.82
8. SIZE	6.917e-004	7.44
9. SIZEDUM	1.517e-005	.85
10. SIZESQ	-3.717e-006	6.40
11. SIZESQDUM	1.641e-008	.37

3. **Dependent Variable NIEE/A**

	Observations	614
	R-squared	.783
	Durbin-Watson Statistic	2.04

Variable	Coeff	T-Stat
1. MERGED	-5.524e-003	2.13
2. Y88	1.328e-002	4.28
3. Y89	2.383e-002	8.46
4. Y90	2.331e-002	12.35
5. Y91	1.536e-002	9.39
6. Y92	8.978e-003	6.43
7. Y93	2.458e-003	1.72
8. SIZE	1.511e-003	10.80
9. SIZEDUM	2.716e-006	.11
10. SIZESQ	-8.215e-006	9.60
11. SIZESQDUM	5.287e-008	.83

Table 6–8C. Regression Equations:Above and Below Median Size

1. **Dependent Variable ROA**

Observations	615
R-squared	.587
Durbin-Watson Statistic	2.23

Variable	Coeff	T-Stat
1. Y88	.001102	.43
2. Y89	.001224	.53
3. Y90	-.001399	.91
4. Y91	-.000734	.55
5. Y92	.000055	.05
6. Y93	-.000733	.64
7. MERGEA	.000820	.53
8. MERGEB	.005692	3.41
9. LSIZE	.000564	1.54

2. **Dependent Variable NIE/A**

Observations	615
R-squared	.809
Durbin-Watson Statistic	1.89

Variable	Coeff	T-Stat
1. Y88	-.003399	1.50
2. Y89	-.003856	1.86
3. Y90	-.002112	1.53
4. Y91	-.001550	1.29
5. Y92	-.000144	.14
6. Y93	.000178	.17
7. MERGEA	-.000104	.08
8. MERGEB	-.003342	2.24
9. LSIZE	.002308	7.03

3. **Dependent Variable NIE/A**

Observations	614
R-squared	.786
Durbin-Watson Statistic	2.12

Variable	Coeff	T-Stat
1. Y88	.008505	2.68
2. Y89	.018986	6.55
3. Y90	.020131	10.38
4. Y91	.012823	7.67
5. Y92	.006758	4.74
6. Y93	.000645	.45
7. MERGEA	-.004116	2.13
8. MERGEB	-.007716	3.68
9. LSIZE	.005641	11.40

Table 6–8D.

1. **Definition of Explanatory Variables:**

LSIZE	=	natural logarithm of consolidated total assets, in merger year.
MERGED	=	dummy variable, merged or not merged in current year.
SIZE	=	total consolidated assets, in merger year, in $ millions.
SIZESQ	=	SIZE^2.
MERGEA	=	dummy variable for merged, and above median asset size at merger date.
MERGEB	=	dummy variable for merged, and below median asset size at merger date.
Yi	=	dummy variable for year i.

Interaction variables:

LSIZEDUM	= LSIZE*MERGED
SIZEDUM	= SIZE*MERGED
SIZESQDUM	= SIZESQ*MERGED

2. **Sample Means and Medians**

Variable	Mean	Median
ROA	.0095	.0105
NIE/A	.0324	.0301
NIEE/A	.0718	.0711
SIZE ($Mil.)	134.8	94.4

3. **Simple Correlations**

	ROA	NIE/A	NIEE/A	SIZE
ROA	1.00	-.56	-.56	-.16
NIE/A		1.00	.58	.31
NIEE/A			1.00	.10

dummy variable is partitioned into two, distinct classes. The variable MERGEA (B) takes on the value one iff a bank is merged and was above (below) the sample median asset size at the time of merger. In all three regressions, MERGEB is of the expected sign (indicating merger benefits) and significant at the 95 percent confidence level or higher. But only in the NIEE/A regression is MERGEA significant at the 90 percent confidence level. In sum, the benefits of merging are again apparent, but they are concentrated in the smaller firms in the sample – those with total assets of less than the median, which is about $94 million. These tests do not suggest any "merger detriment" for larger sample banks.

Table 6–9. Estimated Merger Benefits: Percentage Increase in Profitability, or Decrease in Expense, Due to Merging*

| | | From Regressions 8A: | | |
| | | Combined Asset Size ($ mil.) | | |
Percentage Change in	From Regressions 8C:**	25.0	50.0	93.8
ROA:	+58.7	+82.5	+57.0	+34.2
NIE/A:	-10.9	-17.0	-11.1	-5.7
NIEE/A:	-10.8	-13.5	-10.7	-8.3

* Estimates based on the Table 8B regressions were not obtained due to the large number of insignificant explanatory variables in those tests.
**Effect for banks below the medium sample size of $93.8 million (combined assets, at meger).

Magnitude of the Merger Effect

The estimated benefits of mergers are highly significant in a statistical sense. As shown in Table 9 they are also quite large in economic terms. Based on the coefficients in regressions for banks below the median sample size, merging results in about an 11 percent average reduction in the noninterest expense ratio (NIE/A), and in the total expense ratio (NIEE/A). In terms of ROA, the estimated merger benefit is almost 60 percent. Table 9 also presents estimates based on the Table 8A regressions, where the merger benefit depends upon the size of the banks involved. These estimates are quite consistent with the Table 8C estimates, indicating a much larger effect on profits than on expenses. We have no idea what accounts for the differential effect, but it is reassuring that both regression specifications produce similar results.

6. CONCLUSION

Except for the work with small banks we have just presented, we see little evidence that consolidation of the U.S. banking industry has been particularly helpful over any performance dimension. In our assessment, there are several possible explanations for this negative finding, which are not mutually exclusive.

First, we don't believe that it is socially desirable to marshall resources out of banking and into other sectors of the economy. The data do not indicate that the banking industry is declining or losing market share over the long haul. If anything, the banking industry appears to have been a growth sector, as has been the financial intermediary sector.

A second possible explanation for the weak performance record of consolidation may lie in the incentive structure which has caused it. As we have argued elsewhere (Boyd and Graham 1991) it is vexing to explain consolidation in banking as a response to market forces. But it may be that managerial hubris, as opposed to ownership interests, is the driving force (Gorton and Rosen 1995). With only a few exceptions, bank mergers have been friendly ones, and these are almost always financially rewarding to senior managements on both sides. In such combinations, branches and staff may get cut substantially (Savage 1991), but there is little trimming of dead wood at the top.

A third possible explanation, the one emphasized in this study, is that the consolidation trend has been concentrated in the acquisition of medium-sized or large banks. These are the ones which present the *least* potential for gains due to scale efficiencies. The new empirical work we have presented is suggestive that when small banks have combined, the average result has been considerable improvement in performance. Undoubtedly, more empirical work needs to be done before that conclusion can be accepted as final. But it is reassuring that our findings are consistent with the empirical literature on economies of scale, which essentially predicted our results.

Looking to the Future
The United States will enter the next banking downturn, whenever that occurs, with a much more concentrated industry than it had the last time. Boyd and Gertler (1993) investigated the last downturn and what they found was not reassuring – especially not in the context of a now even more concentrated banking industry. Their study concluded that banks with assets in excess of $1 billion contributed a wildly disproportionate amount of total losses, even after controlling for systematic size differences in asset mix and geographic location. They calculated that over the period 1983–91, if large banks (over $1 billion) had done as well as medium-size banks ($250 million-$1 billion), loan losses of the industry would have been reduced by $45 billion (or about 20 percent of total industry capital). They attributed this poor performance record of large banks to the TBTF policy and to bad luck. "Of course, it is the case that large banks were unlucky, since they were heavily invested in assets which experienced negative shocks during the 1980s. However, a similar statement could be made about the savings and loans." (op. cit., p. 20).

An interesting and important question is whether recent policy changes – especially the Basle Accord of 1988 and the Federal Deposit Insurance Corporation Improvement Act of 1991 (FDICIA) – will help to reduce the risk exposure of large banks. FDICIA explicitly recognizes the distortions caused by the TBTF policy, and attempts to attenuate them. However, the TBTF policy still exists and market participants are well aware of that. Therefore, it is hard to predict the net effect of these policy changes. We simply have no experience under the new regime, and in a difficult macroeconomic environment.

NOTES

1. Merger data have been constructed by Rhoades (see Rhodes 1996). They exclude mergers where the acquiring and acquired banks were commonly owned prior to merger. They also exclude mergers where the target was a failing or likely-to-fail bank.
2. This computation is not exactly the rate of acquisitions by size class, since the numerator size is at the time of acquisition (anytime from 1980 to 1994) and the denominator is fixed in 1980.
3. This is admittedly a "back of the envelope" computation. The more precise alternative would be to tally up all mergers over the 1980–94 period, record the size of each target bank, and then sum the acquired assets within each size class. For a variety of reasons this is a difficult and labor-intensive task. It seemed not worth the effort given the striking nature of the computations presented, even under the most conservative of assumptions.
4. Calculated as the dollar value of assets of acquired banks (from Table 4) as a percent of the dollar value in 1980.
5. This ex post correction of the data is of little consolation to the many economists who did empirical studies of the "Credit Crunch" during that period. They were attempting to explain an apparent contraction in bank lending which was largely ephemeral.
6. Boyd and Gertler (1995) also looked at banks' share of value added to GDP, and banks' share of factor inputs (labor and capital) relative to factor inputs of the national economy. According to these measures, commercial banking has actually been a "growth industry," substantially expanding its share of value added, employment, and net investment in capital and equipment. Although we have not reproduced these computations here, the same is true with our updated data.
7. From an antitrust perspective (not the perspective of this study) what is alarming in the recent data is the rising concentration levels in rural markets, and in small urban markets. For example, between 1984 and 1994 the average Herfindahl-Hirschman Index (HHI) for all rural markets increased from 3,584 to 3,724, or 140 points. Over the same period, the average HHI for small urban markets, (those with populations less than 100,000) increased from 1,715 to 1,810, or 95 points (Amel 1996). This is above the 1,800 threshold level above which the Justice Department defines bank markets as "highly concentrated." Note that these are averages, so that in something like half of all markets the actual HHI is higher. The implication is that in many small markets, be they rural or urban, there are competitive problems which are getting worse.
8. Although this large literature is interesting and informative, we believe it is best viewed as a form of "statistical cost accounting," not really "economies of scale measurement." We say that because, the "output level" or "product" of financial intermediary firms is extremely difficult to define, let alone measure. The output measures typically employed in these statistical cost studies bear almost no relationship to the output measures suggested by the modern theory of financial firms (for example, Diamond 1984 or Boyd and Prescott 1986). Interestingly, the same conceptual issues are present in national income accounting for the financial intermediary sector. One study which rigorously investigates some of these issues is Hornstein and Prescott (1991).
9. As indicated above, Rhoades identifies one study which examines the mergers of small banks (O'Keefe 1992). It examined mergers involving failed banks and thus is quite different from ours.

SANDRA L. CHAMBERLAIN

7. The effect of bank ownership changes on subsidiary-level earnings

ABSTRACT

This paper investigates whether mergers improve the profitability of 180 bank subsidiaries acquired between 1981 and 1987. Although profitability is unchanged for acquired subsidiaries relative to non-acquired counterparts, specific earnings components improve. In particular, net interest margins widen, and premises expenses and salaries expenses are reduced in the post-merger period. However, these gains are offset by increases in other non-interest expenses, an amalgamation of expenses related to centralized management such as a management fees, advertising expense, research and development expense, director's fees, and data processing charges. The change in bank ownership is also associated with increases in loan loss provisions and losses from sales of securities in the year the merger is consummated, raising the possibility that ownership changes lead to changes in subsidiary-level earnings management.

1. INTRODUCTION

This paper examines whether mergers and acquisitions improve the operating efficiency of acquired banks, and if not, why not. Press announcements and proxy statements concerning bank acquisitions frequently project merger-related cost savings due to actions such as the laying-off of employees, elimination of overlapping branches, or consolidation of back office

This paper is based on my dissertation completed at the University of Chicago. I thank my dissertation committee: R. Beatty, R. Leftwich, L.M. Marais, S. Peltzman, A. Smith, and especially the chairman Katherine Schipper. I have benefitted from comments from A. Alford, A. Beatty, P. Berger, R. Bliss, G. Clinch, B. Holthausen, C. Ittner, S. Kole, M. Lang, L. Maines, J. Magliolo, K. McGahren, R. Sloan and M. Zmijewski. I also acknowledge comments received from members of the Chicago Federal Reserve Bank and Stephen Rhoades, and from seminar participants at Columbia U., Cornell U., Duke U., the U.'s of California, at Berkeley, at Davis, and at Los Angeles; U. of Southern California; U. of Texas, Austin; Washington U. and the Wharton School.

137

Y. Amihud and G. Miller (eds.), Bank Mergers & Acquisitions, 137–172
© *1998 Kluwer Academic Publishers. Printed in the Netherlands.*

operations. If mergers and acquisitions do yield such benefits that are not offset by other costs, then they ought to be associated with improved earnings. This study analyses the earnings and earnings components of bank subsidiaries involved in ownership changes between 1980 and 1988.

Mergers and acquisitions by banks and bank holding companies out-numbered consolidations in every other industry, in each year 1981 to 1989, and ranked among the top five industries based on the value of consideration for each of these years as well. The increase in merger activity seen in the 1980's has been ascribed to state level relaxation of merger laws, changes in federal regulation, and changes in antitrust policies by the Department of Justice and the Federal Reserve Board.[1] Deregulation has continued into the 1990's with a focus on the sanctioning of interstate branching. These efforts culminated in the passage of the Interstate Banking and Branching Efficiency Act of 1995. This legislation is likely to continue the trend towards industry consolidation.

The increase in merger activity over the last decades has heightened interest in determining whether bank consolidations are beneficial and has spawned a large body of research papers focused on detecting such benefits. Surprisingly, the results of this research are generally negative, failing to find evidence of significant operating efficiencies in merged banks. Some studies analyze merger announcement share price reactions to gauge the long run performance effects of mergers. These studies find that the overall reaction to merger announcements tends to be neutral or negative, suggesting no gains in performance.[2] These studies, though useful in establishing the effects of mergers and acquisitions when both acquirer and acquiree are publicly traded, cannot be used to analyze merger effects for non-publicly traded entities and cannot by themselves be used to determine the source of any merger gain or loss.[3]

To address these concerns, other studies have used accounting performance measures to gauge efficiency effects. Some, such as Cornett and Tehranian [1992], Srinivasan and Wall [1992] and Pilloff [1996] have studied the pre- and post-merger performance of earnings and earnings components at the consolidated bank holding company level. Additional research, notably Linder and Crane [1992], Rhoades [1993], and Spindt and Tarhan [1991] examine merged banks, as opposed to merged bank holding companies. However, like the share price reaction studies, whether mergers are examined at the consolidated bank holding company level, or at the bank level, the accounting-based literature has uncovered very little direct evidence that mergers increase the operating efficiency of banks.[4, 5]

One contribution of this paper is that it examines a new sample of acquired firms. Like Linder and Crane [1993], Rhoades [1993] and Spindt and Tarhan [1991], the paper takes an accounting-based approach and examines the effect of ownership changes at the bank level as opposed to the consolidated bank holding company level. However, whereas these prior business-unit-level studies focused on legal mergers, this study focuses on an alternative form of acquisition wherein the newly acquired firm is retained as a legal subsidiary. The distinction between legal mergers and legal acquisitions is important because in states with either unit banking laws or limited branching laws, the acquiring bank holding company can be unable to structure a combination as a legal merger. Yet, acquisitions in states with unit banking laws and limited branching laws comprise a significant percentage of total bank acquisitions during the last decade; Rhoades [1985] documents more acquisitions in Texas (a unit banking state) between 1980 and 1983 than in any other state. Moreover, during the sample period certain bank holding companies, such as Banc One Corporation voluntarily chose the legal subsidiary form of acquisition under the belief that it would yield superior operating results.

Examining the performance of acquired bank subsidiaries is possible because banks file annual reports with regulators, known as call reports, regardless of whether the bank is independent, or a subsidiary of a multibank holding company. These reports include an income statement, balance sheet and supplementary disclosures, similar in detail to those reported to external investors for the consolidated firm. Call report data, measured at year-end 1980 to 1988, are used to evaluate the performance of 180 bank subsidiaries acquired by fifty distinct acquiring organizations. The research method matches each acquired subsidiary with a non-acquired control bank located in the same market, and of the same approximate size and leverage. Inferences are based on non-parametric statistics from sample distributions of matched-pair differences in accounting ratios.

The analysis centers on a break-down of subsidiary accounting earnings into a number of components: the net interest margin, non-interest income, non-interest expense (salaries, premises and other non-interest expenses) the provision for loan losses, and gains (losses) on sales of investment securities. This break-down helps to separate real cost or revenue improvements due to a change in control from the transitory effects of earnings management on reported earnings. The paper finds that although changes in ownership do not lead to improvements in bottom-line profitability, they yield specific cost and revenue improvements. The evidence suggests that premises expenses and to a lesser extent salaries expenses decline and the net interest margin widens for acquired firms relative to their non-acquired counterparts. However, these gains are offset by increases in the provision for loan losses for Texas banks, as well as an increase in *other non-interest expenses* for the sample as a whole. Other non-interest expenses is an amalgamation of expense items partly related to organizational complexity, such as data processing charges, directors fees and legal costs, and partly containing items subject to managerial discretion such as restructuring charges and fees charged to the bank holding company.

The finding that gains derived from improved labor, capital, and loan usage are off-set by other non-interest expenses is new to this paper. The result potentially helps to reconcile conflicting conclusions presented by papers claiming that bank mergers increase employee productivity (Cornett and Tehranian [1993] and Spindt and Tarhan [1992]) and by papers which conclude that total non-interest expense is unchanged by mergers (Crane and Linder [1992], Srinivasan and Wall [1992], Rhoades [1990], and Rhoades [1993]). The analysis presented here suggests the improvement in operating performance which would have been yielded through increased employee and premises cost efficiencies and improved net interest margins are partially offset by the combination of organizational costs and discretionary expense items included in other non-interest expenses. Unfortunately, the level of detail provided in call reports does not allow for a determination of whether this increase in other non-interest expense is mainly due to discretionary or non-discretionary earnings components.

The remainder of the paper is organized as follows. Section 2 explains the research design and its associated costs and benefits relative that used in other studies. Section 3 outlines the sample selection procedures. Section 4 reports the main empirical results and Section 5 examines the sensitivity of these results to alternative sample selection criteria. Section 6 concludes the paper.

2. HYPOTHESES AND EMPIRICAL METHOD

2.1 Hypotheses

Improved subsidiary-level earnings performance is consistent with at least three merger motivations – mergers to replace incompetent management, to realize economies of scale, or to achieve market power. Other merger motives, such as size maximization by acquiring companies, make no predictions for acquired firm post-merger performance.[6] Accordingly, the main hypothesis tested in this paper, H1, is that the earnings performance of the acquired firm will improve after the merger. The paper also examines if acquiring firms pick out poor performers, H2, a prediction yielded from the management replacement motivation. H2 derives from the notion that merger gains from making management more efficient will be greatest if management was very inefficient to begin with.

Since mergers can result in changes in managers (Martin and McConnell [1991]), their compensation plans, or both, the incentive to manage earnings may also change. If so, apparent changes in relative post-merger performance will not necessarily indicate real changes in efficiency. This paper also examines a third hypothesis, that acquired firms engage in different earnings management behavior than their non-acquired counterparts. H3 is analyzed using two components of net income previously assumed to contain large discretionary components, securities gains (losses) and the provision for loan losses (e.g. Moyer [1990] or Scholes, Wilson, and Wolfson [1990].)

2.2 The unit of analysis: the acquired firm

There are two primary benefits, and one major cost, to studying merger effects at the subsidiary level. First, focusing on a subsidiary can make detection of performance improvements easier to measure. The gain to a merger will be easier to detect if it is large relative to the unit examined. In this paper the unit of analysis is small, so improved performance need not be very large in order to detect it. Of course, the size of the subsidiary-level effect will depend partly on what motivates the merger to begin with. If bank mergers are partly motivated by multi-plant economies of scale or scope, performance benefits will be spread out across the organization, and the advantage to evaluating subsidiary-level effects may be small. For example, suppose that acquisitions simply spread fixed centralized costs such as data processing, headquarter staff costs, or advertising costs across more subsidiaries, and that overlaps in these activities are successfully eliminated in the acquired organization. All subsidiaries of the consolidated firm will benefit from the acquisition through lower charges for these services, and no one subsidiary will be the sole locus of gains in efficiency. If instead, some of the gains derive from directly managing the subsidiary more efficiently, then the performance improvement may be easy to detect in the subsidiary, even though the improvement could be small relative to the operations of the consolidated firm.

A second benefit of call reports is that the choice of purchase versus pooling is expected to have no impact on post-merger performance measures. Usually, post-merger balance sheets and income statements will differ depending on whether purchase or pooling techniques are employed. If the price paid for the company exceeds the book value of equity, the purchase method results in higher assets and lower net income (due primarily to goodwill amortization and increased depreciation) relative to the assets and income had the same transaction been accounted for as a pooling of interests. Purchase accounting thus tends to attenuate increases in accounting ratios, such as returns on assets, relative to a non-acquired firm, biasing test statistics towards the null. However, in this sample purchase accounting does not have this effect because subsidiary-level reports typically do not reflect these purchase accounting adjustments.[7]

A potential drawback to analyzing subsidiary-level reports is that inferences can hinge on whether transfer prices reflect in an unbiased manner the value of goods and services exchanged between units of the consolidated entity. If they do not, the post-merger profits of an acquired bank could be an artifact of arbitrary transfer pricing arrangements. Importantly, in this industry there is at least some regulatory oversight regarding transfer prices. Nevertheless, it is likely that this oversight is imperfect. However, the matched-paired design used in this study should help to alleviate this concern. In order for transfer pricing arrangements to influence the conclusions of this paper, there would have to be systematic differences in transfer pricing policies of recently-acquired subsidiaries relative to the independent banks and seasoned subsidiaries used as benchmarks in the empirical section. I am unaware of arguments that would suggest such a bias.

2.3 Construction of a Benchmark

In order to examine if mergers improve performance, researchers must measure what performance would have been, had the merger not occurred. Some studies use an industry index for this purpose (e.g. Healy, Palepu and Ruback [1992], Cornett and Tehranian [1991], Linder and Crane [1992]); others control for non-merger factors using multiple regression (e.g. Srinivasan and Wall [1992] and Rhoades [1990]). This paper adopts a matched-pair research design, measuring the counterfactual benchmark as the performance of a non-acquired bank from the same market area, with a similar production technology as the acquired bank. Market area is measured by the Metropolitan Statistical Area (MSA) or county of the acquired subsidiary and production technology is assumed to be summarized by asset size and leverage, measured in 1980. This approach has the advantage over the industry index approach of better controlling for geographic-specific market variables, such as the extent of markets for consumer, commercial or other types of loans.

The effect of the merger is estimated by subtracting the control firm's performance from the acquired firm's performance. This *relative* performance is than aligned in event time, defining the merger-year as year zero. Since the financial statements available to me are confined to 1980 through 1988, data for only one pre-merger year are available if the merger is consummated in 1981; however seven years of post-merger data are available for the same acquisition. Similarly a merger consummated in 1987 would provide seven years of pre-merger data and only one of post-merger data. Pre-merger performance for a particular acquired subsidiary is summarized by the average relative performance for all pre-merger years available, excluding year zero. Post-merger performance is computed analogously.

The hypothesis that performance improves following mergers, H1, is investigated by analyzing the distribution of averaged relative pre-merger performance subtracted from averaged relative post-merger performance computed for each matched-pair. Tests of H2 are computed using the sample distribution of the pre-merger relative performance. H3 is tested using pre-, post- and merger-year relative performance distributions of security gains (losses) and the provision for loan losses.

To avoid cross-sectional dependence, the sample includes only one acquired subsidiary for each acquired bank holding company. Specifically, when a multibank holding company is acquired, as opposed to an independent bank or one-bank holding company, more than one subsidiary is acquired; however only one, randomly-selected, subsidiary per acquired bank holding company is included in the sample. In addition, because the paired differences of accounting ratios in this study tend to be skewed, standard parametric statistical tests can be inappropriate. Instead, I use the Sign Test which examines the null hypothesis that the number of positive and negative paired differences are equal, to assess the statistical significance of the paired differences. This test requires only that the observations be independent and drawn from continuous distributions.

To illustrate the computation of performance measures, assume that a particular merger involves three banking subsidiaries, all held by an acquired bank holding company (z), and that each subsidiary is matched with one control bank (j).

$a_{tz} \equiv$ the acquired subsidiary performance at event time (t) in transaction (z)

$c_{tj} \equiv$ the control firm (j)

For the pre-merger period, the acquired firm performance is assumed to comprise a treatment effect (μ_b) which is assumed to be constant across all pre-merger years, an unobserved subsidiary specific control effect (c_{tz}), and a transaction specific error (η_{tz}) term.[8] The subsidiary specific control effect is what performance would have been, had the merger not occurred.

$$a_{tz} = \mu_b + c_{tz} + \eta_{tz}$$

I also assume that a particular control firm (j) measures c_{tz} with error.

$$c_{tj} = c_{tz} + \epsilon_{tj}$$

The error components ϵ_{tj} and η_{tz} are assumed to be cross-sectionally and mutually independent, but possibly correlated over time. Notice that

$$a_{tz} - c_{tj} = \mu_b + \eta_{tz} - \epsilon_{tj} = \widehat{\mu_{tz}} .$$

Again, only one subsidiary is included in the sample for each acquired bank holding company to preserve cross-sectional independence.

The pre-merger relative performance measure, $\widehat{\mu_{bz}}$, is computed as the average of all $\widehat{\mu_{tz}}$ in the pre-merger period. The post-merger measure $\widehat{\mu_{az}}$ is computed analogously. Based on the assumptions made, $\widehat{\mu_{bz}}$ measures the pre-merger treatment effect, μ_b, with an error which is independent across observations. In order to use the sample distribution of $\widehat{\mu_{bz}}$ or $\widehat{\mu_{az}}$ to form a Sign Test, the error associated with each observation must come from a median zero distribution, although the distribution need not be the same for each observation (Hollander and Wolfe, [1973] pp 39-43). H2 can be investigated using the Sign Test on the observed values, $\widehat{\mu_{bz}}$.

Test of H1 are conducted using the distribution of the post-merger measure minus the pre-merger measure. This measure contains the change in relative performance $\mu_{az} - \mu_{bz} = \delta$ plus a noise term, τ_z. That is,

$$\widehat{\mu_{az}} - \widehat{\mu_{bz}} = \delta + \tau_z = \widehat{\delta_z}$$

where $\widehat{\delta_z}$ is the observed relative change for transaction z. Again, the Sign Test can be used to infer whether the relative change in performance, δ, is greater than zero, as long as each τ_z comes from a continuous median zero distribution.

2.4 Components of Earnings Examined

Net income is used as a summary measure of subsidiary-level merger effects. The empirical tests examine after-tax net income divided by assets, by equity and by operating revenues (i.e. the sum of interest and non-interest income). Different divisors are used because of the interaction of leverage and profitability. For a manufacturing firm, operating profit (profit gross of interest) is the natural numerator when defining return on assets. However, this form of operating profit has little meaning for a bank because interest income and interest expense are more than just financing charges; they are also the operating expenses for a bank.[9] Return on assets, as defined for a bank, will tend to be negatively related to the debt to assets ratio while return on equity will tend to be positively related to this ratio.

Call reports also break-down after-tax earnings into six less aggregated components:

$$
\begin{array}{ccc}
(1) & (2) & (3)
\end{array}
$$

net interest margin $-$ loan loss provision $+$ non-interest income

$$
\begin{array}{cc}
(4) & (5)
\end{array}
$$

$+$ gains (losses) on sales of securities $-$ non-interest expenses

$$
(6)
$$

$-$ taxes $=$ after tax net income

In addition to after-tax net income, I investigate pre-tax earnings before securities gains and before the provision for loan losses. Since the paper focuses on real efficiencies from mergers, adding back these two components allows me to separate at least some discretionary components in evaluating performance changes. Securities gains (losses) (4), the provision for loan losses (2), and the sum of these two components are also separately analyzed in the context of H3.

Like Linder and Crane [1992], this paper views potential sources of merger efficiencies as deriving from three main net income components, all scaled by revenues: the net interest margin (the difference between interest income and interest expense)(1); non-interest expense (the sum of salaries expenses, premises expenses and other non-interest expenses) (5); and non-interest income (income from fiduciary activities, service charges, trading gains and losses etc)(3). Non-interest expense is in turn broken-down into its components, salaries, premises expenses and other non-interest expenses. This final analysis provides evidence on claims found in the popular press and elsewhere that reductions in non-interest expenses are a main source of bank merger benefits.[10] Extended definitions of these components are contained in the appendix.

3. SAMPLE SELECTION

The empirical method just described implicitly assumes that a bank is acquired only once, an assumption which does not hold in practice. For example, in 1986 the Conifer Group acquired Patriot Bancorporation, and in 1987, the Conifer Group was in turn acquired by the Bank of New England Corp. Since the subsidiaries of the Patriot Bancorporation were actually acquired twice, there is ambiguity about when the pre- and post-merger periods begin. As a result, I eliminate such subsidiaries from my sample. That is, the sample would potentially include any subsidiaries of the Conifer Group which were acquired by the Bank of New England as long as those subsidiaries were not previously a part of the Patriot Bancorporation. This requirement creates a need to trace merger histories for each acquiring organization.

Since a merger history is hand-collected for each acquiring bank holding company, I initially limit the set of acquiring bank holding companies to those making acquisitions in 1983 from *Mergers and Acquisitions*. I choose acquiring bank holding companies from 1983 so that there will be relatively long pre- and post-merger performance histories for each acquired subsidiary. (Recall that the data tapes cover 1980 to 1988). Generally if an acquiring bank holding company is acquired by second acquiring bank holding company, a merger history is collected for the second firm as well. For example, I have collected merger histories of the Conifer Group and of Bank of New England Corp. All acquisitions made by these bank holding companies between 1981 and 1987 are initially eligible for sample inclusion.

Table 1, Panel A summarizes the sample selection results. Of 709 acquired bank holding companies identified through the merger histories of 98 acquiring firms, 277 involved subsidiaries acquired more than once during the sample period. This leaves 569 subsidiaries held by 432 acquired organizations. If possible, each of these acquired subsidiaries is matched with a non-acquired control bank of the same approximate size and located in the same market.[11] A qualifying control bank must be located in the same MSA or county as the acquired bank and must not differ in asset size by more than a factor of four. If more than one control bank is identified on the basis of size and market area, I select the control bank which most closely matches the acquired subsidiary on the basis of leverage.

Matches are obtained for 434 acquired subsidiaries (representing 327 acquired bank holding companies). In branching states bank holding companies usually have the option to convert subsidiaries into branches. If a conversion occurs, the acquired entity will not file call reports in the post-merger period. Of 327 acquired bank holding companies with subsidiaries matched with control banks, only 180 file call reports for at least one post-merger year. All statistics except those in table 1 are based on the 180 transactions with post-merger data.

Table 1, Panel B shows that, relative to the general population of mergers, the sample acquisitions are disproportionally distributed in 1983; almost 25%

Table 7–1. Sample Characteristics

	Panel A: Sample Selection Criteria			
	Number Acquiring Organizations	*Number Acquired Organizations*	*Number Acquired Subsidiaries*	*Number States (of Subsidiaries)*
Original[1]	98	709	1023	39
minus Multiple[2]	-30	-277	-454	-2
Subtotal	68	432	569	37
minus No Match[3]	0	-105	-135	0
Subtotal	68	327	434	37
minus No Post-Merger[4]	-18	-147		-11
Total	50	180		26

[1] The original sample includes the acquisitions between 1981 and 1987 of 98 acquiring firms with at least one acquisition in 1983.
[2] The sample is reduced due to eliminating subsidiaries acquired more than one time during the sample period.
[3] Acquired subsidiaries with no control banks are deleted. A control bank must be located in the same county or MSA as the acquired bank and must differ in size by no more than factor of four.
[4] These are the sample acquisitions that ceased filing call reports in the post-merger period.

	Panel B: Distribution of Mergers by Year							
	81	*82*	*83*	*84*	*85*	*86*	*87*	*Total*
Population of Mergers[1]	335	426	331	251	381	415	262	2401
% of Total	14.0	17.7	14.0	10.5	15.9	17.3	10.9	
Obs. with Pre-Merger Data[2]	40	51	80	44	46	38	28	327
% of Total	12.2	15.6	24.5	13.5	14.1	11.6	8.6	
Obs. with Post-Merger Data[3]	27	27	44	19	29	20	14	180
% of Total	15.0	15.0	24.4	10.6	16.1	11.1	7.8	

[1] Entries in this row are the total number of bank mergers reported in various issues W T Grimm's *Mergerstat.*
[2] Entries in this row are the number of sample acquisitions per year with pre-merger data. Not all observations have post-merger data due to conversions of subsidiaries to branches.
[3] These are the number of sample acquisitions completed in each year which continue to file call reports in the post-merger period.

Table 7-1. Sample Characteristics continued

	Panel C: Ten States with Greatest Number of Targets			
	Pre-Merger		Post-Merger	
	Number	Percent (of 327)	Number	Percent (of 180)
Texas	53	16.2	46	25.6
Florida	39	11.9	7	3.9
Ohio	30	9.2	13	7.2
Georgia	29	8.9	6	3.3
Alabama	19	5.8	6	3.3
Illinois	16	4.9	12	6.7
Missouri	15	4.6	12	6.7
Pennsylvania	15	4.6	8	4.4
Michigan	14	4.3	12	6.7
New Jersey	11	3.4	1	0.6
Tennessee	11	3.4	6	3.3

This panel shows how the target banks are distributed across the ten sample states with the highest number of acquisitions. For example fifty-three of the 327 targets (16.2%) shown in panel A are located in Texas. Of these, forty-six continue to file call reports after the merger, making up 25.6% of the 180 observations reported in panel A.

	Panel D: Relative Size of Sample Observations				
	Mean	Std Dev	Q3	Median	Q1
Total Assets of Acquiring Org. (in Millions $)	3719.17	4544.96	4770.33	2093.32	1040.67
Total Assets of Target Org. (in Millions $)	360.15	1207.31	154.86	74.46	40.01
Target Assets/Acquiring Assets (in %)	11.09	20.55	10.81	3.64	1.63

Based on 180 observations with post-merger data. Although the unit of analysis in this study is a single acquired subsidiary, the actual acquired organization can be a target bank holding company made up of many bank subsidiaries. Call reports identify subsidiaries held by a common bank holding company through a data field called the *Highest Holding CompanyNumber*. This table reports the aggregate asset size of the target organization and acquiring organization by adding up all assets in all subsidiaries across the *Highest Holding Company Number*. In the last row the relative size of the two organizations is reported. In this table assets are measured the year before the merger.

of the sample acquisitions are consummated in 1983 whereas only 14% of the roughly 2,400 bank acquisitions occurring between 1981 and 1987 actually took place in 1983. The remaining 75% of the sample acquisitions are distributed fairly uniformly in the remaining years.

Panel C shows that the sample mergers are concentrated in Texas and Florida. Acquisitions in Texas and Florida make up approximately 28% of the sample observations with pre-merger data. However, branching laws result in increased sampling from Texas in the post-merger data. Specifically, Panel C shows that only seven of thirty-nine Florida acquisitions continue to file call reports in the post-merger period, due to the conversion of subsidiaries into branches. In contrast forty-six of fifty-three Texas acquisitions file data in the post-merger period. Thus in comparison to the pre-merger period, Texas is over-represented in the post-merger period with states such as Florida, New Jersey, and Georgia under-represented.

The sample mergers examined in this paper are non-random both due to the investigation of bank holding companies with at least one acquisition in 1983 and due to state branching regulations which allow for the conversion of acquired subsidiaries into branches. While these sample selection biases limit the generalizability of my findings, the biases incorporated in this study are different from the biases inherent in other studies, so that ultimately perhaps the overall body of literature can be generalized. A key difference in this sample versus others is that it focuses on situations where the merger does not result in increased numbers of branches held by the acquiring company, but instead focuses on situations where the number of subsidiaries are increased. Linder and Crane [1992] conjecture that the ability to legally merge may provide opportunities for operational efficiencies that cannot be realized with the subsidiary form. If they are correct, the sample selection criteria used in this study would bias against finding gains to mergers.

Table 1 Panel D shows that the sample acquired organizations are small. The median size of the acquired organizations is $74.4 million in assets compared with $312.7 million in Srinivasan and Wall (240 mergers) and with $3,551 million reported in Cornett and Tehranian (30 mergers). However, the sample also includes forty-eight mergers with post-merger data where the size of the acquired organization is at least 10% of the size of the acquiring organization. In Section 5 I examine whether variation in the significance of the acquisition to the acquiring company, measured by relative size of the acquiring and acquired organization, is associated with subsequent merger benefits.

3.1 Assessment of the Control Firms

The goal of isolating control firms of the same approximate size and leverage and in the same location as acquired subsidiaries is to assure that the control firm has the same production function and market characteristics as the acquired counterpart. Since market area is observable, the most difficult task is to assure that production functions are similar; Table 2 provides some evidence in this regard. Table 2 assumes that the production of the bank is a function of asset mix (e.g. the loan to deposit ratio and the mix of loans), the deposit structure of the bank, size and number of branches.

Table 2 Panel A indicates that the sample comprises acquired subsidiaries which are systematically somewhat larger than their non-acquired counterparts. The median acquired subsidiary has assets prior to the merger of $57 million whereas the median control bank has assets of approximately $44 million. Fifty-nine percent of acquired subsidiaries have more assets than their non-acquired counterparts. In addition, acquired banks differ from control banks at conventional levels of significance along the dimensions of agricultural and real estate loan concentrations (where acquired firms have de-emphasized these loans relative to control banks) and along the dimension of large deposits (acquired banks have more large deposits than control banks.) Acquired banks do not differ in a statistical sense in leverage (measured by primary capital), in their emphasis on commercial and consumer loans, in the loan to deposit ratio and in the number of branches.[12]

The results in Table 2 suggest that perhaps the matched-pair approach has not adequately controlled for differences in risk. It is comforting that the matched-pairs do not differ in leverage given the interaction of leverage with net income scaled by assets or equity. However, agricultural and real estate loans tend to be riskier than commercial and consumer loans, so the control banks could be viewed as having higher loan default risk than their acquired counterparts. This would increase the expected return to the loan portfolio for control banks relative to acquired banks.

Relatedly, the empirical tests do not control for changes in risk. Table 2 panel B shows how the balance sheets of the matched-pairs change relative to one another from the pre-merger to post-merger period. Although loan mix does not change, acquired banks do change their financial risk, becoming more leveraged after the acquisition. As discussed in section 2.4 this change in leverage potentially biases the profitability results towards increased relative returns on equity and decreased returns on assets for acquired subsidiaries in the post-merger period.

4. THE PERFORMANCE EFFECTS OF MERGERS

4.1 Preliminary Analysis

Measuring merger effects by averaging across the pre- and post-merger paired differences smooths over any time-series variation in performance. In addition, as shown in Table 1, the post-merger sample is over-represented by Texas in part because Texas banks were not allowed to branch until 1987. Figure 1 provides plots of median earnings scaled by assets over time for three samples – for all 180 transactions with post-merger data (Plot A), for all non-Texas

Table 7-2. Profile of Acquired and Control Banks

Panel A: Pre-merger Balance Sheet Characteristics

		Matched Variables		Loan Mix				Other Characteristics		
		Total Assets Millions $	Primary Capital %	Comm'l to Tot Loans %	Cons to Tot Loans %	Agri to Tot Loans %	Real Es to Tot Loans %	Lg Dep to Tot Deposits %	Loan to Tot Deposits %	Number Branches
Acquired	Mean	188.02	8.66	29.48	29.50	3.91	37.70	13.09	57.58	5.1
	Std. Dev.	635.68	2.91	14.86	12.41	8.91	15.62	9.23	11.98	14.2
	Median	56.95	8.15	28.36	28.68	0.56	35.38	11.28	58.67	1.7
Control	Mean	241.87	8.63	28.57	29.33	4.40	39.16	11.56	57.94	5.4
	Std. Dev.	1416.87	2.43	14.61	12.95	8.52	15.67	9.45	11.55	16.9
	Median	44.01	8.21	27.65	26.78	1.11	38.15	9.25	59.39	1.0
Acq-Con	Mean	-53.85	0.03	0.92	0.16	-0.49	-1.45	1.53	-0.36	-0.3
	Std. Dev.	898.13	1.71	16.12	14.52	7.36	16.37	9.70	15.00	6.5
	Q1	41.24	0.85	9.53	9.00	0.57	8.09	6.81	7.85	1.0
	Median	11.61	0.02	0.97	0.44	-0.00	-3.73	1.46	-0.10	0.0
	Q3	-14.84	-0.94	-7.60	-9.17	-1.76	-11.73	-2.94	-9.43	-1.0
	Stu Rng	14.66	8.69	5.90	6.57	9.68	7.34	6.98	5.73	12.97
	Frac > 0	0.587	0.506	0.544	0.517	0.430	0.417	0.606	0.494	0.528
	t(Mean)	-0.80	0.25	0.76	0.15	-0.89	-1.19	2.11	-0.32	-0.67
	Sign Test	2.34*	0.15	1.19	0.45	-1.75+	-2.24*	2.83**	-0.15	0.62

Footnotes are contained on next page.

Table 7–2. Profile of Acquired and Control Banks continued

Panel B: The Change (Post minus Pre-Merger) in Balance Sheet Characteristics

		Matched Variables		Loan Mix				Other Characteristics		
		Total Assets Millions $	Primary Capital %	Comm'l to Tot Loans %	Cons to Tot Loans %	Agri to Tot Loans %	Real Es to Tot Loans %	Lg Dep to Tot Deposits %	Loan to Tot Deposits %	Number Branches
Acquired	Mean	153.25	-0.68	3.09	-5.17	-1.07	5.19	1.26	7.33	1.3
	Std. Dev.	614.06	2.70	19.04	11.46	3.60	13.06	7.72	12.70	3.8
	Median	30.13	-0.20	4.92	-5.51	-0.02	5.16	0.45	7.02	0.0
Control	Mean	111.31	-0.13	2.93	-5.02	-0.77	5.00	0.85	3.25	1.0
	Std. Dev.	454.87	2.24	18.84	9.86	3.14	11.32	5.18	10.70	3.9
	Median	22.27	0.09	0.79	-5.08	-0.05	4.28	1.15	3.55	0.0
Acq-Con	Mean	41.94	-0.55	0.16	-0.15	-0.30	0.19	0.41	4.08	0.4
	Std. Dev.	267.48	2.33	16.01	12.88	4.26	14.31	8.55	14.88	3.5
	Q1	31.18	0.74	9.29	7.38	0.77	8.47	4.83	13.48	0.8
	Median	5.68	-0.37	1.36	-0.22	0.00	0.11	0.50	3.39	0.0
	Q3	-7.93	-1.39	-9.32	-7.76	-0.69	-8.74	-5.13	-5.78	-0.3
	Stu Rng	12.19	7.85	6.60	7.33	9.29	5.43	7.55	5.78	13.25
	Frac > 0	0.587	0.417	0.539	0.494	0.524	0.506	0.522	0.583	0.567
	t(Mean)	2.10	-3.16	0.13	-0.16	-0.95	0.18	0.65	3.68	1.34
	Sign Test	2.34*	-2.24*	1.04	-0.15	0.62	0.15	0.60	2.24*	1.51

These distributions are based on the 180 acquisitions with post-merger data. All pre-merger characteristics are measured as the average of all available pre-merger years (Panel A). The change in the characteristic (Panel B) is the post merger characteristic minus the pre-merger characteristic. *Acquired*, *Control* and *Acq-Con* refer to the target subsidiaries, their matched pairs, and the paired differences respectively. Stu Rng is the studentized range for the distribution of paired differences in the relevant row. Frac > 0 is the fraction of paired differences which are positive. t (Mean) is the standard t-statistic testing the hypothesis that the mean of the paired difference is equal to zero. Sign Test is the z-statistic testing the hypothesis there are equal numbers of positive and negative paired differences. **, *, and + denote 1%, 5% and 10% significance using two tailed tests in all columns. Significance levels are reported on Sign Test statistics only due to skewed distributions. Extended variable definitions are contained in the appendix.

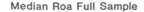

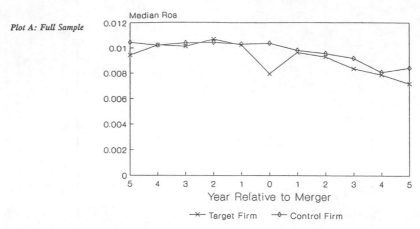

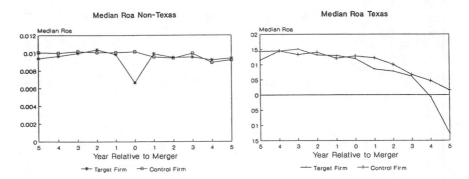

Figure 7–1. Median Return on Assets

transactions (Plot B) and for the Texas transactions alone (Plot C).[13] These figures provide some assurance that averaging does not result in a loss of important information.

The plots forecast many of the main empirical results documented later in this section. First, profitability does not appear to improve for acquired banks relative to their controls. If anything, acquired subsidiaries lose ground in the post-merger period. Second, in the merger year itself, profitability ratios drop sharply for acquired firms. Third, Plots B and C, which compare the sub-sample of Texas mergers with those of other states, suggest that state environments are related to merger performance.

Table 7-3. Analysis of Profitability

		ROA After Tax (%)				ROE After Tax (%)				ROR After Tax (%)			
		Bef	Yr 0	Aft	Chg	Bef	Yr 0	Aft	Chg	Bef	Yr 0	Aft	Chg
Acquired	Mean	1.00	0.74	0.47	-0.53	12.43	9.94	-2.65	-15.07	9.40	6.43	4.75	-4.65
	Std Dev	0.56	1.70	1.41	1.52	7.08	34.12	85.66	86.47	5.35	10.62	14.55	15.28
	Median	1.01	0.79	0.82	-0.13	13.01	10.68	11.67	-0.36	9.15	7.66	8.17	-0.70
Control	Mean	1.03	1.00	0.73	-0.30	13.03	12.15	8.01	-5.02	9.55	9.34	7.44	-2.11
	Std Dev	0.45	0.70	0.94	0.95	5.68	10.36	19.46	19.38	4.52	6.12	9.05	9.04
	Median	1.00	1.04	0.93	-0.13	13.26	13.34	11.71	-1.54	9.52	10.03	9.34	-0.70
Acq - Con	Mean	-0.03	-0.26	-0.26	-0.23	-0.60	-2.22	-10.66	-10.05	-0.16	-2.91	-2.69	-2.53
	Std Dev	0.58	1.74	1.47	1.49	7.82	34.88	85.97	86.01	5.68	11.82	14.66	14.73
	Median	0.03	-0.27	-0.08	-0.01	0.39	-3.13	0.31	0.71	0.08	-2.25	-0.77	0.01
	Frac > 0	.511	.356	.456	.494	.506	.361	.511	.533	.506	.372	.456	.500
	Stu Range	6.72	13.90	9.64	9.71	7.55	14.27	13.67	13.62	7.29	11.33	9.80	9.69
	T(Mean)	-0.61	-2.00	-2.36	-2.09	-1.04	-0.85	-1.66	-1.57	-0.37	-3.30	-2.46	-2.31
	Sign Test	0.30	-3.88**	-1.19	-0.15	0.15	-3.73**	0.30	0.89	0.15	-3.43**	-1.19	0.00

This table presents tests of H1, that the change in relative profitability is positive and H2, that pre-merger relative profitablity is negative. The Sign Test under the column labelled 'Bef' tests Hypothesis 2 and the Sign Test under the column labelled 'Chg' tests H1.

All distributions are based on the 180 acquired subsidiaries with post-merger data. Bef, Yr0, Aft refer to the pre-, year of-, and post-merger distributions. (For each sample acquired subsidiary, pre-merger performance is the average for a particular performance measure across all available pre-merger years, excluding the merger year. Post-merger performance is computed analogously.) Chg refers to the difference in performance (i.e. Aft - Bef). Acquired, Control and Acq - Con refer to the target subsidiaries, their control firms, and the paired differences respectively. Stu Rng is the studentized range for the distribution of paired differences in the relevant column. Frac > 0 is the fraction of paired differences which are positive. t(Mean) is the standard t-statistic testing the hypothesis that the mean of the paired differences is equal to zero. Sign Test is the z-statistic testing the hypothesis that there are equal numbers of positive and negative paired differences. **, *, and + denote 1%, 5% and 10% significance using two tailed tests in all columns except Bef and Chg which test H2 and H1 respectively. Significance levels are reported on Sign Test statistics only due to skewed distributions. Extended variable definitions are contained in the appendix.

4.2 Effects on Earnings and Earnings Components

Tables 3, 4 and 5 contain evidence of the effects of acquisitions on the distribution of earnings and earnings components. Each of these tables is organized in the same way. Distributional facts are provided on the acquired subsidiaries (*Acquired*), on control firms (*Control*) and on the paired differences (*Acq - Con*). The column headings indicate pre-merger (Bef), post-merger (Aft), merger-year (Year 0), and changes (Chg) in the performance measure. Tests that mergers improve performance (H1) are conducted by the Sign Test under the column labelled Chg. Tests that acquired firms under-perform their control firms are conducted by the Sign Test under the column labelled Bef.

4.2.1 Test of H1

Tables 3 and 4 provide almost no support for the hypothesis that performance improves for acquired subsidiaries in the post-merger period. Profitability generally declines (see Table 3) for both acquired and control firms. For example, the median return on assets is approximately 1% for both acquired and control firms in the pre-merger period. The median return declines by about .13% for both groups of firms. Only forty-nine percent of the matched-pairs exhibit positive changes in earnings performance, rejecting the hypothesis that performance improves. Similar results are shown for the other two earnings ratios.

This finding is repeated in Table 4 which reports that two of three main earnings components also do not improve. Non-interest expense tends to increase for both acquired and control firms, and acquired firms improve relative to control firms in roughly 50% (i.e. 1.0–.494) of the cases. Non-interest income also increases for both sets of firms (from about 7.5% of revenues to somewhat greater than 7.6% of revenues); again though, improvement by acquired firms relative to control firms occurs in just 51% of the paired differences. There is however, weak evidence that net interest margins widen for acquired banks relative to control banks. The median acquired firm improves its net interest margin as a fraction of revenues by approximately 3% whereas control firms improve their net interest margins by about 2%. This improvement in net interest margin possibly results from the increased loan levels intimated in Table 2, Panel B (see the loan to deposit ratio). However, positive paired differences are found in only 56% of the observations yielding one-tailed significance at only the 10% level.

The finding that non-interest expenses do not decline is puzzling given that other studies, particularly Cornett and Tehranian [1992] and Spindt and Tarhan [1992] report evidence that salaries are reduced in their samples. In this sample, there is only very weak evidence that salaries expenses decline after mergers. Panel B in Table 4 reports that the median salary expense increases for both acquired and control banks, and that fifty-five percent of acquired firms improve their ratios of salaries expenses to revenues relative to control banks.

The evidence that premises expenses are reduced following acquisitions is somewhat stronger. Premises expenses for acquired banks are reduced by approximately .23% whereas they are increased by .23% for the control sample. Over 60% of the acquired firms improve their ratio of premises expenses relative to their control firms, statistically significant at greater than the 1% level.

These gains are offset, however, by increases in other non-interest expenses, where over 65% of acquired firms increase relative to control firms. The increase in other non-interest expense is difficult to interpret without additional disclosure. One possibility is that acquisitions yield specific cost reductions in labor and capital, but that informational and other organizational costs are increased as the number of subsidiaries are increased. For example, data processing charges and other back office expenses might increase even as employees are layed-off and investment and expenditures on fixtures and buildings are reduced. However, a second possibility is that the increase in other non-interest expense is simply a transfer of costs from premises expenses and salaries expenses to the other non-interest expense category. For example, suppose that the acquisition was followed by large lay-offs and write-downs of fixed assets. These charges could be labelled restructuring costs and would increase other non-interest expenses while reducing premises and salaries expenses. Unfortunately, call reports do not disclose the level of detail that would be needed to separate these two scenarios. To sort out these explanations it would be necessary analyze the merger at the level of the consolidated bank holding company where 10-k reports disclose some details on the composition of other non-interest expenses. To my knowledge, the effect of mergers and acquisitions on the composition of these expenses has not been explored.

4.2.2 Hypothesis 2

Tables 3 and 4 provide almost no evidence that acquiring firms choose poorly performing targets. Sign Tests indicate acquired firms are equally likely to underperform control firms as they are to outperform control firms in the pre-merger period. Counter to the prediction that acquired subsidiaries are inefficiently managed before the merger, Table 4 indicates that 58% of acquired firms actually have lower non-interest expenses than their non-acquired counterparts. The only evidence of sub-normal, pre-merger performance by acquired firms is that approximately 57% of acquired firms have lower net interest margins than the control firms (significant at greater than the one-tail 5% significance level).

4.2.3 Merger Effects on Loan Loss Provisions and Securities Gains

Figure 1 reveals a drop in merger-year net income for the acquired firms relative to control firms. Tables 3 and 4 show that acquired firms are out-performed by control firms for approximately 64% of the matched-pairs in the merger year. The statistics reject the hypothesis of no differences in the merger-year profitability (at the 1% level) across all net income measures. However,

Table 7-4. Analysis of Profitability Components

Panel A: Non-interest and Interest Components

		Non-Interest Exp to Revenues (%)				Non-interest Inc to Revenues (%)				Net Interest Margin to Revenues (%)			
		Bef	Yr 0	Aft	Chg	Bef	Yr 0	Aft	Chg	Bef	Yr 0	Aft	Chg
Acquired	Mean	29.99	30.24	33.05	3.05	8.29	8.96	8.51	0.23	36.37	35.91	38.49	2.12
	Std Dev	8.78	8.22	8.70	8.37	3.87	7.14	3.97	3.00	8.05	7.63	5.55	8.49
	Median	28.72	29.59	31.86	3.03	7.54	7.73	7.60	-0.04	35.30	36.28	38.89	3.11
Control	Mean	30.77	30.51	32.84	2.07	7.98	8.48	8.72	0.74	37.38	36.96	38.85	1.46
	Std Dev	8.89	8.26	8.82	7.11	3.56	5.11	4.64	3.54	8.52	8.57	5.89	8.01
	Median	29.19	28.96	31.81	2.02	7.55	7.49	7.67	0.45	36.30	37.12	38.78	2.13
Acq - Con	Mean	-0.78	-0.27	0.21	0.98	0.31	0.47	-0.21	-0.51	-1.01	-1.05	-0.36	0.66
	Std Dev	9.58	10.56	11.65	8.63	4.23	6.92	5.11	4.19	8.19	8.04	5.64	7.51
	Median	-0.88	-0.83	0.13	-0.05	-0.06	-0.16	-0.49	0.06	-1.26	-1.06	-0.51	1.20
	Frac > 0	0.422	0.456	0.506	0.494	0.489	0.489	0.433	0.511	0.433	0.433	0.450	0.561
	Stu Rng	7.97	7.01	7.51	8.15	8.23	11.71	7.32	8.16	7.10	5.95	5.78	5.66
	T(Mean)	-1.09	-0.34	0.24	1.53	0.98	0.92	-0.54	-1.64	-1.66	-1.75	-0.85	1.17
	Sign Test	-2.09	-1.19	0.15	-0.15	-0.30	-0.30	-1.79+	0.30	-1.79*	-1.79+	-1.34	1.64+

This table presents tests of Hypothesis 1, that the change in the relative net income (expense) component is positive (negative), and Hypothesis 2, that the pre-merger relative net income (expense) is negative (positive). The Sign Test under the column labelled 'Bef' ('Chg') tests Hypothesis 2 (Hypothesis 1). All distributions are based on the 180 acquired subsidiaries with post-merger data. Bef, Yr0, Aft refer to the pre-, year of-, and post-merger distributions. (For each sample acquired subsidiary, pre-merger performance is the average for a particular performance measure across all available pre-merger years. Post-merger performance is computed analogously.) Chg refers to the difference in performance (i.e. Aft minus Bef). Acquired, Control and Acq - Con refer to the target subsidiaries, their control firms, and the paired differences respectively. Stu Rng is the studentized range for the distribution of paired differences in the relevant column. Frac > 0 is the fraction of paired differences which are positive. t(Mean) is the standard t-statistic testing the hypothesis that the mean of the paired differences is equal to zero. Sign Test is the z-statistic testing the hypothesis that there are equal numbers of positive and negative paired differences. **, *, and + denote 1%, 5% and 10% significance using two tailed tests in all columns except Bef and Chg which test H2 and H1 respectively. Significance levels are reported on Sign Test statistics only due to skewed distributions. Extended variable definitions are contained in the appendix.

Table 7-4. Analysis of Profitability Components cont.

Panel B: Analysis of Non-interest Expense Components

		Salaries to Rev (%)				Premises Exp to Rev (%)				Other Exp to Rev (%)			
		Bef	Yr 0	Aft	Chg	Bef	Yr 0	Aft	Chg	Bef	Yr 0	Aft	Chg
Acquired	Mean	14.96	14.53	15.01	0.04	5.05	4.87	4.77	-0.28	9.98	10.85	13.27	3.29
	Std Dev	3.89	3.49	3.05	3.14	2.36	2.39	2.06	2.08	3.56	3.96	5.37	5.24
	Median	14.64	14.32	14.91	0.44	4.65	4.32	4.56	-0.23	9.26	10.09	12.28	2.96
Control	Mean	15.48	15.14	16.04	0.56	4.88	4.81	5.12	0.24	10.41	10.56	11.68	1.27
	Std Dev	4.31	4.07	4.12	3.21	2.03	1.96	2.30	2.04	3.94	3.97	3.94	3.59
	Median	15.03	14.77	15.59	0.75	4.50	4.60	4.89	0.23	9.54	10.03	10.99	1.17
Acq - Con	Mean	-0.52	-0.61	-1.03	-0.52	0.17	0.06	-0.35	-0.52	-0.43	0.29	1.59	2.02
	Std Dev	4.79	4.88	4.94	3.48	2.62	2.86	3.02	2.68	4.08	5.29	6.32	5.52
	Median	-0.70	-0.64	-0.90	-0.53	0.15	0.13	-0.12	-0.37	-0.21	-0.02	0.83	1.21
	Frac > 0	0.433	0.450	0.417	0.450	0.522	0.522	0.472	0.394	0.456	0.500	0.606	0.656
	Stu Rng	7.36	6.37	6.38	6.53	6.69	6.62	7.85	6.47	7.70	8.21	7.69	7.97
	T(Mean)	-1.45	-1.69	-2.30	-1.99	0.87	0.26	-1.55	-2.60	-1.42	0.73	3.37	4.90
	Sign Test	-1.79	-1.34	-2.24*	-1.34+	0.60	0.60	-0.75	-2.83**	-1.19	0.00	2.83**	4.17

This table presents tests of Hypothesis 1, that the change in the relative expense component is negative and Hypothesis 2, that pre-merger relative expense component is positive. The Sign Test under the column labelled 'Bef'('Chg') tests Hypothesis 1).

All distributions are based on the 180 acquired subsidiaries with post-merger data. Bef, Yr0, Aft refer to the pre-, year of-, and post-merger distributions. (For each sample acquired subsidiary, pre-merger performance is the average for a particular performance measure across all available pre-merger years, excluding the merger year. Post-merger performance is computed analogously.) Chg refers to the difference in performance (i.e. Aft minus Bef). Acquired, Control and Acq - Con refer to the target subsidiaries, their control firms, and the paired differences respectively. Stu Rng is the studentized range for the distribution of paired differences in the relevant column. Frac > 0 is the fraction of paired differences which are positive. t(Mean) is the standard t-statistic testing the hypothesis that the mean of the paired differences is equal to zero. Sign Test is the z-statistic testing the hypothesis that there are equal numbers of positive and negative paired differences. **, * and + denote 1%, 5% and 10% significance using two tailed tests in all columns except Bef and Chg which test H2 and H1 respectively. Significance levels are reported on Sign Test statistics only due to skewed distributions. Extended variable definitions are contained in the appendix.

Table 7-5. Analysis of Discretionary Earnings Components

Panel A: Effect of Discretionary Components on Return on Assets

		ROA Before Sec Gn (%)				ROA Before Sec Gn and Prov (%)			
		Bef	Yr 0	Aft	Chg	Bef	Yr 0	Aft	Chg
Acquired	Mean	1.29	1.34	1.35	0.06	1.61	1.91	2.10	0.49
	Std Dev	0.76	2.28	0.88	1.07	0.67	2.08	0.88	0.93
	Median	1.27	1.36	1.40	0.19	1.60	1.75	1.99	0.48
Control	Mean	1.33	1.41	1.43	0.11	1.61	1.81	2.00	0.39
	Std Dev	0.65	0.92	0.66	0.75	0.67	0.88	0.81	0.81
	Median	1.32	1.45	1.47	0.11	1.58	1.73	1.85	0.34
Acq - Con	Mean	-0.03	-0.07	-0.08	-0.05	-0.00	0.11	0.10	0.10
	Std Dev	0.82	2.28	1.05	1.14	0.71	1.95	1.09	1.10
	Median	-0.04	-0.22	-0.01	0.08	-0.03	-0.02	0.19	0.13
	Frac > 0	.483	.411	.489	.533	.483	.489	.561	.556
	Stu Rng	6.27	14.30	8.31	6.82	6.61	12.52	8.86	8.09
	T(Mean)	-0.55	-0.42	-1.04	-0.56	-0.07	0.73	1.20	1.24
	Sign Test	-0.45	-2.39*	-0.30	0.89	-0.45	-0.30	1.64+	1.49+

This panel presents tests of Hypothesis 1, that the change in relative profitability before discretionary components is positive and Hypothesis 2, that pre-merger relative profitablity is negative. The Sign Test under the column labelled 'Bef' ('Chg') tests Hypothesis 2 (Hypothesis 1). All distributions are based on the 180 acquired subsidiaries with post-merger data. Bef, Yr0, Aft refer to the pre-, year of-, and post-merger distributions. (For each sample subsidiary, pre-merger performance is the average for a particular performance measure across all available pre-merger years, excluding the merger year. Post-merger performance is computed analogously.) Chg refers to the difference in performance (i.e. Aft minus Bef). Acquired, Control and Acq - Con refer to the target subsidiaries, their control firms, and the paired differences respectively. Stu Rng is the studentized range for the distribution of paired differences in the relevant column. Frac > 0 is the fraction of paired differences which are positive. t(Mean) is the standard t-statistic testing the hypothesis that the mean of the paired differences is equal to zero. Sign Test is the z-statistic testing the hypothesis that there are equal numbers of positive and negative paired differences. **, *, and + denote 1%, 5% and 10% significance using two tailed tests in all columns except Bef and Chg which test H2 and H1 respectively. Significance levels are reported on Sign Test statistics only due to skewed distributions. Extended variable definitions are contained in the appendix.

Table 7–5. Analysis of Discretionary Earnings Components cont.

Panel B: Analysis of Individual Components

		Provision to Rev (%)				Security Gains to Rev (%)				Prov plus Sec Gn to Rev (%)			
		Bef	Yr 0	Aft	Chg	Bef	Yr 0	Aft	Chg	Bef	Yr 0	Aft	Chg
Acquired	Mean	2.88	5.39	7.50	4.62	-0.26	-1.78	0.35	0.61	3.14	7.17	7.15	4.01
	Std Dev	2.64	9.23	9.92	9.63	1.68	5.04	1.19	1.86	3.06	10.44	9.92	9.63
	Median	2.32	2.85	3.87	1.61	0.00	0.00	0.07	0.25	2.50	3.85	3.73	1.27
Control	Mean	2.67	3.64	5.50	2.83	-0.29	0.25	0.41	0.70	2.96	3.39	5.09	2.13
	Std Dev	2.42	4.37	6.43	6.02	1.17	1.96	1.49	1.75	2.59	4.13	6.53	6.14
	Median	1.96	2.33	3.27	1.09	0.00	0.00	0.07	0.26	2.44	2.06	3.09	0.88
Acq - Con	Mean	0.21	1.75	2.00	1.79	0.03	-2.03	-0.05	-0.08	0.18	3.78	2.05	1.88
	Std Dev	3.34	10.17	8.97	9.21	1.89	5.19	1.94	2.54	3.80	11.18	9.16	9.47
	Median	0.12	0.63	0.89	0.40	0.00	-0.19	0.00	-0.00	-0.04	1.81	1.02	0.42
	Frac > 0	.533	.600	.617	.528	.482	.313	.515	.492	.494	.683	.606	.533
	Stu Rng	9.49	10.30	8.11	7.89	10.43	7.09	15.73	10.31	8.32	8.53	8.36	7.97
	T(Mean)	0.84	2.31	2.99	2.61	0.23	-5.26	-0.35	-0.44	0.63	4.54	3.01	2.66
	Sign Test	0.89	2.68**	3.13**	0.75	-0.47	-4.74**	0.38	-0.22	-0.15	4.92**	2.83**	0.89

This panel presents evidence regarding whether managers manipulate earnings before or after acquisitions. Two components of earnings are analyzed, the provision for loan losses and gain (losses) from sales of investment securities.

All distributions are based on the 180 acquired subsidiaries with post-merger data. Bef, Yr0, Aft refer to the pre-, merger year, and post-merger distributions. (For each sample acquired subsidiary, pre-merger performance is the average for a particular measure across all available pre-merger years, excluding the merger year. Post-merger performance is computed analogously.) Chg refers to the difference in an earnings component (i.e. Aft minus Bef). *Acquired, Control* and *Acq-Con* refer to the target subsidiaries, their control firms, and the paired differences respectively. Stu Rng is the studentized range for the distribution of paired differences in the relevant column. Frac > 0 is the fraction of paired differences which are positive. *t*(Mean) is the standard *t-statistic* testing the hypothesis that the mean of the paired differences is equal to zero. Sign Test is the *z-statistic* testing the hypothesis that there are equal numbers of positive and negative paired differences. ** , * , and − denote 1%, 5% and 10% significance using two tailed tests in all columns. Significance levels are reported on Sign Test statistics only due to skewed distributions. Extended variable definitions are contained in the appendix.

the components of net income shown in Table 4, (with the exception of the net interest margin) do not display these merger-year effects.

Table 5 reports the effects of mergers on income with and without provisions for loan losses and securities gains (losses), components of net income which can be managed. Panel A shows that when earnings are measured before securities gains, only 59% of acquired firms are outperformed by their controls in the merger year (significant at greater than 5% level, two-tailed significance), and when earnings are measured before both the provision and securities gains 49% of acquired firms are outperformed by control firms failing to reject the null of that performance is equal between acquired and control firms. Panel B confirms that the provision for loan losses is higher for 60% of the matched-pairs and security losses are larger for approximately 69% of the matched-pairs in the merger year. This combined evidence suggests that the merger year decline in profitability is a result of increases in components of earnings thought to contain large discretionary parts.

The merger-year decline in profitability could reflect earnings management (---) either as a response to over-statements of earnings prior to the merger, or in an attempt to improve perceptions of performance after the merger. Notice however, there is no difference in pre-merger securities gains (losses) and loan loss provisions for acquired firms relative to their matched-pairs. This goes against the notion that earnings were over-stated prior to the merger. There is some evidence that provisions for loan losses are higher in the post-merger period for acquired firms relative to their controls; however, this would suggest, if anything, an understatement of earnings after the merger (and perhaps overstatement prior to the merger). Finally there is no relative change in discretionary earnings components from the pre- to post-merger period.

The merger-year decline in profitability, if it does reflect earnings management, potentially biases inferences regarding merger-related performance changes because it is not possible to tell whether the merger-year performance reflects past actions that should be included in the pre-merger measures or future costs that have been improperly recorded in the merger year. To assess the sensitivity of measured performance to the merger-year drop in profits, I recompute the paired differences in the performance measures described in section 2, first attributing merger year performance to pre-merger management and then to post-merger management. Under the first assumption, merger year relative performance is averaged into pre-merger performance and will drive down $\widehat{\mu}_{bz}$. Under the second assumption, merger year performance becomes a part of $\widehat{\mu}_{az}$. These tests show that inferences for the overall sample remain unchanged by this assumption. Thus although the merger-year dip in profitability raises additional research issues regarding the interaction of earnings management and ownership changes, it does not substantially affect the interpretation of results regarding the existence of benefits from bank mergers.

4.2.4 Summary of Evidence

There is little evidence that mergers generate improved earnings in acquired subsidiaries. Although there is some evidence that net interest margins, salaries expenses, and premises expenses are improved, these gains are offset by increases in other non-interest expenses. Unfortunately, call reports do not disclose sufficient information to discern the reason for the increase in other non-interest expenses. The data also reveal no evidence that acquired subsidiaries are poor performers before-hand, reducing the likelihood that management replacement is the sole motive in bank mergers. Finally, the merger-year coincides with increased loan loss provisions and securities losses, components of net income assumed to contain large discretionary factors. This finding suggests an association between earnings discretion and changes in ownership.

The results for the sample of legal acquisitions in this paper are generally consistent with much of the other research which has focused on legal mergers. For example, Srinivasan and Wall [1992] report no reduction (except for intra-market mergers) in non-interest expenses for a sample of acquired firms with assets greater than $100 million. Similarly Linder and Crane [1992] find that New England interfirm bank mergers do not yield improved profitability, non-interest expense or net interest margins. Of the prior papers, only Cornett and Tehranian [1992] and Spindt and Tarhan [1992] report performance improvements. However, neither paper explores the behavior of total non-interest expense, raising the possibility that employee cost savings would be offset by increases in other costs as found in this paper. Taken together, this body of research suggests that the hoped-for operating gains claimed by acquiring companies are not realized, regardless of state-level branching and holding company laws. This paper contributes to this research by isolating a potential culprit for the failure to realize gains, the increase in other non-interest expenses. However, to fully explore the underlying cause for this increase, 10-k disclosures on the components of other non-interest expense need to be analyzed.

5. SAMPLE SELECTION CRITERIA AND INFERENCES

Even if acquiring firms rationally expect that acquisitions will improve the performance of the acquired entity, there is some probability that this expectation will not be realized. Ex-post measures will reflect the ex-ante expectations provided there is sufficient cross-sectional and cross-temporal dispersion. For this reason sample selection criteria, because they tend to reduce cross-sectional and (or) cross-temporal dispersion can yield inferences which do not generalize to the population of bank mergers. This section analyses whether sample selection criteria influence inferences. Two analyses are conducted. The first examines the weighting of sample firms to one geographic region, and the second examines sensitivity of results to selection by acquisition size.

Table 7-6. Comparison of Texas with other States

Comparison of Change in Relative Performance, H1

All measures scaled by total of interest and non-interest revenues.

		Mean	Std Dev	Median	Q1	Q3	Frac >0	Sign	Wilcoxon	Median
Net Income (%)	Texas	-13.37	22.08	-9.29	-20.52	-0.49	0.239	-3.54	-4.72**	-4.09**
	Non-Texas	1.19	8.52	1.17	-3.17	4.04	0.590	2.07*		
Provision (%)	Texas	7.54	13.22	5.56	-0.96	14.75	0.652	2.06*	3.46**	1.70+
	Non-Texas	-0.18	6.30	-0.12	-2.54	2.01	0.485	-0.35		
Security Gains(%)	Texas	-0.11	2.74	0.04	-0.63	1.07	0.556	0.75	0.75	1.02
	Non-Texas	-0.07	2.48	-0.02	-0.81	0.95	0.470	-0.69		
Net Interest Margin(%)	Texas	-2.74	8.99	-1.47	-6.60	2.25	0.435	-0.88	-2.97**	-2.04*
	Non-Texas	1.82	6.57	2.12	-2.47	6.22	0.604	2.42*		
Non-Interest Income (%)	Texas	-0.93	3.68	-0.71	-2.87	1.66	0.391	-1.47	-1.17	-2.04*
	Non-Texas	-0.37	4.36	0.42	-2.17	1.78	0.552	1.21		
Non-Interest Exp (%)	Texas	3.80	12.08	1.05	-3.82	8.24	0.587	1.18	1.52	1.36
	Non-Texas	0.01	6.87	-0.38	-4.40	4.60	0.463	-0.86		
Salaries (%)	Texas	0.03	3.85	-0.28	-2.64	2.58	0.500	0.00	0.85	0.00
	Non-Texas	-0.70	3.34	-0.53	-2.36	1.16	0.433	-1.55+		
Premises Exp (%)	Texas	-0.52	3.24	-0.05	-1.59	1.17	0.457	-0.59	0.69	0.68
	Non-Texas	-0.52	2.47	-0.50	-1.61	1.26	0.373	-2.94**		
Other Exp (%)	Texas	4.29	8.70	2.19	-1.07	6.01	0.652	2.06	1.80+	1.36
	Non-Texas	1.24	3.61	1.02	-0.69	3.22	0.657	3.63		

5.1 Focusing Attention on One Region

As discussed in Section 3, a combination of selection criteria lead to oversampling of Texas acquisitions. Figure 1 suggests that systematically excluding the Texas mergers would result in a more positive view of merger benefits. Table 6 contains a comparison of Texas with all other states and verifies this suspicion. The distribution of relative changes in performance across the two samples are compared using a two sample median test and the Wilcoxon Rank Sum test. This table shows that excluding the Texas acquisitions leads to acceptance of the alternative hypothesis that acquired subsidiaries improved earnings. These performance improvements are due to a median 2% relative improvement in the net interest margin. Although the non-Texas sample shows reductions in salaries and premises expenses relative to the control firms, these reductions again are offset by increases in other non-interest expenses. In contrast, the subsidiaries involved in the Texas acquisitions experience lower profitability relative to the controls. This reduction in profitability is due particularly to increases in loan loss provisions; however, there is a general deterioration across other net income components as well.

There are at least two explanations for the results provided in Table 6. Acquiring firms in Texas may have simply experienced bad luck relative to acquiring firms in other states (and relative to the non-acquired control firms.) That is, possibly the Texas mergers are generally motivated no differently than mergers in other states, and mergers generally are not motivated to improve profitability. For example, suppose that acquiring firm managers attempt to identify and purchase undervalued assets. If so, ex-post some mergers would appear to improve in performance by chance and others, by chance would deteriorate in performance. This explanation is consistent with the findings for the overall sample. However, it requires that sampling variability, and inherently random characteristic, clusters by geographic region.

A second possibility is that merger motives for Texas bank holding companies differ from those in other states. This explanation could be true if state-level regulation and macro-economic conditions interact giving rise to

◄ This panel compares tests of Hypothesis 1, that the change in a relative net income (expense) measure is positive (negative) for acquired banks in Texas (46 observations) versus other states (136 observations).

All distributions are based on acquired subsidiaries with post-merger data. This table reports only on distributions of paired differences, (i.e. *Acq - Con*). For each matched-pair, pre-merger performance is the average paired difference for a particular performance measure across all available pre-merger years, excluding the merger year. Post-merger performance is computed analogously. The change in relative performance is the post-merger minus pre-merger relative performance. Frac > 0 is the fraction of paired differences which are positive. Sign Test is the *z-statistic* testing the hypothesis that there are equal numbers of positive and negative paired differences for a particular sub-sample. **, *, and + denote 1%, 5% and 10% significance using one-tailed significance levels (except for the loan loss provision and securities gains variables which report two-tailed significance levels.)

The last two columns contain the test statistics associated with the two-sample median test and the Wilcoxon Rank sum test. Inferences in these two columns are based on two-tailed significance levels. Extended variable definitions contained in the appendix.

conditions most suitable for a particular motivation. One line of reasoning follows the arguments inherent in Jensen's [1986] free cash flow hypothesis. Texas banks enjoyed prosperity relative to all banks in the U.S. so that bank holding companies in Texas are likely to have had excess free cash flows available to them.[14] At the same time, the banking industry within Texas was declining and acquiring banks were not allowed to acquire firms outside of banking, or even outside of Texas.[15] Banks in Texas may simply have preferred to invest their excess free cash flows in acquisitions (where returns were declining), rather than paying dividends to shareholders.

Since this paper does not provide any direct evidence on acquiring firms, substantiation of these conjectures would have to come from future work in this area. The main point is that, at least in this sample, the inferences are quite sensitive to the systematic exclusion of the highest concentration of mergers. Other studies that select samples either purposely or unwittingly on geographic region, may also find that results do not generalize.

5.2 Does the Relative Size of the Acquired Firm Matter?

Recent studies by Akhavein, Berger, and Humphrey [1997] Cornett and Tehranian [1992], Srinivasan and Wall [1992] and Rhoades [1990] require that acquired organizations meet a size requirement. Cornett and Tehranian [1992] stipulate that the acquisition price be at least $100 million, and, Akhavein, Berger and Humphrey [1997] and Rhoades [1990] require the asset size of both acquiring and acquired organizations to be $1 billion. Srinivasan and Wall [1992] impose a less stringent restriction, requiring that the target organization be at least $100 million in assets. Cornett and Tehranian [1992] argue that inclusion of only very large acquired firms will better enable the detection of merger gains at the consolidated firm level. Moreover, they state that their thirty observations represent a significant portion of merger activity (based on dollar value), and therefore are of interest. Srinivasan and Wall [1992] and Rhoades [1990] argue that large acquisitions are the focus for of policy makers.

I have argued that examining the subsidiary mitigates the measurement problem raised by Cornett and Tehranian. However, there may be some merit to the supposition that big acquisitions are the sample of interest from a policy perspective. The sample used in this study contains forty-eight acquisitions for which the relative size of the acquired firms is 10% or more of the acquiring firm. The median relative size in this subsample is 3.64%, so these acquisitions would be, by almost any measure, significant events in the life of the acquiring firm. In contrast, Table 1 Panel D shows that the relative size of the median acquired subsidiary in the main sample is less than 4% the size of the acquiring organization.

Table 7 compares the distribution of merger gains for acquired subsidiaries which are held by acquired organizations of relatively small size, with those coming from organizations of relatively large size. Changes in relative profitability are positive for subsidiaries of large acquired organizations, and slightly negative for those of smaller organizations. Wilcoxon and Median tests indicate that the distributions of earnings differ between the two groups. Notice however, that the two groups do not differ distributionally along any other measure. This finding is reinforced in Panel B which confines attention to the non-Texas acquisitions. In Panel B, the small acquisitions show significant gains in net interest margins, in non-interest income and reductions in premises and salaries expenses. For subsidiaries of smaller acquired organizations these gains are offset by increases in other non-interest expenses. For large acquisitions, the gains in net interest margins, and premises expenses are not offset by increases in other non-interest expenses.

The evidence in Table 7 has the same flavor as findings by Srinivasan and Wall [1992] who document that the consolidated acquiring firm is less apt to reduce non-interest expenses the more acquisitions the acquiring firm undertakes. Although acquired subsidiaries in small acquisitions benefit from the same gains as those in larger acquisitions (i.e. increases in net interest margins and reductions in salaries and premises expenses), other non-interest expenses are smaller per subsidiary when the acquisition is large.

Perhaps this result is due to a greater incentive for the acquiring firm to generate merger benefits when the acquired organization represents a significant contribution to the operations of the consolidated firm. Alternatively, the bidding market for small organizations may be less competitive than for larger organizations, allowing the acquiring firm to receive a higher premium on the acquisition. If so, the acquiring firm would have less incentive to make the acquired subsidiaries fully efficient.

6. CONCLUSION

This paper examines the effects of acquisitions on the earnings and earnings components of acquired bank subsidiaries. The sample used in this paper differs from that of other papers in that it focuses on legal acquisitions rather than legal mergers. Nevertheless, the findings overall are quite consistent with prior studies. In aggregate, bank merger transactions do not appear to yield operating efficiencies. Though there is evidence of improved net interest margins, and reduced premises and salaries expenses, this paper shows that these gains are offset by increases in other non-interest expenses. There is not sufficient disclosure in the subsidiary-level call reports to discern why other non-interest expenses increase, but the finding does suggest an area of future research. If increases in other non-interest expenses can also be detected at the consolidated bank holding company level, 10-k reports can potentially be used to pinpoint why these expenses increase.

Inferences regarding merger benefits are shown to be sensitive to whether Texas acquisitions are included or excluded from the sample. In the sub-sample of non-Texas mergers, the data support the hypothesis that profitability

Table 7-7. Comparison of Large Acquisitions to Small Acquisitions

Panel A: Comparison of Change in Relative Performance, H1 (Full Sample 180 observations)
All measures scaled by total of interest and non-interest revenues.

		Mean	Std Dev	Median	Q1	Q3	Frac >0	Sign	Wilcoxon	Median
Net Income (%)	Large	-1.89	15.38	2.41	-1.90	4.19	0.652	2.06*	1.98*	2.39*
	Small	-2.75	14.55	-0.78	-6.21	3.70	0.448	-1.21		
Provision (%)	Large	2.49	10.11	0.57	-2.35	2.42	0.543	0.59	-0.29	0.34
	Small	1.55	8.91	0.23	-2.17	4.47	0.522	0.52		
Security Gains (%)	Large	0.10	2.19	0.02	-0.66	1.18	0.533	0.45	0.41	0.68
	Small	-0.15	2.65	-0.01	-0.75	0.89	0.478	-0.52		
Net Interest Margin (%)	Large	1.95	6.88	2.16	-1.96	5.77	0.609	1.47+	1.29	0.68
	Small	0.21	7.69	1.07	-4.46	5.64	0.545	1.04		
Non-Interest Income (%)	Large	-0.81	5.08	-0.46	-3.22	1.61	0.435	-0.88	-0.57	-1.02
	Small	-0.41	3.86	0.25	-2.24	1.75	0.537	0.86		
Non-Interest Exp (%)	Large	0.74	8.01	-0.24	-4.09	3.68	0.478	-0.29	-0.55	-0.34
	Small	1.07	8.87	0.09	-4.32	5.96	0.500	0.00		
Salaries (%)	Large	-0.41	2.94	-0.46	-2.25	0.95	0.391	-1.47+	-0.11	0.00
	Small	-0.55	3.66	-0.53	-2.44	1.83	0.470	-0.69		
Premises Exp (%)	Large	-0.35	2.81	-0.34	-1.42	1.75	0.391	-1.47+	0.68	0.34
	Small	-0.58	2.64	-0.44	-1.68	1.07	0.396	-2.42*		
Other Exp (%)	Large	1.50	6.12	0.40	-1.10	3.30	0.565	0.88	-1.22	-1.02
	Small	2.20	5.32	1.40	-0.58	3.87	0.687	4.32		

This panel compares tests of Hypothesis 1, that the change in a relative net income (expense) measure is positive (negative) for acquired organizations which are at least 10% the size of the acquiring organization (48) observations versus smaller acquisitions (132 observations).

More notes contained on page.000.

Table 7-7. Comparison of Large Acquisitions to Small Acquisitions cont.

Panel B: Comparison of Change in Relative Performance, H1 (Non-Texas Acquisitions 134 observations)

All measures scaled by total of interest and non-interest revenues.

		Mean	Std Dev	Median	Q1	Q3	Frac >0	Sign	Wilcoxon	Median
Net Income (%)	Large	1.61	7.22	2.72	1.52	5.82	0.757	3.12**	2.00*	3.65**
	Small	1.02	9.00	0.31	-3.52	3.92	0.526	0.51		
Provision (%)	Large	0.19	6.20	-0.01	-2.35	1.56	0.486	-0.16	-0.44	0.19
	Small	-0.32	6.37	-0.21	-2.54	2.53	0.485	-0.30		
Security Gains(%)	Large	0.06	2.35	0.04	-0.77	1.14	0.514	0.16	0.32	0.96
	Small	-0.12	2.54	-0.07	-0.85	0.83	0.454	-0.91		
Net Interest Margin(%)	Large	2.76	5.63	2.86	-1.63	5.77	0.649	1.81*	0.94	0.96
	Small	1.47	6.89	1.68	-3.33	6.23	0.588	1.73*		
Non-Interest Income (%)	Large	-1.06	5.25	-0.73	-3.22	1.61	0.432	-0.82	-1.19	-0.96
	Small	-0.11	3.97	0.65	-1.85	1.85	0.598	1.93*		
Non-Interest Exp (%)	Large	-0.10	6.39	-0.05	-4.40	3.39	0.486	-0.16	-0.21	0.19
	Small	0.06	7.08	-0.49	-4.32	5.03	0.454	-0.91		
Salaries (%)	Large	-0.33	2.94	-0.06	-2.06	0.95	0.432	-0.82	0.56	0.96
	Small	-0.85	3.48	-0.72	-2.36	1.16	0.433	-1.32+		
Premises Exp (%)	Large	-0.49	2.79	-0.37	-1.55	1.44	0.378	-1.48*	0.39	0.57
	Small	-0.53	2.36	-0.52	-1.61	0.87	0.371	-2.54**		
Other Exp (%)	Large	0.71	3.68	0.42	-1.00	3.20	0.595	1.15	-0.71	0.34
	Small	1.44	3.58	1.12	-0.43	3.22	0.680	3.55		

Notes on next page

improves through improved net interest margins, reduced salaries and reduced premises expenses. In contrast acquisitions in Texas exhibit performance declines in all components of net income, but especially in the loan loss provision. The paper does not settle the issue of whether these differences are due to random variation or due to clustering of merger motives by state environment. Results are also shown to be sensitive to partitioning the sample between large versus small acquisitions. Large acquisitions in this sample are associated with improved operating performance, whereas small acquisitions are not. The sensitivity of results to relatively minor changes in sample composition highlights how difficult it is to reconcile disparate findings from other studies focusing on different samples based on time, geographic or other selection criteria. In addition, the paper shows that focusing on a narrow set of income components can provide misleading conclusions regarding merger benefits.

APPENDIX

List of Variable Definitions

Balance Sheet Items
1. *Assets* – Total assets minus the balance of goodwill. The goodwill adjustment affects less than 5% of the sample observations because very few acquiring firms *push down* purchase accounting to the subsidiary.
2. *Primary Capital Ratio* – Common plus preferred equity minus goodwill plus the allowance for loan losses all divided by assets plus the allowance for loan losses.
3. *Commercial Loans* – Loans for commercial and industrial purposes whether secured or unsecured, single-payment of installment. Excluded are loans secured primarily by real estate, even if the proceeds are used for commercial purposes.
4. *Consumer Loans* – These are all loans to individuals for medical expenses, personal taxes, vacations, consolidation of personal indebtedness, automobile loans, loans for household appliances, furniture, mobile homes, etc; and loans not secured by real estate, that will be used to purchase real estate to be used as a residence of the borrowers family. Excludes loans secured by real estate.
5. *Agriculture Loans* – Includes all loans to finance agricultural productions, whether secured or

◄ This panel compares tests of Hypothesis 1 for acquisitions non-Texas acquisitions, that the change in a relative net income (expense) measure is positive (negative) for acquired organizations which are at least 10% the size of the acquiring organization (37) observations versus smaller acquisitions (97 observations).

All distributions are based on acquired subsidiaries with post-merger data. This table reports only on distributions of paired differences, (i.e. *Acq - Con*). For each matched-pair, pre-merger performance is the average paired difference for a particular performance measure across all available pre-merger years, excluding the merger year. Post-merger performance is computed analogously. The change in relative performance is the post-merger minus pre-merger relative performance. Frac > 0 is the fraction of paired differences which are positive. Sign Test is the *z-statistic* testing the hypothesis that there are equal numbers of positive and negative paired differences for a particular sub-sample. **, *, and + denote 1%, 5% and 10% significance using one-tailed significance levels (except for the loan loss provision and securities gains variables which report two-tailed significance levels.)

The last two columns contain the test statistics associated with the two-sample median test and the Wilcoxon Rank sum test. Inferences in these two columns are based on two-tailed significance levels. Extended variable definitions contained in the appendix.

unsecured and whether made to farm and ranch owners or non-farmers. Excludes loans secured by real estate.

6. *Real Estate Loans* – Includes all loans, whatever the purpose, secured by real estate. Includes all such loans whether originated by the bank or purchased from another party.

7. *Large Deposits* – Time deposits in denominations $100,000 or more both negotiable and non-negotiable.

Net Income Ratios

1. *ROA After Tax* – After tax net income, before extraordinary items divided by assets.

2. *ROE After Tax* – After tax net income before extraordinary items less preferred dividends divided by common equity adjusted for goodwill.

3. *ROR After Tax* – After tax net income before extraordinary items divided by total interest and non-interest income.

4. *ROA Before Security Gains* – Net income before security gains and losses, before taxes, and before extraordinary items divided by assets.

5. *ROA Before Security Gains and Provision* – Net income, before security gains and losses, taxes, and extraordinary items plus the provision for loan losses divided by assets.

Net Income Components

1. *Salaries to Revenues* – Total salaries and employee benefits divided by the total of interest and non-interest revenues. The numerator includes salaries, wages, overtime, bonuses, incentive compensation and extra compensation for all officers and employees.

2. *Premises Expense to Revenues* – Total expenses of premises and fixed assets divided by the total of interest and non-interest revenues. The numerator includes depreciation expense on buildings and equipment.

3. *Other Non-Interest Expense to Revenues* – This includes among other things, directors fees; federal deposit insurance; legal fees; loss on sale or disposal of loans, fixed assets, other real estate owned or branches; management fees assessed by the parent bank holding company; cost of data processing services performed for the bank by others; advertising and promotional expenses, research and development costs; charge-offs or write-downs on investment securities prior to sale; and training expenses.

4. *Total Non-Interest Expense to Revenues* – The sum of salaries expenses, premises expenses, and other non-interest expenses divided by the total of interest and non-interest revenues.

5. *Non-interest Income to Revenues* – Non-interest income comprises income from fiduciary activities (e.g. trust department income), service charges on deposit accounts, trading gains and losses and fees from foreign exchange transactions, gains (losses) and fees from assets held in trading accounts, and miscellaneous other non-interest income such as fees from safe deposit box rentals, gains on sales of loans or other real estate owned, and fees issued on credit cards. Non-interest income is scaled by the total of interest and non-interest income.

6. *Net Interest Margin to Revenues* – Interest income minus interest expense divided by the sum of interest and non-interest income.

Discretionary Income Components

1. *Provision for Loan Losses to Revenues* – This expense is defined by the call report instructions as follows:

> The estimated amount sufficient to bring the balance in 'Allowance for Loan and Lease Losses' (Loan Loss Reserve) to an adequate level to absorb expected loan and lease losses based upon management's knowledge of the bank's loan portfolio as presently evaluated. It is the responsibility of the management of the reporting bank to determine an adequate loan and lease loss provision based upon their own judgement. Management's judgement as to the adequacy of the loan and lease loss provision is subject to review by examiners during the course of their examination. Management is, therefore, required to maintain a reviewable record of the basis for their determination of the loan and lease loss provision.

This item is scaled by total interest and non-interest revenues.

2. *Security Gains or Losses to Revenues* – This is the gross amount of all investment securities gains and losses realized during the year. These gains and losses arise from the sale, exchange, redemption, or retirement of bonds, stocks and other investment securities at prices above or below book values. This item is also scaled by total interest and non-interest revenues.

NOTES

1 See Golembe and Holland (1981, 1983, and 1988), Hawke (1982), and Amel and Jacowski (1989).

2 Two recent papers are Houstan and Ryngaert [1994] and Pilloff [1996]. Another returns based study by Madura and Wiant [1994] finds a negative drift in returns over the 36 months following bank acquisitions.

3 Some studies such as Pilloff [1996] and Cornett and Tehranian [1993] combine a market based approach with a accounting based approach to examine cross-sectional determinants of announcement returns.

4 Both Spindt and Tarhan [1991] and Cornett and Tehranian [1993] find some evidence of labor cost efficiencies and improvements in return on equity. However, in both papers if net income is scaled by assets instead equity, no improvement is found.

5 A third related literature, also using accounting data, measures cost and (or) profit efficiencies by estimating the distance of merged companies' profit attributes from the efficient cost or profit frontier. This literature is reviewed in Berger, Hunter, and Timme [1993], and in Pilloff and Santomero [1997]. The evidence from the cost frontier studies is generally consistent with the simple ratio studies. However, recent profit frontier studies such as Akhavein, Berger, and Humphrey [1997] detect significant improvements in profit ranks.

While the profit frontier studies offer some advantages, it is unclear whether the profit measures used are as comprehensive as those used in the simple ratio studies. For example, Akhavein, Berger, and Humphrey assume profits can be described by just two outputs, (loans and investment securities), and two variable inputs, (deposit funds and labor), and one fixed netput, (equity capital), and the prices of these netputs are estimated from income and balance sheet data. The limiting of profit sources to just these netputs potentially omits important profit components, such as those associated with other non-interest expense.

6 The literature on merger motivations is extensive. Among others, Manne [1965] proposes the management replacement motive; Scherer [1980] pp 133-138 discusses how mergers might generate multiplant economies of scale or scope; Stigler [1950] explains how mergers might occur to achieve market power; Mandelker [1964] discusses tax motives; Marris [1964] suggests that mergers represent non-value maximizing behavior by the acquiring firm.

7 I thank Maureen Cummings at the Chicago Federal Reserve bank for clarifying this for me.

8 The transaction specific error term corresponds to the intuition that a group of m subsidiaries all held by a single target bank holding company is not likely to provide m independent measures of performance.

9 There is disagreement among economists as to the proper classification of interest expenses in banks. Under the *intermediation* approach, banks are viewed as producing the service of matching borrowers and lenders, and operating expenses include interest expenses. Under the *production* approach, only capital and labor are considered to be operating expenses. (See Clark [1988].)

10 For example, 'Financial Courtship: Wells Fargo Initiated Talks About a Merger That could Signal Start of a Trend' *Wall Street Journal* (Jan. 22,1991 page 1) discusses the potential benefits of merging Wells Fargo and Security Pacific:

"Some of the savings would come from cutting overlapping operations such as branches, headquarters staffs and data processing facilities. But layoffs would save even more. If the merged bank was as efficient as Wells Fargo is, up to 12,000 employees would have to go."

This sentiment is also expressed in the academic literature – for example, James (1984) might ascribe such gains to replacement of management.

11 To identify control banks which are not acquired I use two different filters. Call reports identify banks held under a common bank holding company through the *highest holding company number (HHC)*, so that if a bank is acquired its *HHC* will change. If a control bank has the same *HHC* in 1980 and 1988, I assume the bank was not acquired. Second, if the 1980 and 1988 *HHC's* are different, but the bank is part of a one bank holding company in 1988, I assume that the bank was not acquired, but merely changed its form to a one bank holding company.

12 One question arising from table 2 is whether the observed differences in the matched-pairs are large enough to be economically important. To investigate this I examined the sensitivity of my results to the criterion that the control firms differ from acquired firms by no more that a size factor of 2. The inferences are insensitive to this refinement, but there is a considerable loss in number of observations.

13 There are not necessarily 180 firms generating the median measure in each period because the number of pre- and post-merger years of data for a given transaction depends on when in calendar time the merger occurred.

14 The FDIC's *Bank Operating Statistics* and *U.S. Bank Performance Profile* published by the Bank Administration Institute in Rolling Meadows IL. reports that the median bank in Texas in 1980 earned a return to assets (equity) of 1.51% (17.42%) whereas the median bank in the country earned a return of 1.15% (13.34%).

15 While the median Texas bank out-performed banks in the United States until 1984, median performance steadily declined throughout this period as the oil and gas sectors and real estate sectors suffered a retrenchment. Hawanini and Swary (1990) note that Texas' interstate banking law adopted in 1987 came in response to the poor health of the banking sector in 1987.

REFERENCES

Akhavein, Jalal D., Allen M Berger, and David B. Humphrey, 1997, 'The Effects of Mega-mergers on Efficiency and Prices: Evidence from a Bank Profit Function,' Review of Industrial Organization, 12.

Amel, Dean F. and Michael J. Jacowski, 1989, Trends in banking structure since the mid 1970's, Federal Reserve Bulletin, March, 120-133.

Berger, Allen N., William C. Hunter, and Stephen G. Timme, 1993, 'The Efficiency of Financial Institutions: A Review and Preview of Research Past, Present, and Future,' Journal of Banking and Finance, 17, 221-49.

Clarke, J.A., 1988, "Economies of Scale and Scope at Depository Financial Institutions: A Review of the Literature," The Economic Review, Sept, 16-33.

Cornett, Marcia Millon and Hassan Tehranian, 1992, 'Changes in Corporate Performance Associated With Bank Acquisitions,' Journal of Financial Economics, 3, 211-234.

Golembe, Carter H. and David S. Holland, 1981, Federal regulation of banking (Golembe Associates, Washington).

Golembe, Carter H. and David S. Holland, 1983, Federal regulation of banking 1983-1984 (Golembe Associates, Washington).

Golembe, Carter H. and David S. Holland, 1988, Federal regulation of banking 1986-1987 (Golembe Associates, Washington).

Hawawini, Gabriel and Itzhak Swary, 1990, Mergers and acquisitions in the U.S. banking industry: Evidence from the capital markets, (Elsevier Science Publishers B.V., North-Holland, Amsterdam).

Hawke, John D. ed., 1982, Banking expansion in the 80's (Harcourt Brace Janovich, New York).

Healy, Paul M., Krishna G. Palepu, and Richard S. Ruback, 1992, Do Mergers Improve Corporate Performance?, Journal of Financial Economics 3.

Hollander, Myles and Douglas A Wolfe, 1973, Nonparametric Statistical Methods (John Wiley & Sons, New York).

Houstan, Joel F. and Michael D. Ryngaert, 1994, The overall gains from large bank mergers, Journal of Banking and Finance, 18, 1155-1176.

James, Christopher, 1984, An Analysis of the Effect of State Acquisition Laws on Managerial Efficiency: The Case of Bank Holding Company Acquisitions, Journal of Law and Economics, 27, 211-227.

Jensen, Michael C., 1986, Agency Costs of Free Cash Flow, Corporate Finance, and Takeovers, American Economic Review, 76, 323-329.

Linder, Jane C. and Dwight B. Crane, 1992, Bank mergers: integration and profitability, Journal of Financial Services Research, 7, 35-55.

Madura, J. and Kenneth J Wiant, 1994, Long term valuation effects of bank acquisitions, Journal of Banking and Finance, 18, 1135-1154.

Mandelker, G., 1974, 'Risk and Return: The Case of Merging Firms,' Journal of Financial Economics, 1, 303-335.

Manne, Henry G, 1965, Mergers and the Market for Corporate Control, Journal of Political Economy, 73, 110-120.

Marris, Robin, 1964, The Economic Theory of Managerial Capitalism (Free Press, Glencoe Illinois).

Martin, Kenneth J. and John J. McConnell, 1991, Corporate performance, takeovers, and management turnover, Journal of Finance, 66, 671-687.

Moyer, Susan E, 1990, Capital Adequacy Ratio Regulations and Accounting Choices in Commercial Banks, Journal of Accounting and Economics, 13, 123-154.

Pilloff, Steven J., 1996, Performance changes and shareholder wealth creation associated with mergers of publically traded banking institutions, Journal of Money, Credit and Banking, 28, 294-310.

Pilloff, Steven J., 1997, 'The Value Effects of Bank Mergers and Acquisitions,' in Bank Mergers & Acquisitions (Irwin) Y. Amihud, and G. Miller, eds., ???

Rhoades, Stephan A., 1985, Mergers and Acquisitions by Commercial Banks, 1960-1983, Federal Reserve Board Staff Studies No. 142 (Board of Governors of the Federal Reserve System, Washington).

Rhoades, Stephan A., 1990 'Billion Dollar Bank Acquisitions: A Note on the Performance Effects' Mimeograph, Board of Governors of the Federal Reserve System.

Rhoades, Stephan A., 1993, Efficiency effects of horizontal (in-market) bank mergers, Journal of Banking and Finance, 17, 411-422.

Scherer, F.M., 1980 Industrial Market Structure and Economic Performance, 2nd ed. (Houghton Mifflin Co, Boston).

Scholes, Myron, G. Peter Wilson and Mark A. Wolfson, 1990, Tax planning, regulatory capital planning and financial reporting strategy for commercial banks, The Review of Financial Studies, 3.

Spindt, Paul A. and Vefa Tarhan 1992, 'Are There Synergies in Bank Mergers?' Working Paper Tulane University.

Srinivasan Aruna and Larry D. Wall, 1992, 'Cost Savings Associated with Bank Mergers,' Working Paper 92-2 Federal Reserve Bank of Atlanta.

Stigler, George J, 1950, Monopoly and Oligopoly by Merger, American Economic Review, 40, 23-34.

PART THREE

JONATHAN R. MACEY AND GEOFFREY P. MILLER

8.   Bank mergers and American bank competitiveness

1. INTRODUCTION

In this paper we attempt to elaborate on the observation that "the common environmental feature that underlies mergers and acquisitions throughout the U.S. economy is increased competition."[1] Motivating this paper is the sharp contrast between the high cost of bank mergers and acquisitions and the large number of such transactions. The existing legal rules and regulations that govern bank mergers and acquisitions make such transactions very costly. The legal environment dramatically increases the transaction costs of mergers and acquisitions and especially of hostile takeovers in the field of banking.

It is easy to show that bank acquisitions are dramatically more costly than non-bank acquisitions because a complex and potentially arbitrary set of legal requirements is layered on top of the existing set of rules governing takeovers in general. Indeed, the rules governing bank takeovers are so complex that hostile takeovers are next to impossible. The Bank of New York acquisition of Irving Trust Company is the rare exception that proves the rule.   Despite the high relative and absolute transaction costs of bank mergers, bank mergers have proceeded at a record pace during the 1990s. As the *Economist* magazine recently observed "the urge to merge" has characterized American banking in recent years.[2] In this article we seek to identify the economic sources of these mergers.

It is possible to argue that the recent mergers are a sign of strength. During the 1990s the quality of banks' earnings and assets recovered after the disastrous decade of the 1980s. Indeed industry earnings reached record highs in the 90s, and return on assets also rose to their highest levels in several years. Nonetheless, in this article we argue that the banking industry in the United States remains weak. And we seek to show that the merger wave in banking is more a display of this weakness than of underlying strength.

While it is true that the relaxation of barriers to interstate banking has introduced new competition that has prompted a significant number of mergers, the real problems facing the banking industry, in our view, stem from two sources: (1) changing technology; and (2) inefficient legal rules.

175

Y. Amihud and G. Miller   eds.), Bank Mergers & Acquisitions, 175–190
© *1998 Kluwer Academic Publishers. Printed in the Netherlands.*

Changing technology has led to a diminution in the overall demand for banks' services. This has led to mergers. It is hard to argue that U.S. banks are merging because they are inefficient. At the moment American banks already are among the world's most efficient banks, with a cost-to-income ratio below 60 percent. This rate is compares very favorably with Germany (74%, and Japan (65%) and Switzerland (72%), and indeed every other country in the developed world except Sweden.[3] Rather, we argue that banks are merging as a mechanism for down-sizing.

Besides obsolescence, we argue that banks are merging because of inefficient U.S. laws which make it relatively more difficult for U.S. banks to protect themselves from borrowers' moral hazard. In a nutshell, banks are unable to make contracts with borrowers that permit them to inject themselves in the corporate governance of the firms to which they have loaned money. This, in turn, makes bank loans in the United States relatively more expensive as a source of funding, and helps explain why firms in the U.S. resort to bank borrowing much less than their counterparts in Germany or Japan and why banks in the U.S. are less profitable than their international rivals.

In our view, mergers among banks should be viewed not only as a mechanism by which weak management teams are replaced by stronger managers (although we fully recognize that this is an important feature of the market for corporate control of banks); rather, bank mergers should instead be viewed as a low-cost substitute for bank failures.

Moreover, from an economic perspective, the bank merger wave of the 1990s should be viewed as a natural extension of the bank failure wave of the 1980s. During the 1980s, the number of banks in the United States declined by 12 percent. During the 1980s, the number of banks in the United States declined by 10 percent. In our view, the lesson that bank management learned from the 1980s is that mergers represent a more efficient strategy for redeploying bank assets than bank failure. Consequently, managers in the 1990s began to choose merger as a mechanism for avoiding failure.

This article is organized as follows. In the following section we discuss the economic relationship between bank failures and bank mergers. This analysis is consistent with the observation that competition is the source of bank mergers, but it provides a better account of why U.S. bank mergers have been proceeding at a much faster pace than mergers in other industries. In the second part of the article we argue that the consolidations currently taking place in the banking industry will not be sufficient to solve the industry's problems because these problems are structural problems caused by a regime of inefficient legal rules that prevent banks from protecting themselves from the moral hazard problems presented by borrowers.

2. MERGERS AS A SUBSTITUTE FOR BANK FAILURE

In an earlier article focusing on bank failure, we studied the market for corporate control in the context of banking regulation.[4] We observed that the market for corporate control in general, and the tender offer in particular, serve as mechanisms by which the performance of management can be monitored. The market for corporate control serves to improve managerial performance by providing private parties with incentives to monitor management. However, we also observed that the complex system of regulation that governs the market for control of banks significantly reduces the possibility that a bank can be acquired in a hostile takeover – regardless of how bad the performance of incumbent management has been.

A. The Economics of Bank Failures and Bank Mergers

In analyzing bank mergers, it is important to observe the similar economic characteristics of bank mergers and failures. First, a bank failure, like a bank takeover, is a means for monitoring management. Just as the spectre of failure provides a mechanism for disciplining management, so too does the spectre of a takeover. And, just as it is the weaker firms in an industry that fail, so too it is the weaker firms in an industry that are the most likely candidates for takeover, since it is the weak firms that provide the greatest possibility for arbitrage profits by superior management teams. Indeed, in an insight that is particularly relevant for this discussion, Professor Dewey observed decades ago that takeovers are "merely a civilized alternative to bankruptcy or the voluntary liquidation that transfers assets from falling to rising firms."[5]

A robust market for corporate control is a sign of the vigor of competition in a particular industry. Henry Manne in his seminal article on mergers pointed out that takeovers are not only efficient when the failure of a firm is imminent, but also "before bankruptcy becomes imminent in order to avoid that eventuality."[6] Dean Manne goes on to point out that "if mergers were completely legal, we should anticipate relatively few actual bankruptcy proceedings in any industry which was not itself contracting. The function so wastefully performed by bankruptcies and liquidations would be economically performed by mergers at a much earlier state of the firm's life."[7]

Like, mergers and other sorts of takeovers, bank failures – and the spectre of bank failures – brings about more efficient management of firms, increased protection for non-controlling investors – and a more efficient allocation of resources.[8] In other words, mergers are a substitute for insolvency. But, since mergers are less costly, and involve less waste of assets than either liquidations and insolvencies, they can be viewed as a superior substitute to those alternatives.

Of course, as in the rest of corporate finance, agency costs as well as transaction costs have a role to play in the analysis. But, in this case, we argue that agency costs – as well as transaction costs – prompt bank managers to seek out merger partners. The explanation for this is simple. In an insolvency, top-level bank managers are almost certain to lose their jobs. In addition, such managers will have a very hard time finding another job because of the diminution in the value of their reputation that has been caused by the failure.

In a merger top-level bank managers are less likely to lose their jobs than in an insolvency. This is because hostile takeovers in the banking sector are so costly that outside acquirors almost always will find it in their interest to negotiate a friendly acquisition rather than to launch a hostile takeover bid. Friendly acquirors will need the cooperation of the incumbent management of the target firm, and will offer them employment contracts in order to obtain such cooperation. For example, analysis of nine case studies of bank mergers during the 1990s conducted under the supervision of Charles W. Calomiris and Jason Karceski reveals that the management teams of the target banks remained the same after the merger in every case except where target management had sizeable golden parachute compensation contracts.[9]

B. Why Banks are Failing

Our observation that bank mergers are a substitute for bank failures is only the beginning of the analysis, because this observation merely raises the broader question of why banks feel the need to merge in the first place. Here, the explanation is simple, as capital markets and technology develops, the need for banks diminishes as low-cost substitutes for bank loans begin to emerge.

Banks do three things. First, banks specialize in assessing credit risk. Banks, at least in theory, accumulate money from investors (depositors) on the basis of their ability to identify good, profitable uses for depositors' funds. Depositors are willing to pay for the benefit of banks' financial skills because few individual investors are able to distinguish good loans from bad. By placing their money in a bank, depositors in effect hire the bank to use its know-how in identifying good investment opportunities. The beauty of a properly functioning banking system is that depositors need not – in fact almost never do – know anything about the markets in which the bank invests its assets. Because they need not gain the expertise themselves, the depositors can spend their time doing the things they enjoy.

Second, banks allow depositors to take advantage of economies of scale that otherwise would place many good investment opportunities out of the grasp of ordinary investors. Commercial bank loans often are made to borrowers who need millions of dollars in capital. Most investors are unable to extend this kind of credit, particularly if they want to retain the benefits of a diversified investment portfolio. Because banks pool funds from numerous depositors, the depositors are able to participate in the market for large-scale investments.

Third, banks convert illiquid investments into what are, from the depositors' perspective, liquid investments.[10] A liquid investment is one that the investor can convert to cash quickly in order to meet sudden demands for funds. All else being equal, of course, investors would prefer to hold liquid investments rather than illiquid ones. Consequently, borrowers forced to offer potential investors illiquid investments must offer such investors a greater return to compensate them for the additional inconvenience of illiquidity. Banks, by issuing demand deposits, "can improve on a competitive market by providing better risk sharing among people who need to consume at different random times."[11]

Thus, banks improve the operation of the economy by investing in portfolios of illiquid assets and by offering depositors liquid claims (deposits) on the banks' own assets. This conversion of illiquid investments into liquid ones provides a significant benefit for investors – and for borrowers as well. Consider a manufacturing firm with an asset that cannot be used to pay current operating expenses because it is not generating any income at present. Suppose further that the future income that will be generated by this asset is uncertain and difficult to value. This asset is illiquid. If, however, the firm can obtain a loan from a bank secured by the asset, it can convert a substantial portion of the asset's value into liquid form while continuing to control the plant.

Banks' ability to sell their skill at valuing assets, their ability to allow investors and borrowers to realize economies of scale in investing, and their ability to convert illiquid investments into liquid investments all explain why banks have survived and prospered even though financial intermediation is costly both to lenders (depositors) and to borrowers.

This is a succinct description of the role that banks play in the economy. Notice, however, that because the demand for banks' services arises from imperfect information and from the costliness of arranging direct investor-borrower transactions, the demand for these services will decline as markets develop – and in particular as the costs of organizing and communicating information and arranging financial transactions fall. First, as markets develop, intermediaries other than commercial banks will emerge to provide funds to particularly large borrowers, and banks will cease to be unique in this respect. Life insurance companies, for example, receive funds from purchasers of insurance that they invest in securities, loans, and other productive assets. While insurance companies can "purchase" funds on significantly different terms than banks, they amass substantial resources that allow them to make large-scale investments of the kind banks make. Pension funds can do likewise.[12] Open-end mutual funds, which accept investments from customers and invest these funds in securities, compete even more directly with banks by allowing investors to redeem their shares at any time, and by allowing investors to make redemptions by writing checks to third parties drawn on their mutual fund accounts. Thus, investors now have many mechanisms for pooling their funds with those of other investors to overcome the economies of scale problems described above. As these alternative avenues of financial intermediation emerge, it is only natural that the relative importance of banks as financial intermediaries should decline.

Similarly, the demand for bankers' skill in evaluating particular investments should be expected to decline as secondary and new issue markets develop. As secondary capital markets develop, business firms will find it increasingly easy to raise capital by making public offerings. The sophistication of the trading markets provides a dependable price setting mechanism that permits investors to rely on anonymous market forces rather than on the judgment of particular bankers to determine the appropriate prices for investments.[13] In addition, trading markets such as the New York Stock Exchange enable firms in search of capital to "securitize" their assets. Securitization involves unbundling the earnings stream of a firm into a large number of securities that can be sold to small investors, thus competing directly with banks' ability to transform illiquid investments into liquid investments for the benefit of depositors.

Finally, as trading markets become more developed due to the emergence of more sophisticated mechanisms for processing information, bankers must compete for business against the participants in those markets as well. Businesses in need of capital will be indifferent between borrowing from banks and selling securities in a public offering. They will make their decision on the basis of which form of investment offers them the capital they need at the lowest rate of interest. Consequently, the emergence of well developed capital markets inevitably places downward pressure on banks' rates of return. The emergence of these markets also confronts the specialists who evaluate credit risk for commercial banks (loan officers) with new competition from thousands of financial analysts and amateur investors who are attempting to ferret out information about the earnings streams of publicly traded securities. As a result, the development of securities markets will make it increasingly difficult for banks to uncover profitable investment opportunities.

The development of robust capital markets for equity and debt securities and the growth of pension plans and money market funds are a natural outgrowth of the emergence of new information technologies and the general development of the economy. As information and data processing capabilities have improved, the costs of trading have fallen. These markets developed because investors now can communicate with one another, and can obtain new information about corporate cash flows, quickly and cheaply by using computer-driven trading systems.

Likewise, as the labor force has become more skilled and productive, it has been able to command an increasing share of society's resources. Favorable tax treatment has led to explosive growth in the nation's pension system. Furthermore, as technological developments have caused the nation's capital markets to price securities more efficiently, such markets have become available to smaller and smaller issuers. In 1792, the New York Stock Exchange was the nation's only public securities market.[14] Today there are ten stock exchanges operating in the United States as well as several specialized exchanges that have added trading in options and financial futures to their traditional business of trading in commodities. In addition, the over-the-counter securities market includes three thousand securities firms with six thousand branch offices that deal in securities not traded on an organized exchange.[15] There are no listing requirements for securities traded on the over-the-counter market; all registered securities are entitled to participate in this market. Brokers trade securities in this market "via a complex telephone and telex communications system, by which information is transmitted and trades are consummated."[16]

In a nutshell, as markets become more efficient, the information, evaluation and transaction services provided by commercial banks are increasingly displaced by newer and more efficient forms of financial intermediation. It is important to note, moreover, that bankers historically have specialized in servicing the most inefficient segments of the capital markets. More efficient market segments have been able to securitize themselves and thereby avoid more costly commercial loan markets. As financial markets have developed and as a wider array of assets have become capable of being securitized, bankers have been driven to focus on increasingly uncertain investments that remain incapable of being securitized. Thus, as capital markets and technology have developed, not only have commercial banks' share of investment markets declined, but the portion they have retained has become more risky; lower cost financial intermediaries have skimmed off much of the best business that commercial banks traditionally enjoyed.

The traditional bank loan involves ongoing, continuous monitoring on the part of the bank extending the credit of making the loan. The typical loan document gives banks the right to accelerate the maturity date of their outstanding loans. Banks, seeking to protect their investments carefully monitor the firms to which they loan money on an ongoing basis. By contrast, the process of securitization involves intense monitoring by the underwriters at the time a block of securities initially is offered to the public.[17] After the securities are sold, however, it is expected that the subsequent monitoring of the issuer will be less intense because of the well-known collective action and free-rider problems facing those who invested in the issuers' securities. In particular, unlike banks, many investors who buy securities will engage in little, if any, monitoring of credit because they must incur the full costs of monitoring the issuer, while only capturing a small portion of the gains from such monitoring.[18]

Those firms that cannot obtain credit unless they subject themselves to the continual monitoring performed by banks will continue to seek bank loans. All else being equal, borrowing from a commercial bank will be more costly than raising capital by issuing securities because banks must charge more interest on loans to compensate for the continual monitoring associated with such lending. Of course, all else is not equal. The existence of federally subsidized deposit insurance enables banks to obtain funds more cheaply than securities firms because depositors demand far lower interest rates on demand deposits than they would in the absence of government-backed deposit insurance. These cheaper funds tend to offset banks' increased costs. Moreover, these cheaper, federally insured deposits were used to fund increasingly risky investments throughout the 1980s.

Firms able to obtain credit from the securities markets will do so in order to avoid the burden of bank monitoring and to avoid the concomitantly higher rates charged by banks in many cases. Of course, firms that need only occasional or episodic monitoring are likely to be better credit risks than firms that need constant monitoring. Thus, all else being equal, borrowers that are better credit risks will sell securities rather than borrow from banks because such borrowers will have no desire to pay the higher costs of obtaining the continuous monitoring available from commercial banks.

This process is highlighted by the ability of investment banks, through the underwriting of commercial paper, to capture a large portion of the most basic commercial lending business of the nation's largest commercial banks. Commercial paper is the popular name for the short-term[19] unsecured debt obligations of corporations that have become a common feature in American corporate finance, particularly for large, well capitalized corporations with aggressive asset and liability management strategies. Commercial paper bears similarities to securities such as stocks and bonds, and to commercial loans made by banks.[20] Like stocks and bonds, commercial paper is sold in the secondary market, usually in negotiated underwritings with securities dealers. Like bank loans, commercial paper generally is sold in privately negotiated transactions between a single underwriting firm and a single issuing company. Issuing firms view the sale of commercial paper as a direct substitute for other forms of financing because it provides ready access to capital, does not create long term financial obligations, and does not require extensive and costly negotiations prior to issuance.[21]

Firms in need of capital can choose to issue commercial paper, obtain traditional bank financing, or sell stocks or bonds in the secondary markets. Their choice is significantly affected by federal regulation. Since 1933, the Glass-Steagall Act[22] has imposed a legal separation between commercial banking and securities dealing. With minor exceptions for such things as municipal bonds and U.S. government securities, the Glass-Steagall Act prohibits banks from underwriting, selling, or dealing in securities.[23] Firms that wish to sell securities to raise capital therefore have no choice but to do so through investment banks and securities houses. On the other hand, firms that wish to raise capital by direct borrowing can do so not only from commercial banks but also from any other person or firm willing to extend credit.

This regulatory disadvantage for many years was not a significant impediment to banks' ability to compete in the financial markets against other sorts of financial intermediaries, because of the extensive regulatory costs of raising capital by selling securities. In particular, firms that wished to raise substantial amounts of money by selling securities traditionally were required to make a "public-offering" of securities within the meaning of the securities laws. In 1933, Congress created something of a "level playing field" for commercial banks and securities firms by imposing significant costs on firms that wished to make public offerings of securities. These costs, which come in the form of registration and prospectus delivery requirements of the Securities

Act of 1933,[24] reduced the attractiveness of securities offerings. It is in this sense that the Securities Act of 1933 mitigated the harsh effects of Glass-Steagall's regulatory restrictions by increasing the demand for commercial banks' lending services as against securities dealers' underwriting services.

During the late 1970s and early 1980s, commercial paper became the primary source of short-term financing for publicly held corporations. During this period, commercial paper accounted for one quarter of all short-term corporate debt outstanding.[25] For issuing corporations, commercial paper has distinct advantages over both commercial bank borrowing and public securities offerings. The advantage of commercial paper over a public offering of debt or equity is that commercial paper, by virtue of its short maturity, is exempt from the costly registration requirements of the Securities Act of 1933.[26] Technical improvements in the commercial paper market greatly enhanced the liquidity characteristics of that market and enabled securities firms to sell commercial paper at lower rates of interest. By passing these interest rate savings along to their clients, investment banks selling commercial paper were able to offer corporate borrowers rates of interest on commercial paper significantly below the bank prime rate.

Large corporations increasingly began to turn from commercial bank lending to the commercial paper market to fund their short-term financing needs as "[t]he spreads and placement costs on commercial paper fell low enough that a corporation could often save money by going directly into the commercial paper market rather than by obtaining funds from a bank or other financial intermediary."[27] The difficulties this presented to commercial banks were acute and far-reaching:

> Once having entered the commercial paper market, many firms were reluctant to return to higher-cost bank financing, even when bank funds became readily available again. . . . Banks, to their surprise and dismay, began to see commercial paper as a threatening competitor for their core loan business.
>
> The problem was not simply a loss of loan revenues, although this was bad enough. In addition, commercial banks were deprived of key information about the activities of their loan customers. In the days when corporations returned to their banks frequently to roll over commercial loans, banks were able to maintain regular contact with their customers and thus to obtain reliable, current information about them. That source of information began to dry up as blue chip corporations increasingly turned to the commercial paper market for their short-term financing needs.[28]

Several important points can be gleaned from the commercial paper saga. First, it illustrates how commercial banks' inability to expand their product lines beyond traditional commercial lending made it difficult for them to compete in the rapidly changing financial marketplace. Second, it is a striking example of the earlier theoretical point that the business lost by commercial banks due to regulatory restrictions has not been random. Rather, commercial banks have been losing their best business and their most important customers because as participants in secondary trading markets become more sophisticated they can take advantage of technology. This technology permits them to securitize assets that previously could only be financed through traditional bank lending. Over time, investment bankers developed sophisticated trading strategies that allowed them to sell commercial paper to customers with the express or implied promise that, should the need arise, the investment bank would repurchase the securities at the market price for the remainder of their terms. Ironically, the availability of back-up lines of credit from commercial banks has further enhanced the competitiveness of commercial paper markets. Investment banks thus were able to offer investors in commercial paper meaningful liquidity over the short-term life of the loans, which in turn, enabled them to make credible financing commitments to borrowers. The emergence of commercial paper as an important tool of corporate finance reveals a story about how the nation's major commercial banks lost their most important, profitable, blue-chip clients to a rival industry through a combination of regulatory impediments and technological evolution.

The final chapter in the commercial paper saga concerns the commercial banks' response to the crisis presented by the erosion of their commercial lending customer base. Led by Bankers Trust Company of New York, the commercial banks responded by re-evaluating their "long-accepted notion that the Glass-Steagall Act prohibited them from dealing in commercial paper."[29] Rather than cut their commercial lending rates to compete with the investment banks, they sought to enter the business of underwriting and dealing in commercial paper.

Two important implications can be drawn here. First, the natural response to financial market innovation is not to expand the scope of commercial banking but to diversify into investment banking. Over time, as improved markets and new technologies lead to an increase in the demand for securitized assets and a decrease in the demand for commercial loans, market force should cause the commercial banking industry to shrink rather than to expand. Second, the legal system has placed costly obstacles in the way of banks that wish to pursue this strategy. In our example, Bankers Trust Company had only two options: (1) giving up its traditional core business of lending to large, blue chip clients, or (2) pursuing a risky and costly strategy of litigating the apparent legal restrictions on its ability to deal in commercial paper. Bankers Trust chose the latter strategy.

The commercial paper saga presents a stark example of the competitive dynamic facing the commercial banking industry. As financial markets have developed, the same process has repeated itself, albeit in a more subtle fashion and in numerous ways: bank clients gradually have reduced the portion of their external funding that comes from bank lending and increased the funding they receive from selling securities.

This process simultaneously has reduced the role that commercial banks play in the economy and caused banks to become more risky. The reduced role is a result of a decreased demand for commercial lending. Risk has increased because the assets that have become securitized are the assets for which good information is readily available, i.e., those that present less commercial uncertainty.

We wish to emphasize that the process we are describing is slow and subtle, although rapid advancements in information technology have allowed U.S. securities markets to register dramatic improvements in efficiency in the past decade. For most creditworthy borrowers, the process we are describing has not resulted in a complete shift from bank borrowing to securitization, although for large, publicly held corporations the shift from bank borrowing to commercial paper issuance has been dramatic. Rather, the process of technological evolution we are describing has manifested itself in a gradual change in the overall composition of the liability side of the corporate balance sheet, with bank borrowing assuming a smaller fraction of overall liabilities, and other forms of debt assuming a larger fraction.

Perhaps the best example of this phenomenon involves the securitization of home mortgages and other consumer financial obligations, which began in earnest in the 1980s. Historically, commercial banks carried home mortgages on the asset side of their balance sheets as loans. These mortgages were high profit, low risk assets for banks. But as computer and communications technology made it cheaper to collect and disseminate information, and as interest rates and asset prices became more volatile, it became much more efficient for banks to move these assets off their books by securitizing them. The securitization phenomenon had a profound effect on U.S. capital markets:

> by the third quarter of 1987, mortgage-based securities outstanding exceeded $640 billion, over one-fifth of the total value of all mortgage claims. Since 1982, mortgage-backed securities have accounted for 60 percent of the growth in mortgage debt. The sale of other asset-backed obligations – debt instruments that are claims against a pool of assets such as automobiles, credit-card receivables, or leases – only began in 1985. Yet in just two years the amount of these securities outstanding had risen to almost $12 billion. By the end of 1986, GMAC (General Motors Acceptance Corporation) was the largest issuer of nonmortgage asset-based obligations, with $8 billion outstanding.[30]

The securitization phenomenon was bad for banks in three ways. First, the fees for securitizing a loan are trivial compared to the profits involved in booking the loan as an asset. Unfortunately, the costs of keeping a loan on the books as an asset are also high, particularly when interest rates are rising and the asset has a fixed interest rate. Thus, banks that did not securitize assets that were capable of being securitized could not compete with banks that did so. Second, because commercial banks have no competitive advantage in securitization, the business of originating loans opened up to a myriad of specialized firms, thereby further eroding the market share of commercial banks. Finally, to the extent that banks attempted to continue to book commercial loans, they were forced to concentrate on increasingly risky loans, as the better credit risks came to be securitized.

In summary, during the 1980s, borrowers that traditionally looked to banks for credit began to turn to other, cheaper sources such as securitized assets and commercial paper. This phenomenon left commercial banks a shrinking and increasingly risky segment of the capital markets to service. Problems on the liability side of banks' balance sheets exacerbated the problems on the asset side. Here, the growth of pension funds, mutual funds, and new insurance products has given savers and investors a wide range of new products from which to choose. This has forced banks to pay increasingly high rates to attract depositors, despite the increasing riskiness of the banks' activities. Given such a competitive environment, it would have been surprising had commercial banks not begun to fail in record numbers during the 1980s and to seek merger partners in order to avoid failure.

The most important implication of the above analysis is that the only healthy banking industry is going to be a significantly smaller banking industry. While the firms engaged in commercial banking need not be small, the portion of economic activity conducted by commercial banks, as opposed to other suppliers of credit, is going to continue to shrink. This is why bank mergers have been occurring.

3. BANKING AND CORPORATE GOVERNANCE

The above account is a more or less straightforward account of the diminution in the demand for banks' services brought about by technological change. The story is simple, the demand for banks' services in making commercial loans has been falling. Banks have been merging as a means of dealing with this problem. But technology is not banks' only problem. Shortcomings in the legal system prevent banks from protecting themselves adequately in their shrinking role as commercial lenders.

The American system of corporate governance prevents American financial intermediaries from contractually protecting themselves against the moral hazard problem posed by shareholders. The moral hazard problem facing borrowers largely consists of the danger that *ex post*, i.e. after a loan has been made, borrowers will shift their assets from less risky to more risky investments, thereby transferring wealth from fixed claimants to residual claimants.[31] Of course, banks will attempt to control for moral hazard by contract, but this is difficult to do. Moreover, controlling moral hazard also requires that banks be able to monitor and to exert control over borrowers during the period in which their loan is outstanding.

Legal restrictions prevent American banks from monitoring and controlling borrowers. These legal restrictions cause the moral hazard problem facing American banks to be more serious than the moral hazard problem facing

European and Japanese banks, where bankers routinely serve on corporate boards and actively participate in the governance of the firms to which their banks have lent money. Because of these flaws in the legal system, in the U.S. the moral hazard problem facing U.S. banks is disproportionately large and banking in the United States is riskier than it otherwise would be. This, in turn, leads to an increase in the interest rates that banks must charge to compensate themselves for additional incremental risks they are facing. And, of course, this causes U.S. banks to be less competitive than they otherwise would be.

Several American legal doctrines expose lenders to potential liability if they attempt to write contracts that protect themselves from borrowers' moral hazard. Many of these liability rules derive from the reasonable doctrine that banks have a general obligation of good faith toward borrowers,[32] but courts often interpret them in a manner inconsistent with basic freedom of contract. As a result, expanded rules of lender liability have enabled borrowers to transfer wealth to themselves by opportunistically suing banks when banks threaten to enforce their contracts with borrowers.[33]

When banks have threatened, for example, to enforce a management change clause (a contractual provision ostensibly allowing lenders to declare a default if top officers are appointed who are not approved by lenders), borrowers have been successful in suing banks for interfering with contractual relations between borrowers and their employees.[34] Courts have even forced banks to loan more money or to give more advance notice of termination of a lending relationship than required by contract.[35] Furthermore, banks which become actively involved in the affairs of borrowers in order to protect the value of their security interests may face massive liability for environmental harm the firm causes.[36]

Bankruptcy rules further chill American banks' incentive to take an active role in the affairs of borrowers, thereby discouraging intervention when it would be most helpful – when borrowers are in financial distress. Specifically, U.S. bankruptcy law strips senior lenders of their claims to collateral or subordinates their claims to those of junior lenders, or both, if the lender exercises some degree of control over the borrower. This principle, which is known as equitable subordination, provides a strong disincentive for banks to play an active role in corporate governance. In the classic *American Lumber* case,[37] an American bank assisted in restructuring a troubled debtor after it had advanced the debtor extra funds. When the debtor began to fail despite these efforts, the bank tried to recover its funds. Other creditors complained of preferential treatment, and they persuaded the court to subordinate the bank's claims to theirs:

> While [the bank] argues that subordination will cause members of the financial community to feel that they cannot give financial assistance to failing companies, but must instead foreclose on their security interests and collect debts swiftly, not leaving any chance for survival, the Court is singularly unimpressed.[38]

Thus, America's corporate governance problem may not stem from a lack of concentrated share blocks and powerful financial intermediaries as Mark Roe suggests.[39] Rather, the problem may arise from American courts' and legislatures' unwillingness to enforce the contractual provisions upon which financial intermediaries and borrowers agree. Enforcing such contractual provisions not only would protect the banks from moral hazard but would also help borrowers avoid excessive borrowing costs.

4. CONCLUSION

The banking industry's share of U.S. financial assets has decreased from 66 percent to less than 30 percent in the last twenty years,[40] and American banks have virtually disappeared from the ranks of the world's major financial institutions. Bank mergers and acquisitions have been a natural market response to the circumstances that have caused the decline of banking in the U.S. In this article we identify two reasons why banks are not very important in the U.S., either in absolute or in relative terms. The first reason is technological. U.S. capital markets are so advanced that low-cost, high quality alternatives to bank loans abound. The second reason is legal. U.S. law raises the cost of commercial banking by making it difficult for banks to protect their interests as fixed claimants.

In other words, banks in the U.S. are not merging to achieve greater economies of scale or scope, but as a substitute for other means of shrinking, such as liquidation. Unfortunately, these mergers will not solve banks' core business problems. Instead legal changes to the bankruptcy code, the law of lender liability will be necessary. Above all, universal banking is needed, because if banks could deal in securities, they would not only be able to enter into the high growth areas of corporate finance, they also would be able to use their ability to buy stock as a means to protect their interests as fixed claimants in the firms to which they have loaned money.

NOTES

1. "The Bank Merger Wave of the 90s: Nine Case Studies", Charles W. Calomiris and Jason Karceski, Office for Banking Research, University of Illinois, Urbana/ Champaign, 1995.
2. The Economist, September 7, 1996, at 82.
3. Economist, September 7 at 82.
4. Macey & Miller, "Bank Failures, Risk Monitoring, and the Market for Bank Control," 88 *Columbia Law Review* 1153 (1988).
5. Dewey, "Mergers and Cartels: Some Reservations About Policy," 51 *American Economic Review Paper and Prac,* 255, 257 (1961).
6. Henry Manne, "Mergers and the Market for Corporate Control," 73 *Journal of Political Economy,* 110, 112-13 (1965).
7. *Id.* at 111.

8. Haddock, Macey & McChesney, "Property Rights in Assets and Resistance to Tender Offers," 73 *Virginia Law Review*, 701, 709 (1987).

9. Calomiris and Karceski, *The Bank Merger Wave of the 90s: Nine Case Studies* (1996).

10. Diamond and Dybvig, "Bank Runs, Deposit Insurance, and Liquidity," 91 *J. Pol. Econ.* 401, 403 (1983) ("Banks are able to transform illiquid assets (into liquid assets) by offering liabilities with a different, smoother pattern of returns. . . Illiquidity of assets provides the rationale. . . for the existence of banks. . .").

11. *Id.* at 402.

12. Pension fund assets, which now exceed two trillion dollars, include nearly a quarter of all equity securities and half of all corporate debt. The pension fund, now the dominant player in the world of institutional investing, scarcely existed a century ago, and was unimportant until the latter half of this century. In 1950, pension plans accounted for only 15.3% of the total holdings of institutional investors; by 1983 pension fund holdings had risen to 58.5% of institutional investments. R. Ippolito, *Pensions, Economics, and Public Policy* 157 (1986).

13. *See* Macey & Miller, "Good Finance, Bad Economies: An Analysis of the Fraud on the Market Theory," 42 *Stan. L. Rev.* 1059 (1990).

14. Macey & Haddock, "Shirking at the SEC. The Failure of the National Market System," 1985 *U. Ill. I. Rev.* 315 (describing the origins of the NYSE).

15. R. Sobel, *Inside Wall Street* 67 (1982).

16. Maccy & Haddock, *supra* note 14, at 329-330.

17. Easterbrook, "Two Agency-Cost Explanation of Dividends," 74 *Am. Econ. Rev.* 650, 654 (1984).

18. *Id.* at 653. We wish, however, to emphasize that the reduction in bank monitoring in trading markets is replaced by market mechanisms such as the market for corporate control, incentive-based compensation packages for managers, and competition in internal labor markets.

19. Typically, commercial paper matures in 90 days or less.

20. Litt, Macey, Miller & Rubin, "Politics, Bureaucracies and Financial Markets: Bank Entry into Commercial Paper Underwriting in the United States and Japan," 139 *U. Pa. L. Rev.* 369, 375 (1990).

21. *Id.*

22. The Glass-Steagall Act, officially designated the Banking Act of 1933, is the popular name of Ch. 89, 48 Stat. 162 (codified in amended in scattered sections of 12 U.S.C.).

23. Section 16 is codified at 12 U.S.C. §16 of Glass-Steagall applicable to state banks that are members of the Federal Reserve System.

24. 15 15 U.S.C. §77 et. seq. (1988).

25. Note, "A Conduct Oriented Approach to the Glass-Steagall Act," 91 *Yale L. J.* 102, 115 (1981) (Jonathan R. Macey, author, citing J.P. Judd, "Competition Between Commercial Paper Markets and Commercial Banks," 39, 48 (Staff Paper, Federal Reserve Bank of San Francisco, on file with the *Yale Law Journal*)).

26. The Securities Act of 1933 ' 3(a)(3), 15 U.S.C. §77c(a)(3)(1988) exempts from the registration, prospectus delivery, and anti-fraud provisions of the Act notes, drafts, bills of exchange, and bankers' acceptances arising out of a current transaction that have a maturity at the time of issuance of less than nine months.

27. Litt, Macey, Miller & Rubin *supra note* 20, at 378.

28. *Id.* at 379.

29. *Id.*

30. Haraf & Kushmeider, "Redefining Financial Markets," in *Restructuring Banking and Financial Services in America* 3 (1988).

31. This phenomenon is easy to illustrate. Suppose at the time a loan has been made, a borrower has all of its assets in an investment with a 1.0 probability of returning $1000 at the end of the investment period. Suppose further that $500 of this $1000 must be used to repay the principal and interest which is due to the firms fixed claimants at the end of the investment period. In this investment, the expected value for the fixed claimants is $500, and the

expected value for the shareholders is the residual, or $1000 - $500 = $500. Next, suppose the borrower shifts its investments into a riskier investment, one with a .5 chance of a $2000 payoff, and a .5 chance of a $300 pay off. This investment is worse for the fixed claimants because now the investment has an expected value of $400 instead of $500. The expected value of $400 results from the fact that if the second investment does well and produces a return of $2000, the fixed claimants will be paid in full their $500, while if the investment does poorly and returns only $300, the fixed claimants will be paid only $300. The expected value of this investment is therefore $400 ($500X .5 + $300 X.5 = $400). On the other hand, the shareholders prefer the second investment because it increases their expected return from $500 to $1000 ($2000 X .5 + $0 X .5 = $1000). Thus shareholders have an incentive to shift from the first investment to the second investment after a loan has been made.

32. Macey & Miller, *supra* note 13, at 206.
33. *See* Daniel R. Fischel, "The Economics of Lender Liability," 99 *Yale L.* J. 131, 140-42 (1989) (discussing various interpretations of the duty of good faith and relevance of this duty in deterring opportunistic behavior by both lenders and borrowers).
34. See *e.g. Farah Mfg. Co.*, 678 S.W. 2d at 690.
35. See *e.g., K.M.C. Co.* 757 F. 2d at 759-63.
36. *See Fleet Factors Corp.* 901 F.2d at 1557-68 (noting that a creditor may incur liability for a borrower's affairs if its participation in management indicates ability to intervene in the corporation's affairs). *But see* In re Gergsoe Metal Corp., 910 F.2d 668, 672 (9th Cir. 1990) (stating that "some actual management of the facility" is required to establish liability of secured creditor for a borrower's affairs).
37. *In re American Lumber Co.*, 5 B.R. 470 (Bankr. D. Minn. 1980).
38. *Id.* at 478.
39. Mark J. Roe, "Political and Legal Restraints on Ownership and Control of Public Companies," 27 *J. Fin. Econ.* 7, 9-21 (1990) (describing how law constrains financial institutions' role in the corporate structure).
40. Lise Simmons, "Banking: D'Amato Introduces Sweeping Legislation Aimed at Financial Services Modernization," *1995 Daily Report for Executives* (BNA) No. 23 (February 3, 1995), available in Lexis, News Library, Curnws File.

ANTHONY V. NANNI

9. Consolidation in the banking industry: An antitrust perspective

I am honored to participate in this panel, and welcome the opportunity to share with you the Antitrust Division's perspective – or at least my thinking – on bank consolidation. As you might expect, I will focus on antitrust issues and the Division's bank merger review program.

At the outset, I would like to try to dispel the notion that the Antitrust Division is a traditional regulatory agency or that the antitrust laws are regulatory in format. We do not seek to set rules in order to regulate any industry. Rather, we are a law enforcement agency and we view our role more like that of a baseball umpire. We call the balls and strikes, but we don't set the rules. Our function is to stay out of the way as much as possible in order to let the game unfold on its own.

Having said that, I am not suggesting that antitrust policy does not have an important role to play in the banking industry. Our mission is to ensure that markets remain competitive. Experience has shown, in particular, that when there are multiple and competing sources of credit and financial services, prices for these products tend to be lower while quality and innovation are higher. Banking is clearly an industry whose financial soundness and competitive structure are essential to the fulfillment of our nation's economic potential. Although technology may change the economic role of banks, I believe that a healthy competitive banking industry remains critical to the success of American business.

Two and a half years ago, when I took over responsibility for banking matters at the Division, I had two broad goals: first, to improve the Division's working relationship with the bank regulatory agencies – particularly the Federal Reserve Bank and the Office of the Comptroller of the Currency – as well as with the various State Attorneys General; and, second, to streamline and clarify the Division's review process in order to respond expeditiously and efficiently in all proposed transactions and to avoid confusion concerning our enforcement intentions. These two goals share a common purpose – to coordinate government review as much as possible so that those transactions that are anticompetitive will be challenged while consolidations that offer efficiencies or are otherwise

191

Y. Amihud and G. Miller (eds.), Bank Mergers & Acquisitions, 191–206
© 1998 Kluwer Academic Publishers. Printed in the Netherlands.

lawful may proceed as quickly as possible.

The success of these two initiatives is best illustrated by the Bank Merger Screening Guidelines that were issued jointly last year by the Antitrust Division, the Federal Reserve Bank and the Office of the Comptroller of the Currency. These Guidelines are a significant clarification of the agencies' review process and for the first time in a single document set out the ground rules by which the federal agencies will review bank mergers.

In practice, these Screening Guidelines have ensured that bank merger applications come to us with information necessary for us to review them and reach an initial assessment of a merger's likely competitive effects. The Division has also been willing to meet with parties before they file an application in order to discuss the likely impact of our screening process on a specific transaction. The Guidelines and our openness to advance consultation with the parties have enabled us to identify potential areas of concern and have allowed us and the other agencies to begin an examination and analysis of the competition issues and possible resolutions as early as possible.

In addition, we have sought to make it clear that these screens are not hard and fast rules or bright lines. Rather, they are meant to open the discussion and dialogue. It does not follow that we will challenge a proposed merger merely because it fails the tests in the screens. The screening materials should inform the industry of the factors we will be examining and the issues that are important to our evaluation. Indeed, less than one percent of all applications raise any significant antitrust concern under the screening procedures. The primary effect of our Screening Guidelines is to allow proposed transactions that raise no significant antitrust issues to proceed promptly.

Cooperation among the agencies has also produced a wide range of other benefits. For example, the lines of communication and dialogue among the agencies has improved substantially. To the extent the agencies are aware of each others' concerns, the parties can be more comfortable that the investigations are proceeding on parallel tracks, thereby minimizing the potential for divergent decisions. Each agency also provides its own experience and perspective and often may pursue issues related but not identical to those of other agencies. The communities in which bank mergers occur should be reassured that a variety and range of concerns are being investigated and addressed.

In that connection, the participation of State Attorneys General in joint investigations with the Division has proven to be extremely helpful and productive. The State Attorneys General are able to bring to the investigations knowledge of local market conditions and concerns as well as knowledge of local businesses and their needs. I believe this knowledge has allowed our investigations to proceed more effectively and has resulted in decisions and resolutions which better address local issues.

Turning specifically to our review process for bank mergers, we begin with the same analytic framework (our Merger Guidelines of April 2, 1992) that we use for mergers in other industries. Within this framework, however, we have relied on our experience with numerous banking transactions to develop certain factual conclusions that guide our analysis. In the banking industry, in particular, we have emphasized the availability of banking services, including loans and credit, to small and medium-sized businesses.

Our investigations have suggested that small and medium-sized businesses have few alternatives and options other than commercial banks available to them. Small businesses tend to have credit needs that do not attract banks located in other regions and tend to rely on and value their relationships with their local commercial bankers. Medium-sized businesses may be able to access lenders and providers from larger arenas, but still tend not to have the access to national capital markets that may be available to larger corporations. At least to date, we believe that small and medium-sized businesses will be most affected by the potential loss of competition that bank mergers present.

Given that small businesses tend to bank locally, we have focused our competition analysis for small business banking services primarily within defined local areas such as RMA's (Ranally Metropolitan Areas) or counties as an approximation of the geographic scope of competition. Once we have identified a relevant geographic market we will use the deposits of commercial banks in the area as the best initial proxy to measure the competitive significance of the merging banks. A thrift's deposits are excluded in our first review, but then added if our investigation discloses that the thrift is, in fact, making commercial loans. Although we use the same methodology for our analysis of lending to medium-sized businesses, the effective area of competition by banks for such loans and services tends to be larger than for small businesses because of the greater ability of banks to secure and service those loans over greater distances.

I would like to stress that our focus on business banking services does not mean that we are ignoring the potential effects of bank mergers on retail consumers. We have found that retail consumers have banking alternatives available to them that most business customers do not – such as thrifts and credit unions. Although these factors may diminish potential anticompetitive effects, we have and will continue to screen and investigate for any significant loss of competition in the retail area as well.

Whenever we conduct detailed investigations, we seek to learn as much as we can about competition for banking services in the relevant markets. We specifically take into account, for example, the actual level of commercial loan activity by the market participants. I should add a note of caution on this point – that the loan data may not supersede entirely the deposit data. The deposit data historically have been more reliable and loan data do not necessarily reflect lending capacity or the full competitive significance of a commercial bank in the market.

The future of banking and the future delivery of banking services is a hot topic for speculation and prognostication. Clearly, the issue of how electronic banking will affect the industry is in the forefront of discussion. In some communities, non-bank institutions that traditionally have been weak competitors or have not engaged in commercial lending have also become more active in those areas. Similarly, parties have suggested that some banks are providing loans to small businesses from areas outside of the local markets within which those businesses operate.

This market evolution has given rise to arguments that the Division should change its bank merger program. My response is that antitrust merger analysis is sufficiently flexible and robust that it can readily account for any change in market dynamics that may occur in any industry. We have great confidence in the soundness of the principles that we use to examine potential anticompetitive effects from industry consolidation. We will continue to evaluate our review process and tailor it, as appropriate, to reflect industry conditions. Given the time frame within which we frequently operate, I would encourage parties to begin discussions with us as soon as possible to permit full consideration of these views.

The success of our program, in part, is reflected in the fact that our goal of preventing anticompetitive mergers has been reached without litigation and without the need to use compulsory process to obtain information. Instead, we have been able to enter into constructive dialogue in the context of clearly articulated standards. We do not measure our success by the number of cases filed or mergers restructured. We believe the public benefits if banks and their advisors feel they have clear guidance and if we permit lawful transactions to proceed with minimal delay.

The divestitures we have required, for example, show that we are mindful of both the potential pro-competitive and anticompetitive aspects of a merger. When bank mergers present concerns in certain markets, we try to reach resolutions tailored to the offending portions of the transaction. Fleet's acquisition of Shawmut, Wells Fargo's acquisition of First Interstate and CoreState's acquisition of Meridian all proceeded to closing after we negotiated appropriate divestitures that solved competitive concerns within discrete local markets. Moreover, in the First Interstate transaction, we took care during the phase when the transaction was subject to competing tender offers not to favor one party over the other. Our approach is to be as even-handed as possible so that our review procedures do not provide any unnecessary advantage to either side.

One final point concerning divestitures is that when we construct a network of branch offices to find an appropriate fix to potential competitive concerns, we will look beyond the amount of assets to be divested to the quality and location of the branches that are included in the divestiture package. Because our primary focus is competition for small business loans, we investigate in some detail the characteristics of the parties' branches in those markets, including their deposit and loan make-up, locations and ease of access for businesses. Our goal is to determine and evaluate each branch's overall current use by, and potential attractiveness to, area businesses. We have requested some parties, for example, to provide photographs of the branches. We also obtain significant additional information during our interviews of other participants in the market.

We also spend considerable time evaluating the viability and overall effectiveness of branch networks proposed for divestiture in a market. The issue we address is whether a purchaser of the network would be an effective business banking competitor in the area. The factors we consider include the number of branches, the location of branches, as well as the needed mix of deposits, banking services and personnel. The result is not based solely on concentration figures. We may argue strongly for particular branches or branch locations to be included in the divestiture package. We also require that parties divest the entire relationship for each customer associated with each branch, including deposits, loans and other related services. The final package is intended to reflect the commercial realities of the markets involved as well as to give the purchaser of the divested branches a strong presence in the market.

Overall, I believe that the Division's bank merger program has been a great success. In the past 12 months, we reviewed 1,874 transactions. Of those, seven were restructured. All were disposed of within the time provided by statute. We have been – and will continue to be – aggressive in our mission to preserve competition as well as efficient in our handling of all transactions with the overriding goal of permitting the market to operate on its own as much as possible.

APPENDIX

Bank Merger Competitive Review– Introduction and Overview

The banking agencies and the Department of Justice review the competitive impact of bank and bank holding company mergers under the banking and antitrust laws to proscribe mergers that would tend to substantially lessen competition. To speed this competitive review and reduce regulatory burden on the banking industry, the banking agencies and the Department have developed screens (attached as Screens A and B), to identify proposed mergers that clearly do not have significant adverse effects on competition. In addition to the screens, the banking agencies and the Department have identified information, described below in Section 2, which has proven to be useful in analyzing the competitive effects of proposed mergers highlighted by Screen A or Screen B.

Parties planning a merger transaction may wish to consult with the relevant banking agency or the Department before submitting an application. Where a proposed merger causes a significant anticompetitive problem, it is often possible to resolve the problem by agreeing to make an appropriate divestiture. In such cases, it may be useful to discuss the matter with the Department and the relevant regulatory agency. The Department seeks divestitures that will resolve the loss of competition in the market. A divestiture will resolve the problem if it ensures the presence of a strong and vigorous competitor that replaces the competition lost because of the merger.

Section 1 – Screening

Banking Agencies

The banking agencies rely primarily on Screen A, which looks at competition in predefined markets developed by the Federal Reserve. If the calculation specified in Screen A does not result in a postmerger HHI over 1800 and an increase of more than 200, the banking agencies are unlikely to further review the competitive effects of the merger.[1] If the result of the calculation specified in Screen A exceeds the 1800/200 threshold, applicants may consider providing additional information. See Section 2 for a description of the types of information that may be relevant. Providing such information with a merger application can eliminate delays in the review process and may avoid special requests for additional information.

Department of Justice

The Department initially reviews transactions using data from the banking agencies' screen, Screen A. If a proposed merger exceeds the 1800/200 threshold in Screen A, applicants should consider submitting the calculations set forth in Screen B.

In some cases, the Department may further review transactions which do not exceed the 1800/200 threshold in Screen A. This is most likely when Screen A does not reflect fully the competitive effects of the transaction in all relevant markets, in particular lending to small and medium-sized businesses. For example, the Department is more likely to review a transaction involving two commercial banks if the postmerger HHI approaches 1800 and the HHI increase approaches 200, and screen A includes thrifts which are not actively engaged in commercial lending. In addition, the Department is more likely to review a transaction if the predefined market in which the applicants compete is significantly larger than the area in which small business lending competition may exist (e.g., the predefined market includes multiple counties, or is significantly larger than an RMA in which the applicants are located). In such a case, applicants should consider submitting the calculations set forth in Screen B. Often, the Department will review the information in Screen B and find no need for further review of the proposed merger.

If the calculation specified in Screen B results in an HHI over 1800 and an increase of over 200, applicants may consider providing additional information. See Section 2 for a description of the types of information that may be relevant. Providing such information with a merger application can eliminate delays in the review process and may avoid special requests for additional information.

In some limited instances, the Department may examine a transaction in further detail even though Screen A and Screen B do not identify anticompetitive problems. This is most likely to occur when it appears that:

> *The Screens' market area does not fit the transaction.* Sometimes the geographic market used in the screens may not be an appropriate choice for analyzing the particular merger involved. For example, the Screens' market area is a county, and one merging institution is at the east end of one county and the other merging institution is at the west end of the adjacent county. The institutions may in reality be each other's most important competitors, but the screens would not reflect that fact. Or the Screens' market area may be quite large, but the merger involves two institutions at the center of the market. Institutions at the periphery of the market area may be very improbable substitutes for the competition that would be lost in the transaction and thus the transaction should be scrutinized in a narrower area to ensure that the relevant geographic market is considered.

> *Specialized products are involved.* Sometimes the merging institutions are competitors for a specialized product and few of the institutions included in the Screens compete in offering that product. For example, the Screens likely would not identify a concentrated market for working capital loans to medium-sized commercial customers, if the market area has many institutions but the merging institutions are two of only a few institutions able to compete for such business.

In such cases, applicants may wish to submit additional information. See Section 2 for a description of the types of information that may be relevant. Providing such information with a merger application can eliminate delays in the review process and may avoid special requests for additional information.

Section 2 – Additional Analysis

The Department and the banking agencies are likely to examine a transaction in more detail if it exceeds the 1800/200 threshold in Screen A. The Department is also likely to examine the effect of a proposed merger on competition for commercial loans if the transaction exceeds the 1800/200 threshold in Screen B. In instances where a screen highlights a transaction for further review, the applicant may present additional information not considered in the screen.

In cases where either Screen A or Screen B highlights a transaction for further scrutiny, additional information may establish a clearer picture of competitive realities in the market. Such information may include:

- evidence that the merging parties do not significantly compete with one another;
- evidence that rapid economic change has resulted in an outdated geographic market definition, and that an alternate market is more appropriate;
- evidence that market shares are not an adequate indicator of the extent of competition in the market, such as:
  - evidence that institutions in the market would be likely to expand current levels of commercial lending. Such evidence might include current loan-to-deposit ratios, recent hiring of new commercial loan officers, pending branch applications or significant out-of-market resources that would be shifted into the market in response to new loan opportunities;
  - evidence that a particular institution's market share overstates or understates its competitive significance (such as evidence that an institution is rapidly gaining or losing market share or that the institution is not competitively viable or is operating under regulatory restrictions on its activities);
- evidence concerning entry conditions, including evidence of entry by institutions within the last two years and the growth of those institutions that have entered; evidence of likely entry within the next two years, such as pending branch applications; and expectations about potential entry by institutions not now in the market area and the reasons for such expectations, including legal requirements for entry.

In cases where Screen B highlights a transaction for further scrutiny, applicants may consider preparing an HHI worksheet for the market area using, instead of deposits, data from the relevant Reports of Condition on commercial and industrial loans a) below $250,000 and b) between $250,000 and $1,000,000. Such information can be a useful assessment of actual competition for small business lending.[2]

Additional information that may be relevant includes evidence of competition from sources not included in Screen B, such as:

- evidence that a thrift institution is actively engaged in providing services to commercial customers, particularly loans for business startup or working capital purposes and cash management services;
- evidence that a credit union has such membership restrictions, or lack of restrictions, and offers such services to commercial customers that it should be considered to be in the market;
- evidence of actual competition by out-of-market institutions for commercial customers, particularly competition for loans for business startup or working capital purposes;
- evidence of actual competition by non-bank institutions for commercial customers, particularly competition for loans for business startup or working capital purposes.

If the applicants believe that Screen B does not accurately reflect market concentration and competitive realities in a particular area, they are encouraged to submit additional information explaining the reasons for their belief. This information should include an HHI worksheet which indicates the geographical area that should be covered, the institutions that should be included, the method of calculating the market share of each institution (e.g., deposits, branches, loans), and the reasons why this information is preferable to the information supplied in Screen B. Inclusion of institutions outside the areas identified in Screen B should be supported, wherever possible, by evidence of actual competition by these institutions. Such alternative worksheets should be submitted *in addition to*, rather than in lieu of, the HHI worksheets from Parts A and B.

Part A: Market Screen A

A.1. **List areas.** If there are offices of both[3] merging institutions[4] in any:

      a. Federal Reserve market (contact the relevant Federal Reserve Bank for information on defined markets);

      b. Ranally Metropolitan Area (RMA), if no Federal Reserve market exists;

      c. county, not within any Federal Reserve market or RMA,

then list each such area.   Check one:

_____ □ FRB Market □ RMA □ County

_____ □ FRB Market □ RMA □ County

_____ □ FRB Market □ RMA □ County

_____ □ FRB Market □ RMA □ County

_____ □ FRB Market □ RMA □ County

_____ □ FRB Market □ RMA □ County

A.2. **Calculate HHIs.** For each area listed under item A.1, prepare an HHI worksheet (see next page) covering all banks and thrifts in the area. Follow the instructions accompanying the worksheet (including thrifts at 50 percent as explained in the instructions) to calculate the pre-merger and post-merger HHIs and the HHI increase. Prepare as many worksheets as there are market areas listed above in Item A.1.

HHI Worksheet – Market Screen A

A.3.   Market Area: _____

A.4.   Source and publication date of data used: _____

A.5.   HHI Calculation

Column (a)
Column (b)
Column (c)
Column (d)
Column (e)
Column (f)

Depository institutions (including affiliates)
Number of offices in market area
Total deposits in market area
Market share of deposits (%)

Share squared pre-merger
Share squared post-merger

_____

Merging Institutions

Acquiring institution

_____

_____

_____

_____

Acquired institution

_____

_____

_____

_____

Merged institution

_____

_____

_____

Merged Share

_____

Other Institutions

_____
_____
_____
_____
_____
_____

_____
_____
_____
_____
_____
_____

_____
_____
_____
_____
_____
_____

_____
_____
_____
_____
_____
_____

_____   Pre-merger HHI   _____
                                     Total

                                                                      _____
                                                                      Post-merger HHI

                                                                      _____

                                                                      HHI Increase

Instructions
for preparing HHI Worksheets for Merger Screen A

Item Number

Instruction _____

Item A.3
Prepare a separate HHI Worksheet for each market area listed in A.1.
Item A.5
Calculate an HHI for the market area, as described below.
Item A.5.a
In Column (a), list all the commercial banks and thrift institutions that have offices in the market area, indicating whether each is a bank or a thrift.

Affiliates. For institutions that are affiliated by common control, make only one entry that combines all affiliates together.
Item A.5.b
In Column (b), report the number of offices each listed institution has in the market area.
Item A.5.c
In Column (c), list deposits for each institutions.

For commercial banks, list the total deposits that each institution (including all affiliates) has in the market area.

For thrifts, list 50% of the total deposits that each institution (including all affiliates) has in the market area.

Total. Add all the deposits listed in column (c) (except those in the merged institution) to get the total for the market area.
Item A.5.d
In Column (d), calculate the percentage market share of deposits for each institution. Use the total of column (c) as the basis of the calculation.
Item A.5.e
In Column (e), calculate the square of the percentage figures listed in Column (d) for the acquiring institution, the acquired institution, and the other institutions. Calculate the Pre-merger HHI by adding all of the figures in Column (e).
Item A.5.f
In column (f), calculate the square of the percentage figure listed in column (d) for the merged institution, and enter the figures from column (e) for the other institutions. Calculate the post-merger HHI by adding all of the figures in column (f).

HHI increase. Calculate the HHI increase by subtracting the Pre-merger HHI from the Post-merger HHI.

Part B: Market Screen B

B.1. **List areas.** If there are offices of both[5] merging institutions[6] which make commercial loans[7] in any:

    a.   Ranally Metropolitan Area (RMA); or

    b.   county, but not within any RMA,

then list each such area.   Check one:

_____ □ RMA □ County

_____ □ RMA □ County

_____ □ RMA □ County

_____ □ RMA □ County

_____ □ RMA □ County

_____ □ RMA □ County

B.2. **Calculate HHIs.** For each area listed under item B.1, prepare an HHI worksheet (see next page) covering all commercial banks in the area. Follow the instructions accompanying the worksheet to calculate the pre-merger and post-merger HHIs and the HHI increase. Prepare as many worksheets as there are market areas listed above in Item B.1.

HHI Worksheet – Market Screen B

B.3.　Market Area:_____

B.4.　Source and publication date of data used: _____

B.5.　HHI Calculation

Column　(a)
Column　(b)
Column　(c)
Column　(d)
Column　(e)
Column　(f)

Depository institutions (including affiliates)
Number of offices in market area
Total deposits in market area
Market share of deposits (%)

Share squared pre-merger
Share squared post-merger

_____

Merging Institutions

Acquiring institution

_____

_____

_____

_____

Acquired institution

_____

_____

_____

_____

Merged institution

_____

_____

_____

Merged Share

_____

Other Institutions

_____

_____
_____
_____
_____
_____

_____

_____
_____
_____
_____

_____

_____
_____
_____
_____

_____

_____
_____
_____
_____
_____

_____   Pre-merger HHI   _____
                                 Total

                                                       _____
                                                       Post-merger HHI

                                                       _____
                                                       ## HHI Increase

B.6.   Commercial Loans. For each merging institution, report the outstanding balance of commercial and industrial loans ("C&I loans") originated by offices in the market area.

Acquiring institution: _____

Acquired institution: _____

Instructions
for preparing HHI Worksheets for Merger Screen A

Item Number

Instruction _____

Item B.1
For item B.1, prepare a separate HHI Worksheet for each market area in which both institutions have offices which make commercial loans.

Item B.5
Calculate an HHI for the market area, as described below.

Item B.5.a
In Column (a), list all the commercial banks (but not thrifts) that have offices in the market area. Also list the acquired and acquiring firm, even if both are not commercial banks.

Affiliates. For institutions that are affiliated by common control, make only one entry that combines all affiliates together.

Item B.5.b
In Column (b), report the number of offices each listed institution has in the market area.

Item B.5.c
In Column (c), list the total deposits that each institution (including all affiliates) has in the market area.

Total. Add all the deposits listed in column (c) (except those in the merged institution) to get the total commercial bank deposits for the market area.

Item B.5.d
In column (d), calculate the percentage market share of deposits for each institution. Use the total of column (c) as the basis for the calculation.

Item B.5.e
In Column (e), calculate the square of the percentage figures listed in Column (d) for the acquired institution, the acquiring institution, and the other institutions. Calculate the Pre-merger HHI by adding all of the figures in column (e).

Item B.5.f
In column (f), calculate the square of the percentage figure listed in column (d) for the merged institution, and enter the figures from column (e) for the other institutions. Calculate the post-merger HHI by adding all of the figures in column (f).

HHI increase. Calculate the HHI increase by subtracting the Pre-merger HHI from the Post-merger HHI.

Item B.6
In item B.6, indicate the outstanding balance of commercial loans originated in the market area by the acquiring and the acquired institution. "Commercial loans" are those which fall within the category entitled "commercial and industrial loans" in the FDIC Report of Condition and the category entitled "non-mortgage commercial loans" in the OTS Thrift Financial Report.

NOTES

1. However, if a proposed merger would result in a postmerger market share in excess of 35%, the Federal Reserve is likely to review the transaction further.
2. In preparing such a market share table, parties may estimate another institution's commercial lending in a given market by multiplying the institution's overall ratio of commercial loans to deposits by its deposits in the relevant market, if market-specific information regarding that institution is unavailable. Applicants should indicate which figures are actual and which are estimates.
3. This document is written for a situation in which only two institutions are involved. In a transaction in which more than two institutions are involved, treat each reference to "both" or "two" institutions as if it referred to "two or more" institutions.
4. Including their affiliates. All subsequent references to "institutions" include all affiliates.
5. This document is written for a situation in which only two institutions are involved. In a transaction in which more than two institutions are involved, treat each reference to "both" or "two" institutions as if it referred to "two or more" institutions.
6. Including their affiliates. All subsequent references to "institutions" include all affiliates.
7. As defined in the FDIC Report of Condition as "commercial and industrial loans," and in the OTS Thrift Financial Report as "non-mortgage commercial loans."

JOHN C. COATES IV

10. Reassessing risk-based capital in the 1990s: Encouraging consolidation and productivity

This paper reassesses the risk-based capital rules, as they have been implemented in the 1990s, in light of ongoing consolidation in the banking industry. After briefly reviewing the theory behind the risk-based capital rules, the paper observes that although the risk-based capital rules have not been generally binding on US banks, they soon may become binding as a result of market forces that are pressuring banks to take steps that result in lower risk-based capital ratios. The paper then argues against past and likely future proposals to raise capital minimums on the ground that higher ratios would interfere with the healthy, ongoing consolidation in the banking industry. Next, the paper briefly reviews the status and treatment of three types of risk under the risk-based capital rules – concentration risk, innovation risk and acquisition risk – and argues that current rules perversely encourage the most risky type of bank growth (product innovation) while discouraging the least risky type of bank growth (acquisitions that produce greater geographic diversification). The paper concludes by calling for a re-evaluation of the way in which the risk-based capital rules apply to acquisitions, with a view toward better discriminating between risk-increasing and risk-decreasing transactions.

1. RISK-BASED CAPITAL RULES IN THEORY

Tradition holds that the moral hazards created by deposit insurance and implicit government guarantees (such as a "too big to fail" policy) create incentives for banks to hold less capital than is socially optimal. Taxpayers protect the downside; shareholders get the upside; and the combined effect leads banks to take "excessive" risks.[1] Without some form of binding regulatory constraint on their activities, banks can thus be expected to produce a net loss to society, ceteris parilous.

Regulatory constraints take two theoretical forms: (1) ex ante rules and (2) ex post monitoring. In their theoretically pristine form, ex ante rules are fixed in advance of their application, are (relatively) unchanging over time, and (relatively) objective, with regulators having no ability to impose greater or

207

Y. Amihud and G. Miller (eds.), Bank Mergers & Acquisitions, 207–220
© 1998 Kluwer Academic Publishers. Printed in the Netherlands.

lesser constraints except at relatively infrequent intervals and on a general basis. "Ex post" monitoring, by contrast, constrains banks on a continual (if not continuous) basis, and is characterized by flexibility and subjectivity, with regulators having the power to heighten, modify or reduce constraints on individual banks. Ex ante rules may provide a more reliable, objective system of incentives and disincentives to encourage banks to take optimal levels of risk, and so permit better planning, reduce the risk of enforcement bias (or unjustifiable forbearance) and reduce costs.[2] Ex post monitoring, on the other hand, may provide better information to devise more particularized constraints, and may better prevent "gaming" and "loophole lawyering."

In practice, regulatory constraints designed to address the moral hazard of deposit insurance have fallen into three types: (1) activity restrictions, (2) capital requirements and (3) ongoing examination and supervision. The first two types have generally functioned as ex ante rules; the third type has generally functioned as ex post monitoring. The bank and thrift crises of the 1980s led commentators to attack exclusive reliance on ex post examination and supervision on the grounds that regulators had both the opportunity and the incentive to defer imposing needed constraints on banks engaged in excessive risk-taking. At the same time, commentators renewed the attack on activity restrictions as being more likely to reduce than increase bank safety, given accelerating technological change and heightened competition in the financial services industry. Instead, Congress directed regulators to rely to a greater extent than ever before on capital rules as the primary line of defense against excessive risk-taking.

The "risk-based" capital rules adopted by federal banking regulators[3] pursuant to the Basle accord[4] are defended as both an improvement on traditional "one size fits all" regulatory capital minimums[5] and a rational compromise between the desire for more objective, transparent constraints (limiting the ability of regulators to forbear) and the desire to provide banks with more flexibility at the operational level (reducing the risk that regulatory constraints will unintentionally decrease bank competitiveness). By tailoring capital standards to the credit risk characteristics of a given bank's asset portfolio (including off-balance sheet credit exposures), the risk-based capital rules limit the opportunities for "gaming" and so reduce perverse incentives that uniform capital rules create.

2. RISK-BASED CAPITAL RULES IN PRACTICE

Since their full phase-in in 1992, the risk-based capital rules have not generally been binding on US banks.[6] Although some feared that the risk-based capital rules would be binding on a large number of banks and so would exacerbate the "credit crunch" that accompanied the last recession, in fact this does not appear to have been the case. Investors, reacting to high level of bank losses and failures during the late 1980s, rewarded banks that held capital at levels higher than the 4%/8% Tier 1/total risk-based capital floors. During the early 1990s, higher capital ratios correlated with higher price/earnings multiples, giving acquirors stronger deal currency and reluctant sellers the best of all takeover defenses – a high stock price. Market incentives, in other words, were sufficiently strong to induce banks to raise capital ratios so that the risk-based capital rules have not generally been binding.[7]

But as the credit cycle has progressed, market incentives to *reduce* capital have grown. Among other factors, technological innovation and the relaxation of legal barriers to competition have made "all forms of financial capital ... irreversibly more expensive."[8] Market incentives have affected both the denominator and the numerator of the risk-based ratios. In the denominator, five years of economic growth have enabled high-yielding loans (risk-weighted at 100%) to displace low-yielding investment securities (risk-weighted as low as 0%). In the numerator, banks have used stock buybacks[9] and cash or part-cash acquisitions[10] to reduce equity and so increase EPS and ROE. Banks that might otherwise have been reluctant to reduce their capital ratios voluntarily have been forced to do so by activist shareholders such as Michael Price, who in 1994 successfully pressured Michigan National to undertake a large one time buyback in the form of a Dutch auction self-tender, and CAI Investors, which this year was able to sell a sizeable block of stock back to Commercial Federal after winning a proxy fight in 1995.

As recently noted by bank analyst David Berry, the banking "industry's capital strength has eroded materially over the past two years." The typical large bank (assets > $25 billion) has reduced its risk-based ratios 100 basis points since the end of 1993. (See Appendix A.) At 8.1% at June 30, 1996, the average large bank Tier 1 ratio is still well above the 6% "well capitalized" regulatory floor. But the trend suggests that absent structural change in the economy or the industry, the regulatory floors may begin to become binding in the not-so-distant future.

3. The Regulatory Dilemma

Orthodoxy would call for regulatory intervention to slow or reverse this trend. Calls for higher capital levels continue despite the low level of failures in recent years and apparent industry-wide vigor. The Shadow Financial Regulatory Committee has proposed raising all floors 100 basis points.[12] Even if political considerations make formal increases infeasible, regulators may push for higher ratios informally, through the exam process, in reviewing merger applications, and by informal jawboning.

However, we are living in unorthodox times. The nation remains overbanked. Even after 15 years of interstate consolidation, the US has over 12,000 independent banking organizations, compared to 600 each in the United Kingdom and France.[13] At 21% of total bank assets, the top 10 US banks hold the smallest portion of national banking assets of all the industrial countries; the top 10 Canadian banks hold nearly 90%.[14] If non-bank financial assets were included, US industry fragmentation would be even more pronounced.

Private consolidation, it has been suggested, is the best method for reducing overcapacity.[15] Large banks fails less often than small banks, in part because large banks tend to be better diversified.[16] Although the absolute amount of assets involved in large bank failures is larger (since large banks hold more assets), the ratio of resolution costs to assets at the time of failure is lower for large banks than for small banks.[17] Even the Bank for International Settlements has touted mergers and hostile takeovers as means of resolving future problem banks early and cheaply.[18]

Before any action is taken to increase capital requirements, consideration should be given to how such an increase would affect banks generally and consolidation activity in particular. Proponents of a capital increase reason that since existing ratios are not binding, an increase would have little impact. The Shadow Committee argues that a 100 basis point increase would "demote only a few institutions to the undercapitalized category."[9]

This focus is too narrow. An increase in capital requirements would have an immediate, negative effect on bank stock prices. The same market forces that are encouraging banks to lower their ratios would cause the markets to react adversely to any new legal impediment to the ongoing restructuring of the industry. Buybacks and cash acquisitions would dwindle. Investors would quickly see that banks' ability to continue to deliver high returns was in jeopardy.

The next logical effect of higher regulatory floors would be on bank management. In an effort to increase earnings to maintain returns, management can be expected to push for yield. Credit standards would slip. Yet because the risk-based ratios are only crudely calibrated to credit risk, banks could lend to riskier borrowers without incurring a greater near-term capital cost. Corporate and real estate loans, for example, carry the same risk weight as secured credit card loans; loss rates on the former remain well above those on the latter (despite the recent up-tick in credit card losses). To be sure, examiners would have some opportunity to react to obvious signs of greater risk-taking. But on the margin, across the system, credit risk would increase.[20]

Worse, higher ratios could interfere with industry consolidation.[21] Hannan & Rhoades note that "smaller banks ... [are] generally ... better capitalized than larger banks."[22] (See Appendix A.) This capital differential is voluntary and healthy; it reflects higher loss rates in smaller, less diversified banks. To the extent that a capital requirement increase would be binding on the lower capitalized, less risky large banks, but not binding on smaller banks, an increase could erase this differential. The predictable stock market reaction noted above would fall most heavily on larger banks. Thus, large regional banks – which have been the main engines of industry consolidation – would lose acquisition capacity and turn their focus inward. As Hannan & Rhoades conclude, "it seems likely that ... higher capital requirements ... will ... slow bank expansion both geographically and in new product lines."[23]

Regulators thus appear to face a dilemma: acquiesce as capital ratios fall, or intervene and risk choking off acquisition activity.

4. CONCENTRATION RISK, INNOVATION RISK AND ACQUISITION RISK

Regulators have a potential way out of the dilemma posed by falling capital levels. Rather than increasing requirements generally, they could refocus on risk-related characteristics. As noted at the outset, better tailoring *is* the principal justification for risk-based capital rules. Yet current rules are both incomplete and, in some respects, perverse. Commentators have noted numerous examples of the incompleteness of the risk-based rules, from interest-rate risk to market risk.[24] The remainder of this paper focuses on the impact on capital requirements of three risk characteristics that directly relate to industry consolidation: concentration risk, innovation risk, and acquisition risk.

Initially, the Basle accords (and FDICIA) were thought to mandate capital supplements for concentration risk – whether due to geographic or industry concentrations – and risks arising from non-traditional activities.[25] In December 1994, however, US banking regulators announced their decision to defer indefinitely any attempt to develop any specific capital rules related to such risks.[26] Instead, they adopted vague "standards"[27] giving supervisory officials discretion to impose – or not impose – capital requirements related to such risks.[28] It appeared that regulators intended to treat such risks as they had treated acquisition risk: existing policy mandates that active participants in the bank acquisition market must maintain additional capital to support those activities.

In practice, however, the story has been different. Based on interviews with officials at regulatory agencies and affected banks, it is fair to say that the regulators have only sparingly imposed higher capital levels for concentration risk and innovation risk. It is true that examiners review geographic risk in connection with establishing a bank's supervisory (*e.g.*, CAMEL) rating, and have encouraged banks to develop their own models for monitoring concentration and non-traditional product risk. Only in the case of troubled or inadequately capitalized banks, however, have regulators appeared to specify specified additional capital requirements related to concentration risk. Banks have been deemed "well capitalized" under the prompt corrective action rules promulgated under FDICIA[29] – with the benefit of lower deposit insurance premiums[30] and greater operational flexibility – as long as they have had risk-based capital ratios of 6%/10% (and a 5% leverage ratio). Yet few banking organizations can be said to be truly diversified from a geographic point of view. Banks based in a single state, for example, are generally more geographically concentrated than multistate bank holding companies.

Similarly, while innovative products and services have attracted supervisory attention in the last few years, this attention has been confined to the exam process and to general policy directives that banks develop adequate controls and procedures to monitor innovation. Banks have been rapidly pushing into new lines of business. From securities and insurance to electronic banking and derivatives, banks have all been searching for the Holy Grail of high-margin, growth businesses. As with geographic concentration, however, innovation – prudent or not – has not affected banks' capital categories. As long as management has shown "progress" in managing these risks, regulators have relied on the risk-based capital rules and have not attempted to specify capital supplements on the basis of non-credit-related risk.

In contrast, regulators *have* enforced their older policy on acquisition risk. Banks that experience significant growth through acquisition are expected to maintain capital levels 100 to 200 basis points above the minimum ratios, and these ratios should not decline as a result of an acquisition.[31] In 1993, the Federal Reserve Board refused to permit Bank of Boston (BKB) to proceed with an acquisition until the bank committed to raise $170 million in additional capital, even though (1) the transaction was an all-stock transaction that would not have diminished BKB's capital ratios; (2) BKB would have had, on a pro forma basis following the acquisition, capital in excess of the 5%/6%/10% regulatory floors; and (3) BKB had a track record of successfully accomplishing acquisitions.

If industry capital levels continue to decline, the disparate regulatory treatment of geographic and innovation risk, on the one hand, and acquisition risk, on the other hand, will be put to the test. Every bank that does not hold a geographically diversified portfolio of assets should in theory hold *more* capital than 5%/6%/10% to be deemed "well capitalized" under FDICIA. If regulators continue to forbear on concentration risk while enforcing the requirement of higher capital for acquisition risk, banks will face a disincentive to achieving geographic diversification through acquisition. Similarly, under current regulatory practices, banks will have an incentive to withdraw from traditional horizontal consolidation and instead build innovative businesses. If – as expected – the regulators and Congress continue to relax activity constraints, this incentive will grow all the more important.

An Illustration

To illustrate the foregoing, assume that Bank A (a large bank holding company with assets primarily in Region A and a proven acquisition track record) is considering two projects:

- Project 1 is the acquisition of Bank B, which is a "plain vanilla" mid-sized bank holding company with assets located in Region B.
- Project 2 is a de novo start-up operation providing investment advice on derivatives to retail customers via the Internet.

Assume that, based on the information that Bank A has and all *known* risks, each project has a net present value (NPV) of $100 million. Finally, assume that either project will tie up management time sufficiently that no other project may be undertaken for the foreseeable future.

Which should Bank A choose? Which would expose the taxpayer to more risk?

A good argument could be made that Project 1 is the better choice. Although the NPV of the two projects is the same, it appears to involve fewer uncertainties (*i.e.*, unknown risks, including operational risk) than Project 2. Bank A's acquisition experience suggests that its information about Project 1 is better. Hence, it should in theory carry a lower capital charge than Project 2. In fact, the current capital rules should *in theory* benefit Bank A for pursuing Project 1 to the extent that it would lower Bank A's geographic concentration risk.

However, existing capital rules *as applied* make Project 2 the better choice. Project 2 will produce few balance sheet assets, and little or no credit-related capital charge; in effect, it would have a risk-weighting of zero under the current capital rules. Project 1 would *not* provide Bank A will more favorable capital treatment due to the lack of attention currently given to geographic concentration risk. Notwithstanding Bank A's experience in acquiring targets like Bank B, Project 1 will require Bank A to maintain *more* capital than it would otherwise have to maintain because of current regulatory policy on acquisition risk.

Of course, examiners may take ex post action to encourage Bank A to develop appropriate risk management procedures to help assure that Project 2 plays out as expected. The geographic diversification provided by Project 1 may turn out to be illusory if regional recessions are a thing of the past. Bank A's past success in integrating acquisitions may have been dumb luck. The illustration may be exaggerated. Still, given the nature of bank missteps in the 1990s – from Barings to Daiwa to Bankers Trust, all of which involve non-traditional activities – it at least gives one pause.

In sum, to the extent capital rules are or become binding, they will interfere with consolidation as currently applied, just as would higher capital minimums.

5. CONCLUSION

Regulators can respond to both problems described in this paper – the dilemma posed by declining capital levels and the perverse effects of existing rules – in the same way. Greater attention could be given to the risks posed by poor diversification and product innovation. There is no good reason why geographic diversification could not be modeled and weighted in the capital rules. As with existing credit weightings, no such model will be perfect, but any set of reliable weights will represent an improvement over the status quo.

Conversely, less anxiety should surround "plain vanilla" horizontal acquisitions, which for all the major industry players have become routine and comparatively safe. Regulators could safely eliminate acquisition risk as a reason for requiring higher capital levels for seasoned participants in the M&A arena that have developed rigorous acquisition plans and procedures (including procedures addressing due diligence, integration and cost savings). Such changes would be small but useful steps toward insuring that safe consolidation activity is rewarded and not punished under the capital rules.

In closing I would note that it is extremely difficult, if not impossible, for regulators to choose minimum capital ratios rigorously.[32] It should be recalled that the 4%/8% ratios contained in the Basle accord were – by admission of the Basle negotiators – arbitrary.[33] They were little more than a "seat of the pants" guess of appropriate capital minima, based on limited studies of capital levels that markets have historically required.[34] By imposing operational constraints and higher deposit insurance assessments on banks that are merely "adequately capitalized" under FDICIA, the US banking regulators have effectively raised the risk-based floors from 4%/8% to 6%/10%. If regulators are correct about the benefits of "prompt corrective action" in lowering the costs of bank failures,[35] the minimums established in 1988 may now be "too high" from a social point of view. As existing capital rules begin to bind banks, no dogmas should be beyond question, particularly when they threaten to distort the long-term trends – consolidation and innovation – that promise to keep the financial services industry healthy into the future.

NOTES

1. See Lovett, Moral Hazard, Bank Supervision and Risk-Based Capital Requirements, 49 Ohio St. L.J. 1365 (1989); Macey & Garrett, Market Discipline by Depositors: A Summary of the Theoretical and Empirical Arguments, 5 Yale J. on Reg. 215 (1988).
2. See Sunstein, Problems with Rules, 83 Calif. L. Rev. 955, 1003 (1995) (contrasting costs and benefits of rules and standards).
3. Final Rule – Amendment to Regulations H and Y, 75 Fed. Res. Bull. 156 (Mar. 1989) (announcing adoption of risk-based capital rules).
4. See Bank for International Settlements Committee on Banking Regulation and Supervisory Practices, Report on International Convergence of Capital Measurements and Capital Standards, American Society of International Law (July 1988).
5. O'Keefe, Risk-Based Capital Standards for Commercial Banks: Improved Capital-Adequacy Standards?, Federal Deposit Insurance Corporation Publication (Spring/Summer 1993) ("risk-based capital standards are an improvement over the former primary and secondary capital constraints they replaced"); Greenspan, "Innovation and Regulation of Banks in the 1990s," 74 Fed. Res. Bull. 783 (Dec. 1988) ("Everyone realizes that the [risk-based capital rules are] far from perfect ... [but they are] clearly an improvement."). At the regulatory level, a similar compromise seems to be made by bank examiners, who punish relatively inefficient banks for engaging in risky behavior, regardless of the impact on returns, but do not similarly penalize efficient banks. DeYoung, Hughes & Moon, Evidence on the Objectives of Bank Regulators, Working Papers (Oct. 7, 1996).
6. The average Tier 1 ratio for the top 20 public bank holding companies, for example, was over

6.60% in 1990, two years ahead of the full phase-in at 4%; for all banks, the average was even higher, at 10.64%. Total capital ratios were similarly well above regulatory minimums well prior to 1992. See Appendix A. Claims that the risk-based capital rules caused or materially contributed to the last recession appear in retrospect to have been instances of special pleading, cf. Soft on Banks?, The Economist (Feb. 23, 1991), at 20, and in any event were simply wrong. Berger & Udell, Did Risk-Based Capital Allocate Bank Credit and Cause a "Credit Crunch" in the United States?, 26 J. Money, Credit & Banking 585 (1994).

7. See Garten, Whatever Happened To Market Discipline of Banks?, 1991 Ann. Surv. Am. L. 749, 765. By contrast, the regulatory leverage ratio, which does not weight assets on the basis of credit risk, has been more of a constraint for some banks, although average leverage ratios have remained 150 basis points above the "well capitalized" 5% regulatory floor.

8. Bank for International Settlements, 66th Annual Report, at 84 (June 10, 1996).

9. See Herlihy, et al., Mergers and Acquisitions of Financial Institutions 1995, Securities Activities of Banks Fifteenth Annual Institute (Nov. 1995), at 118 ("Banks announced buybacks in 1994-95 of over $7 billion.").

10. Id., at 33 ("There has been an increasing incidence of part-cash ... transactions.").

11. Berry, Levering Up: Declining Capital Ratios in the Banking Industry, 44 Keefe Bruyette & Woods, Inc. Analyst Report (Sep. 13, 1996).

12. Shadow Financial Regulatory Committee, Statement No. 126 (Dec. 11, 1995); "Shadow Group Urges Rise in Risk-Based Capital Ratio," The American Banker (Dec. 12, 1995).

13. Bank for International Settlements, supra note 8, at 86.

14. Id.

15. Macey & Miller, Bank Mergers and American Bank Competitiveness, Conference on Mergers of Financial Institutions (Oct. 11, 1996), at 3 ("bank mergers should ... be viewed as a low-cost substitute for bank failures").

16. Cole & Gunther, When Are Failing Banks Closed?, Fed. Res. Bk. of Dallas Report (Apr. 19, 1995), Table 5; Failed Banks, Congressional Budget Office Study (June 1994), Table 8; Modernizing the Financial System, Dept. of Treas. (Feb. 1991), at II-5.

17. Bovenzi & Murton, Resolution Costs and Bank Failures, 1 FDIC Banking Rev. 1, 10 (1988) (1985 and 1986 data); Failed Banks, supra note 16, Tables 8 and 10, and accompanying text (presenting FDIC data on resolution costs of failed banks 1987-1992 and 1992-1993).

18. Bank for International Settlements, supra note 8, at 90-92, 167 ("The risk is that consolidation will proceed too slowly ... [T]he reduction of excess capacity is essential. ... Regulatory ... obstacles to hostile takeovers in the banking industry ... deserve more attention [from regulators]. ... [T]he reduction of artificial barriers to takeovers and mergers ... would be helpful.") .

19. See note 12 supra.

20. See Modernizing the Financial System, supra note 16, at II-14; Rose, Higher Capital May Impair Bank Safety, Amer. Banker (1990), at 1, 4; Wall & Peterson, The Effect of Capital Adequacy Guidelines on Large Bank Holding Companies, 11 J. Banking & Fin. 581 (1987).

21. When the risk-based capital rules were first implemented, there was some concern that higher requirements would have the opposite effect – i.e., encourage consolidation (which was opposed by smaller banks). See Modernizing the Financial System, supra note 16, at II-16. However, at that time, the concern was more that the new rules would immediately put a large number of banks into capital noncompliance, thereby pushing them into failure or sale. Given that smaller banks generally hold capital well above any potential increased requirement, that result now seems unlikely.

22. Future U.S. Banking Structure: 1990 to 2010, Antitrust Bull. 737 (Fall 1992).

23. Supra note 22. See also 58 Fed. Reg. 17,533 (1993) (describing likely negative impact of higher capital requirements on acquisitions).

24. See Garten, supra note 7; Jackson, The Expanding Obligations of Financial Holding Companies, 107 Harv. L. Rev. 509 (1994). Cf. Risk-Based Standards; Market Risk, Joint Final Rule (Aug. 29, 1996) (requiring banks with significant exposure to market risk associated with foreign exchange, commodity positions, and debt or equity trading positions, measure that risk

using its own internal value-at-risk model, and hold a commensurate amount of capital to support such activities).

25. See, *e.g.*, Conroy, Risk-Based Capital Adequacy Guidelines, 63 Fordham L. Rev. 2395, 2437; Garten, supra note 7, at n.67.

26. *E.g.*, Risk-Based Capital; Concentrations of Credit and Nontraditional Activities, OCC-94-71 (Dec. 23, 1994). Regulators defended their decision on the ground that a formula-based capital calculation for such risks were infeasible because "there [was] no generally accepted approach to identifying and quantifying" such risks. While this may be true, it is also true that existing risk-based capital standards do not reflect any generally accepted approach for identifying and quantifying credit risk. A commercial real estate loan, for example, has the same risk-weighting as a credit card loan, even though losses on the two types of loans differ dramatically. Nevertheless, even rough risk-related adjustments to capital minimum are – if directionally accurate – arguably an improvement over uniform capital rules.

27. See Sunstein, supra note 2, at 964-65.

28. See, *e.g.*, 12 C.F.R. § 3.10.

29. 57 Fed. Reg. 44,866 (1992) (adopting prompt corrective action rules).

30. See 12 C.F.R. Part 327.

31. *E.g.*, 12 C.F.R. Part 225, App. A and D (setting forth Federal Reserve policy).

32. See Jackson, supra note 24, at n.294.

33. See Fairlamb, Beyond Capital, Institutional Investor, (Aug. 1994) at 42 ("'That figure was seat-of-the-pants stuff," admits Peter Cooke, the former Bank of England official who chaired the BIS Committee on Banking Supervision that hammered out the Basle Agreement.") (cited in Conroy, supra note 25, at n.160)); Scott, Scholarship in Banking Law, 49 Ohio St. L.J. 1183, 1186 (1989).

34. Conroy, supra note 25, at 2418. Moreover, the studies on which the risk-based capital rules were based dated from the now-distant 1960s and 1970s, a period in which the banking landscape was entirely different. Id.

35. Average resolution costs have fallen dramatically since the enactment of FDICIA. See Proposed Rule: Assessments; New Assessment Rate Schedule for BIF Member Institutions, 60 Fed. Reg. 32 (Feb. 23, 1995) (losses per insured deposits averaged 16 basis points 1981-1993 and fell to less than one basis point in 1994). Studies of stock market reactions to FDICIA suggest that the prompt corrective action rules are expected to benefit shareholders, presumably by lowering resolution costs. Liang, Mohanty & Song, The Effect of the Federal Deposit Insurance Corporation Improvement Act of 1991 on Bank Stocks, 19 J. Fin. Res. 229 (1996).

APPENDIX A

Aggregates and Averages
for Top 20 Public Banks by Asset Size and For All 424 Public Banks

	Total Assets ($000) Mst RctQ	Total Assets ($000) 1995	Total Assets ($000) 1994	Total Assets ($000) 1993	Total Assets ($000) 1992	Total Assets ($000) 1991	Total Assets ($000) 1990
Average for Top 20 Public Banks	120,078,016	112,972,384	104,967,021	89,225,942	80,946,722	75,703,767	66,691,742
Aggregate for Top 20 Public Banks	2,401,560,328	2,259,447,688	2,099,340,426	1,784,518,832	1,618,934,438	1,514,075,334	1,333,834,835
Average for All 424 Public Banks	8,483,099	8,031,412	7,427,582	6,479,876	5,982,965	5,775,653	5,546,971
Aggregate for All 424 Public Banks	3,596,833,973	3,405,318,647	3,141,867,344	2,734,507,708	2,494,896,210	2,327,588,355	2,080,113,997

Aggregates and Averages
for Top 20 Public Banks by Asset Size and For All 424 Public Banks

	Gross Loans ($000) Mst RctQ	Gross Loans ($000) 1995	Gross Loans ($000) 1994	Gross Loans ($000) 1993	Gross Loans ($000) 1992	Gross Loans ($000) 1991	Gross Loans ($000) 1990
Average for Top 20 Public Banks	66,157,148	61,689,729	56,629,209	48,684,654	47,067,452	45,995,169	41,773,261
Aggregate for Top 20 Public Banks	1,323,142,963	1,233,794,589	1,132,584,171	973,349,081	941,349,046	919,903,384	835,465,225
Average for All 424 Public Banks	4,910,096	4,607,715	4,215,378	3,642,585	3,484,199	3,496,946	3,470,128
Aggregate for All 424 Public Banks	2,081,880,651	1,953,671,282	1,783,104,829	1,537,170,728	1,452,910,803	1,409,269,091	1,301,298,186

Aggregates and Averages
for Top 20 Public Banks by Asset Size and For All 424 Public Banks

	Total Deposits ($000) Mst RctQ	Total Deposits ($000) 1995	Total Deposits ($000) 1994	Total Deposits ($000) 1993	Total Deposits ($000) 1992	Total Deposits ($000) 1991	Total Deposits ($000) 1990
Average for Top 20 Public Banks	70,354,507	66,516,283	64,075,056	56,976,792	54,831,675	53,286,448	46,475,602
Aggregate for Top 20 Public Banks	1,407,090,149	1,330,325,658	1,281,501,129	1,139,535,849	1,096,633,507	1,065,728,961	929,512,031
Average for All 424 Public Banks	5,453,328	5,192,009	4,915,048	4,465,364	4,332,204	4,283,984	4,098,066
Aggregate for All 424 Public Banks	2,312,210,938	2,201,411,981	2,079,065,147	1,884,383,771	1,806,529,225	1,726,445,604	1,536,774,934

Aggregates and Averages
for Top 20 Public Banks by Asset Size and For All 424 Public Banks

	Total Equity ($000) Mst RctQ	Total Equity ($000) 1995	Total Equity ($000) 1994	Total Equity ($000) 1993	Total Equity ($000) 1992	Total Equity ($000) 1991	Total Equity ($000) 1990
Average for Top 20 Public Banks	9,079,844	8,313,353	7,458,809	6,641,415	5,624,877	4,512,612	3,751,491
Aggregate for Top 20 Public Banks	181,596,871	166,267,065	149,176,173	132,828,295	112,497,536	90,252,245	75,029,810
Average for All 424 Public Banks	663,948	619,783	550,225	498,681	428,862	366,246	334,222
Aggregate for All 424 Public Banks	281,513,882	262,788,174	232,745,364	210,443,578	178,835,551	147,597,115	125,333,373

Aggregates and Averages
for Top 20 Public Banks by Asset Size and For All <24 Public Banks

	Tier 1/ Risk-Adj Assets (%) Mst RerQ	Tier 1/ Risk-Adj Assets (%) 1995	Tier 1/ Risk-Adj Assets (%) 1994	Tier 1/ Risk-Adj Assets (%) 1993	Tier 1/ Risk-Adj Assets (%) 1992	Tier 1/ Risk-Adj Assets (%) 1991	Tier 1/ Risk-Adj Assets (%) 1990	Total Cap/ Risk-Adj Assets (%) Mst RctQ	Total Cap/ Risk-Adj Assets (%) 1995	Total Cap/ Risk-Adj Assets (%) 1994	Total Cap/ Risk-Adj Assets (%) 1993
Average for Top 20 Public Banks / Aggregate for Top 20 Public Banks	8.42	8.56	9.00	9.31	8.78	7.65	6.60	12.74	12.80	13.34	13.73
Average for All 424 Public Banks / Aggregate for All 424 Public Banks	12.65	12.87	12.96	12.88	11.99	11.25	10.64	14.32	14.54	14.67	14.61

Aggregates and Averages
for Top 20 Public Banks by Asset Size and For All 424 Public Banks

	Total Cap/ Risk-Adj Assets (%) 1992	Total Cap/ Risk-Adj Assets (%) 1991	Total Cap/ Risk-Adj Assets (%) 1990	Tier 1/ Avg Qrtrly Tang Assets (%) Mst RctQ	Tier 1/ Avg Qrtrly Tang Assets (%) 1995	Tier 1/ Avg Qrtrly Tang Assets (%) 1994	Tier 1/ Avg Qrtrly Tang Assets (%) 1993	Tier 1/ Avg Qrtrly Tang Assets (%) 1992	Tier 1/ Avg Qrtrly Tang Assets (%) 1991
Average for Top 20 Public Banks / Aggregate for Top 20 Public Banks	13.22	11.57	10.27	6.85	6.82	6.87	7.04	6.62	5.86
Average for All 424 Public Banks / Aggregate for All 424 Public Banks	13.73	12.92	12.42	8.56	8.64	8.48	8.21	7.72	7.36

Aggregates and Averages
for Top 20 Public Banks by Asset Size and For All 424 Public Banks

	Tier 1/ Avg Qrtrly Tang Assets (%) 1990	Return on Avg Equity (%) Mst RctQ	Return on Avg Equity (%) 1995	Return on Avg Equity (%) 1994	Return on Avg Equity (%) 1993	Return on Avg Equity (%) 1992	Return on Avg Equity (%) 1991	Return on Avg Equity (%) 1990	Price/ EPS (x) Mst RctQ	Price/ EPS (x) 1995
Average for Top 20 Public Banks Aggregate for Top 20 Public Banks	5.30	16.55	15.16	15.82	16.25	13.36	8.52	10.22	10.90	14.11
Aerage for All 424 Public Banks Aggregate for All 424 Public Banks	7.19	13.11	11.93	11.13	10.83	9.90	7.28	8.31	13.03	14.13

Aggregates and Averages
for Top 20 Public Banks by Asset Size and For All 424 Public Banks

	Price/ EPS (x) 1994	Price/ EPS (x) 1993	Price/ EPS (x) 1992	Price/ EPS (x) 1991	Price/ EPS (x) 1990
Average for Top 20 Public Banks Aggregate for Top 20 Public Banks	8.68	10.23	14.28	18.69	10.33
Average for All 424 Public Banks Aggregate for All 424 Public Banks	12.68	14.52	13.88	13.21	10.67

GREGORY F. UDELL

11. The consolidation of the banking industry and small business lending

ABSTRACT

This paper examines the issue of the impact of the consolidation of the U.S. banking industry on the supply of bank credit to small businesses. It reviews the popular argument that bank mergers and acquisitions create larger institutions that may be less inclined to lend to small business. In particular, these institutions may lose their local community identity and refocus their franchises toward providing capital market services to large corporate clientele. Theoretical arguments that provide economic content to this view are synthesized. The paper then reviews the extant empirical literature which generally provides support for the contention that larger banks, and the merger of larger banks, are associated with a lower allocation of bank assets to small business lending. However, the empirical evidence also suggests that increased lending by other banks in the local market, as well as other factors, may likely offset reductions in small business lending by the consolidating institutions.

I. INTRODUCTION

The banking industry is consolidating at an extraordinary pace. Precipitated by the liberalization of geographic restrictions in the early 1980s, banking organizations were able to circumvent the McFadden Act by acquiring banks across state lines through holding company acquisitions. As a result merger and acquisition activity has reached extraordinary levels. So far in the 1990s about 20% of the banking industry's assets have been involved in a merger *each year*.[1] Another 20% of the industry's assets have been in holding companies that acquired other banks *each year*.[1] As a result, the number of independent banking organizations (independent banks plus holding companies that are not owned by other holding companies) fell from 12,647 to 8,838 from 1979 to 1994. Mergers within states over the same period have reduced the number of banking charters from 14,336 to 10,367. The passage of the Reigle-Neal Act will only accelerate this process by permitting nationwide interstate branching in 1997.

221

Y. Amihud and G. Miller (eds.), Bank Mergers & Acquisitions, 221–235
© 1998 Kluwer Academic Publishers. Printed in the Netherlands.

222   *Gregory F. Udell*

Many observers have expressed concern that the consolidation of the banking industry may come at the expense of small business. Those holding this view typically argue that banking is a declining industry and in order to preserve its franchise the industry needs to focus on nontraditional activities including the provision of capital market services to larger companies. In fact, there is much evidence to suggest that the industry has been quite successful in reinventing itself – so much so that when the size of the banking industry is recalibrated taking into account these new nontraditional activities (many of which are off-balance sheet), the banking industry isn't declining at all (see Boyd and Gertler 1995). However, if the banking industry refocuses itself to compete in the capital markets, the provision of banking services to small business may be relegated to second order importance. More specifically, if smaller banks are swallowed up by large banking organizations they may be stripped of their community identity – and their comparative advantage in making local business loans may be sacrificed on the alter of a centralized, long distance management structure.

This concern about the effect of bank consolidation on small business lending comes on the heals of a credit crunch during the early 1990s that was associated with a precipitous drop in bank lending. While part of that drop may have been the result of a decrease in loan demand, recent empirical evidence suggests that banking regulation and shocks to bank capital may have played a significant role (see, for example, Berger and Udell 1994, Hancock, Liang and Wilcox 1995, and Peek and Rosengren 1995). This in turn created a heightened sensitivity to the banking industry's propensity to lend – particularly to small businesses – that in turn resulted in a number of initiatives that focused on small business lending including: expanded Small Business Administration loan programs[2], increased reporting requirements by banks to measure small business lending[3], and commitments from merger and acquisition participants for future small business lending.[4]

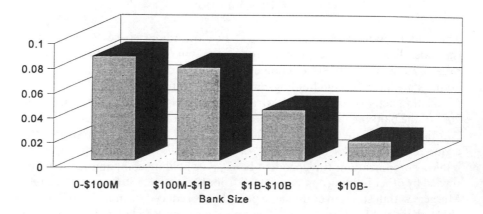

Figure 11–1. Small Business Lending (Fraction of Assets in Loans <$1 million)

At its most fundamental level, the concern about bank consolidation and small business lending stems from the historical fact that large banks tend to allocate a much smaller fraction of their assets to small business lending than large banks. Because mergers and acquisitions create larger banking organizations out of smaller ones, this suggests that small business lending may decline in the future if lending propensities by bank size stay the same. The potential magnitude of this effect is reflected in Figure 1 which shows small business lending as a fraction of bank assets by bank size where small business lending is defined as less than $1 million of credit capacity.

Figure 2 shows the dollar amount of lending by bank size category and reflects the fact that a significant percentage of small business loans are extended by small and mid-sized banks. The smallest banks with assets less than $100 million dollars extended in aggregate about $28 billion in small business loans as of June 1994; banks with assets between $100 and $1 billion extended $51 billion; banks with assets between $1 billion and $10 billion, about $45 billion; and banks with assets above $10 billion extended about $30 billion in small business loans. Thus, over half of all small business lending is extended by banks with asset size less than $1 billion.

If lending propensities remain the same then we can use statistics reflected in Figure 1 to roughly estimate extreme case scenarios. If, for example, all banks less than $1 billion in asset size were to have merged into banks with asset size between $1 billion and $10 billion, and lending propensities remain the same, then small business lending would have been only $117 billion in 1994 instead

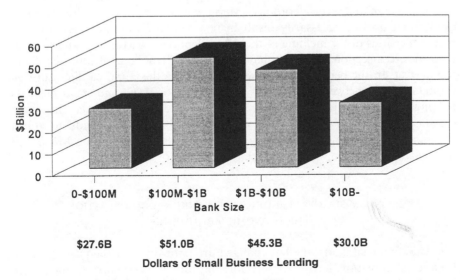

Source: Consolidated Report of condition and Income, June 1994

Figure 11–2. Small Business Lending (Total Small Business Lending by Bank Size Category)

of $154 billion. If all banks had merged into banks with assets greater than $10 billion then small business lending would have fallen from $154 billion to $64 billion! While this is an admittedly "worst case" scenario, it does capture the spirit of the popular argument against banking industry consolidation as it relates to credit availability and probably represents a reasonable estimate of the upper limit of the small business effect.

The problem with this extrapolation exercise is that it ignores other effects. For instance: To what extent will other banks in the market increase small business lending when consolidating banks decrease theirs? Are there limits to consolidation that suggest that many small banks will survive industry consolidation? Fortunately recent empirical evidence sheds considerably light on this issue.   In the remainder of this paper we will examine more closely the issue of banking consolidation and small business lending and synthesize the extant empirical evidence on the subject. Specifically, in the next section we will develop more rigorously the economic foundations of the argument that the current wave of consolidation in the banking industry may lead to a decline in small business lending. In the third section of the paper we will examine the empirical literature on the relationship between bank size and complexity and small business lending. We will note that the conclusions drawn in this literature on the cross-sectional relationship between institutional size and small business lending, for the most part, reflect (a less extreme) version of the conclusion suggested by Figures 1 and 2 – that larger banks, and possibly more complex banking organizations, tend to allocate a lower fraction of their assets to small business lending. However, static analysis of the cross-sectional relationship between bank size and lending propensities tends to suppress important dynamic considerations. Mergers and acquisitions are dynamic events that do not necessarily result in new banking organizations that are mere reflections of the melding of the antecedent banks. Moreover, these types of static cross-sectional analyses have ignored the reactions of other banks in the market. In the penultimate section we examine the empirical literature on the relationship between the merger and acquisition *event* and small business lending. This literature highlights important dynamic effects the most significant of which is the reaction of other banks that tends to offset reductions in small business lending by the banks participating in M&As. In the concluding section, we offer some predictions for the future.

2. SMALL BUSINESS LENDING AND BANKING CONSOLIDATION: THE ECONOMIC ARGUMENT

The U.S. financial landscape has changed dramatically over the past 25 years. Financial innovation, information technology and global competitiveness have dramatically altered the environment in which commercial banks operate. These changes have forced banks to significantly alter their product mix in order to preserve their franchise value. In particular, banks now offer a much expanded menu of nontraditional products that include brokerage services, corporate underwriting, financial derivatives, venture capital, capital market advisory services – just to name a few. This could be viewed as a trend away from a focus on traditional on-balance sheet lending activity to fee-generating off-balance sheet activity.

These changes have occurred at the same time as, and have been encouraged by, significant regulatory changes. The Federal Reserve's transition over the past decade from a narrow interpretation of Glass-Steagall to a much more liberal interpretation has been a key factor in promoting the transformation of the industry from traditional to nontraditional banking. Equally significant has been the concomitant collapse of the McFadden Act. This stalwart of twentieth century U.S. banking began to unravel as bank holding companies took advantage of reciprocity agreements among groups of states with regional banking compacts. This lead to the formation of large regional bank organizations, many of which in turn were consolidated into gigantic supperregional banks such as NationsBank and Fleet. Not to be outdone, large money center banks have combined to form even larger money center banks the most notable being Chase Manhattan. The regulatory framework for consolidation has now been rationalized by the passage of the Interstate Banking and Branching Efficiency Act of 1994 (the Reigle-Neal Act) which effectively permits nationwide branch banking in 1997. This can only accelerate the industry's consolidation. When combined with the increasing likelihood that Congress will soon pass some form of universal banking, it is reasonable to predict that the average banking organization will become even larger and more complex in the future.

The argument that these trends may come at the expense of small business is based in part on the possibility that the proliferation of new bank product lines associated with larger and more complex banking institutions may have forced an internal competition for scarce capital and managerial attention – a competition in which the small business component of banking may be a loser. In addition, the formation of banking organizations that are increasingly geographically dispersed may have fundamentally changed banking's governance structure. Specifically, acquired banks may lose their local identity as local management is replaced by the acquired bank's management. In the process the acquiring bank may impose its own policies and procedures, stripping the acquired bank of its autonomy as well as it management. This loss of community identity may significantly diminish the banking industry's appetite for loans to small local businesses.

This argument is predicated on the notion that selling banking services to small businesses is fundamentally different from sell banking services to mid-size and large corporate clients – otherwise it would be easy for banks to jointly serve both clienteles. Academic work in this area suggests, however, that the difference might be significant.[5] A number of recent papers have emphasized that firms lie on an information continuum with the smallest most informationally opaque firms at one end, and the largest most informationally

226   *Gregory F. Udell*

transparent firms at the other end (see Berger and Udell 1993, and Carey et al. 1993). The position of a firm on this continuum will determine its access to markets for external finance (see Figure 3) and the type of contracts it will likely be required to utilize.[6] The smallest new venture firms may not even have access to the bank loan market. Later stage new venture firms and smaller nonventure firms are likely to be entirely bank dependent for external (nontrade) debt finance. Larger mid-sized firms will have access to long term debt in the private placement market and only the largest firms will have access to the public bond market (see Carey et al. 1993).

Because smaller firms are so informationally opaque, the financial intermediaries who provide their external financing frequently impose costly contract features to address problems associated with adverse selection and moral hazard. Most notably these include collateral, personal guarantees and covenants. To the extent that these nonprice elements cannot eliminate problems associated with asymmetric information, lenders will be forced to lend at higher interest rates or to deny credit altogether (i.e., credit ration). If, however, a small firm can develop a relationship with a commercial bank, then dependence on costly contracting mechanisms can be minimized as the bank acquires more information about the firm – that is, as the firm acquires a private reputation

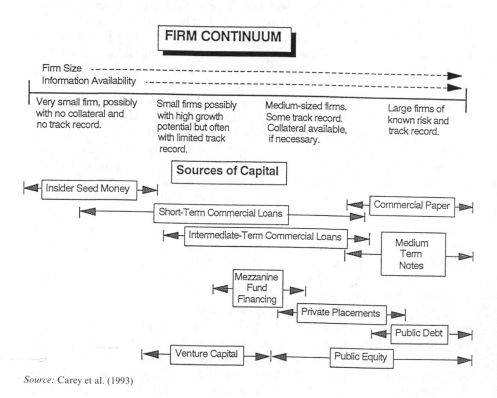

Source: Carey et al. (1993)

Figure 11–3.

with the bank. The development of such a relationship is likely to require a bank with a strong knowledge of the firm, the firm's owner, its suppliers, its customers, etc. – all of which, in turn, are likely to require a thorough knowledge of the borrower's local community. Persuasive evidence that for small firms banking relationships provide value is offered by Petersen and Rajan (1993, 1994) and Berger and Udell (1995).[7] Taken together these papers show that the stronger a small firm's relationship with a bank, i) the lower the interest rate on firm's bank loans; ii) the less likely that the firm will be required to pledge collateral; and, iii) the less dependent the firm will be on trade credit.[8]

Thus bank lending to small firms appears to be distinctly different from bank lending to larger firms who typically borrow from multiple banks under much less restrictive and much more generic contracts, and whose nonbank debt is likely to be monitored by a rating agency. Moreover, the nonloan services offered to larger corporate customers are quite different from the menu of nonloan products banks sell to small companies. For instance, while banks sell derivatives, sophisticated cash management services, capital market advisory services, private placement agenting, and corporate underwriting to large and midsize companies, these services are mostly irrelevant to small businesses.

Given these differences between selling banking services to small firms versus large firms, organizational inefficiencies might result for those institutions who choose to provide them jointly. Organizational models of firm behavior usually associated with Williamson (1967) emphasize managerial diseconomies associated with the provision of multiple activities in large, complex organizations.[9] This implies that large, complex banking organizations may attempt to minimize the managerial diseconomies associated with providing banking services to both large and small firms by reducing the amount of these services offered to the latter. This would avoid managing the transaction-related product menu associated with large corporate clients *along with* managing the relationship-oriented services offered to small businesses. It would also avoid a management structure that needs to be national (indeed global) in orientation to market successfully to large companies, and yet local in orientation to sell to small companies.[10]

To the extent that the banking industry is characterized by these type of organizational diseconomies we would expect to see a negative cross-sectional relationship between bank size and small business lending and a negative cross-sectional relationship between bank organizational complexity and small business lending. The existence of these diseconomies also suggest that as banking organizations grow in size and complexity through mergers and acquisitions, the propensity of the participating (i.e., consolidating) banks to lend to small businesses should decline. However, offsetting effects are possible. For example, merging banks may choose to downsize after the merger and/or they may choose to become less complex by focusing on a specific niche. Moreover, other banks in the market may choose to pick up the slack, offsetting any decline in small business lending by the merging banks. To examine these possibilities, we now turn to the empirical evidence.

3. The Empirical Evidence on Bank Size and Small Business Lending

A number of papers have examined the effects of banking organization size on small business lending. Berger, Kashyap, and Scalise (1995) and Berger and Udell (1996) found evidence that larger banking organizations tend to lend much more to medium and large business borrowers, whereas small banking organizations tend to invest much higher proportions of their assets in small business loans. These studies were based on data from the Federal Reserve's Survey of Terms of Bank Lending (STBL). The STBL is a quarterly survey of approximately 300 banks, including the 50 largest, that report detailed contract information on each loan. Keeton (1995), Levonian and Soller (1995), Peek and Rosengren (1996), and Strahan and Weston (1996) found the same result using the small business lending section of the Call Report. (The Call Report is the detailed financial information supplied by banks to their regulators.) The small business Call Report data has the virtue of including all banks in the U.S. Unfortunately, it was not available until 1993.

In addition to finding that larger banks tend to lend less to smaller firms, Berger and Udell (1996) found evidence to suggest that they tend to lend to a different *type* of small business than small banks. Specifically, they concluded that because the small business loans made by larger banks are less likely to be collateralized and tend to be associated with a lower interest rate, they are less likely to be relationship-driven loans to informationally opaque borrowers. In addition, Berger and Udell (1996) found some evidence (although not as strong as in the case of bank size) that organizational complexity is associated with less small business lending. They define organizational complexity in terms of the number of layers of holding company management structure, the extent of its branching structure, and the breadth of its "nonbanking" activities. Keeton (1995) found evidence that out-of-state ownership and a high degree of branching tended to reduce small business lending.[11]

Taken together these studies suggest that small banks tend to focus on lending to informationally-opaque small business borrowers that are likely to require a strong bank-borrower relationship. Large and more complex banks, on the other hand, are likely to lend proportionately less to small businesses; and to the extent that they do, they tend to lend to a more informationally transparent type of small business that is less likely to need a strong bank-borrower relationship.[12]

4. The Empirical Evidence on Mergers and Acquisitions and Small Business Lending

Papers that examine the impact of mergers and acquisitions on small business lending fall into two categories: a) those that indirectly examine impact of M&As by comparing banks in markets more conducive to M&A activity with banks in more restrictive markets; and b) examining the dynamic effect of the merger or acquisition itself.

In the former category, several studies have examined the effects of liberalizing state geographic banking restrictions on small business lending behavior. Berger, Kashyap, and Scalise (1995) found evidence that past relaxation of geographic restrictions has been associated with less small business lending. Other studies have found that geographic liberalization has been associated with an increase in the average quality of small business bank loans (Jayaratne and Strahan 1995) and an increase in bank profitability (Schranz 1993 and Jayaratne and Strahan 1996). This suggests that geographical liberalization encourages organizational complexity (through geographic dispersion) which in turn results in banks shifting out of lower quality smaller business loans (and possibly more informationally opaque relationship borrowers) to higher quality small business loans (consistent with Berger and Udell 1996) and larger business loans – suggestive of a relative shift in the supply of small business lending away from lower quality.

In the latter category are several studies that specifically focus on the dynamic effect of bank mergers and acquisitions – that is, studies that examine banks *before and after* mergers and acquisitions to determine the impact on business lending. These studies can be viewed as providing direct evidence on the merger or acquisition event.

Akhavein, Berger, and Humphrey (1996) analyzed 69 'megamergers' of the 1980s. They defined a megamerger as a merger or acquisition in which all parties had over $1 billion in assets. They found evidence of a substantial increase in *overall* lending as a percent of assets relative to other large banking organizations but did not examine the impact on *small* business lending. Peek and Rosengren (1996) used the June 1993 and June 1994 Call Report data to specifically evaluate the change in small business lending associated with 13 M&As in New England over the one year period between the two Call Report dates. They generally found a decrease in the proportion of assets devoted to small business lending except when the smallest banks acquired other small banks, in which case there was an increase in the small business ratio. Although they did not make a formal comparison with other banks, the same type of lending pattern was reflected in New England banks in general.

Strahan and Weston (1996) analyzed the impact on small business lending using a much larger national sample of 180 mergers in a study that followed the sample and some control groups over a two-year period, using the June 1993 and June 1995 small business lending sections of the Call Report. For small banks they found that participation in a merger or acquisition increased lending (consistent with the findings of Peek and Rosengren 1996) while for large banks they found no clear effect (inconsistent with the findings of Peek and Rosengren 1996).

In a study of banks in the Tenth Federal Reserve district Keeton (1996) analyzed the lending behavior of 652 rural banks involved in acquisitions and 467 urban banks involved in acquisitions over the period 1986 to 1995. Because

Keeton did not use the new lending sections of the Call Report he was not limited to the post 1993 period. However, he was not able to directly isolate small business lending from large business lending. However, because most of the banks in the Tenth Federal Reserve District are relatively small, their legal lending limits necessarily limit them to smaller loans. Keeton's results indicated that banks in his sample tended to reduce their (probably mostly local) business lending when they are acquired by distant organizations. The results were strongest for out-of-state organizations buying (either rural or urban) banks from urban organizations – although the result was weaker in the 1990s than in the 1980s. Although Keeton's study did not analyze lending changes by participating bank size, his results appear to be consistent with Strahan and Weston (1996) – at least to the extent that out of state organizations and urban organizations are likely to be the largest in the sample.[13]

The three previous studies are limited in terms of either their sample period and/or their sample size and coverage. The most comprehensive analysis to date in terms of sample coverage is by Berger et al. (1996). This paper's methodology permits the authors to analyze virtually all mergers *and* acquisitions since 1980. That is, it permits them to overcome the fact that their data on small lending propensities come from the STBL which surveys only about 300 banks per year. Specifically, they use data on STBL-surveyed banks to estimate a model of lending propensities in which the proportion of loans in different loan size categories is a function of bank financial characteristics, organizational characteristics, market structure and participation in mergers or acquisitions. They also estimate a model of how banks change their characteristics after they participate in a merger or acquisition. Then they use estimated coefficients from these two models to calculate predicted M&A-induced changes in lending and to isolate the causes of those changes for the vast majority of *all* mergers and acquisitions over the sample period.

The Berger et al. methodology isolates changes in lending that are associated with just the static melding of two banks by either an acquisition or a merger. For example, in the case of a merger of two $500 million banks, they estimate the impact of forming a new $1 billion bank (and the effects associated with a simple melding of all of the characteristics of the merging banks). This *aggregation effect* would reflect any difference in lending propensities associated with banks whose size is $1 billion versus the lending propensities of banks whose size is $500 million.[14] Then they estimate the predicted changes that result from any post-M&A refocusing that could operate through changes in the financial and organizational characteristics of the bank, or any changes in lending policy, that are typically associated with a merger or acquisition. This could occur in the previous example if the typical merger of two $500 million banks is soon followed by a downsizing of the post-merger bank from $1 billion to $800 million. These could be referred to as dynamic *refocusing effects*.[15] Finally, they estimate the predicted reaction of *other* banks in the market which they call the *external effects*. Berger et al. find that in the case of mergers that a relatively large negative external effect offsets a relatively large aggregation effect. The refocusing effects had a positive but minor impact on small business lending. In the case of acquisitions, a relatively large negative aggregation effect is offset by both a relatively large refocusing effect and a large external effect. Inconsistent with Keeton (1996) they do not find that out-of-state acquisitions are associated with less lending by the participating banks. However, consistent with both Peek and Rosengren (1996) and Strahan and Weston (1996), Berger et al. find that smaller banks participating in mergers tend to increase their small business lending.

5. CONCLUSION

At first blush theoretical arguments appear to provide some support for the conventional wisdom that consolidation of the banking industry could lead to an overall reduction in small business lending. Williamson-type organizational and managerial diseconomies could force the increasing number of larger banks to focus away from small business lending. Critics of consolidation who make this argument can make a strong case that lending to small firms is distinctly different from lending to large firms. Because small businesses are informationally opaque they require complex loan contracts and strong bank-borrower relationships that may be best offered by banks with a strong community identity. For large and complex banking organizations the provision of this type of service to small companies, while simultaneously providing capital market services to large national and multinational corporate clients, could siphon away scarce managerial resources. Static analyses provides some empirical support for this view. Summary statistics of bank lending by asset-size category indicate that large banks tend to allocate significantly less assets to small business lending. In addition, cross-sectional analyses which control for other factors also indicate that larger, and possibly more complex, banks lend less proportionately to small businesses than smaller more focused banks.

However, studies that analyze the impact of mergers and acquisitions on small business lending in a *dynamic* framework paint a different picture. While this work shows that banks participating in *mergers* tend to decrease small business lending, there is also evidence to suggest that other banks in the market are likely to offset this effect. Moreover, for small bank *mergers*, the merging banks tend to *increase* their small business lending – not decrease it. For *acquisitions*, the evidence is mixed on the behavior of the acquired and acquiring institutions. However, the evidence also indicates that any reduction in small business lending by the combining institutions is likely to be offset by other banks in the local market who increase their small business lending. There is also some evidence that indicates that in recent years any negative effect of *acquisitions* has likely diminished.

What does this suggest for the future? One interpretation of the extant empirical evidence is that there may be limits to the banking industry's consolidation. If small business lending is a positive net present value activity, and if it is best supplied by banking organizations with a local identity, then we should not expect to see small banking organizations entirely disappear from the landscape. That small banks have not disappeared in states like California with a long history of state-wide branching lends support to this view (see Berger, Kayship and Scalise 1995). Thus the smaller banks that remain should continue to be the beneficiaries of larger bank consolidations. Moreover, we might also expect to see an increase in de novo banks in areas where M&A activity has been the greatest.[16] New U.S. bank charters, in fact increased significantly in 1995.

We should also be cautious in predicting the future solely based on the past. Regulators and community organizations have in recent years successfully extracted commitments from merging and acquiring banks to continue lending to small businesses. In addition, as the banking industry evolves it may develop organizational forms better equipped to minimize organizational diseconomies associated with nationwide branching and expansive product lists. Merrill Lynch, for instance, represents a stunning example of a mega financial institution that successfully competes in both retail and wholesale markets. It also seems reasonable to expect that regulatory barriers that may have in the past inhibited the adoption of an optimal organizational form, and possibly discouraged small business lending, are likely to continue to decrease.

NOTES

1. A merger is defined as a combination of banks where a bank charter disappears while an acquisition involves the purchase of a bank by a holding company such that the acquired bank's charter survives.
2. The SBA created a new program for guaranteeing asset-based lines of credit, historically one of the most risky kinds of small business lending.
3. The June Call Report for all banks now includes a schedule in which banks report the level of their small business lending defined as the dollar level of loans where the total credit capacity is less than $1 million.
4. In the recent Wells Fargo-First Interstate merger, for example, Wells Fargo pledged to make $25 billion in small business loans in the ten years following the merger (see Smith 1996).
5. This literature is a natural extension of the more general literature on the role of financial intermediaries as information producers (e.g., Diamond 1984, 1991, Ramakrishnan and Thakor 1984, and Boyd and Prescott 1986).
6. The continuum should not be viewed as static. In particular, changes in technology could alter the relationship between the size of the firm and the type of markets to which it has access. Innovations in information and analytical technology, for example, might decrease the minimum size of firms with access to the traded securities markets. This implies an increase in the size of the capital markets at the expense of the banking industry (see Macey and Miller 1997). However, this could be offset by innovations that make formerly nonbankable small business bankable (see Berger and Udell 1993).
7. See Greenbaum et al. (1989), Sharpe (1990), Wilson (1993), Petersen and Rajan (1993), Boot and Thakor (1994) for theoretical information-based models of relationship lending.
8. The establishment of a relationship with a single bank may introduce some costs associated with the acquisition of an information monopoly (see, for example, Rajan 1992 and Houston

and James 1996). It is likely for small borrowers, however, that these costs are more than offset by the benefits of a private reputation that develops over the course of a single bank-borrower relationship.

9. These managerial diseconomies can be rationalized in a transactions cost framework or an agency theory framework. For a discussion of the distinction between these approaches, see Williamson (1988).

10. At first blush it would seem that the same argument might apply to consumer services because consumer banking requires local branches. However, consumer banking is arguably much more generic than small business lending. Consumer lending is based on credit scoring and does not require the analytical skills associated with making five and six figure business loans secured by collateral and personally guaranteed by the owner. Likewise selling checking accounts and CDs is straightforward. Moreover, an increasing volume of consumer services are sold by phone, mail or electronically.

11. Keeton (1995) analyzed the June 1994 Call Report data on small business lending in the 10th Federal Reserve District. In contrast to Keeton, Whalen (1995) examined the June 1993 Call Report information for three states (Illinois, Kentucky, and Montana) and found that banks owned by out-of-state BHCs did not have lower levels of small business lending than other banks.

12. A recent increase in small business lending by large banks has been widely reported in the popular press. It is also often trumpeted by larger banks to such an extent that "... small business banking [has become] a kind of fad in the industry – virtually every bank claims to be focusing on it ..." (Cline 1995, p. 5). Cline (1995) reports in his article in the *American Banker* entitled "Small Business is Booming at Biggest Banks" that banks with more than $1 billion of small business loans increased their lending by nearly 10% between June 30, 1994 and June 30, 1995. However, he also reports that total domestic business lending increased by a substantially higher amount, nearly 20%. The recent availability of Call Report data on small business lending has quite probably increased the attention on small business lending. It is also possible that by making small business lending more visible, the new Call Report data has had a positive effect on the actual volume of lending.

13. Keeton (1996) excluded all mergers – about a third of all M&A activity. In a merger the bank charter disappears.

14. In addition to size Berger et al. examine other financial characteristics and organizational characteristics as determinants of lending propensities.

15. Specifically, Berger et al. decompose these dynamic refocusing effects econometrically into those that operate through changes in the combined banks' financial and organizational characteristics and those that are unrelated to any post-M&A alteration of financial and organizational characteristics (i.e., changes that are idiosyncratic to post M&A banks with the same characteristics as those banks who did not participate in an M&A).

16. See Deogun for a discussion in the popular press of de nova banks filling the gap in local markets created by consolidating banks.

REFERENCES

Akhavein, Jalal D., Allen N. Berger, and David B. Humphrey, 1996, "The Effects of Bank Megamergers on Efficiency and Prices: Evidence from the Profit Function," *Review of Industrial Organization* 11.

Berger, Allen N., Anil K Kashyap, and Joseph M. Scalise, 1995, "The Transformation of the U.S. Banking Industry: What A Long, Strange Trip It's Been," *Brookings Papers on Economic Activity* (2:1995): 55-218.

Berger, Allen N., Anthony Saunders, Joseph M. Scalise, and Gregory F. Udell, 1996, "The Effects of Bank Mergers on Small Business Lending," New York University working paper.

Berger, Allen N., and Gregory F. Udell, 1993, "Securitization, Risk, and the Liquidity Problem in

Banking," in *Structural Change in Banking*, edited by Michael Klausner and Lawrence J. White. New York: Business One Irwin.

Berger, Allen N., and Gregory F. Udell, 1994, "Did Risk-Based Capital Allocate Bank Credit and Cause a 'Credit Crunch' in the U.S.," *Journal of Money, Credit and Banking*, (August).

Berger, Allen N., and Gregory F. Udell, 1995, "Relationship Lending and Lines of Credit in Small Firm Finance," *Journal of Business* 68 (July): 351-82.

Berger, Allen N., and Gregory F. Udell, 1996, "Universal Banking and the Future of Small Business Lending", edited by Anthony Saunders and Ingo Walter, *Financial System Design: The Case for Universal Banking*, Burr Ridge, IL, Irwin Publishing.

Boot, Arnoud, and Anjan V. Thakor, 1994, "Moral Hazard and Secured Lending ina an Infinitely Repeated Credit Market Game," *International Economic Review*, 35 (November) 899-920.

Boyd, John H., and Mark Gertler, 1995, "Are Banks Dead? Or are the Reports Greatly Exaggerated?" working paper 5045. NBER.

Boyd, John H., and Edward C. Prescott, 1986, "Financial Intermediary-Coalitions," *Journal of Economic Theory*, 38:211-232.

Carey, Mark, John Rea and Stephen Prowse and Gregory Udell, 1993, "The Economics of Private Placements: A New Look," *Financial Markets, Institutions and Instruments*, 2 (August).

Cline, Kenneth, 1995, "Small Business is Booming at Biggest Banks," *American Banker*, (November 21) 5.

Deogun, Nikhil, 1996, "Displaced by Mergers, Some Bankers Launch Their Own Start-Ups," *Wall Street Journal* (March 4), 1.

Diamond, Douglas W., 1984, "Financial Intermediation and Delegated Monitoring," *Review of Economic Studies*, 51: 393-414.

Diamond, Douglas W., 1991, "Monitoring and Reputation: The Choice Between Bank Loans and Directly Placed Debt," *Journal of Political Economy*, 99:688-721.

Greenbaum, Stuart I., George Kanatas and I. Venezia, 1989, "Equilibrium Loan Pricing Under the Bank-Client Relationship," *Journal of Banking and Finance* 13: 221-35.

Hancock, Diana, Andrew J. Liang and James A. Wilcox, 1995, "Bank Capital Shocks: Dynamic Effects on Securities, Loans, and Capital," *Journal of Banking and Finance* 19 (June): 661-677.

Houston, Joel F., and Christopher M. James, 1996, "Bank Information Monopolies and the Mix of Private and Public Debt Claims," *Journal of Finance* 51 (December): 1863-1889.

Jayarantne, Jith, and Philip E. Strahan, 1996, "Entry Restrictions, Industry Evolution and Dynamic Efficiency: Evidence from Commercial Banking," Federal Reserve Bank of New York Working Paper (August).

Keeton, William R., 1995, "Multi-Office Bank Lending to Small Businesses: Some New Evidence," Federal Reserve Bank of Kansas City *Economic Review* 80 (2): 45-57.

Keeton, William R., 1996, "Do Bank Mergers Reduce Lending to Businesses and Farmers? New Evidence from Tenth District States," Federal Reserve Bank of Kansas City *Economic Review* 81 (3): 63-75.

Levonian, Mark, and Jennifer Soller, 1995, "Small Banks, Small Loans, Small Business," Federal Reserve Bank of San Francisco Working Paper, (December).

Macey, Jonathan R., and Jeoffrey P. Miller, "Bank Mergers and American Bank Competitiveness," this issue 1997.

Peek, Joe, and Eric S. Rosengren, 1995, "The Capital Crunch: Neither a Borrower or Lender Be," *Journal of Money, Credit and Banking* 26.

Peek, Joe, and Eric S. Rosengren, 1996, "Small Business Credit Availability: How Important is Size of Lender?" edited by Anthony Saunders and Ingo Walter, *Financial System Design: The Case for Universal Banking*, Burr Ridge, IL, Irwin Publishing.

Petersen, Mitchell A. and Raghuram G. Rajan, 1993, "The Effect of Credit market Competititon on Firm-creditor Relationships," University of Chicago working paper (February).

Petersen, Mitchell A. and Raghuram G. Rajan, 1994, "The Benefits of Firm-Creditor Relationships: Evidence from Small Business Data," *Journal of Finance* 49 (March): 3-37.

Ramakrishnan, S., and Anjan V. Thakor, 1984, "Information Reliability and a Theory of Financial Intermediation," *Review of Economic Studies* 51: 415-32.

Rajan, Raghuram G., 1992, "Insiders and Outsiders: The Choice Between Informed and Arm's Length Debt," *Journal of Finance* 47: 1367-1400.

Schrantz, Mary S., 1993, "Takeovers Improve Firm Performance: Evidence from the Banking Industry," *Journal of Political Economy*, 101 (April): 299-326.

Sharpe, Steven A., 1990, "Asymmetric Information, Bank Lending, and Implicit Contracts: A Stylized Model of Customer Relationships," *Journal of Finance* 45 (September): 1069-87.

Smith, Roy C., 1996, "Wells Fargo and First Interstate," New York University Salomon Center Case Series in Finance and Economics, Case No. C61.

Strahan, Philip E., and James Weston, 1996, "Small Business Lending and Bank Consolidation: Any Cause for Concern?" New York Federal Reserve Bank *Current Issues in Economics and Finance* 2 (March).

Wilson, Patricia F., 1993, "The Pricing of Loans in a Bank-Borrower Relationship," Indiana University working paper (July).

Whalen, Gary, 1995, "Out-of-State Holding Company Affiliation and Small Business Lending," Comptroller of the Currency working paper 95-4.

Williamson, Oliver, 1967, "The Economics of Defense Contracting: Incentives and Performance" in *Issues in Defense Economics*, ed. R. McKean. New York: Columbia University Press.

Williamson, Oliver, 1988, "Corporate Finance and Corporate Governance," *Journal of Finance* 43 (July): 567-91.